1 MONTH OF
FREE
READING

at

www.ForgottenBooks.com

By purchasing this book you are eligible for one month membership to ForgottenBooks.com, giving you unlimited access to our entire collection of over 1,000,000 titles via our web site and mobile apps.

To claim your free month visit:

www.forgottenbooks.com/free919098

ISBN 978-0-265-98382-9
PIBN 10919098

[Oct 1976]

The University Record
University of Florida

CORRESPONDENCE DIRECTORY

Graduate School
Harry H. Sisler, Dean
223 Grinter Hall - (904) 392-1281
University of Florida, Gainesville, Florida 32611

Application for Admission
Office of the Registrar - Admissions Section
135 Tigert Hall - (904) 392-1361

Assistantships
Chairman of the department in which the student wishes to enroll

Graduate Student Loans
Director, Student Financial Affairs
23 Tigert Hall - (904) 392-1275

Housing
University **or** Off-Campus
Division of Housing - (904) 392-2161
S. W. 13th St. & Museum Road

International Student Advisement
Adviser, International Students
Building AE - (904) 392-1345

This public document was promulgated at a total cost of $26,275.00 or $.75 per copy to provide official information describing the Graduate Program at the University of Florida, including admission requirements, facilities, fees, fields of instruction and course listings.

This publication has been adopted as a rule of the University pursuant to the provisions of Chapter 120 of the Florida Statute. Addenda to the University Record Series, if any, are available upon request to the Office of the Registrar. '

UNIVERSITY OF FLORIDA RECORD

Vol. LXXI—Series 1, No. 4   October, 1976
Published quarterly by the University of Florida, Gainesville, Florida zip code 32611. Office of Publications, Gainesville, Florida. Second class postage paid at Gainesville, Florida, 32601.

MANUFACTURED BY CONVENTION PRESS. INC., JACKSONVILLE, FLORIDA

Graduate School Information

UNIVERSITY OF FLORIDA RECORD

GAINESVILLE 1976 / 1977

Contents

GENERAL INFORMATION

FIELDS OF INSTRUCTION

Officers of Administration

FLORIDA STATE BOARD OF EDUCATION

REUBIN O'D. ASKEW
Governor

BRUCE SMATHERS
Secretary of State

ROBERT SHEVIN
Attorney General

PHILIP E. ASHLER
Acting State Treasurer

RALPH D. TURLINGTON
Commissioner of Education

GERALD A. LEWIS
Comptroller

DOYLE CONNER
Commissioner of Agriculture

BOARD OF REGENTS OF FLORIDA

MARSHALL M. CRISER
Chairman, Palm Beach

JAMES J. GARDNER
Vice Chairman, Fort Lauderdale

J. J. DANIEL
Jacksonville

JACK McGRIFF
Gainesville

CHESTER HOWELL FERGUSON
Tampa

JULIUS F. PARKER, Jr.
Tallahassee

MARSHALL S. HARRIS
Miami

BETTY ANNE STATON
Orlando

E. W. HOPKINS, Jr.
Pensacola

E. T. YORK, Jr.
Chancellor, Tallahassee

UNIVERSITY OF FLORIDA

ROBERT QUARLES MARSTON, M.D.; B.Sc. (Oxonian); D.Sc.
President of the University

HAROLD PALMER HANSON, Ph.D.
Executive Vice President

DON L. ALLEN, D.D.S., *Dean, College of Dentistry*

CLIFFORD ALLEN BOYD, Ed.D., *Dean, College of Physical Education, Health, and Recreation*

CHARLES BENTON BROWNING, Ph.D., *Dean for Resident Instruction, Institute of Food and Agricultural Sciences*

ROBERT ARMISTEAD BRYAN, Ph.D., *Vice President for Academic Affairs*

WILLIAM E. CARTER, Ph.D., *Director, Center for Latin American Studies*

WAYNE H. CHEN, Ph.D., *Dean, College of Engineering* and *Director, Engineering and Industrial Experiment Station*

CHARLES E. CORNELIUS, Ph.D., *Dean, College of Veterinary Medicine*

JOSHUA CLIFTON DICKINSON, JR., Ph.D., *Director, Florida State Museum*

WILLIAM EARL ELMORE, B.S., *Vice President for Administrative Affairs*

KENNETH FRANKLIN FINGER, Ph.D., *Dean, College of Pharmacy* and *Associate Vice President for Health Affairs*

JOHN LEWIS GRAY, D.F., *Director, School of Forest Resources and Conservation*

GUSTAVE ADOLPHUS HARRER, Ph.D., *Director, University Libraries*

GENE W. HEMP, Ph.D., *Assistant Vice President for Academic Affairs*

MARK T. JAROSZEWICZ, M.A.U.D., *Dean, College of Architecture*

JOSEPH RICHARD JULIN, J.D., *Dean, College of Law*

ROBERT FRANKLIN LANZILLOTTI, Ph.D., *Dean, College of Business Administration*

RALPH L. LOWENSTEIN, Ph.D., *Dean, College of Journalism and Communications*

JOSEPH J. SABATELLA, M.F.A., *Dean, College of Fine Arts*

C. ARTHUR SANDEEN, Ph.D., *Vice President for Student Affairs*

BERT LAVON SHARP, Ed.D., *Dean, College of Education*

BETTY LENTZ SIEGEL, Ph.D., *Dean for Continuing Education*

HARRY HALL SISLER, Ph.D., *Dean, Graduate School* and *Director, Division of Sponsored Research*

JOHN WILBUR SITES, Ph.D., *Dean for Research, Institute of Food and Agricultural Sciences*

CHANDLER A. STETSON, M.D., *Dean, College of Medicine* and *Vice President for Health Affairs*

HOWARD KAZURO SUZUKI, Ph.D., *Dean, College of Health Related Professions*

KENNETH R. TEFERTILLER, Ph.D., *Vice President for Agricultural Affairs*

BLANCHE I. UREY, Ed.D., *Dean, College of Nursing*

CALVIN ANTHONY VANDERWERF, Ph.D., *Dean, College of Arts and Sciences*

RICHARD HOLMES WHITEHEAD, B.A., *Dean of Admissions and Records*

THE GRADUATE SCHOOL

HARRY H. SISLER, Ph.D. (Illinois), *Dean, Graduate School; Director, Sponsored Research;* and *Professor of Chemistry*

LINTON E. GRINTER, Ph.D. (Illinois), *Dean Emeritus, Graduate School* and *Professor of Engineering*

F. MICHAEL WAHL, Ph.D. (Illinois), *Associate Dean, Graduate School* and *Professor of Geology*

JOHN M. NEWELL, Ph.D. (Texas), *Assistant Dean, Graduate School* and *Professor of Education*

MADELYN L. LOCKHART, Ph.D. (Ohio State), *Assistant Dean, Graduate School* and *Professor of Economics*

JIMMY C. PERKINS, B.S., *Assistant to the Dean*

THE GRADUATE COUNCIL

HARRY H. SISLER (Chairman), Ph.D. (Illinois), *Dean, Graduate School; Director, Sponsored Research;* and *Professor of Chemistry*

STANLEY S. BALLARD, Ph.D. (California), *Professor of Physics*

YVONNE BRACKBILL, Ph.D. (Stanford), *Graduate Research Professor of Psychology* and *Professor of Obstetrics and Gynecology*

MELVIN FRIED, Ph.D. (Yale), *Professor of Biochemistry* and *Assistant Dean for Graduate Education in the Medical Sciences*

HARRY H. GRIGGS, Ph.D. (Iowa), *Professor of Journalism and Communications*

SAMUEL S. HILL, JR., Ph.D. (Duke), *Chairman* and *Professor of Religion*

LAWRENCE E. MALVERN, Ph.D. (Brown), *Professor of Engineering Sciences*

CARTER C. OSTERBIND, Ph.D. (American University), *Professor of Economics* and *Director of Bureau of Economic and Business Research* and *Director of Center for Gerontological Studies and Programs*

WILLARD W. PAYNE, Ph.D. (Michigan), *Chairman* and *Professor of Botany* and *Interim Director of Biological Sciences*

JOHN E. REYNOLDS, Ph.D. (Iowa State), *Associate Professor of Food and Resource Economics*

GARETH L. SCHMELING, Ph.D. (Wisconsin), *Chairman* and *Professor of Humanities* and *of Classics*

RICHARD B. STEPHENS, LL.B. (Michigan), *Director, Graduate Program in Taxation*

HANNELORE L. WASS, Ph.D. (Michigan), *Professor of Foundations of Education*

CRITICAL DATES FOR GRADUATE STUDENTS

Deadline:	Fall	Winter	Spring	Summer
University Dates				
Admission Application Deadlines:	July 2	Nov. 14	Feb. 18	May 6
Classes Begin:	Sept. 20	Jan. 5	Mar. 28	June 20
Late Registration Dates:	Sept. 17-24	Jan. 5-11	Mar. 28-Apr. 1	June 20-24
Admission to Candidacy Deadline for Master's Degrees:	Aug. 20	Dec. 3	Mar. 11	June 3
Midpoint of Quarter:	Oct. 29	Feb. 9	May 4	July 20
Classes End:	Dec. 3	Mar. 11	June 3	Aug. 19
Graduation:	Dec. 11	Mar. 19	June 11	Aug. 27
Thesis and Dissertation				
Submission of Master's Abstracts:	Nov. 1	Feb. 7	Apr. 25	July 18
First Submission of Dissertation:	Nov. 8	Feb. 14	May 2	July 25
Submit Signed Original Copy of Thesis:	Nov. 24	Mar. 2	May 27	Aug. 19
Submit Signed Original Copy of Dissertation:	Nov. 29	Mar. 7	May 31	Aug. 22
GSFLT and GRE Test Dates				
GRE Application Deadlines:	Sept. 20 May 11	Nov. 10	Dec. 7	Jan. 26 Mar. 23
GRE Examination Dates:	Oct. 16 June 11	Dec. 11	Jan. 8	Feb. 26 Apr. 23
GSFLT Examination Dates:	Oct. 9	Feb. 5	Apr. 9	June 25

University of Florida Calendar*

FALL QUARTER

1976

July 2, Friday, 4:00 p.m.	Last day for currently enrolled students to file application at Registrar's Office for admission to Graduate School.
July 30, Friday, 4:00 p.m.	Last day for those not previously in attendance at the University of Florida to file application for admission for Fall Quarter, and for those previously in attendance to apply for registration appointments.
August 20, Friday, 4:00 p.m.	Last day to file application for **Admission to Candidacy** for master's degree to be conferred at end of Fall Quarter.
September 3, Friday, 4:00 p.m.	Last day for those whose application was filed by above deadline to clear admissions. All credentials must have been received and college changes approved. Those who clear after this date will be assigned late registration appointments.
September 13-16, Monday-Thursday	Registration (including payment of fees) according to assigned appointments. No one permitted to start regular registration after 3:00 p.m., Thursday, September 16.
September 17-24, Friday-Friday ...	Late registration. Students subject to $25 late registration fee.
September 20, Monday	Classes begin.
September 20, Monday	Last day for receipt by the Educational Testing Service, Princeton, N. J. of Registration Form for October 16 Graduate Record Examination. Registration fee increases $4 after this date up to closing date of September 24, 1976.
September 24, Friday, 4:00 p.m. ...	Last day for DROP/ADD and for changing sections.
September 27, Monday, 3:30 p.m. .	Last day to pay fees without being subject to $25 late fee.

*This *Calendar* may be subject to change. Should subsequent notices be in conflict with the dates listed herein, the latest information should be followed. *Deadline Dates* are available each quarter from the Graduate School Office.

October 8, Friday, 4:00 p.m. ...... Last day to apply at Registrar's Office for degree to be conferred at end of Fall Quarter.

October 8, Friday, 4:00 p.m. ...... Last day for currently enrolled students to file application at Registrar's Office for admission to Graduate School.

October 8, Friday, 4:00 p.m. ...... Last day to file application with Office of the Registrar to change college or major department for the Winter Quarter.

October 9, Saturday, 9:00 a.m. .... Foreign language reading knowledge examination (GSFLT) in French, German, and Spanish.

October 16, Saturday, 8:30 a.m. ... Graduate Record Examination.

October 29, Friday .... Midpoint of term for completing doctoral qualifying examination.

November 1, Monday .... Last day for master's candidates to file abstracts and fee receipt for library hardbinding with the Graduate School.

November 8, Monday .... Last day for candidates for doctoral degrees to file dissertations, fee receipts for library hardbinding and microfilming, and all doctoral forms with the Graduate School.

November 10, Wednesday .... Last day for receipt by ETS of Registration Form for December 11 Graduate Record Examination. Fees increase $4 after this day and up to closing date of November 17.

November 11, Thursday,
Veterans Day .... Classes suspended.

November 19-20, Friday-Saturday,
Homecoming .... Classes suspended.

November 19, Friday, 4:00 p.m. ... Last day to withdraw without receiving failing grades in all courses.

November 24, Wednesday .... Last day to submit signed original copies of master's theses and Final Examination Reports to the Graduate School.

November 25-27, Thursday-Saturday,
Thanksgiving .... Classes suspended.

November 29, Monday .... Last day to submit signed original copies of dissertations and Final Examination Reports to the Graduate School.

November 29, Monday .... Final Examination Report for nonthesis degrees due in Room 288 GRI by this date.

December 3, Friday .... All classes end.

December 6, Monday .... Final examinations begin.

December 7, Tuesday .... Last day for receipt by the Educational Testing Service, Princeton, N. J of Registration Form for January 8 Graduate Record Examination. Registration fee increases $4 after this date up to closing date of December 13, 1976.

December 9, Thursday,
10:00 a.m. .... Grades for degree candidates due in Registrar's Office.

December 10, Friday, Noon ...... Report of colleges on candidates for degrees due in Graduate School Office.

December 11, Saturday .... Commencement Convocation.

December 11, Saturday,
8:30 a.m. .... Graduate Record Examination.

December 13, Monday,
9:00 a.m. .... All grades for Fall Quarter due in Registrar's Office.

WINTER QUARTER

1976

November 12, Friday, 4:00 p.m. ... Last day for those not previously in attendance at the University of Florida to file application for admission Winter Quarter, and for those previously in attendance to apply for registration appointments.

December 3, Friday, 4:00 p.m. .... Last day to file application for **Admission to Candidacy** for master's degree to be conferred at end of Winter Quarter.

December 10, Friday, 4:00 p.m. ... Last day for those whose application was filed by above deadline to clear admissions. All credentials must have been received and college changes approved. Those who clear after this date will be assigned late registration appointments.

1977

January 4, Tuesday	Registration (including payment of fees) according to assigned appointments. No one permitted to start regular registration after 3:00 p.m.
January 5, Wednesday	Classes begin.
January 5-11, Wednesday-Tuesday .	Late registration. Students subject to $25 late registration fee.
January 8, Saturday, 8:30 a.m.	Graduate Record Examination.
January 11, Tuesday, 4:00 p.m. . . .	Last day for DROP/ADD and for changing sections.
January 12, Wednesday, 2:30 p.m. .	Last day to pay fees without being subject to $25 late fee.
January 21, Friday, 4:00 p.m.	Last day for currently enrolled students to file application at Registrar's Office for admission to Graduate School.
January 21, Friday, 4:00 p.m.	Last day to apply at Registrar's Office for degree to be conferred at end of Winter Quarter.
January 21, Friday, 4:00 p.m.	Last day to file application with Office of the Registrar to change college or major department for the Spring Quarter.
January 26, Wednesday	Last day for receipt by ETS of Registration Form for February 26 Graduate Record Examination. Fees increase $4 after this day and up to closing date of February 2.
February 5, Saturday, 9:00 a.m. . . .	Foreign language reading knowledge examination (GSFLT) in French, German, and Spanish.
February 7, Monday	Last day for master's candidates to file abstracts and fee receipt for library hardbinding with the Graduate School.
February 9, Wednesday	Midpoint of term for completing doctoral qualifying examination.
February 14, Monday	Last day for candidates for doctoral degrees to file dissertations, fee receipts for library hardbinding and microfilming, and all doctoral forms with the Graduate School.

February 25, Friday, 4:00 p.m.	Last day to withdraw without receiving failing grades in all courses.
February 26, Saturday, 8:30 a.m. ..	Graduate Record Examination. (Aptitude Test only.)
March 2, Wednesday	Last day to submit signed original copies of master's theses and Final Examination Reports to the Graduate School.
March 7, Monday	Last day to submit signed original copies of dissertations and Final Examination Reports to the Graduate School.
March 7, Monday	Final Examination Reports for nonthesis degrees due in Room 288 GRI by this date.
March 11, Friday	All classes end.
March 14, Monday	Final examinations begin.
March 17, Thursday, 10:00 a.m. ...	Grades for degree candidates due in Registrar's Office.
March 18, Friday, 10:00 a.m.	Report of colleges on candidates for degrees due in Graduate School Office.
March 19, Saturday	Commencement Convocation.
March 21, Monday, 9:00 a.m.	All grades for Winter Quarter due in Registrar's Office.

SPRING QUARTER

1977

February 18, Friday, 4:00 p.m.	Last day for those not previously in attendance at the University of Florida to file application for admission for Spring Quarter, and for those previously in attendance to apply for registration appointments.
March 11, Friday, 4:00 p.m.	Last day for those whose application was filed by the above deadline to clear admissions. All credentials must have been received and college changes approved. Those who clear after this date will be assigned late registration appointments.
March 11, Friday, 4:00 p.m.	Last day to file application for **Admission to Candidacy** for master's degree to be conferred at end of Spring Quarter.

March 23, Wednesday . . . . Last day for receipt by the Educational Testing Service, Princeton, N. J. of Registration Form for April 23 Graduate Record Examination. Registration fee increases $4 after this date up to closing date of March 30, 1977.

March 25, Friday . . . . Registration (including payment of fees) according to assigned appointments. No one permitted to start regular registration after 3:00 p.m.

March 28, Monday . . . . Classes begin.

March 28-April 1, Monday-Friday . Late registration. Students subject to $25 late registration fee.

April 1, Friday, 4:00 p.m. . . . . Last day for DROP/ADD and for changing sections.

April 4, Monday, 3:30 p.m. . . . . Last day to pay fees without being subject to $25 late fee.

April 9, Saturday, 9:00 a.m. . . . . . . Foreign language reading knowledge examination (GSFLT) in French, German, and Spanish.

April 15, Friday, 4:00 p.m. . . . . Last day to file application with Office of the Registrar to change college or major department for the Summer Quarter.

April 15, Friday, 4:00 p.m. . . . . Last day for currently enrolled students to file application at Registrar's Office for admission to Graduate School.

April 15, Friday, 4:00 p.m. . . . . Last day to apply at Registrar's Office for degree to be conferred at end of Spring Quarter.

April 23, Saturday, 8:30 a.m. . . . . . Graduate Record Examination.

April 25, Monday . . . . Last day for master's degree candidates to file abstracts and fee receipt for library hardbinding with the Graduate School.

May 2, Monday . . . . Last day for candidates for doctoral degrees to file dissertations, fee receipts for library hardbinding and microfilming, and all doctoral forms with the Graduate School.

May 4, Wednesday . . . . Midpoint of term for completing doctoral qualifying examination.

May 11, Wednesday	Last day for receipt by the Educational Testing Service, Princeton, N. J. of Registration Form for June 13 Graduate Record Examination. Registration fee increases $4 after this date up to closing date of May 18, 1977.
May 27, Friday	Last day to submit signed original copies of master's theses and Final Examination Reports to the Graduate School.
May 30, Monday, Memorial Day . .	Classes suspended.
May 31, Tuesday	Last day to submit signed original copies of dissertations and Final Examination Reports to the Graduate School.
May 31, Tuesday	Final Examination Reports for nonthesis degrees due in Room 288 GRI by this date.
June 3, Friday	All classes end.
June 6, Monday	Final examinations begin.
June 9, Thursday, 10:00 a.m.	Grades for degree candidates due in Registrar's Office.
June 10, Friday, Noon	Report of colleges on candidates for degrees due in Graduate School Office.
June 11, Saturday	Commencement Convocation.
June 11, Saturday, 8:30 a.m.	Graduate Record Examination.
June 13, Monday, 9:00 a.m.	All grades for Spring Quarter due in Registrar's Office.

SUMMER QUARTER

1977

May 6, Friday, 4:00 p.m.	Last day for those not previously in attendance at the University of Florida to file application for admission for Summer Quarter, and for those previously in attendance to apply for registration appointments.
June 3, Friday, 4:00 p.m.	Last day to file application for **Admission to Candidacy** for a master's degree to be conferred at end of Summer Quarter.

June 3, Friday, 4:00 p.m. . . . . Last day for those whose application was filed by the above deadline to clear admissions. All credentials must have been received and college changes approved. Those who clear after this date will be assigned late registration appointments.

June 11, Saturday, 8:30 a.m. . . . . . . Graduate Record Examination.

June 17, Friday . . . . Registration (including payment of fees) according to assigned appointments. No one permitted to start regular registration after 3:00 p.m.

June 20, Monday . . . . Classes begin.

June 20-24, Monday-Friday . . . . . . Late registration. Students subject to $25 late registration fee.

June 24, Friday, 4:00 p.m. . . . . Last day for DROP/ADD and for changing sections.

June 25, Saturday, 1:30 p.m. . . . . . . Foreign language reading knowledge examinations (GSFLT) in French, German, or Spanish.

June 27, Monday, 3:30 p.m. . . . . . . Last day to pay fees without being subject to $25 late fee.

July 4, Monday,
Independence Day . . . . Classes suspended.

July 8, Friday, 4:00 p.m. . . . . Last day to file application with Office of the Registrar to change college or major department for the Fall Quarter.

July 8, Friday, 4:00 p.m. . . . . Last day for currently enrolled students to file application at Registrar's Office for admission to Graduate School.

July 8, Friday, 4:00 p.m. . . . . Last day to apply at Registrar's Office for degree to be conferred at end of Summer Quarter.

July 18, Monday . . . . Last day for master's candidates to file abstracts and fee receipt for library hardbinding with the Graduate School.

July 20, Wednesday . . . . Midpoint of term for completing doctoral qualifying examination.

July 25, Monday . . . . Last day for candidates for doctoral degrees to file dissertations, fee receipts for library hardbinding and microfilming, and all doctoral forms with the Graduate School.

August 5, Friday, 4:00 p.m. .... Last day to withdraw without receiving failing grades in all courses.

August 19, Friday .... Last day to submit signed original copies

August 19, Friday .... Last day to sumbit signed original copies of master's theses and Final Examination Reports to the Graduate School.

August 22, Monday .... Final examinations begin.

August 22, Monday .... Last day to submit signed original copies of dissertations and Final Examination Reports to the Graduate School.

August 22, Monday .... Final Examination Report for nonthesis degrees due in Room 288 GRI by this date.

August 25, Thursday, 10:00 a.m. .. Grades for degree candidates due in Registrar's Office.

August 26, Friday, Noon .... Report of colleges on candidates for degrees due in Graduate School Office.

August 27, Saturday .... Commencement Convocation.

August 29, Monday, 9:00 a.m. .... All grades for Summer Quarter due in Registrar's Office.

General Information

THE GRADUATE SCHOOL

ORGANIZATION AND HISTORY

The Graduate School consists of the dean, associate dean, assistant deans, the Graduate Council, and the graduate faculty. General policies and standards of the Graduate School are established by the graduate faculty. The Graduate School is responsible for the enforcement of minimum general standards of graduate work in the University and for the coordination of the graduate programs of the various colleges and divisions of the University. The responsibility for the detailed operations of graduate programs is vested in the individual colleges, divisions, and departments. In most of the colleges an assistant dean or other official is directly responsible for graduate study in his college.

The Graduate Council, of which the graduate dean is chairman, assists him in being the agent of the graduate faculty for execution of policy related to graduate study and associated research. The Council considers petitions and recommends the award of graduate degrees. Members of the graduate faculty, who are appointed by the dean with the approval of the Graduate Council, fall into two categories in accordance with their function: the Graduate Studies Faculty (GSF), who are appointed to teach graduate courses and to direct master's theses, and the Doctoral Research Faculty (DRF), who are appointed in addition to direct doctoral dissertations. No staff member is expected to perform any of these functions without having been appointed to the graduate faculty, though temporary exceptions may be made in unusual circumstances.

In the beginning the organization of graduate study was very informal. Control was in the hands of a faculty committee which reported directly to the President. In 1910, however, James N. Anderson, head of the Department of Ancient Languages, was appointed Dean of the College of Arts and Sciences and Director of Graduate Work, and in 1930 he became the first dean of the Graduate School. He was succeeded upon his retirement in 1938 by T. M. Simpson, head of the Department of Mathematics, who held the position until 1951. C. F. Byers, head of the Department of Biological Sciences in the University College, served as acting dean from June, 1951, until August, 1952, when he was succeeded by L. E. Grinter, who came from the Illinois Institute of Technology, where he had been Vice President, Dean of the Graduate School, and Research Professor. Upon becoming Acting Executive Vice President in 1969, Dr. Grinter was named dean *emeritus* of the Graduate School. He was succeeded by Harold P. Hanson, who came to Florida from the University of Texas, where he had served as Chairman of the Department of Physics. In 1971, Dr. Hanson was appointed Vice President for Academic Affairs. Dr. Alexander G. Smith, of the Department of Physics and Astronomy and a former assistant dean of the Graduate School, served as acting dean until the appointment of Dr. Harry H. Sisler. Dr. Sisler served as Chairman of the Department of Chemistry for twelve years, as Dean of the College of Arts and Sciences, and as Executive Vice President of the University of Florida until he became Dean of the Graduate School in March, 1973.

Study leading to graduate degrees has existed at the University of Florida from the date of the establishment of the University on its present campus. The first M.A. was awarded in 1906, the major being English, and the first M.S. in 1908, with a major in entomology. The first programs leading to the Ph.D. were initiated in 1930, and the first degrees were awarded in 1934, one with a major in chemistry and the other with a major in pharmacy. The first Ed.D. was awarded in 1948. Graduate study has had a phenomenal growth at the University ·of Florida. In 1930, 33 degrees were awarded in 12 fields. In 1940, 66 degrees were awarded in 16 fields. In 1974-1975 the total number of graduate degrees awarded was 1,747 in more than 90 fields. The proportion of doctoral degrees has increased steadily. In 1950, 18 Ph.D.'s and 5 Ed.D.'s were awarded. In 1974-1975 the total was 292 Ph.D.'s and 61 Ed.D.'s.

GRADUATE DEGREES AND PROGRAMS

Refer to the section of this *Catalog* **entitled** *Fields of Instruction* **for specializations in the approved programs.**

NONTHESIS DEGREES
(Asterisk (*) indicates thesis option)

Master of Agriculture (M.Ag.), with program in one of the following:

Agricultural and Extension
  Education
Agronomy
Animal Science
Botany
Dairy Science
Entomology and Nematology
Food Science

General Agriculture
Horticultural Science:
  Fruit Crops
  Ornamental Horticulture
  Vegetable Crops
Plant Pathology
Poultry Science
Soil Science

Master of Agricultural Management and Resource Development (M.A.M.R.D.), with program in Food and Resource Economics.

Master of Arts in Teaching (M.A.T.), with program in one of the following:

Anthropology
English
French
Geography
German
History
Latin
Latin American Area Studies
Linguistics

Mathematics
Philosophy
Political Science
Political Science
  International Relations
Psychology
Sociology
Spanish
Speech

Master of Building Construction (M.B.C.)

Master of Business Administration (M.B.A.), with program in one of the following:

Accounting
Business Administration
Economics
Finance
Health and Hospital
  Administration

Insurance
Management
Marketing
Real Estate and
  Urban Land Studies

Master of Education (M.Ed.), with program in one of the following:

Business Education
Childhood Education

Educational Administration
Foundations of Education

Counselor Education
  (available only in conjunction with the Ed.S. degree)
Curriculum and Instruction

Music Education
Secondary Education
Special Education
Vocational, Technical, Adult
  Education

Master of Engineering (M.E.), with program in one of the following:
Aerospace Engineering*
Agricultural Engineering*
Chemical Engineering*
Civil Engineering*
Coastal and Oceanographic
  Engineering*
Electrical Engineering*
Engineering Mechanics*

Engineering Science*
Environmental Engineering
  Sciences*
Industrial and Systems
  Engineering*
Mechanical Engineering*
Metallurgical and Materials
  Engineering*
Nuclear Engineering Sciences*

Master of Forest Resources and Conservation (M.F.R.C.)
Master of Health Education (M.H.Ed.)
Master of Health Science (M.H.S.), with program in one of the following:
Occupational Therapy   Rehabilitation Counseling
Master of Laws in Taxation (LL.M. in Tax.)
Master of Nursing (M.Nsg.)
Master of Physical Education (M.P.E.)
Master of Science in Teaching (M.S.T.), with program in one of the following:
Astronomy
Botany
Chemistry
Geography
Geology

Mathematics
Microbiology
Physics
Psychology
Zoology

Master of Statistics (M.Stat.)
Engineer (Engr.)—A special degree requiring one year of graduate work beyond the master's degree. For a list of the approved programs, see those listed above for the Master of Engineering degree. (Thesis optional.)
Specialist in Education (Ed.S.)—A special degree requiring one year of graduate work beyond the master's degree. For a list of the approved programs, see those listed below for the Doctor of Education degree.

THESIS DEGREES
(Dagger (†) indicates nonthesis option)

Master of Arts (M.A.), with program in one of the following:
Accounting†
Anthropology†
Business Administration:
  Finance
  Insurance
  Management
  Marketing
  Real Estate and Urban
    Land Studies
Economics†
English†

History
Latin
Latin American Area
  Studies
Linguistics
Mathematics†
Philosophy†
Political Science†
Political Science
  International Relations†
Psychology†

French†	Sociology
Geography	Spanish†
German	Speech

Master of Arts in Architecture (M.A.Arch.)

Master of Arts in Education (M.A.E.). For a list of the programs, see those listed above for the Master of Education degree.

Master of Arts in Health Education (M.A.H.Ed.)

Master of Arts in Journalism and Communications (M.A.J.C.), with program in Communication.

Master of Arts in Physical Education (M.A.P.E.)

Master of Fine Arts (M.F.A.), with program in one of the following:

Art	Music	Theatre

Master of Arts in Urban and Regional Planning (M.A.U.R.P.)

Master of Science (M.S.), with program in one of the following:

Aerospace Engineering†	Horticultural Science:
Agricultural Engineering†	*Fruit Crops*
Agricultural and Extension	*Ornamental Horticulture*
Education	*Vegetable Crops*
Agronomy	Industrial and Systems
Animal Science	Engineering†
Astronomy†	Mathematics†
Biochemistry	Mechanical Engineering†
Botany	Medical Sciences:
Chemical Engineering†	*Anatomical Sciences*
Chemistry	*Immunology and Medical*
Civil Engineering†	*Microbiology*
Coastal and Oceanographic	*Neuroscience*
Engineering†	*Pathology*
Dairy Science	*Pharmacology*
Electrical Engineering†	*Physiology*
Engineering Mechanics†	Metallurgical and Materials
Engineering Science†	Engineering†
Entomology and Nematology	Microbiology
Environmental Engineering	Nuclear Engineering
Sciences†	Sciences†
Food and Resource	Physics†
Economics	Plant Pathology
Food Science	Poultry Science
Forest Resources and	Psychology†
Conservation	Soil Science
Geography	Veterinary Sciences
Geology	Zoology†

Master of Science in Building Construction (M.S.B.C.)

Master of Science in Nursing (M.S.Nsg.)

Master of Science in Pharmacy (M.S.P.), with program in Pharmaceutical Sciences:
Pharmaceutical Chemistry
Pharmacy

Master of Science in Statistics (M.S.Stat.)

Doctor of Education (Ed.D.), with program in one of the following:

Counselor Education   Educational Administration
Curriculum and Instruction   Foundations of Education
                              Special Education

Doctor of Philosophy (Ph.D.), with program in one of the following:

Aerospace Engineering   Mathematics
Agronomy   Mechanical Engineering
Animal Science   Medical Sciences:
Anthropology   *Anatomical Sciences*
Astronomy   *Immunology and*
Biochemistry   *Medical Microbiology*
Botany   *Neuroscience*
Business Administration   *Pathology*
Chemical Engineering   *Pharmacology*
Chemistry   *Physiology*
Civil Engineering   Metallurgical and Materials
Counselor Education   Engineering
Curriculum and Instruction   Microbiology
Economics   Nuclear Engineering Sciences
Educational Administration   Pharmaceutical Sciences:
Electrical Engineering   *Pharmaceutical Chemistry*
Engineering Mechanics   *Pharmacy*
English   Philosophy
Entomology and Nematology   Physics
Environmental Engineering   Plant Pathology
   Sciences   Political Science
Food and Resource Economics   Political Science—
Foundations of Education   International Relations
Geography   Psychology
History   Romance Languages:
Horticultural Science: *French*
   Fruit Crops   *Spanish*
   Ornamental Horticulture   Sociology
   Vegetable Crops   Soil Science
Industrial and Systems   Special Education
   Engineering   Speech
Linguistics   Statistics
                              Zoology

ADMISSION TO THE GRADUATE SCHOOL

Application for Admission.—Admission forms and information concerning admission procedures may be obtained from the Registrar and Admissions Office, 135 Tigert Hall. Prospective students are urged to apply for admission as early as possible. For some departments, deadlines for receipt of admission applications may be earlier than those stated in the current *University Calendar;* prospective students should check with the appropriate department. Applications which meet minimum standards are referred to the graduate selection committees of the various colleges and departments for approval or disapproval.

To be admitted to graduate study in a given department, the prospective student must satisfy the requirements of the department as well as those of the Graduate

School. In some departments, the available space and facilities limit the number of students that can be admitted.

General Requirements.—The Board of Regents has established the following minimum standards for first-time admission to a master's or doctoral degree program in the State University System: a grade average of B or better for all upper-division undergraduate work or a total Verbal-Quantitative score of 1000 or higher on the Aptitude Test of the Graduate Record Examination. It must be emphasized that these are *minimum* standards for the State University System, and satisfaction of these Board of Regents minimum criteria is not sufficient for admission to graduate study at the University of Florida.

The Graduate School, University of Florida, requires *both* a minimum grade average of B for all upper-division undergraduate work *and* a minimum of a Verbal-Quantitative total score of 1000 on the Aptitude Test of the Graduate Record Examination. For some departments, and in more advanced levels of graduate study, an undergraduate average or Graduate Record Examination scores above those stated for the Graduate School may be required. Some colleges and departments require a reading knowledge of at least one foreign language. Exceptions to the above requirements are made only when these and other criteria such as letters of recommendation are reviewed by the department, recommended by the department, and approved by the Dean of the Graduate School.

Unqualified admission to the Graduate School is dependent upon the presentation of a baccalaureate degree from an accredited college or university. No application will be considered unless the complete official transcript of all the applicant's undergraduate and graduate work are in the possession of the Registrar, and no transcript will be accepted as official unless it is received directly from the registrar of the institution in which the work was done. Official supplementary transcripts are required as soon as they are available for any work completed after application for admission has been made. In general, no student who is a graduate of a non-accredited institution will be considered for graduate study in any unit of the University.

The University of Florida encourages applications from qualified persons without respect to race, sex, religion, cultural, or ethnic background.

Graduate Record Examination (GRE)

In addition to the Aptitude Test of the Graduate Record Examination which is required of all applicants, some departments encourage the applicant to submit scores on one or more advanced subject tests of the Graduate Record Examination. The scores on all tests taken will be considered in regard to admission.

Postponement of the Graduate Record Examination.—In the event that an applicant takes the GRE Aptitude Test too late for the results to reach the Admissions Office before the proposed date of entry, the student may apply for conditional admission to the Graduate School with postponement of the GRE Aptitude Test provided satisfactory scores on the Miller Analogies Test (MAT) are submitted. The scores on the Miller Analogies Test will be used as a partial basis for deciding whether conditional admission may be granted. The Miller Analogies Test is *not* a substitute for the Graduate Record Examination. In cases where conditional admission is granted based on the scores of the Miller Analogies Test, it is for *one* term only. Satisfactory scores on the GRE Aptitude Test must be submitted before a second registration will be permitted.

The decision on postponing the Graduate Record Examination Aptitude Test will be based on the scores on the Miller Analogies Test and the academic credentials submitted. If these scores and academic credentials are not satisfactory, submission of the results of the GRE Aptitude Test will be required before an admission decision is reached. It should be noted that the Miller Analogies Test may not be repeated until at least one year has elapsed.

Graduate Study in Business Administration.—Students applying for admission to the Graduate School for study in the College of Business Administration may substitute satisfactory scores on the Graduate Management Admission Test (GMAT) for the Graduate Record Examination. Applicants are requested to contact the Educational Testing Service, Princeton, New Jersey for additional information.

FOREIGN STUDENTS

All foreign students seeking admission to the Graduate School are required to submit satisfactory scores on the GRE Aptitude Test and on the TOEFL (Test of English as a Foreign Language) with the following exceptions:

1. Foreign students whose native tongue is English or who have studied at a United States college or university for one year or more need not submit TOEFL scores but must submit satisfactory scores on the Aptitude Test of the Graduate Record Examination before their application for admission can be considered.

2. Students educated in foreign countries who apply for admission while residing outside the United States may be granted a one-quarter postponement of the GRE but not the TOEFL. Permission to register for subsequent quarters will depend upon the submission of scores on the Graduate Record Examination.

3. All foreign students applying for admission to the Master of Business Administration program must submit satisfactory scores from either the Graduate Record Examination Aptitude Test or the Graduate Management Admission Test before their application for admission can be considered. The Graduate Management Admission Test is recommended.

Applicants are requested to write TOEFL, Educational Testing Service, Princeton, New Jersey, for registration forms.

CONDITIONAL ADMISSION

Students may be given conditional admission to the Graduate School to ascertain their ability to pursue graduate work successfully where previous grade records or Graduate Record Examination scores are on the borderline of acceptability.

Students granted conditional admission should be notified by the major department of the conditions under which they are admitted. When these conditions have been satisfied, the department must notify the student in writing, sending a copy of notification to the Graduate School. Work taken while a student is in conditional status may be applied toward a graduate degree.

POSTBACCALAUREATE STUDENTS

Students who have received a bachelor's degree but have *not* been admitted to the Graduate School are classified as postbaccalaureate students (6—) and may enroll in courses for any of the following reasons: (1) to validate undergraduate records from nonaccredited and unevaluated colleges; (2) to provide a means for students *not seeking a graduate degree* to enroll in courses—included in this category would be students who change their professional goals or wish to expand their academic background; and (3) to accommodate students who *do intend* to enter a graduate program at some future date, but need a substantial number of prerequisite courses.

Postbaccalaureate students may enroll in graduate courses but the work taken will not normally be transferred to the graduate record if the student is subsequently admitted to the Graduate School. By petition in clearly justified cases, it is possible to transfer up to but no more than 10 quarter hours of course work earned with a grade of A or B.

Students in the College of Education who desire postbaccalaureate classification to obtain teacher certification must provide the college with a clear statement of certification goals as a part of the requirements for admission. Interested students should contact the Graduate Studies Office, 134 Norman, for further information.

Faculty Members as Graduate Students

Members of the faculty of the University of Florida with the rank of instructor or above (or equivalent), except county extension directors in the Agricultural Extension Service, may not receive or be a candidate for a graduate degree from this institution. They may, however, register for work in the Graduate School.

State University System Programs

Traveling Scholar Program.—The State University System affords, under the Traveling Scholar Program, an opportunity for graduate students to take courses or conduct research activities at any of the universities in the State System. Course work taken under the auspices of the Traveling Scholar Program at another university in the State System will apply for graduate credit at the student's home campus. The deans of the graduate schools of the state universities are the coordinators of the program, and interested students should contact the dean of the graduate school on their home campus for additional information.

Cooperative Degree Programs.—In certain degree programs, faculty in the State University System hold graduate faculty status at the University of Florida. In those approved areas, the intellectual resources of these external graduate faculty members are available to students at the University of Florida.

GENERAL REGULATIONS

It is the responsibility of the graduate student to become informed concerning, and to observe, all regulations and procedures required by the program the student is pursuing. The student must be familiar with those sections of the *Graduate Catalog* that outline general regulations and requirements, specific degree program requirements, and the offerings and requirements of the major department. **Ignorance of a rule does not constitute a basis for waiving that rule.** Any exceptions to the policies stated in the *Graduate Catalog* must be approved by the Dean of the Graduate School.

After admission to the Graduate School, but before the first registration, the student should consult the college and/or the graduate coordinator in the major department concerning courses and degree requirements, deficiencies if any, and special regulations of the department. The dean of the college in which the degree program is located must approve all registrations.

STUDY LOADS

The University of Florida operates on a quarter system consisting of four 10-week periods of instruction and examination. A credit under the quarter system is equal to 2/3 of a semester credit.

Maximum Registration.—Maximum registration for a graduate student is 20 credits. This number will be reduced for those students who hold graduate student appointments. Guidelines for adjusting the maximum registration in such instances are provided in the *Graduate Coordinators' Manual,* and students on appointment should consult the graduate coordinator in their respective departments.

Minimum Registration.—Graduate students who receive any of the various types of graduate stipends must meet certain minimum registration requirements. Information concerning these minima is available in the Graduate School or from the graduate coordinator of the student's major department.

Any graduate student who is utilizing University facilities and/or faculty time must register for an appropriate course load and *in no case for less than three quarter hours.*

COURSES AND CREDITS

Courses numbered 500 and above are limited to graduate students, with the exception described under *Undergraduate Registration in Graduate Courses.* Courses numbered 700 and above are designed primarily for advanced graduate students.

A complete list of approved graduate courses appears in the section of this *Catalog* entitled *Fields of Instruction.* Departments reserve the right to decide which of these graduate courses will be offered in a given quarter and the departments should be consulted concerning available courses.

Correspondence and Extension Work.—No courses may be taken for graduate credit by correspondence. No extension courses may be used for graduate credit except in programs for the M.Ag., M.Ed., M.A.E., M.H.Ed., M.P.E., and Ed.S. degrees. Extension work taken at another institution, except through the Board of Regents Office for Continuing Education, may not be transferred to the University of Florida for graduate credit.

State Centers for Continuing Education.—Course work is available in the graduate residence centers established in the state. The amount of credit acceptable for transfer to a degree program varies according to the degree sought. Residence center work is not transferable to all degree programs and the student should consult the requirements for specific degrees in this *Catalog* for additional information.

GRADES

Passing grades for graduate students are A, B, C, and S (satisfactory). Grades of D, E, U (unsatisfactory), I (incomplete), X (absent from examination), EW (dropped for nonattendance or unsatisfactory work), or WF (withdrew failing) cannot be used to satisfy any of the requirements of a graduate degree. Grade points are not designated for S and U grades; these grades are not used in calculating grade-point average.

Grades of S and U are the only grades awarded in courses numbered 697 (Supervised Research), 698 (Supervised Teaching), 699 (Master's Research), and 799 (Doctoral Research). Additional courses for which S and U grades apply are noted in the departmental course offerings. With the exception of those courses listed in the Graduate Catalog for which S and U grades apply, no course may be taken by a graduate student for an S or U grade.

Deferred Grade H.—In special situations where it is not possible to assign a regular grade at the end of a term, a deferred grade (H) may be assigned. This grade may be used only in special situations where the expected unit of work may be developed over a period of time greater than a single term. The grade of H is *not* a substitute for a grade of S, U, or I. Courses for which H grades are appropriate must be so noted in their catalog descriptions, and must be approved by the Graduate Curriculum Committee.

Incomplete Grades.—Grades of I (incomplete) must be removed no later than the last day of classes of the first term in which the student registers following receipt of the I grade. If the I grade has not been changed accordingly, the Office of the Registrar will be requested to record a grade of E for the course. Exceptions to this policy will be made by the Graduate School only if written justification from the department chairman, approved by the college dean, is received by the Graduate School four weeks prior to the last day of classes. **All grades of I must be removed prior to the award of a graduate degree.**

UNDERGRADUATE REGISTRATION IN GRADUATE COURSES

With permission of the instructor and the college concerned, an undergraduate student at the University of Florida may enroll in graduate-level courses (500 and 600 level) if the student has senior standing and an upper-division grade-point average of at least 2.8. After a student has been accepted in the Graduate School, up to 10 hours of graduate-level courses earned with a grade of A or B taken under this provision may be applied toward a graduate degree at the University of Florida provided credit for the course has not been used for an undergraduate degree.

CONCURRENT GRADUATE PROGRAMS

A graduate student who is pursuing graduate degrees in two programs must have the approval of the chairman of both departments involved and the Dean of the Graduate School. No more than 10 hours of course work may be applied toward meeting the requirements of each degree program.

INFORMATION FOR VETERANS

The University of Florida is approved for the education and training of veterans under all public laws in effect; i.e., Chapter 31, Title 38, U.S. Code (Disabled Veterans); Chapter 34, Title 38, U.S. Code (Cold-War G.I. Bill); and Chapter 35, Title 38, U.S. Code (Children of Deceased or Disabled Veterans).

Students who may be eligible for educational benefits under any Veterans Administration program are urged to contact the Veterans Affairs Office, 123 Tigert Hall, or the Veterans Administration Regional Office, P. O. Box 1437, St. Petersburg, Florida 33700, well in advance of the date of registration.

Students expecting to receive benefits under one of these programs must file with the Office of the Registrar their Certificate of Eligibility which is issued by the Veterans Administration. No certification can be made until the Certificate is on file. Benefits are determined by the Veterans Administration, and the University certifies according to these rules and regulations.

Unsatisfactory Scholarship

Any graduate student may be denied further registration in the University or in a graduate program should progress toward completion of the planned program become unsatisfactory to the department, college, or Dean of the Graduate School. Failure to maintain a B average in all work attempted is, by definition, unsatisfactory progress.

Change of Major or College

Graduate students who wish to change their major or college must make formal application through the Office of the Registrar and receive approval of the appropriate department chairman, college dean and the Dean of the Graduate School. Deadline dates for such changes as specified in the current *University Calendar* must be met.

Foreign Language Examination

A foreign language examination is not required for all degree programs and the student should contact the graduate coordinator in the appropriate department for specific information regarding any requirement of a foreign language.

If a department requires that a student meet the foreign language requirement by satisfactory performance on the Graduate School Foreign Language Tests (GSFLT) in French, Spanish, or German, the student should contact the Graduate School for applications and payment of fees. The application deadline dates and examination times, dates and places are listed in the *University Calendar*. Educational Testing Service (ETS) no longer administers this examination and does not accept application fees or issue tickets of admission for these tests.

Admission to Candidacy

Admission to candidacy is not automatic. **It requires a formal application distinct from registration** on or before the dates stipulated in the current *University Calendar*. Admission to candidacy depends, among other requirements, upon the maintenance of a B average or higher in the major and in all work attempted. All grades of I and X must be removed.

Examinations

The student's supervisory committee is responsible for the administration of the written and oral qualifying examinations as well as the final oral examination for the defense of the thesis or dissertation. *All* members of the supervisory committee must sign the appropriate forms, including the signature pages, in order for the student to satisfy the requirements of the examination.

Procedure for Final Quarter

It is the student's responsibility to ascertain that all requirements have been met and that every deadline is observed. Deadline dates are set forth in the *University Calendar* and by the college, school, or department. Regular issues of *Deadline Dates* are available each quarter.

When the dissertation or thesis is ready to be put in final form, the student should get instructions from the Graduate School Editorial Office, and should request the Student Information and Records Office to check the student's folder to make certain that *all* requirements for graduation have been fulfilled.

When a student registers for the last term, the appropriate fees for the Library permanent binding of two copies and for microfilming the dissertation must be paid by the deadline specified in the *University Calendar*.

A student must be registered for an appropriate load (in no case fewer than three credits) in the University for the term in which the final examination is given and at the time the degree is received.

AWARDING OF DEGREES

The Graduate School will authorize a candidate to be awarded the degree appropriate to the course of study under the following conditions, the details of which can be found under the descriptions of the several degrees.

1. The candidate must have completed all course requirements, including an internship or practicum if required, in the major and minor fields, observing time limits, limitations on transfer credit, on nonresident work, and on level of course work.

2. The candidate must have a grade average of B or better in all work attempted in the graduate program. All grades of I and X must be removed.

3. The candidate must have satisfactorily completed all required examinations, qualifying, comprehensive, and final, and be recommended for the degree by the supervisory committee, major department, and college.

4. The dissertation or, if required, thesis or equivalent project, must have been approved by the supervisory committee and accepted by the Graduate School. Recommendations for the awarding of a degree include meeting all academic and professional qualifications as judged by the faculty of the appropriate department.

5. All requirements for the degree must be met while the candidate is a fully registered graduate student. Students who have been registered in the Graduate School at least one quarter of each successive calendar year may graduate according to the curriculum under which they entered, provided the courses are still offered by the University.

ATTENDANCE AT COMMENCEMENT

Graduates who are to receive advanced degrees are urged to attend Commencement in order to accept personally the honor indicated by the appropriate hood. The student may arrange through the University Bookstore for the proper academic attire to be worn at Commencement.

REQUIREMENTS FOR MASTER'S DEGREE
GENERAL REGULATIONS

The following regulations represent those of the Graduate School. Colleges and departments may have additional regulations beyond those stated below. **Unless otherwise indicated in the following sections concerning master's degrees, these general regulations apply to all master's degree programs at the University.**

Course Requirements.—Courses numbered 500 and above are open for graduate credit. At least 50% of the minimum course work for a master's degree must be in courses numbered 500 and above. Courses numbered 300 and above may be acceptable for minor credit when taken as a part of an approved graduate program. The program of course work for a master's degree must be approved by the student's adviser, supervisory committee, or representative of the department. No more than 10 credits from a previous master's degree program may be applied toward a second master's degree.

If a minor is chosen, at least 8 credits of work are required in the minor field. Two 8-credit minors may be taken with departmental permission. Minor work must be in a department other than the major; in special cases this requirement may be modified, but only with the written permission of the Dean of the Graduate School.

Degree Requirements.—Unless otherwise specified, for any master's degree, the student must earn a minimum of 45 credits as a graduate student at the University of Florida of which no more than 10 quarter hours of course work earned with a grade of A or B may be transferred from institutions approved for this purpose by the Dean of the Graduate School.

Transfer of Credits.—Courses open only for graduate credit to the extent of 10 quarter hours earned with a grade of A or B may be transferred from an institution approved for this purpose by the Graduate School. Acceptance of transfer credit requires approval of the student's supervisory committee and the Dean of the Graduate School. Nonresident or extension work taken at another institution, with the exception of work taken through the Board of Regents Office for Continuing Education, may not be transferred to the University of Florida for graduate credit.

Supervisory Committee.—Supervisory committees for graduate degree programs are nominated by the representative department chairman, approved by the college dean, and appointed by the Dean of the Graduate School. Only members of the graduate faculty may be appointed to supervisory committees. The Dean of the Graduate School is an ex-officio member of all supervisory committees.

The supervisory committee for a master's degree with a thesis must consist of at least two members selected from the graduate faculty. The supervisory committee for a master's degree without a thesis may consist of one member of the graduate faculty who advises the students and oversees the program. If a minor is designated, the committee should include one member of the minor department who has been appointed to the graduate faculty.

Admission to Candidacy.—Application should be made through the department no later than the last day of classes in the quarter **preceding** the quarter in which the student expects to receive the degree. The Graduate Council reserves the right to deny degrees to persons who have failed to comply with this regulation at the proper time. The student must have a B average for all graduate work completed and in all work attempted in order to be admitted to candidacy.

Language Requirements.—(1) The requirement of a reading knowledge of a foreign language is at the discretion of the department. The foreign language requirement varies from department to department and the student should check with the appropriate department for specific information. (2) The ability to use the English language correctly and effectively, as judged by the supervisory committee, is required of all candidates.

Examination.—A final comprehensive examination, oral, written or both, must be passed by the candidate. This examination will cover at least the candidate's field of concentration, and in no case may it be scheduled earlier than six months before the degree is to be conferred.

Time Limitation.—All work counted toward the master's degree must be completed during the seven years immediately preceding the date on which the degree is to be awarded.

Master of Arts and Master of Science

The requirements for the Master of Arts and the Master of Science degrees also apply to the following degrees, except as they are individually described hereafter: Master of Arts in Education, Master of Arts in Health Education, Master of Arts in Journalism and Communications, Master of Arts in Physical Education, Master of Science in Building Construction, and Master of Science in Pharmacy.

Course Requirements.—The minimum course work required for a master's degree with thesis is 45 credits which may include up to 9 hours of the research course numbered 699. The minimum course work requirement for a master's degree without a thesis or the master's taken with the nonthesis option is 48 credits excluding credits for which grades of S and U are given. Students pursuing the nonthesis option may not use courses numbered 699 or 799 to meet the credit requirement. Nonthesis degree or nonthesis option students may enroll for courses 697 Supervised Research, or 698—Supervised Teaching, in their final term. Since 697 and 698 courses are graded S/U, registration in these courses must be *in excess of* the 48 credit minimum requirement for the degree.

For both nonthesis and thesis degrees at least half the required credits, exclusive of 699 or 799, must be in a field of study designated the major. One or two minors of at least 8 credits each may be taken, but a minor is not required by the Graduate School. Minor work must be in a department other than the major. The work in the major field must be in courses numbered 500 or above. For work outside the major, courses numbered 300 or above may be taken.

Thesis.—Candidates for the master's degree with thesis are required to prepare and present a thesis (or equivalent in creative work) acceptable to their supervisory committees and the Graduate School. The candidate should consult the Graduate School on or before the dates specified in the *University Calendar*. The college copy should be submitted to the college or department by the specified date. Two separate copies of the abstract, must be in the office of the Dean of the Graduate School on or before the dates specified in the *University Calendar*. The college copy should be submitted to the college or department by the specified date. Two title pages should be inserted in the original and college copies. After the thesis is accepted, these two copies will be permanently bound and deposited in the University Libraries.

Change from Thesis to Nonthesis Option.—A student who wishes to change from the thesis to the nonthesis option for the master's degree must obtain the permission of the supervisory committee to make such a change. This permission must be forwarded to the Graduate School at least one full quarter prior to the intended date of graduation. The candidate must meet all the requirements of the nonthesis option as specified above. A maximum of 5 credits earned in 699 (Master's Research) can be counted toward the degree requirements only if converted to credit as Individual Work. The supervisory committee must indicate that the work was productive in and by itself and warrants credit as a special problem or special topic course.

Supervisory Committee.—The student's supervisory committee should be appointed as soon as possible after the student has been admitted to the Graduate School but, in no case, later than the end of the second quarter of study. The duties of the supervisory committee are to advise the student, to check on the student's qualifications and progress, to supervise the preparation of the thesis, and to conduct the final examination.

Admission to Candidacy.—Application for admission to candidacy for the master's degree should be made no later than the last day of classes in the quarter prior to the quarter in which the student plans to receive the degree.

The Graduate Council may deny degrees to persons who have failed to comply with this regulation at the proper time. In order to be admitted to candidacy, the student must have (1) maintained a B average or higher in the major and in all work attempted, (2) chosen a thesis topic, (3) satisfied the supervisory committee, department chairman, and the college dean that the student is qualified to become a candidate for the degree. It is the responsibility of the supervisory committee at this time to make such investigation as is necessary to determine the student's eligibility.

Final Examination.—When the student's course work is completed, or practically so, and the thesis is in final form, the supervisory committee is required to examine the student orally or in writing on (1) the thesis, (2) the major subjects, (3) the minor or minors, and (4) matters of a general nature pertaining to the field of study.

At least three faculty members must be present at the student's final examination, but only the members of the official supervisory committee are required to sign the final examination report. The thesis must be approved unanimously and signed by the supervisory committee members. A written announcement of the examination must be sent to the Dean of the Graduate School. Using the form provided for the purpose, the supervisory committee shall report in writing to the Dean of the Graduate School not later than one week before the time for conferring the degree whether all work has been completed in a satisfactory manner and whether on the basis of the final examination the student is recommended for a degree. This examination may not be scheduled earlier than six months before the degree is to be conferred without special approval of the Graduate Council.

Master of Arts in Teaching and Master of Science in Teaching

These degrees are designed for graduate students majoring in departments of the various colleges of the University who intend to teach in junior or four-year colleges. Requirements for admission are the same as those for the regular M.A. and M.S. degrees in the various colleges, and programs leading to the M.A.T. and M.S.T. may, with proper approval, be incorporated into programs leading to the Ph.D.

The requirements for the degrees are as follows:

1. A reading knowledge of one foreign language if required by the student's major department.

2. Satisfactory completion of at least 54 credits of work while registered as a graduate student; at least 50 percent of these credits must be in courses open only for graduate credit, with work distributed as follows:

   a. At least 28 credits in the major and 8 credits in the minor.

   b. Nine credits in a departmental internship in teaching. Three years of successful teaching experience may be substituted for the internship requirement, and credits thus made available may be used for further work in the major, the minor, or in education.

   c. At least one course in each of the following: educational psychology, sociology, and curriculum dealing with the community college. These courses may be used to comprise a minor.

3. **Off-Campus Work:** A minimum of 12-25 credits (at the department's discretion), including registration for at least 9 credits hours in a single quarter, must

be earned on the Gainesville campus. Beyond that, credits, including those at the 500 and 600 level, earned in courses offered off-campus by the University of Florida which have been approved by the Graduate School shall be accepted, provided they are appropriate to the student's degree program as determined by the supervisory committee.

4. At the completion of this degree, the student, for certification purposes, must present from the undergraduate and graduate degree programs no fewer than 54 quarter credits in the major field.

5. A final comprehensive examination, either written, oral, or both, must be passed by the candidate. This examination will cover the field of concentration and the minor.

MASTER OF AGRICULTURE

The degree of Master of Agriculture is designed for those students who wish additional training for business occupations or professions, rather than for those interested primarily in research.

The general requirements are the same as those for the Master of Science degree without thesis except that 18 credits of graduate courses in a department constitute a major. Credit toward the degree for courses taken through the Division of Continuing Education is limited to 25 credits. The student's supervisory committee must consist of at least two members of the graduate faculty. A comprehensive written qualifying examination, given prior to the beginning of the quarter of graduation, and a final oral examination are required.

MASTER OF AGRICULTURAL MANAGEMENT AND RESOURCE DEVELOPMENT (M.A.M.R.D.)

The M.A.M.R.D. degree program provides an opportunity for graduate study for students who plan to enter management careers in business firms or government agencies; it is not recommended for those who plan careers in research and university teaching. Areas of concentration include farm management, agricultural marketing, and resource planning and economic development.

The general requirements are the same as those for the Master of Science degree without thesis except that 18 credits of graduate courses in food and resource economics constitute a major. The supervisory committee and examination requirements are the same as those for the Master of Agriculture degree.

MASTER OF ARTS IN ARCHITECTURE

The degree of Master of Arts in Architecture is a professional degree for those students who wish to qualify for registration as an architect or for the teaching profession.

The general requirements are the same as those for other Master of Arts degrees with thesis except that the minimum registration required is 76 credits including no more than 9 credits in AE 699. In some areas, with permission from the departmental graduate faculty, a terminal project requiring 9 credits in AE 629 may be elected in lieu of a thesis.

MASTER OF ARTS IN URBAN AND REGIONAL PLANNING

The degree of Master of Arts in Urban and Regional Planning is a professional degree for students who wish to qualify for full membership in the American Institute of Planners.

The general requirements are the same as those for other Master of Arts degrees with thesis except that the minimum registration required is 72 credits including no more than 9 credits in URP 699. In some study areas, with permission from the departmental graduate faculty, a terminal project requiring 9 credits in URP 629 may be elected in lieu of a thesis.

MASTER OF BUILDING CONSTRUCTION

The degree of Master of Building Construction is designed for those students who wish to pursue advanced work in management of construction, construction techniques, and research problems in the construction field.

The general requirements are the same as those for other Master of Science degrees without thesis except that a minimum of 50 credits is required. At least 37 credits must be in the School of Building Construction in graduate level courses of which at least 25 credits must be earned at the 600 level. The remaining 13 credits may be earned in other departments at the 300 level or above when these courses are included as a part of an approved program of study. A thesis is not required. A final comprehensive examination is required of all students.

MASTER OF BUSINESS ADMINISTRATION

The requirements for the Master of Business Administration degree are designed to give students (1) the conceptual knowledge for understanding the functions and behavior common to all organizations, and with (2) the analytical, problem-solving, and decision-making skills essential for effective management. The emphasis is upon developing the student's capacities and skills for business decision making.

The structure of the curriculum is designed so students may deepen their knowledge in a specialized field by selecting an approved concentration. Included in these concentrations are accounting, economics, finance, health and hospital administration, insurance, management, marketing, and real estate and urban land studies. Several areas of specialization having different emphases are offered within some concentrations. Students may also expand their knowledge in several areas instead of specializing, and pursue a generalist option by selecting approved courses from more than one field of business administration.

The required courses in the curriculum consist of the foundation sequence, advanced graduate sequence, and the concentration credits.

Minimum Requirements.—The Master of Business Administration degree requires a minimum of 51 credits in approved courses, excluding credits earned in the foundation sequence or other preparatory courses. A thesis is not required. The typical Master of Business Administration candidate has earned more than 51 credits at the time the degree is awarded.

Admission.—Applicants for admission must submit satisfactory scores on either the Graduate Management Admissions Test or the Graduate Record Examination Aptitude Test. The Graduate Management Admissions Test is recommended. Applicants whose native language is not English are required to submit, in addition, scores on the Test of English as a Foreign Language (TOEFL).

Information on admission as well as other aspects of the Master of Business Administration program may be obtained by contacting the Director of the Master of Business Administration Program, College of Business Administration, Matherly Hall.

Foundation Sequence.—The following courses constitute the minimum foundation sequence requirements:

.ATG 510—Financial Accounting
BA 560—Computer Concepts in Business
BA 564—Introduction to Managerial Statistics
BA 591—Mathematical Methods and Their Application to Business and Economic Theory
ES 501—Macroeconomic Theory
ES 502—Microeconomic Theory
FI 590—Financial Management
MTG 510—Foundations of Management and Organizational Behavior
MKG 531—Marketing Principles and Institutions
Legal Environment of Business (one course selected from a list of approved courses)

The above courses are required for all Master of Business Administration candidates except where a student, as a result of prior preparation, demonstrates a satisfactory level of understanding of course material by passing a course exemption examination. Students may waive all or part of the required courses in the foundation sequence by passing exemption examinations.

Students who are qualified for admission to the M.B.A. program, but whose undergraduate work was outside business administration, may obtain the necessary preparation through the foundation sequence for advanced graduate study.

Advanced Graduate Sequence.—The following courses are required of all M.B.A. candidates and are not subject to waiver by examination:
BA 610—Managerial Accounting
BA 620—Advanced Finance Topics
BA 630—Problems and Methods of Marketing Management
BA 661—Managerial Quantitative Analysis
BA 664—Analysis of Decisions Under Uncertainty
BA 665—Statistical Analysis for Managerial Decisions
BA 671—Human Behavior in Organizations
BA 679—Business Policy
Applied Economics in Decision Making (selection of either ES 615—Economics of Business Decisions, or ES 616—Macroeconomic Models and the Firm)

These courses comprise between one half and two thirds of the student's program of graduate study beyond the foundation sequence.

Concentration.—A minimum of 18 credits is required in the concentration. At least half of these credits must be in courses approved for graduate credit. A maximum of 9 credits earned as an undergraduate may be counted toward the concentration if approved by the adviser, but credits so used *do not* count toward the minimum number of 51 credits required for the degree. All courses to be counted toward satisfying the concentration requirement must be approved by the adviser. Some concentrations require more than the minimum of 18 credits and students may be required to take additional preparatory courses if their background is not sufficient.

Concentration in Health and Hospital Administration.—The Master of Business Administration degree with a concentration in health and hospital administration is offered by the College of Business Administration. The foundation sequence is required and the course work in the concentration area is offered through the College of Health Related Professions.

In addition to meeting the usual requirements for admission to the Graduate School, students who apply for this concentration must communicate directly with the Chairman of the Program in Health and Hospital Administration, who will arrange for a personal interview with members of a faculty selection committee. Students are accepted for the Fall quarter only. The number of students accepted for each class is limited and applications submitted after April 1 may not be considered.

Comprehensive Examination.—A proficiency examination for all students in the Master of Business Administration program, including the Health and Hospital Administration concentration, is administered by an examining committee appointed from the graduate faculty of the College of Business Administration in the latter part of the term in which the student expects to complete the course work. This examination will cover the student's entire program.

MASTER OF EDUCATION

The degree of Master of Education is a professional degree designed to meet the need for professional personnel to serve a variety of functions required in established and emerging educational activities of modern society. A thesis is not required.

A minimum of 50 credits is required in all master's programs with at least half of these credits in courses at the 500 level or above. Thirty-two credits in education, with 24 at the graduate level, and 8 credits in courses outside education are included. Two exceptions are (1) only 16 credits in education, all at the graduate level, are required for students having at least 32 credits in a baccalaureate program for teacher preparation, and (2) 24 credits in courses outside education are required for these same students if their master's program is in subject specialization teacher education, vocational, technical and adult education, and foundations of education.

At least 25 credits must be earned while enrolled as a graduate student in courses offered on the Gainesville campus of the University of Florida, including registration for at least 9 credits in a single quarter.

MASTER OF ENGINEERING

A student seeking a master's degree in the field of engineering may become a candidate for the Master of Engineering degree with or without thesis, provided such a candidate has a bachelor's degree in engineering from an ECPD-accredited curriculum or has taken sufficient articulation course work to meet the minimum requirements specified by ECPD. Students who do not meet these requirements may become a candidate for the Master of Science degree, provided they meet departmental requirements for admission. The general intent in making this distinction is to encourage those who are professionally oriented to seek the Master of Engineering degree, and those who are more scientifically oriented and those who have science-based backgrounds to seek the Master of Science degree.

Work Required.—The minimum course work required for the master's degree with thesis is 45 credits which may include up to 9 credits of the research course numbered 699 in all departments. A minimum of 48 credits of course work is required, with at least 24 credits in the student's major field for both of the above degrees without thesis. At least 50% of the required 48 credits must be in courses open only for graduate credit, excluding those graded as S/U. Courses in the major must be selected from those open for graduate credit. If a minor is chosen, at least 8 credits of work are required; two 8-credit minors may be taken. In addition, a multidisciplinary minor in departments other than the major may be authorized by the supervisory committee or program adviser. Courses numbered 300 and above may be taken for the minor.

Degree Credit.—In order to qualify for course work toward the Master of Engineering degree, a student must first be admitted to the Graduate School at the

University of Florida. The amount of course work toward this degree that may be taken at an off-campus center will depend upon the student's individual program and the courses provided through the center.

Examinations.—A student seeking the Master of Engineering degree with or without thesis is required to pass a comprehensive oral or written examination at the completion of the course work. A student who takes less than half the course work on the Gainesville campus will be required to pass a comprehensive written examination administered on the University of Florida campus by an examining committee recommended by the Dean of the College of Engineering and appointed by the Dean of the Graduate School. At least one member of the examining committee must be either the student's program adviser or a member of the supervisory committee. If a minor is taken, another member selected from the Graduate Studies Faculty must be chosen from outside the major department to represent the student's minor.

Examination requirements for the Master of Science degree are covered in the preceding section under Master of Arts and Master of Science.

MASTER OF FINE ARTS

The College of Fine Arts offers the Master of Fine Arts degree with majors in art, music, and theatre. The requirements for this degree are the same as those for the Master of Arts with thesis except that a minimum of 72 credits is required, including 9 credits in the master's research course 699. Two years of work are normally required for completion of the degree requirements.

Students applying for admission to the Master of Fine Arts program should have an undergraduate major or its equivalent in their area of specialization. In addition, candidates may be requested to submit samples of their creative work prior to being accepted into the program.

Art.—The M.F.A. degree with a major in art is designed primarily for those who wish to prepare themselves as teachers of art in colleges and universities. Specialization is offered in art history, ceramics, creative photography, drawing, painting, print making, and sculpture. The M.F.A. is generally accepted as the terminal degree in the studio area.

In addition to the general requirements stated above, course work must include ART 500—4 credits; ART 611 and 621—4 credits each; a minimum of 32 credits in the major and a minimum of 9 credits in non-art electives. The remaining credits may be taken in advanced courses in the areas of specialization listed above or general non-art electives.

Music.—The M.F.A. degree with a major in music is designed primarily for those who wish to prepare themselves for careers as teachers in colleges and universities, performers, music historians, music critics, church musicians, composers, and conductors. Recipients of the M.F.A. degree will be prepared to continue doctoral study in the various areas of music listed above.

In addition to the general requirements stated above, registration in courses numbered MSC 611—4 credits; MSC 615 and 616—12 credits; and MSC 609—8 credits are required.

Theatre.—The M.F.A. degree with a major in theatre is designed primarily for those interested in production-oriented theatrical careers. Specialization is offered in the areas of directing-acting and design and technical theatre, and advanced training is offered in the craft skills essential to the theatre artist and their subsequent application in public and studio productions.

In addition to the general requirements stated above, course work must include THE 626—4 credits; THE 628—4 credits; a total of 32 credits of theatre practicum activities; and a total of 17 credits of advanced study in the student's area of specialization. The balance of the program is to be completed with elective theatre courses.

MASTER OF FOREST RESOURCES AND CONSERVATION

The Master of Forest Resources and Conservation program is designed for those students who wish additional professional preparation, rather than for those interested primarily in research. The basic requirements, including those for admission, supervisory committee, plan of study, and admission to candidacy, are the same as those indicated under *General Regulations* for master's degrees in this *Catalog*.

Work Required.—A minimum of 48 credits of course work is required, with at least 24 credits in courses open only for graduate credit. A minimum of 18 credits must be in a selected area of concentration in courses open only for graduate credit. A thesis is not required, but the student must submit reports, term papers, and records of work accomplished. A comprehensive written qualifying examination, given by the supervisory committee, is required one quarter prior to graduation. A final oral examination, covering the candidate's entire field of study, is required.

MASTER OF HEALTH EDUCATION

The program leading to the degree of Master of Health Education is designed to meet the need for advanced preparation of health educators to serve in positions of leadership in schools and communities.

Work Required.—A minimum of 51 credits of course work is required, of which at least 50% must be courses at the graduate level in health education. Of the remaining 50% at least three courses in health sciences must be taken outside the College of Physical Education, Health, and Recreation, and courses from two of the following areas in professional education: curriculum, psychological foundations, social foundations, and measurement and statistics.

Off-Campus Work.—The regulations governing the use of off-campus work are the same as those for the Master of Education degree.

Supervisory Committee.—A committee of the faculty of the College of Physical Education, Health, and Recreation, with the dean of the college, or some person designated by him, serving as chairman and the Dean of the Graduate School as an ex officio member, will supervise the work of students registered in this program, subject to the approval of the Graduate Council.

Admission to Candidacy.—Admission to this program is *not* a guarantee of admission to candidacy. Application should be made no later than the last day of classes in the term **prior** to that in which the student expects to graduate.

Final Examination.—The candidate must pass a final written or oral examination at the close of the course work.

MASTER OF HEALTH SCIENCE

The Master of Health Science degree is designed to meet the need for leadership personnel in allied health to serve a variety of functions required in established and emerging health care programs. The areas of concentration are in occupational therapy and rehabilitation counseling.

A foundation program is required in occupational therapy; i.e., evidence of completion of an accredited basic professional curriculum in occupational therapy. Rehabilitation counseling requires evidence of experience, education, and interest in the profession.

The work required is satisfactory completion of a minimum of 54 credits of academic course work. At least 50% of these credits must be at the 500 level or above, including at least 32 credits in the major area. In addition, the concentration in rehabilitation counseling requires appropriate clinical practicum experiences over four quarters and an internship, usually off campus, of one quarter. The clinical practicums usually require an additional 7 credit hours, and the internship an additional 10 credit hours.

A thesis is not required but the candidate must complete an approved departmental study or research project as a part of the degree requirements. Additional requirements are listed under the section *General Regulations* for all master's degrees.

MASTER OF LAWS IN TAXATION (L.L.M. IN TAX.)

The instructional program leading to the degree Master of Laws in Taxation offers advanced instruction in taxation, with emphasis on federal taxation and particularly federal income taxation, for law graduates who plan to specialize in such matters in the practice of law.

Work Required.—Degree candidates must complete 36 credit hours in courses open only for graduate credit, 30 of which are in law college courses in taxation, including a research course in which the candidate is enrolled for an entire academic year.

MASTER OF NURSING

The program leading to the degree Master of Nursing is designed to give students the basic knowledge and professional skills essential to the three areas of nursing activity: teaching, research and practice.

Work Required.—A minimum of 50 credit hours is required for graduation, at least half of which must be in courses open only for graduate credit. There is no thesis or foreign language requirement.

Final Examination.—Each student must pass a comprehensive written or oral examination during the final quarter of study.

MASTER OF SCIENCE IN NURSING

The program leading to the degree Master of Science in Nursing is designed to provide experience in conducting and reporting research in addition to professional education essential to clinical nursing.

Work Required.—A minimum of 50 credit hours is required for graduation, at least half of which must be in the College of Nursing, and 50% of courses taken must be from those open only for graduate credit.

Final Examination.—During the final quarter of study, each student must pass an oral examination in defense of the thesis.

MASTER OF PHYSICAL EDUCATION

Work Required.—A minimum of 51 credits of course work is required, of which at least 50% must be graduate-level courses in physical education. Of the remaining 50%, at least three courses must be taken outside the College of Physical Education, Health, and Recreation.

Off-Campus Work.—The regulations governing the use of off-campus work are the same as those for the Master of Education degree.

Supervisory Committee.—A committee of the faculty of the college of Physical Education, Health, and Recreation, with the dean of the college, or some person designated by him, serving as chairman and the Dean of the Graduate School as an ex officio member, will supervise the work of students registered in this program, subject to the approval of the Graduate School.

Admission to Candidacy.—Admission to this program is *not* a guarantee of admission to candidacy. Application should be made no later than the last day of classes in the term **prior** to that in which the student expects to graduate.

Final Examination.—The candidate must pass a final examination at the close of the course work. This written or oral examination will be confined largely to the student's major field of study.

MASTER OF STATISTICS

The minimum registration required for the Master of Statistics degree is 54 credits, including no less than 30 credits in the major field. Courses in the degree program will be selected in consultation with the major adviser and approved by the student's supervisory committee. One 9-credit minor is required. The work in the major field must be in courses approved for graduate major credit. For the minor, courses numbered 300 and above may be taken. At least half the 54 credits must be in courses open only for graduate credit. The student will be required to pass, as judged by the supervisory committee, a comprehensive written examination covering the major and minor subjects. In addition, the student will be examined orally on the major subjects.

REQUIREMENTS FOR THE DEGREE OF ENGINEER

For those engineers who need additional technical depth and diversification in their education beyond the master's degree, the College of Engineering offers the degree of Engineer.

This degree requires a minimum of 45 quarter hours of graduate work beyond the master's degree. It is not to be considered as a partial requirement toward the Ph.D. degree. The student's objective after the master's degree should be the Ph.D. *or* the Engineer degree.

Admission to the Program.—To be admitted to the program, students must have completed a master's degree in engineering at an accredited institution approved by the Graduate School, University of Florida, and apply for admission to the Graduate School of the University of Florida. The master's degree is regarded as the essential foundation for the degree of Engineer.

Course and Residence Requirements.—A total registration in an approved program of at least 45 quarter credit hours beyond the master's degree is required. This minimum requirement must be earned through the University of Florida. These credits may be completed in any graduate program administered by the College of Engineering. The last 45 quarter credit hours must be completed within five calendar years.

Supervisory Committee.—Each student admitted to the program will be advised by a supervisory committee consisting of at least three members of the graduate faculty. Two members are selected from the major department and at least one from a supporting department. In addition, every effort should be made to have a representative from industry as an external adviser for the student's program.

This committee will inform the student of all regulations pertaining to the degree program. The committee is nominated by the department chairman, approved by the Dean of the College of Engineering, and appointed by the Dean of the Graduate School. The Dean of the Graduate School is an ex officio member of all supervisory committees and should be notified in writing in advance of all committee meetings. If a thesis or report is a requirement in the plan of study, then the committee will approve the proposed thesis or report and the plans for carrying it out. The committee will also conduct the final examination when the plan of study is completed.

Plan of Study.—Each plan of study is developed on an individual basis for each student. Thus, there are no specific requirements for the major or minor; each student is considered as a separate case. If the plan of study includes a thesis, the student may register for from 9 to 15 quarter credit hours of thesis research in a course numbered 699.

Admission to Candidacy.—Application for admission to candidacy should be made no later than the beginning of the term in which the student intends to graduate. If a thesis is required, the topic must also have been approved by the supervisory committee.

Thesis.—The thesis should represent performance at a level above that ordinarily associated with the master's degree. It should clearly be an original contribution; this may take the form of scientific research, a design project, or an industrial project approved by the supervisory committee. Work on the thesis may be conducted in an industrial or governmental laboratory under conditions stipulated by the supervisory committee.

Final Examination.—After the student has completed all work on the plan of study, the supervisory committee conducts a final comprehensive oral or written examination, which also involves a defense of the thesis if one is included in the program.

REQUIREMENTS FOR THE ED.S. AND ED.D.

The Advanced School of the College of Education offers programs leading to the degrees Specialist in Education, Doctor of Education, and Doctor of Philosophy. These programs are available in five areas: administration and supervision, curriculum and instruction, foundations of education, counselor education, and special education. The Specialist in Education degree is awarded for a two-year program of graduate study. The Doctor of Education degree requires writing a doctoral dissertation. Foreign languages are not required. The Doctor of Philosophy degree in the College of Education is described under *Requirements for the Ph.D.*

Programs leading to these degrees are administered through the Office of Graduate Studies in Education, which carries out the policies of the Graduate School and the graduate committee of the College of Education. Further information may be obtained from that office. Students are advised to familiarize themselves with the various programs and requirements of their department of specialization before applying to the Advanced School of Education.

Admission to the Advanced School of Education.—Admission to the Advanced School is open only to persons who have met the following requirements:

1. Successfully completed 50 credits of professional course work in education. Applicants for admission to the Advanced School of the College of Education who meet all the requirements except for successfully completing 50 credits of professional education courses may be given provisional admission, and full admission when they have completed the required 50 credits.

2. Presented a record of successful professional experience, the appropriateness of which will be determined by the instructional department passing on the applicant's qualifications for admission. In some instances, departments may admit students with the understanding that further experience may be required before the student will be recommended for the degree.

Admission to the Advanced School is based on the following criteria:

1. High scholastic average for previous graduate work (3.5 grade-point average or above, as computed at the University of Florida, will be considered evidence of good scholarship).

2. Satisfactory scores on the Aptitude Test of the Graduate Record Examination (GRE).

The judgment concerning admission of an individual student is made according to the above criteria by the major department. The department will certify to the admissions committee that the student has met the criteria for admission to the Advanced School. In all cases the record, experience, and other relevant qualifications of the person applying for admission are subject to approval of the admissions committee.

All persons admitted to the Advanced School of Education must also apply for and be admitted to the Graduate School of the University.

SPECIALIST IN EDUCATION

Primary emphasis in a Ed.S. program is placed on the development of the competencies needed for a specific job. Programs are available in the various areas of concentration within the Departments of Administration and Supervision, Foundations of Education, and Counselor Education, the Division of Curriculum and Instruction, and Special Education. The Florida State Department of Education recognizes this degree for purposes of granting Rank IA certification.

To study for this degree, the student must apply for and be admitted to the Advanced School of the College of Education. The student must also apply for and be admitted to candidacy for the degree no later than the term prior to that in which the degree is to be awarded. All work for the degree must be completed within seven years of admission to the Advanced School.

The Ed.S. degree is awarded at the completion of a planned program with a minimum of 100 credits beyond the bachelor's degree or a minimum of 50 credits beyond the master's degree. All credits accepted for the program must contribute to the unity and the stated objective of the total program. Students are examined (in no case earlier than 6 months prior to receipt of degree) on both a written and oral examination by a committee selected by the department chairman. A thesis is not required; however, each program will include continuing attention to a research component relevant to the professional role for which the student is preparing.

Students who enter the program with an appropriate master's degree from another accredited institution must complete a minimum of 50 credits of post master's study to satisfy the following requirements.

1. 32 credits in courses open only for graduate credit.

2. At least 16 credits in professional education courses open only for graduate credit.

3. At least 2 quarters of full-time residence on campus in Gainesville.

Eighteen credits for appropriate courses offered off-campus by the University of Florida may be transferred to the program. Nine credits may be transferred from another institution of the State University System or from any institution offering a doctoral degree; however, credit transferred from another institution reduces proportionately the credit transferred from University of Florida off-campus courses.

Students who enter the program with a bachelor's degree only must, during their 100-credit program, satisfy these requirements in addition to the requirements of the Master of Education degree or its equivalent.

DOCTOR OF EDUCATION

A doctoral candidate is expected to achieve understanding of the broad field of education and competence in an area of specialization. Programs are available in the various areas of concentration within the Departments of Administration and Supervision, Foundations of Education, Counselor Education, Special Education, and the Division of Curriculum and Instruction.

Admission to a program of work leading to the degree of Doctor of Education requires admission to the Advanced School of the College of Education, described previously, as well as admission to the Graduate School.

All courses beyond the master's degree taken at another institution, to be applied toward the Doctor of Education degree, must be taken at an institution offering the doctoral degree and must be approved for graduate credit by the Graduate School of the University of Florida.

Minors.—Minor work or work in cognate fields is required. If one minor is selected, at least 24 credits of work therein will be required; if two minors are chosen, one must have at least 18 credits of course work, the other at least 8 credits.

Courses in physical education approved by the College of Physical Education, Health, and Recreation and the Graduate School as subject matter or content courses may be used in the cognate work or as a minor.

In lieu of a minor or minors, the candidate may present a suitable program of no fewer than 24 credits of cognate work in at least two or more departments. If two fields are included, there shall be no fewer than 8 credits in either field. If three or more fields are included, the 8-credit requirement for each field does not apply. This program must have the approval of the student's supervisory committee. The College of Education faculty will expect the candidate to be prepared to answer questions, at the time of his oral examination, in any of the areas chosen.

Admission to Candidacy.—Admission to candidacy for the degree of Doctor of Education rests on successful completion of the qualifying examinations and approval of a dissertation topic. Recommendation to the Graduate School for admission to candidacy is based on the action of the supervisory committee, subject to the approval of the graduate committee of the College of Education. The Florida State Department of Education recognizes this admission to candidacy for purposes of granting Rank 1A certification.

Qualifying Examination.—The applicant is recommended for the qualifying examination by the supervisory committee after completion of sufficient course work.

The examination, administered by the student's major department of the College of Education, consists of (1) a general section; (2) a field of specialization section; (3) examination in the minor or minors, where involved; and (4) an oral examination conducted by the applicant's supervisory committee.

If the student fails the qualifying examination, a reexamination will not be given unless recommended for special reasons by the supervisory committee and approved by the Graduate School. At least one quarter of additional preparation is considered essential before reexamination.

Research Preparation Requirement.—EDF 760—Methods of Educational Research, or its equivalent, for which a basic course in statistics is a prerequisite, is a minimum requirement in all programs. Additional requirements will vary with the department and with the student's plans for doctoral research.

For information relating to *Residence,* the *Supervisory Committee, Time and Lapse Limitation,* the *Dissertation,* and the *Final Examination,* the student is referred to the material presented under the heading *Doctor of Philosophy.* These statements are applicable to both degrees.

REQUIREMENTS FOR THE PH.D.

Doctoral study consists of the independent mastery of a field of knowledge and the successful pursuit of research. For this reason, doctoral students act, in large measure, on their own responsibility and doctoral programs are more flexible and varied than those leading to other graduate degrees. The Graduate Council does not specify what courses will be required for the Ph.D. degree. The general requirement is that the program should be unified in relation to a clear objective and that it should have the considered approval of the student's entire supervisory committee.

COURSE REQUIREMENTS

The course requirements for doctoral degrees vary from field to field and from student to student. The student's supervisory committee has the responsibility for recommending individual courses of study for each doctoral student subject to the approval of the Dean of the Graduate School. A minimum of 135 credits beyond the bachelor's degree is required for the doctoral degree.

Major.—The student working for the Ph.D. must elect to do the major work in a department specifically approved for the offering of doctoral courses and the supervision of dissertations. These departments are listed under *Graduate Programs.*

Minor.—With the approval of the supervisory committee, the student may choose one or more minor fields. Minor work may be completed in any department, other than the major department, approved for master's or doctor's degree programs as listed in this *Catalog.*

If one minor is chosen, the representative of the minor department on the supervisory committee shall suggest from 18 to 36 credits as preparation for a qualifying examination. Of course, a part of this background may have been acquired in the master's program. If two minors are chosen, each must include at least 12 credits. Competence in the minor area may be demonstrated through a written examination conducted by the minor department or through the oral qualifying examination.

Course work in the minor at the doctoral level need not be restricted to the courses of one department, provided that the minor has a clearly stated objective and that the combination of courses representing the minor shall be approved by the Graduate School before registration beyond 6 credits of course work applicable to the minor. This procedure is not required for a departmental minor.

SUPERVISORY COMMITTEE

Supervisory committees are nominated by the department chairman, approved by the dean of the college concerned, and appointed by the Dean of the Graduate School. The committee should be appointed as soon as possible after the student has begun doctoral work, and in general no later than the end of the third quarter of equivalent full-time study. The Dean of the Graduate School is an ex officio member of all supervisory committees and should be notified in writing well in advance of all examinations conducted by such committees.

Duties and Responsibilities.—Duties of the supervisory committee follow:

1. To inform the student of all regulations governing the degree sought. It should be noted, however, that this does not absolve the student from the responsi-

bility of informing himself concerning these regulations. (See *Student Responsibility.)*

2. To meet immediately after appointment to pass on the qualifications of the student and to discuss and approve a program of study.

3. To meet to discuss and approve the proposed dissertation project and the plans for carrying it out.

4. To conduct the qualifying examination or, in those cases where the examination is administered by the department, to take part in it. In either event, no fewer than five faculty members shall be present for the oral portion of the examination.

5. To meet when the work on the dissertation is at least one-half completed to review procedure, progress, and expected results, and to make suggestions for completion.

6. To meet when the dissertation is completed and conduct the final oral examination to assure that the dissertation is a piece of original research and a contribution to knowledge. No fewer than five faculty members shall be present for this examination, but only the members of the official supervisory committee are required to sign the dissertation. The dissertation must be approved unanimously by the official supervisory committee.

Membership.—The supervisory committee for a candidate for the doctoral degree shall consist of no fewer than three members selected from the graduate faculty. At least two members will be from the college or department recommending the degree, and at least one member will be drawn from a different educational discipline. The chairman and at least one additional member of the committee will be members of the Doctoral Research Faculty of the University of Florida.

If a minor is chosen, the supervisory committee will include at least one person selected from the graduate faculty from outside the discipline of the major for the purpose of representing the student's minor. In the event that the student elects more than one minor, each minor area may, at the discretion of the departments concerned, be represented on the supervisory committee.

When a minor is not designated, the supervisory committee will include at least one member of the graduate faculty from outside the discipline of the major. The Graduate Council desires each supervisory committee to function as a university committee, as contrasted with a departmental committee, in order to bring university-wide standards to bear upon the various doctoral degrees.

In unusual cases the doctoral research may require the guidance of a specialist from an area of study other than that of the chairman of the supervisory committee. In such cases the department chairman may recommend appointment of a chairman and a cochairman, with the latter being a member of the graduate faculty, but not necessarily of the Doctoral Research Faculty. A cochairman may also be appointed for the purpose of serving during a planned absence of the chairman; in this case both the chairman and the cochairman shall have been appointed to the Doctoral Research Faculty.

LANGUAGE REQUIREMENT

The foreign language requirement, or a substitute therefor, for the Ph.D. degree is completely optional with the major department. The student should check with the graduate coordinator of the major department for specific information about the foreign language requirements.

The foreign language departments offer special classes for graduate students who are beginning the study of a language. See the current *Schedule of Courses* for the languages in which this assistance is available.

RESIDENCE

Candidates for the doctoral degree must satisfy the minimum residence requirements by completing beyond the master's degree (1) 45 quarter hours in one calendar year, or (2) 52 quarter hours in no more than six quarters within a period of two calendar years on the Gainesville campus of the University of Florida. This requirement was formerly referred to as the period of concentrated study.

In some cases a student may be employed on a sponsored project from which his thesis or dissertation will be drawn. Upon written recommendation of the chairman of the supervisory committee, residence credit may be permitted for the time devoted to such research. This recommendation must be made during the quarter in which the work is done. All time devoted to routine duties, or to research not related directly to the dissertation or thesis, should be removed from consideration.

Candidates in the College of Agriculture may do their research at certain branch stations of the University of Florida Agricultural Experiment Station where adequate staff and facilities are available.

QUALIFYING EXAMINATION

The qualifying examination, which is required of all candidates for the degree of Doctor of Philosophy, may be taken during the third term of the second year of graduate study. The examination, conducted by the supervisory committee, with the aid of the major and minor departments, is both written and oral and covers the major and minor subjects. At least five faculty members must be present at the oral portion. The supervisory committee has the responsibility at this time of deciding whether the student is qualified to continue his work toward the Ph.D. degree.

If a student fails the qualifying examination and requests a reexamination, such a reexamination must be recommended by the supervisory committee and approved by the Graduate School. At least one quarter of additional preparation is considered essential before reexamination.

An announcement of the scheduling of each student's qualifying examination must be submitted in writing to the Dean of the Graduate School. If the student does not file for admission to candidacy immediately after the qualifying examination, a written report of the result of the examination must be filed with the Graduate School Office.

Time Lapse.—Between the qualifying examination and the date of the degree there must be a minimum of two quarters if the candidate is in full-time residence, or three quarters if the candidate is on less than a full-time basis. The quarter in which the qualifying examination is passed is counted, provided that the examination occurs before the midpoint of the term.

ADMISSION TO CANDIDACY

A graduate student does not become an actual candidate for the Ph.D. degree until granted formal admission to candidacy. Such admission requires the approval of the student's supervisory committee, the chairman of the department, the college dean, and the Dean of the Graduate School. The approval must be based on (1) the academic record of the student, (2) the opinion of the supervisory committee concerning overall fitness for candidacy, (3) an approved dissertation topic, and (4) a qualifying examination as described above. Application for admission to candidacy should be made as soon as the qualifying examination has been passed and a dissertation topic has been approved by the student's supervisory committee.

DISSERTATION

Every candidate for a doctoral degree is required to prepare and present a dissertation that shows independent investigation and is acceptable in form and content to the supervisory committee and to the Graduate School. Since all doctoral dissertations will be published by microfilm, it is necessary that the work be of publishable quality and that it be in a form suitable for publication.

The original copy of the dissertation must be presented to the Dean of the Graduate School on or before the date specified in the *University Calendar*. It must contain an abstract and be accompanied by four unpaged separate copies of the abstract, a letter of transmittal from the supervisory chairman, and all doctoral forms. After corrections have been made, and no later than the specified formal submission date, the fully signed copy of the dissertation, together with the signed Final Examination Report, should be returned to the Graduate School. The original copy of the dissertation is sent by the Graduate School to the Library for microfilming and hardbinding. A second signed copy, reproduced on required thesis paper, should be given the office of the college dean or the graduate coordinator for subsequent delivery to the Library for hardbinding. The supervisory chairman and the candidate will each need a copy and, if required, another should also be provided for the departmental library.

Publication of Dissertation.—All candidates for the Ph.D. and Ed.D. degrees are required to pay the sum of $25 to Student Accounts, the Hub, for microfilming their dissertations, and to sign an agreement authorizing publication by microfilm.

Copyright.—The candidate may choose to copyright the microfilmed dissertation for a charge of $15 payable by a certified or cashier's check or money order to University Microfilms attached to the signed Microfilm Agreement Form. To assure receipt of the valuable Copyright Registration Certificate, candidates must give a permanent address through which they can always be reached.

FINAL EXAMINATION

After submission of the dissertation and the completion of all other prescribed work for the degree, but in no case earlier than six months before the conferring of the degree, the candidate will be given a final examination, oral or written or both, by the supervisory committee. An announcement of the scheduled examination must be sent to the Dean of the Graduate School. At least five faculty members must be present at the oral portion of this examination. At the time of the defense all committee members should sign the signature pages and all committee and attending faculty members should sign the Final Examination Report. These may be retained by the supervisory chairman until acceptable completion of corrections.

Satisfactory performance on this examination and adherence to all Graduate School regulations outlined above complete the requirements for the degree.

Time Limitation.—All work for the doctorate must be completed within five calendar years after the qualifying examination, or this examination must be repeated.

CERTIFICATION

Doctoral candidates who have completed all requirements for the degree, including satisfactory defense and final acceptance of the dissertation, may request certification to that effect prior to receipt of the degree. Certification Request Forms, available in the Graduate School Editorial Office, should be filled out by the candidate, signed by the college dean, and returned to the Graduate School for verification and processing.

EXPENSES

APPLICATION FEE

Each application for admission to the University must be accompanied by an application fee of $15. Application fees are nonrefundable. Further instructions will be found in the *Admissions* section of this *Catalog.*

CLASSIFICATION OF STUDENTS—FLORIDA OR NON-FLORIDA

For the purpose of assessing fees, applicants are classified as Florida or non-Florida students. A Florida student is a person who has been a citizen of the United States or a resident alien and who has resided and had a permanent home in the State of Florida for at least twelve months immediately preceding the current registration. If the student is an unmarried minor, the parents or legal guardian must meet the foregoing residence requirements. All other persons are non-Florida students. A written statement concerning residence must be made under oath at the time of application for admission.

In determining Florida residence for the purpose of assessing fees, the burden of proof is on the applicant. Under law an applicant can change a place of residence from another state to the State of Florida only by actually and physically coming into the state and establishing residence with the intention of permanently residing within the state. The spouse of any person who is classified or is eligible for classification as an in-state student is likewise entitled to classification as an in-state student. The legal residence of a minor is that of the parents or legal guardian.

Non-Florida students may apply in writing for reclassification after they or, if minors, their parents have resided in Florida for twelve months, and have filed a declaration of intent to become residents of the state with the Clerk of the Circuit Court in the county of permanent residence. In addition, the student must file with the Registrar's Office a completed Residence Affidavit Form which is available in the Registrar's Office. An alien must have resided in Florida for twelve consecutive months and must present U.S. Immigration and Naturalization certification that he is a resident alien. Those students who are nonresident aliens or who are in the United States on a nonimmigration visa will not be entitled to reclassification. However, for fee-paying purposes, Cuban nationals will be considered as resident aliens. If the application is supported by evidence satisfactory to the University that the student qualifies as a Florida student, classification will be changed for future registrations.

For more detailed information see the section in the *Undergraduate Catalog* entitled *Classification of Students.*

REGISTRATION AND INSTRUCTIONAL FEES

The *University Calendar* appearing at the front of this *Catalog* sets forth the beginning and ending dates of each quarter.

The following fees and charges are proposed at this time. However, since the *Catalog* must be published considerably in advance of its effective date, it is not always possible to anticipate changes, and the fee schedule may be revised. Every effort will be made to publicize changes for any quarter in advance of the registration date for that quarter.

Fees are payable on the dates listed in the *Calendar* or the date given on the statement sent those participating in advance registration. Payment of fees is an integral part of the registration process. Registration (including payment of fees) must be completed on or before the proper due date. Mail payments must be received at Student Accounts, the Hub, by that date. All payments, or properly executed authorization for payment in cases where fees are to be paid by a previously approved loan, scholarship, etc., whether for full- or part-time students, received after the due date are subject to a $25 late fee. The fees charged are based on the classification of a student as Florida or non-Florida, full-time or part-time. Unless otherwise noted, the fees for each quarter include fees for matriculation, student health services, student activities, and a general building fee.

Fees are assessed graduate students as follows:

	Florida Students	Non-Florida Students
Courses numbered 300-499. *Per credit:*	$16.50	$51.50
Courses open only for graduate credit (500- and above). *Per credit:*	$22.00	$62.00
Thesis and dissertation courses (699 and 799). *Per credit:*	$24.00	$64.00

Any graduate student who is utilizing University facilities and/or faculty time must register for an appropriate load, in no case less than three credits.

SPECIAL FEES

Audit Fee.—$16.50 per credit hour for courses numbered 300-499 and $24 per credit hour for courses numbered 500 and above.

Student Health Fee.—Students registered for nine or more credits per quarter are required to pay a $10 Student Health Fee. This fee is optional for students registered for eight credits or less.

Late Registration Fee.—A fee of $25 will be assessed for failure to initiate registration during the registration period or failure to pay fees within the time period specified.

Reinstatement Fee.—A fee of $25 will be assessed a student reinstated after the initial registration during a quarter was cancelled for nonpayment of fees.

Graduate Record Examination.—The Aptitude Test of the Graduate Record Examination is required for admission to the Graduate School. A fee of $10.50 covers the cost of this examination. Students who take one of the Advanced Tests of the GRE in combination with the Aptitude Tests pay a fee of $21. These fees are payable to the Educational Testing Service, Princeton, New Jersey 08540.

Graduate School Foreign Language Test.—A fee of $12.50 is assessed to cover the cost of this examination. This fee is payable to Student Accounts, the Hub. Administrative arrangements to register for this examination and the payment of fees must be made through the Graduate School.

Library Permanent Binding Fee.—Each candidate for a degree with a thesis or dissertation must pay a fee of $10 for the permanent hardbinding of the two copies of the thesis or dissertation deposited in the University Libraries. This fee is payable at Student Accounts, the Hub. A copy of the receipt for this fee must be presented at the Graduate School Editorial Office.

Microfilm Fee.—A fee of $25 is charged for the publication of the doctoral dissertation by microfilm. This fee is payable at Student Accounts, the Hub. A copy of the receipt for this fee must be presented at the Graduate School Editorial Office.

REFUND OF FEES

Fees will be refunded under certain conditions upon presentation at Student Accounts, the Hub, of a Registration Status form issued by the Registrar and the current Certificate of Registration. No refund will be made under this policy except upon proper application.

A full refund of tuition, registration, and instructional fees will be made if a student withdraws from the University or if the registration is cancelled by the University on or before the final day of the drop/add period.

A full refund of tuition, registration, and instructional fees, less $43, will be made if withdrawal is due to involuntary call to active military service or due to death or illness of the student. Illness must be confirmed by the student's physician.

Except as noted above, no refund will be made if the student withdraws after the final day of the add/drop period.

Commensurate refunds will be made to part-time students.

Deductions will be made from refunds for unpaid accounts due the University.

PAST DUE STUDENT ACCOUNTS

All student accounts are due and payable at Student Accounts, the Hub, when charges are incurred.

Delinquent accounts will be considered sufficient cause for cancellation of registration, as University regulations prohibit registration, graduation, granting of credit, or release of transcript for any student whose account with the University is delinquent.

TRAFFIC AND SAFETY REGULATIONS

All students must register their automobiles or motorcycles at the University Traffic and Parking Department during their first registration period at the University. There is a fee for registration and schedule of fines for on-campus vehicle violations. A complete set of rules governing traffic, parking, and vehicle registration may be secured at the Traffic and Parking Office, Room 108B, Johnson Hall. Each student should become familiar with these regulations upon registering at the University.

HOUSING

For Married Graduate Students.—Apartment accommodations on the University campus are available for some married graduate students. Applications should be made as soon as possible.

For Single Graduate Students.—Two modern, air conditioned residence halls are reserved for upper-division and graduate students, one hall for men and one for women. Housing agreements for all single students are for the agreement year of four quarters (September to August), if enrolled.

APPLICATIONS

Each student must make personal arrangements for housing, either by applying to the Office of the Director of Housing for assignment to University housing facilities or by obtaining accommodations in private housing. All inquiries concerning University housing facilities should be addressed to the Director of Housing, University of Florida, Gainesville 32611. Inquiries about private housing accommodations should be addressed to the Off-Campus Housing Office, Division of Housing, University of Florida, Gainesville 32611.

An application for housing may be filed at any time after application for admission to the University. Prospective students are urged to apply as early as possible because of the housing demand.

Graduate students living in University housing are required to qualify as full-time students as defined by their college or school, and they must continue to make normal progress toward a degree as determined by the head of their college or school.

Roommate requests are honored wherever possible, provided the individuals wishing to room together submit their applications at the same time, clearly indicate on their respective applications their desire to room together, and are within similar academic classifications. Any student interested in a room assignment with a foreign student should indicate this preference on the application.

RESIDENCE HALLS FOR SINGLE STUDENTS

Certain floors of the Beaty Towers residence halls (one hall for men and one hall for women) are designated for graduate students. Eight suites accommodating four students each are located on each floor. A suite includes two bedrooms, a private bath, and a study-kitchenette. The rooms provide several study locations so that students studying will not disturb students sleeping. The kitchenettes, with a refrigerator and range, allow students to prepare light meals. The Towers are entirely carpeted and air-conditioned. Other special features for residents include a library, social room, sundry shop, and lounges, as well as laundry, vending, and seminar rooms. The quarterly rent rate, including utilities, is $215 per student.

FACILITIES FOR FAMILIES

The University operates six apartment villages for married students or divorced or widowed students with dependent children. Because of the demand for housing and the limited supply, **application should be made at least one year prior to the time housing is needed.** To be eligible to apply for and occupy apartment housing on campus, the following requirements must be met.

Married students must meet the requirements for admission to the University of Florida, qualify as full-time students as defined by their school or college, and continue to make normal progress toward a degree as determined by the head of their college or school.

The married student must be part of a family unit, defined as husband and wife with or without children, or divorced or widowed students with dependent children. No relatives or housekeepers can be included as part of the family unit. No pets are allowed. In view of the limited size of on-campus apartments, applications from families having more than four children cannot be accepted.

The married, widowed, or divorced student must be part of a family with a combined gross annual income (including grants-in-aid, scholarships, fellowships, and grants) which does not exceed, during the period of occupancy, the following maximum income limitations.*

	2 persons	3 & 4 persons	5 & 6 persons
Undergraduate	$7900	$9100	$10,300
Graduate	$8100	$9310	$10,510

*For Maguire Village residents, the combined gross annual income for each family unit is limited to $7400, $8700, and $10,000 respectively.

Since on-campus apartments are intended to provide relatively low-cost housing for married students, a family with a combined gross annual income in excess of the above scale cannot apply for or occupy an apartment except in unusual circumstances. Exceptions may be granted only by the Committee on Student Housing.

Residents in all villages must furnish their own linens, dishes, rugs, curtains, and similar items.

Corry and Schucht Memorial Villages, of brick, concrete, and wood construction, contain one- and two-bedroom units, 312 total units. There are eight three-bedroom units in Corry only. These apartments are furnished with basic equipment in living room, kitchen, dining area, and one bedroom. Rent rates (subject to change) are $80, $90 and $100 per month.

Diamond Memorial Village consists of 208 apartments similar in construction, furnishings and equipment to those in Corry and Schucht Villages. Special features include a community building with air-conditioned study-meeting room, and a study cubicle in each two-bedroom apartment. Rent rates (subject to change) are $80 and $90 per month for one- and two-bedroom apartments, respectively.

Maguire Memorial Village consists of 220 centrally heated and air-conditioned one- and two-bedroom apartments. Community facilities include a large meeting room and a laundromat. With the exception of wall-to-wall carpeting and kitchens equipped with stove and refrigerator, individual apartments are not furnished. Rent rates (subject to change) are $92.85 and $114.55 per month for one- and two-bedroom apartments, respectively.

University Village South Apartments contain 128 one- and two-bedroom unfurnished units with central heat and air-conditioning, wall-to-wall carpeting, stove, refrigerator, and disposal. Rent rates (subject to change) are $92.50 and $112.50 per month for one- and two-bedroom apartments, respectively.

Tanglewood Manor Apartments, located about 1¼ miles south of the central campus, contain 208 furnished and unfurnished efficiency, one- and two-bedroom, and two-bedroom townhouse units. All are carpeted, centrally heated and air conditioned and have disposals. Two-bedroom units have dishwashers. All one- and two-bedroom units have 1½ baths. Special features include two swimming pools, laundry facilities, and a large recreation building. Rent rates are on a monthly basis and are subject to change. Rates per unit are given below.

	Efficiency	One Bedroom	Two Bedroom	Townhouse
Unfurnished	$80.00	$107.50	$125.00	$147.50
Furnished	$90.00	$117.50	$140.00	$162.50

OFF-CAMPUS HOUSING

The Off-Campus Housing Office maintains extensive records on apartments, houses, rooming units, trailers, and trailer park lots offered for rent to students, faculty, and staff members. It compiles an annual comprehensive list of major apartment developments, rooming houses, and trailer parks accepted by it for referral. This list will be sent upon request to anyone who has completed a Request for Assistance with off-campus housing. In addition to the units contained in the comprehensive list, the office has on record several hundred units in small establishments to which referrals are made after notice of availability is received from the owners.

Since mutually satisfactory rentals can usually be arranged only after personal inspection of facilities and conference with the owners, persons seeking off-campus housing are advised to come to Gainesville at an appropriate time in advance of the term for which they need housing. Such visits should be made on week days not on weekends or holidays—and after advance information has been secured. Appointments may be made for consultation on particular problems.

FINANCIAL AID

Qualified graduate students in every department are eligible for a number of fellowships, assistantships, and other awards. In general, such awards are available to students pursuing either a master's or a doctoral degree. Unless otherwise specified, all applications for financial support should be made to the chairman of the appropriate department, University of Florida, by February 15 of each year.

Fellows and graduate assistants must pay the appropriate Florida or non-Florida tuition. Fellows and trainees are expected to devote full time to their studies and their stipend is "excludable from income for tax purposes." Graduate assistants who have part-time teaching or research duties should register for appropriately reduced study loads. Income received from their services is subject to withholding tax.

Graduate students with an assistantship, fellowship, or traineeship must not accept other employment. Registration will be in accordance with the following schedule.

	Minimum Credit Registration	Maximum Credit Registration
Students not on appointments	3	20
Fellows and Trainees	12	20
1/4-time Assistants	12	17
1/3-time Assistants	10	17
1/2-time Assistants	8	17
3/4-time Assistants	6	14
Full-time Assistants	3	6

UNIVERSITY-WIDE AWARDS

Graduate Council Fellowships are available annually to academically superior students at stipends ranging from $3,400 to $4,300 for 9 months. These awards require no service and provide full academic residence. All Fellows must pay the appropriate Florida or non-Florida tuition, unless a non-Florida student is awarded a tuition waiver.

Non-Florida Tuition Waivers may be available for non-Florida students who hold assistantships of one-third time and above.

One-Fourth-Time Assistantships provide a stipend from $2,340 to $2,925 for 9 months. Assigned duties in teaching or research amount to 10 hours a week.

One-Third-Time Assistantships provide a stipend from $3,120 to $3,900 for 9 months. An academic year of graduate residence may be completed in 4 quarters. Assigned duties in teaching or research amount to 13½ hours a week.

One-Half-Time Assistantships provide a stipend from $4,680 to $5,850 for 9 months. A year of graduate residence may be completed in 5 quarters. Assigned duties amount to 20 hours a week.

Interested students should inquire at their department offices concerning the availability of assistantships and the procedure for making application. Prospective students should write directly to the chairman of their major departments as well as to the Admissions Office. *Early inquiry is essential in order to be assured of meeting application deadlines.* Appointments are made on the recommendation of the department chairman, subject to admission to the Graduate School and to the approval of the Dean of the Graduate School. Clear evidence of superior ability and promise is required. Reappointment to assistantships requires evidence of continuation of good scholarship.

NATIONAL DEFENSE EDUCATION ACT FELLOWSHIPS

Title VI NDEA Fellowships.—These are available for students whose proposed programs emphasize the learning of Spanish, Portuguese, or Aymara through courses in the language or, in the case of doctoral candidates working on the dissertation, through research dealing with the language or research in which the language is an indispensible tool. Fellows are expected also to study other fields needed for a fuller understanding of the area, region, or country in which such a language is commonly used. These related studies may include such fields as anthropology, economics, geography, history, linguistics, literature, political science, and sociology.

The basic stipend will comprise the cost of tuition and all required fees, plus $2,000 for the first academic year of postbaccalaureate study, $2,200 for each subsequent academic year, and $2,400 for the terminal academic year.

NDEA-RELATED FULBRIGHT-HAYS GRADUATE FELLOWSHIPS FOR STUDY ABROAD

The purpose of this program is to enable graduate students who plan to teach in U.S. institutions of higher education to undertake non-Western language and area study and research abroad.

In general, Fellows will be expected to study in the world area of their academic interests during their periods abroad, and Fellows following a full-time program of formal study will normally be expected to carry on their studies in a single country. In certain cases, however, approval may be given for dissertation research which would involve (a) visits to several countries, or (b) study outside the geographic area involved if it is demonstrated that specialized or superior research facilities exist elsewhere.

Stipends will be individually computed on the basis of the cost of living in the foreign country. The award will also cover travel expenses, fees for tuition which the Fellow may need to carry out the approved program, and an allowance to help meet the cost of research and incidental expenses.

AGRICULTURE

H. Harold Hume Fellowship of the Florida Federation of Garden Clubs.— This fellowship, established by the Florida Federation of Garden Clubs, has for its object the investigation of special problems of ornamental horticulture in Florida. The work is under the direction of the Department of Horticultural Science. The fellowship carries a stipend of $2,700 annually.

EDUCATION

Many graduate students in education receive financial aid through assistantships and traineeships made available by federal and foundation grants for research and special programs. The number and nature of these awards vary with each academic year and during the year. Qualified students interested in financial support should maintain contact with the Office of Graduate Studies in Education.

ENGINEERING

Financial aid to graduate students in engineering is available through between 250 and 300 research and teaching assistantships requiring one-third- to one-half-time work loads with stipends of $320 per month and up. Information regarding application for these positions may be obtained from the graduate coordinator of the department of interest or from the Office of the Dean, College of Engineering.

Florida Steel Fabricators and Florida Rock Industries each provide $5,000 for a one-year fellowship for civil engineering students pursuing a Master of Engineering degree.

LAW

Some part-time assistantships and research positions are available for graduate students who have made outstanding records in their studies leading to the first degree in law. In addition, a limited number of University of Florida Law Center Association merit loans of $750 per academic year (3 quarters) may be awarded to needy entering applicants. Merit loans are not available for nonresidents of Florida who have been awarded nonresident tuition waivers.

MEDICINE

Predoctoral fellowships and part-time assistantships and research positions are available for graduate students in the various basic medical science departments participating in the Ph.D. program. In addition some clinical and basic science departments offer postdoctoral fellowships to selected recent recipients of the M.D. or Ph.D. degree who wish extensive research experience in these disciplines.

NURSING

Financial aid is sometimes available. For information contact the Assistant Dean, Graduate Program, College of Nursing, J. Hillis Miller Health Center, Gainesville, Florida 32610.

PHARMACY

American Foundation for Pharmaceutical Education Fellowships.—A number of graduate fellowships are offered by the American Foundation for Pharmaceutical Education, which carry stipends up to $3,000 for married Fellows and up to $2,400 for single Fellows. In addition, allowances up to $800 may be granted annually for tuition, fees, and academic expenses. Holders of these fellowships may pursue graduate work at the University of Florida. Application should be made to the Foundation, 777 14th Street, N.W., Room 330, Washington, D. C. 20005.

PSYCHOLOGY

Financial support is available to assist students to pursue graduate work leading to the master's or doctor's degree. In addition to University-wide awards, current financial assistance includes U.S. Public Health Traineeships, Florida Mental Health Fellowships, Graduate Teaching and Research Assistantships, and the Center for Neurobiological Sciences Fellowships. For information write the Chairman of the Stipend Committee, Department of Psychology.

SPEECH

The Department of Speech administers a number of traineeships, fellowships, and assistantships from such sources as the National Institutes of Health, Social Rehabilitative Services Administration, Alachua County Easter Seal Society, and the University of Florida.

Additional information may be obtained from the Chairman of the Department of Speech.

LOANS

Long-term loans are available to graduate students from five sources: United Student Aid Funds, Federally Insured Loans, University of Florida Long-Term Loans, Florida Insured Student Loans, and Direct Student Loans. All programs are basically the same, but each has limiting eligibility requirements such as residency, family income, etc.

Loan maximums range from $1,000 to $2,500 per academic year, repayable after termination of enrollment, at interest rates varying from 3% to 7% annually. The actual amount of each loan award is determined by assessment of individual need by a uniform formula. Application should be made to the Office for Student Financial Affairs between November 1 and February 28 for the following academic year. Applications received after this date will be honored if sufficient funds remain after processing those arriving during the regular period.

No deadlines exist for the Federally Insured Loan, the United Student Aid Fund Loan, or the Florida Insured Student Loan. Applications may be obtained from the Office for Student Financial Affairs, 23 Tigert Hall.

SPECIAL FACILITIES AND PROGRAMS

RESEARCH AND TEACHING FACILITIES

THE ARTS

The University Center of the Arts is the coordinating facility, administered by the Colleges of Architecture and Fine Arts, to serve the students, faculty, and the general public by presenting exhibitions and performances of the best works in the visual and performing arts. These works include all programs in the Building Arts and Fine Arts such as those in Architecture, Interior Design, Landscape Architecture, Building Construction, Art, and Music. Various other programs are given in cooperation with different departments throughout the University and the community.

ART GALLERIES

The University Gallery is an integral part of the Architecture and Fine Arts complex. The Gallery is located on the campus facing S. W. 13th Street (U.S. 441). An atrium and reflecting pool are two pleasing features of the Gallery's distinctive architectural style. The Gallery, with 3000 square feet of display space, is completely modern, air-conditioned, and maintains a varied exhibition schedule of the visual arts during the year. The contents of exhibitions displayed in the University Gallery range from the creations of traditional masters to the latest and most experimental works by the modern avant-garde. The minor arts of yesterday and today, along with the creations of oriental and primitive cultures, form topics for scheduled exhibitions. Each exhibition shows for approximately a month, and the Gallery's hours are from 9 A.M. to 5 P.M. daily except Sunday, when they are from 1 P.M. to 5 P.M. The Gallery is closed Saturdays, holidays, and during the month of September.

The Teaching Gallery of the Department of Art is located adjacent to the department's office area, on the third floor of the classroom building in the Colleges of Architecture and Fine Arts complex. As a direct and physical adjunct to the Art Department's teaching program, this gallery displays smaller traveling exhibitions of merit, as well as student exhibitions and one-man shows by faculty artists. The

Gallery is open Monday through Friday from 9 A.M. to noon and from 1:30 P.M. to 4:30 P.M. It is closed Saturdays and Sundays.

COMPUTATIONAL FACILITIES

In addition to numerous small digital computers and at least three hybrid computers located on the campus, the University of Florida houses the central facilities of the Northeast Regional Data (Processing) Center (NERDC) of the State University System of Florida. These facilities—which are available to students and faculty at the University—include an IBM System/370-165 computer with 2 megabytes of high-speed core, several IBM 3330 disk drives and a 2311 drive, plus a number of 9-track tape drives and a 7-track unit. In addition to the 165 and its peripheral devices, facilities also include an IBM 1401 and an off-line Calcomp drum plotter.

NERDC supports batch processing and well over a hundred low-speed interactive terminals serving almost all areas of the campus. These terminals support APL, Coursewriter III, FLORTRAN (a locally written interactive FORTRAN interpreter), BASIC, and ATS, and have an interactive file generation, editing capability, and the ability to be used for submission of batch jobs. Limited output from batch jobs may also be routed to such terminals. More extensive output is printed on either of the two centrally located high-speed printers or at one of several on-campus high-speed remote batch terminals available for submission of batch jobs. Extensive software support is provided for batch processing, including the major high-level languages and a large number of program packages and special-purpose languages.

The NERDC facilities are used for instructional, research and administrative computing. In addition to the hardware and software support, they include consulting and programming services by highly qualified applications and systems programmers. The staff of the NERDC also endeavors to facilitate communication among users of its facilities and to disseminate to them information from off campus which may prove valuable to local computational endeavors.

More information about the NERDC is available through its manuals and its newsletter, / Update.

LIBRARIES

The library system consists of two central units, Library West and Library East, and branch libraries in the Colleges of Architecture and Fine Arts, Education, Engineering, and Law; the Institute of Food and Agricultural Sciences, the J. Hillis Miller Health Center, the Department of Chemistry, and the P. K. Yonge Laboratory School. In addition, reading room facilities have been provided for Journalism and Communications, Health and Physical Education, Music, and the dormitory areas.

The holdings of the Libraries number over 1,425,000 cataloged volumes and a large number of uncataloged documents and newspapers.

Library West, opened in 1967, houses 600,000 books, has a seating capacity of 910, and contains 120 conference rooms and studies.

The main reference and bibliography collection, which includes the basic bibliographies, abstracting and indexing services, and catalogs of other libraries, is located on the first floor of Library West. Another basic collection of reference materials is located on the second floor of Library East. In both places librarians are available for consultation and assistance.

Among the special collections in Library West are the Rare Book Collection, the Dance-Music-Theater Archives, the P. K. Yonge Library of Florida History, the Marjorie Kinnan Rawlings Collection, which consists of manuscripts, typescripts, and memorabilia of one of America's distinguished novelists, and the Collection of Creative Writing, which includes work sheets, manuscripts, and other literary papers of significant contemporary American and British authors. The Libraries' outstanding Latin American Collection, which has been steadily strenthened in recent years, especially in the areas of West Indian and Caribbean materials, is housed in Library East.

MONOGRAPH SERIES

The Graduate School sponsors two monograph series devoted to the publication of research primarily by present and former members of the scholarly community of the University. The *Social Sciences Monographs* are published four times each year with subjects drawn from anthropology, economics, history, political science, sociology, education, geography, law, and psychology. The *Humanities Monographs* are published three times each year with subjects drawn from art, language and literature, music, philosophy, and religion.

FLORIDA STATE MUSEUM

The Florida State Museum was created by an act of the Legislature in 1917 as a department of the University of Florida. Through its affiliation with the University it carries dual responsibility as the State Museum of Florida and as the University Museum.

The Museum operates as a center of research in anthropology and natural history. Its accessory functions as an educational arm of the University are carried forward through interpretive displays and scientific publications. Under the administrative control of the director are the three departments of the Museum: Natural Sciences, staffed by scientists and technicians concerned with the study and expansion of the research collections of animals; Social Sciences, whose staff members are concerned with the study of historic and prehistoric cultures; Interpretation, staffed by specialists in the interpretation of knowledge through museum exhibit techniques. Members of the scientific and educational staff of the Museum hold dual appointments in appropriate teaching departments. Through these appointments they participate in both the undergraduate and graduate teaching programs.

Graduate assistantships are available in the museum in areas emphasized in its research programs.

The Museum is located at the corner of Museum Road and Newell Drive in a modern facility completed in 1970. The public halls are open from 9:30 A.M. until 5 P.M. The Museum is closed on Christmas Day. There is no admission charge.

The research collections are under the care of curators who encourage the scientific study of the Museum's holdings. Materials are constantly being added to the collection both through gifts from friends and as a result of research activities of the Museum staff. The archaeological and ethnological collections are noteworthy. There are extensive study collections of birds, mammals, mollusks, reptiles, amphibians, fish, and invertebrate and vertebrate fossils. Opportunities are provided for students, staff, and visiting scientists to use the collections. Research and field work are presently sponsored in the archaeological, paleontological, and zoological fields. Students interested in these specialities should make application to the appropriate teaching department.

The purpose of the University Press is to encourage, seek out, and publish original and scholarly manuscripts which will aid in developing the University as a recognized center of research and scholarship.

In addition to its broad range of state, regional, and Latin American titles, the Press publishes books of general interest and five separate series in Floridiana, gerontology, humanities, Latin American studies, and social sciences. It is also the publisher of *The Handbook of Latin American Studies,* sponsored by the Library of Congress.

The Press Board of Managers, including the director and fourteen faculty experts appointed by the President of the University, determines policies of publication relating to the acceptance or rejection of manuscripts and the issuance of author contracts. Each year the board examines numerous manuscripts submitted not only by the University faculty but by authors from all over the United States, Europe, and Latin America.

The Press is a member of the Association of American University Presses and of the Association of American Publishers, Inc.

Students and members of the faculty and staff are cordially invited to visit the Press offices at 15 N. W. 15th Street, adjacent to the campus.

INTERDISCIPLINARY GRADUATE STUDIES PROGRAMS

INTERNATIONAL STUDIES

As the leading institution of higher education in the state, the University of Florida has long been aware of Florida's unique international position. By the beginning of this century, the University had begun to focus its attention on the Latin American nations. Advanced degrees were given in Latin American studies as early as 1927, and by the midcentury a School of Inter-American Studies had been formed.

During the last two decades, the University of Florida's commitment to international studies has expanded rapidly. This expansion has resulted in the creation of a Center for Latin American Studies, a Center for African Studies, a Center for Tropical Agriculture, a program in International Relations, and an English Language Institute for speakers of other languages. Programs in Asian Studies, Soviet and East European Studies, and West European Studies have been added to the undergradute curriculum. The University of Florida has participated in programs of assistance and development in many major areas of the world: Africa, South America, Central America, and Southeast Asia. There has also been a corresponding increase in the number of faculty members involved in teaching and in research within the field of international studies.

As evidence of its commitment to international programs, the University opened, in January, 1971, the $1.6 million federally funded Graduate School and International Studies Building, dedicated and named Linton E. Grinter Hall. The modern four-story building contains 60 faculty offices, 102 study cubicles, and 9 seminar rooms, as well as the offices of the Graduate School and the Division of Sponsored Research.

The expansion of efforts in these directions represents a conviction on the part of the University that today's students must be aware, in more than a superficial way, of developments and trends outside our national boundaries if they are to live in a world of peace and harmony. International education is essential for the citizenry and leaders of the twenty-first century—the students of today.

The Center for African Studies, established with financial assistance under Title VI of the National Defense Education Act, is responsible for the direction and coordination of interdisciplinary instructional and research activities related to Africa. It cooperates with departments in administering and staffing a coordinated Certificate Program in African Studies. This program provides a broad foundation for students preparing for teaching or other professional careers in which a knowledge of Africa is essential. University fellowships and assistantships are available on a competitive basis to students in the degree programs described below. The Center sponsors conferences and visiting lecturers. It supports directly as well as through various departments selective library acquisitions to meet the instructional and research needs of the Center's faculty and students.

Graduate Degree Programs.—The African Studies Center does not offer interdisciplinary graduate degrees. With the cooperation of its participating departments, if offers a Certificate in African Studies in conjunction with the M.A. and Ph.D. degrees.

Requirements for the Certificate in African Studies with the Master of Arts degree are (a) at least 24 credits of course work in a departmental major, 20 of which should relate to Africa; (b) 12 credits of course work related to Africa and distributed in at least two other departments; (c) a structural knowledge of an African language; and (d) a thesis on an African topic.

Requirements for the Certificate in African Studies with the doctoral degree are (a) the doctoral requirements of the major department; (b) 27 credits of African language or area course work in two or more departments outside the major; (c) 5 credits in an area seminar; (d) a dissertation on an African topic based on field work in Africa; (e) knowledge of a language appropriate to the area of specialization.

Inquiries about the various programs and activities of the Center should be addressed to the Director, Center for African Studies, 470 Grinter Hall, University of Florida.

The English Language Institute offers a noncredit, nondegree program in English as a second language for students with some knowledge of the language who wish to increase their competence. The program, which may be taken any quarter of the academic year, emphasizes the oral and written skills needed by students who plan to attend a university in the United States. In addition to regular English Language Institute testing, institutional administration of TOEFL is given near the end of each quarter.

Further information is available from the Director, English Language Institute, Grinter Hall, University of Florida.

International Relations, a field of specialization leading to the M.A. and Ph.D. degrees, is offered in programs through the Department of Political Science. In addition to the M.A. and Ph.D. with a major in political science which may emphasize international relations, the University offers an M.A. and Ph.D. with a major in international relations. For the M.A. the requirements are the same as for the M.A. in political science. For the Ph.D. the student has the option of taking either 1) four fields of political science and a single or composite minor, or 2) three fields of political science (plus two graduate courses in a fourth field) and two minor fields or a composite minor.

The Center for Latin American Studies is responsible for directing and coordinating graduate training, research, and other academic activities related to the Latin American area.

Master of Arts in Latin American Studies.—This is an interdisciplinary area degree offered directly by the Center. Requirements are (a) a major of 21 credits consisting primarily of Latin American language or area courses in one department, which may be food and resource economics, anthropology, economics, Romance languages (Spanish and Portuguese), geography, history, political science, and sociology; (b) 18 credits of Latin American language or area courses in at least two other departments; (c) a thesis on a Latin American topic for which up to 9 credits are given through registration in LA 699; (d) a reading, writing, and speaking knowledge of a Latin American language. The M.A. in Latin American Studies is intended primarily as a terminal degree for persons who, initially in their graduate program, are not aiming at a teaching career in traditional academic departments but who require a broad knowledge of Latin American cultures and appropriate language competence for their career objectives. It is so structured, however, that students may move directly from it into departmental Ph.D. programs without interrupting their academic progress.

Master's Degree with Certificate in Latin American Studies.—Through agreement with the Center, the departments named in the preceding paragraph as well as the Colleges of Business Administration and Education permit a Latin American concentration in the major and minor fields. A Certificate in Latin American Studies may be awarded to students who complete the master's program in one of the participating departments and meet the following requirements: (a) 30 credits in the major department; (b) a 9-credit minor in another department; (c) a thesis on a Latin American topic for which 9 credits are given; (d) a reading knowledge of a Latin American language.

A certificate may also be awarded to those students in a department permitting the master's degree without thesis who meet the following requirements: (a) departmental requirements for the major and minor; (b) 18 hours of Latin American content courses divided between at least two disciplines; (c) 54 credits of graduate course work; (d) a reading knowledge of a Latin American language. In choosing area courses, the student should work closely with the graduate coordinator of the Center for Latin American Studies. Only those courses specifically approved by the coordinator will be counted toward the required 18 hours of Latin American concentration.

The Ph.D. Program.—The Center does not offer an interdisciplinary Latin American area degree at the doctoral level. Through agreement with participating departments, however, it does provide a Certificate in Latin American Studies which is awarded in conjunction with Ph.D. degrees in food and resource economics, anthropology, economics, education, geography, history, political science, sociology, and Spanish. Requirements for the certificate are (a) Latin American concentration within the major department; (b) an area minor of at least 30 credits consisting principally, if not exclusively, of Latin American language and area courses in two or more departments outside the major and including at least 5 credits of LA 640, Latin American Area Seminar; (c) a dissertation on a Latin American subject; (d) a reading, speaking, and writing knowledge of one Latin American language and a reading knowledge of another; (e) residence in Latin America normally of at least six months' duration and devoted primarily to dissertation research.

A Certificate in Latin American Demographic Studies may be earned in conjunction with an M.A. or Ph.D. program in economics, geography, or sociology.

Graduate Fellowships and Assistantships.—In addition to University fellowships and assistantships available to students on a competitive basis in the programs described above, the Center for Latin American Studies administers financial assistance from outside sources, including Title VI, NDEA Fellowships.

Research.—The Center supports or participates in a number of interdisciplinary research programs which, in addition to their primary objectives, provide opportunities for training and financial support of graduate students.

Library Resources.—The several libraries on the campus of the University of Florida have Latin American holdings totaling over 145,000 volumes as well as important manuscript materials in the original, in transcription, and on microfilm. In terms of subject matter, holdings are strongest in history and the social sciences, but increasing attention is being given to the environmental sciences and to literature. In terms of region, they are strongest in the Caribbean and circum-Caribbean, but Brazilian materials are being augmented rapidly.

Other Activities.—The Center sponsors conferences on Latin American topics, supports publication of scholarly books, monographs, and papers, and cooperates with other University units in conducting developmental programs in Latin America.

Inquiries about the various programs and activities of the Center should be addressed to the Director, Center for Latin American Studies, Grinter Hall, University of Florida.

The Center for Tropical Agriculture, within the Institute of Food and Agricultural Sciences seeks to stimulate interest in research and curriculum related to the tropical environment and its development.

Minor in Tropical Agriculture.—An interdisciplinary minor in tropical agriculture may be planned at both the master's and doctoral levels by students majoring in agriculture, forestry, and other fields where knowledge of the tropics is relevant. The minor may include courses treating characteristics of the tropics: its soils, water, vegetation, climate, agricultural production, and the language and culture of tropical countries.

Certificate Programs.—A program for a specialization (with certificate) in tropical agriculture for graduate students in the College of Agriculture is available. The program provides course selection to broaden the normal degree requirements for those interested in specializing in tropical agriculture. Approved courses must be selected from four basic groups as follows: area studies, international economics, tropical ecosystems, and tropical agriculture. For nonagriculture students a similar program with a Certificate in Tropical Studies is available. Students interested in these programs should consult the Dean of the College of Agriculture.

Research.—The Center provides research grants to faculty members and their graduate students and assists in the coordination of interdisciplinary research funded elsewhere. Development assistance contracts in agriculture and related fields frequently have research components.

Student Support.—Students within the College of Agriculture and the School of Forest Resources and Conservation pursuing a minor in tropical agriculture are eligible for assistantships awarded by the Center through academic departments.

Other Activities.—The Center seeks a broad dissemination of knowledge about tropical agriculture through the sponsoring of conferences and seminars featuring leading authorities on the tropics; publication of books, monographs, and proceedings; and through acquisition of materials for the library and the data bank.

The Organization for Tropical Studies (OTS) is a consortium of major educational and research institutions in the United States and abroad, created to promote understanding of tropical environments and their intelligent use by man. The University of Florida is a charter member. Graduate field courses in Central

America are coordinated from the regional office in Costa Rica. Courses with varying content are offered in the agricultural sciences, earth sciences, forestry, geography, marine science, meteorology, and terrestrial biology during the winter, spring, and summer terms. Additional courses are being planned. Students are selected on a competitive basis from universities throughout the country. OTS provides round-trip transportation and maintenance in the field. A University of Florida graduate student may register for 12 credits in an appropriate departmental course cross-listed with OTS, such as ZY 605 or GPY 690. The University of Florida does not require tuition for OTS courses. OTS offers pilot-study research grants to junior faculty and graduate students who have had limited tropical experience. Further information can be obtained from the OTS campus office located in the Center for Tropical Agriculture.

BIOLOGICAL SCIENCES

Biophysics is an interdisciplinary program of graduate studies and research within a number of departments in the Colleges of Agriculture, Arts and Sciences, Engineering, and Medicine. The Biophysics Council is responsible for coordinating graduate training and other academic activities related to biophysics within the University. Each graduate student must qualify within the participating departments. The Council then provides individual guidance and a biophysics core curriculum. The master's or doctoral degree is offered by the participating department. Certification of biophysical studies is provided by the Graduate Council at the recommendation of the Biophysics Council, in conjunction with the Ph.D. degree within each participating department. This is a developing interdisciplinary field, and at present the following departments have either approved graduate studies in this area or are participating in the program: Biochemistry, Chemistry, Chemical Engineering, Electrical Engineering, Entomology, Materials Science and Engineering, Physics, and Zoology.

For additional information, write the Chairman of the Biophysics Council, Department of Physics, or the representative of the Biophysics Council in any of the above departments.

The Division of Biological Sciences is organized within the College of Arts and Sciences to provide coordination in the biological sciences. The Division, with a staff from many disciplines, has organized faculties in cellular biology, molecular biology, developmental biology, parasitology, marine biology, and radiation biology. Each faculty is responsible for developing and supervising a core program in its special area. In addition to the cross-department programs, the Division serves to coordinate biological science wherever it exists in the University, and to operate marine research stations on the east and west coasts of Florida. The Departments of Zoology, Botany, Microbiology, and Biochemistry are the units composing the Division of Biological Sciences.

The University of Florida Marine Laboratory at Seahorse Key is located 57 miles west of Gainesville on the Gulf Coast, three miles offshore, opposite Cedar Key. Facilities include a 20x40-ft. research and teaching building, and a 10-room residence, with two kitchens and a dining-lounge, which provides dormitory accommodations for 24 persons. The laboratory, which owns a 32-ft. research vessel equipped for offshore work and several smaller outboard-powered boats for shallow water and inshore work, is used for research by graduate students from the various departments of the Division of Biological Sciences.

The University of Florida Cornelius Vanderbilt Whitney Marine Laboratory at Marineland is designed for research and instruction in marine biological sciences.

Facilities are available for research in all fields of modern biology encompassing the techniques of biophysics, biochemistry, microbiology, morphological and functional biology, pathology, marine medicine, pharmacology, and nutrition. Field studies involve both ecological and environmental problems. Research opportunities for graduate students are available through faculty members who use this laboratory.

THE CENTER FOR ALLIED HEALTH INSTRUCTIONAL PERSONNEL

The Center (CAHIP) is a project jointly sponsored by the Colleges of Education and Health Related Professions, and was originally funded under the terms of a grant from the W. K. Kellogg Foundation.

Persons who desire to enroll in graduate programs for the master's or doctor's degree as preparation for careers in teaching or administration in the allied health professions should possess (a) a baccalaureate degree, (b) credentials acceptable for admission to the Graduate School of the University of Florida, and (c) a stated plan for teaching or leadership positions in the allied health fields in two-year or four-year colleges or universities.

Students accepted for admission to any advanced degree program will fulfill the basic requirements of that program and such other courses of study relating to allied health as may be appropriate for their stated goals. Each individual's program is planned, insofar as possible, according to these objectives.

Applicants who desire to assume teaching responsibilities should have a minimum of two years' employment experience in a clinical field, and should possess appropriate licensure, registration, or certification in that field. Those who have had no previous teaching experience will be required to complete a two-quarter teaching practicum. Examples of a few of the clinical fields from which students will be considered (but not limited to) include medical technology, nursing, occupational therapy, physical therapy, radiologic technology, and respiratory therapy technology.

Requests for further information should be sent to the Director, Center for Allied Health Instructional Personnel, Norman Hall, University of Florida.

ENGINEERING: STATE CENTER

The College of Engineering has established an off-campus graduate engineering education center at Eglin Air Force Base where qualified personnel may enroll in courses leading to the master's degree. For admission to the graduate program, the prospective student must file an application with the Graduate School as outlined in the *Admissions Section* of this *Catalog.*

For additional information, visit the Eglin Air Force Base, or write the Dean, College of Engineering, University of Florida.

THE OAK RIDGE ASSOCIATED UNIVERSITIES

The University of Florida is one of the sponsors of Oak Ridge Associated Universities (ORAU), a nonprofit education and research management corporation of 43 colleges and universities. ORAU, which was established in 1946, conducts programs of research, education, information, and human resource development for a variety of government and private organizations. It is particularly interested in three areas: energy, health, and the environment.

Among ORAU's activities are competitive programs to bring undergraduates, graduate students, and faculty members to work on research problems at the research facilities of the Energy Research and Development Administration. Participants are selected by ORAU and the staffs of the facilities participating in the ORAU programs— Oak Ridge National Laboratory; the Oak Ridge Y-12 Plant; the Oak Ridge Gaseous Diffusion Plant; the Atmospheric Turbulence and Diffusion Laboratory in Oak Ridge; the Savannah River Laboratory and Savannah River Ecology Laboratory in Aiken, S.C.; the Comparative Animal Research Laboratory in Oak Ridge; the Puerto Rico Nuclear Research Center; and the Energy Research Centers at Bartlesville, Okla., Pittsburgh, Pa., and Morgantown, W. Va. The ORAU Institute for Energy Analysis, the Special Training Division and the Medical and Health Sciences Division are also open to qualified students and faculty members.

Undergraduate. The ORAU Undergraduate Research Training Program offers juniors majoring in the sciences, engineering, and mathematics an opportunity to spend 10 weeks during the summer working in directed research programs at these sites.

Graduate. The ORAU Laboratory Graduate Participation Program enables a candidate for an advanced degree, upon completion of all requirements for work-in-residence except research, to work toward completion of a research problem and preparation of the thesis at one of the participating sites.

Faculty. University of Florida faculty members under the ORAU Faculty Research Participation Program can go to an Energy Research and Development Administration facility for varying periods up to three months for advanced study and research. It is also possible to combine a University of Florida faculty development grant with a longer ORAU Faculty Research Participation appointment.

Stipends are available. The student stipends are at fixed rates that change from time to time. Faculty stipends are individually negotiated, based upon the current university salary.

A copy of the bulletin and announcement of the ORAU-ERDA university-laboratory programs is available in the offices of the Graduate School and the Department of Nuclear Engineering Sciences. Bulletins also may be obtained by writing to the University Programs Office, Oak Ridge Associated Universities, Inc., P. O. Box 117, Oak Ridge, Tenn. 37830.

Interested persons should ask for assistance from the Chairman of the Department of Nuclear Engineering Sciences who serves as the ORAU Counselor at the University of Florida. All arrangements for these research programs will be made between the Dean of the Graduate School and Oak Ridge Associated Universities.

PUBLIC ADMINISTRATION

Training in this area leads to positions in local, state, and federal government agencies. The curriculum consists of seminars in planning, public administration, and public law and recommended courses in statistics, accounting, economics, sociology, geography, and public works engineering. Supervised internships in selected agencies in Florida are arranged by the Department of Political Science as an integral part of the training program.

Graduate work leads to an M.A. in political science. In most cases, students are advised to pursue the M.A. without thesis, with a total of 60 hours of course work in political science and related outside fields. There is no foreign language requirement.

URBAN AND REGIONAL RESEARCH CENTER

The Center stimulates and coordinates interdisciplinary graduate training, applied research and service activities in urban and regional affairs and works closely with staff and graduate students in any discipline concerned with international, national, state, and local problems of human settlement.

Graudate Program.—The graduate certificate program in the Urban and Regional Research Center (URRC) supplements the student's primary discipline and provides additional training and research opportunities for those who wish to pursue a career related to urban and regional problems. With the cooperation of participating departments, colleges, and centers the URRC offers an interdisciplinary Urban Studies Certificate in conjunction with master's and doctoral degrees.

Requirements for the Urban Studies Certificate: (a) Admission to the Graduate School and a department as a candidate for a graduate degree; (b) completion of departmental degree requirements; (c) completion of departmental requirements to become an urban specialist in the chosen field of study; (d) at least 24 credits of course work outside the major department in courses principally concerned with the major social, political, economic, and technological aspects of contemporary urban growth and planning, including US 600, US 602, and US 610; (e) a master's thesis or doctoral dissertation presented in partial fulfillment of the degree requirements. Optional field work in an urban setting available in several departments and in the Center, is strongly recommended.

Graduate students working toward the Master of Arts in Urban and Regional Planning (M.A.U.R.P.) in the College of Architecture may be credited for specific courses taken in the URRC's Certificate curriculum. For further information consult the Center's course description in this *Catalog.*

Internships and Practical Experience: Under a comprehensive program between the University and participating local, regional, and state governmental units, graduate and advanced undergraduate students may apply through the URRC to work in practical situations on a quarterly basis. Credit for such experience may be given.

Research.—The Center supports or participates in interdisciplinary research programs involving both faculty and students. These projects provide opportunities for additional training in urban and regional affairs and for financial support of graduate students.

Library and Laboratory Resources.—The University Libraries, working with the Urban and Regional Research Center, have accumulated a major collection of volumes and data in all areas related to urban and regional development, including urban government, urban social issues, housing, population problems, environmental issues, and many others.

The Library is an official national depository for the HUD 701 Comprehensive Planning Reports, with a collection of more than 10,000 such reports. The Urban and Regional Research and Documentation Laboratory services this collection and is building a unique collection of national and local-level documentation.

Inquiries about the various programs and activities of the Center should be addressed to the Director, Urban and Regional Research Center, Room 125, Building E, University of Florida.

RESEARCH ORGANIZATIONS

AGRICULTURAL RESEARCH AND EDUCATION CENTERS

The stations are responsible for research leading to the improvement of all phases of Florida's widely varied agricultural production, processing, and marketing. The stations are administered from the University of Florida campus by the

Dean for Research and include main station departments as well as Agricultural Research and Education Centers operating as an integral administrative unit. As a statewide agency having agricultural research as its primary objective, each station cooperates closely with numerous Florida agricultural agencies and organizations.

Many members of the research staff of the Agricultural Experiment Stations are also members of the faculty of the College of Agriculture as are some in the Cooperative Extension Service and the Center for Tropical Agriculture. These three agricultural units of the University of Florida Institute of Food and Agricultural Sciences work cooperatively in many areas under the administration of the Vice President for Agricultural Affairs.

Funds for graduate assistants are made available to encourage graduate training and professional scientific improvement.

Research at the main station is conducted within 18 areas—Agricultural Engineering, Agronomy, Animal Science, Botany, Dairy Science, Entomology and Nematology, Food and Resource Economics, Food Science, School of Forest Resources and Conservation, Fruit Crops, Microbiology, Ornamental Horticulture, Plant Pathology, Poultry Science, Soil Science, Statistics, Vegetable Crops, and Veterinary Science. In addition to the above, the main station has four units vital to its research programs; namely, editorial, library, field services, and business service.

The Agricultural Research Centers are located at Monticello, Brooksville, Ft. Pierce, Immokalee, Dover, Ft. Lauderdale, Hastings, Ona, Apopka, Marianna, Live Oak, Leesburg, Lakeland, Jay, and Ocala.

The locations of the Agricultural Research and Education Centers are at Homestead, Belle Glade, Bradenton, Lake Alfred, Quincy, Sanford, and Tallahassee (F.A.M.U.).

The Florida Agricultural Experiment Stations are cooperating with the Brooksville Beef Cattle Research Station, Brooksville, a USDA field laboratory, in its beef cattle and pasture production and management programs and with the National Weather Service, Lakeland, in the Federal Frost Warning Service for fruit and vegetable producers and shippers.

DIVISION OF SPONSORED RESEARCH

The Division has two general functions: (1) the administration and promotion of the Sponsored Research Program and (2) the support of the total research program of the University in a manner which produces maximum benefit to the University and the greatest service to the State of Florida. All proposals for the sponsorship of research, grants-in-aid, or training grants must receive the approval of the Division Director. Subsequent negotiations with potential contracting agencies or sponsors of research projects are carried on under the Director's supervision.

The activities of the Division of Sponsored Research are intended to stimulate growth and to assist in expanding a balanced research program throughout the University. These activities are intimately related to the support of the graduate program. They are also intended to relieve principal investigators and departments of many of the detailed administrative and reporting duties connected with some sponsored research. The duties and responsibilities of the Division, of course, are designed to supplement the prerogative of the principal investigator to seek sponsors for his own projects and the responsibility of the researcher for the scientific integrity of a project. In direct contacts between a principal investigator and a potential sponsor, however, prior clearance should be obtained from the Division to insure a uniformity in contract requirements and to avoid duplication of negotiations with the same sponsor.

The Division of Sponsored Research is administratively responsible to the Vice President for Academic Affairs through the Dean of the Graduate School. Policies and procedures for the operation of the Division are developed by a Board of Directors working with the Division Director within the general framework of the administrative policies and procedures of the University. The Research Council serves as adviser on scientific matters. The Graduate Council serves as adviser on matters relating to the graduate program.

The law establishing the Division of Sponsored Research enables the utilization of some recovered indirect cost funds in the support of innovative research. The Board of Directors of the Division has the responsibility for the award of these funds. For information write the Director, Division of Sponsored Research, 219 Grinter Hall, University of Florida.

FLORIDA ENGINEERING AND INDUSTRIAL EXPERIMENT STATION

The Station (EIES) developed from early research activities of the engineering faculty and was officially established in 1941 by the Legislature as an integral part of the College of Engineering. Its mandate is "to organize and promote the prosecution of research projects of engineering and related sciences, with special reference to such of these problems as are important to the industries of Florida."

The college and the Station are inextricably intertwined—the two activities cannot be separated functionally; they comprise the two arms of the whole engineering body. This is particularly true at the graduate level. In many instances a program initiated primarily as a research activity has developed into a full-fledged academic department of the college, demonstrating the close interlocking relationship of the research and teaching functions.

Since the fall term of 1967, seven departments of the College of Engineering and the Experiment Station have moved into some 310,000 sq. ft. in seven modern new buildings and one remodeled building. These improvements, including equipment, have raised the value of the physical plant of the college to over $13 million.

The laboratories, staff, and facilities of other divisions of the University are also available to the Station research faculty through many outstanding interdisciplinary programs which provide Station support of graduate students in the physical sciences such as physics and chemistry, as well as in engineering. With the close relationship that exists between teaching and research, students are exposed to many engineering and industrial problems normally not encompassed in a college program.

The Station receives only a small portion of its operating revenue from the state. The major support of its research activities is derived from contracts with government agencies, foundations, and industrial organizations. Large and small manufacturers avail themselves of the finest engineering research laboratories in the Southeast. The Station has superior facilities and staff in such fields as microelectronics and integrated circuits, power systems, metallurgy, ceramics, coastal engineering, soil mechanics, transport phenomena and fluid dynamics, energy conversion, air and water pollution control, electrochemistry, fast neutron physics, nuclear rocket propulsion, dynamics and vibrations, communications, kinetics, ionics, gaseous electronics and plasmas, computer and information science, and systems analysis.

The Coastal and Oceanographic Engineering Laboratory, a unit of EIES, conducts research on problems of the shoreline and of coastal and inland waters, and renders advisory service to public agencies and industry. Interdisciplinary and multidisciplinary research and graduate instruction are closely coordinated and related to applications of the coastal zone. Many graduate students are supported by research programs of the COE Laboratory which include (1) air-sea interaction and the generation of surface waves; (2) scale models of inlets and shore structures; (3) transportation of sediment by waves and currents; (4) wave and current effects at offshore nuclear power plants; (5) water temperature variations near power-generating plants; (6) tidal variations in inland waters; (7) littoral transport under wave action and many others; (8) coastal defense measures.

Laboratory research facilities include (1) a large area for carrying out hydraulic model studies of coastal phenomena; (2) an air-sea interaction facility to investigate wave generation phenomena; (3) an internal wave facility to investigate subsurface wave phenomena; (4) a wave tank in which the effects of waves on structures, sand motion, etc., can be investigated; and (5) a hydraulic tilting flume for basic studies of the interaction of flows with sediments. Field investigations, representing a substantial portion of the research effort, are supported by a mobile field station, three small boats, and a complete range of tide recorders, current meters, sounding and other auxiliary equipment.

INTERDISCIPLINARY RESEARCH CENTERS

The following centers, developed at the University of Florida and approved by the State Board of Regents, function primarily to increase knowledge in specific fields of study and to apply this knowledge to solve many of the crucial problems that our society now faces. Each center is listed in alphabetical order by the first substantive in the title.

CENTER FOR AERONOMY AND OTHER ATMOSPHERIC SCIENCES

The Center (ICAAS) is a community of scholars drawn from many disciplines represented at the University of Florida. Each scholar has an established professional knowledge and research capability in the atmospheric sciences or in physical, biological, or societal disciplines that relate closely to our atmospheric environment. As an interdisciplinary center, ICAAS promotes pure and applied research in the atmospheric sciences and provides machinery for translating research into forms relevant to societal needs. The aeronomical research of the Center deals with physical, chemical, and electrical processes in the upper atmosphere; e.g., the stratospheric, ionospheric, and thermospheric regions of the earth. Other activities include a diverse range of tropospheric and micrometeorological research as well as biological, ecological, and technological research related to the quality of the air we breathe. These activities are dispersed widely in the Colleges of Arts and Sciences, Agriculture, Engineering, Medicine, Law, and Business Administration. Current research deals with ultraviolet radiation levels which might reach the earth's surface should our stratospheric ozone layer be depleted by the effluents from a future supersonic transport fleet. Of specific concern are the potential effects of changes in UV upon the incidence of skin cancer, agricultural productivity, cells and insects. A second active area of research encompasses community noise measurements and abatement projects. With the support of the Florida Department of Pollution Control assistance is being given twenty-two counties in Northern Florida in the development of noise ordinances and instrumentation for noise control. The primary function of ICAAS is to provide coordination, direction, and focus to strengthen existing programs and to expand them in directions that will help mitigate the socio-technical problems arising from the degradation of our atmospheric environment. ICAAS will also help the training of able students at the undergraduate, graduate, and postdoctoral levels in various pure and applied aspects of the atmospheric sciences. For information, write the Director, Center for Aeronomy and Other Atmospheric Sciences, 221 Space Sciences Research Building, University of Florida.

CENTER FOR APPLIED MATHEMATICS

The Center consists of faculty from the Departments of Engineering Science and Mathematics. These faculty are interested in the application of mathematics to research problems in the physical, engineering, social, and biological sciences. Codirectors are Professors A. J. Bednarek and K. T. Millsaps.

CENTER FOR APPLIED THERMODYNAMICS AND CORROSION

The Center facilitates cooperation between research teams at the University of Florida and the Belgian Corrosion Research Center at Brussels. Research is conducted in electrochemistry, in high temperature oxidation, and in physical and process metallurgy, with applications in corrosion-related environmental problems, such as pollution, water desalination, atomic energy, and surgical implants. For information, write the Director, Center for Applied Thermodynamics and Corrosion, 132 Metallurgical Engineering Building, University of Florida.

CENTER FOR AQUATIC SCIENCES

The Center is responsible for intensive development and coordination of University-wide activities in the freshwater, estuarine, and coastal marine sciences. With major emphasis on Florida and contiguous waters, the Center provides leadership for interdisciplinary programs of benefit to the state. The broad spectrum of curricula, facilities, and faculty at the University allows students great latitude in developing their specific interests in the aquatic sciences. Undergraduate and graduate support is provided by the Center, enabling students in cooperating departments to investigate problems related to Florida's aquatic resources. Field research facilities are available at nearby Cedar Key, Welaka, and Marineland. Interested persons should contact the Director, Center for Aquatic Sciences, 2001 McCarty Hall, University of Florida.

CLINICAL RESEARCH CENTER

The Center program, designed around patients, provides a carefully controlled research environment in which physicians and scientists can define and attempt to conquer unsolved disease problems affecting humans.

A discrete unit, funded entirely through a grant by the National Institutes of Health, the Center is administered through the College of Medicine of the University of Florida. The grant provides for a metabolic kitchen and its staff, a laboratory and staff, and nursing and administrative personnel. Through negotiations between NIH and the Shands Teaching Hospital, a per diem rate and ancillary service charges paid to the hospital for patient care result in no charge to the research patient.

COMMUNICATION RESEARCH CENTER

The Center conducts pure and applied research in a variety of fields of mass communication. It also serves as a resource for college faculty and students in their own research, assists the media and other organizations in their research pursuits, and sponsors other programs related to the mass communication needs of the many communities served by the University. For information, write the Director, Communication Research Center, 400 Stadium Building, University of Florida.

CENTER FOR CONSUMER RESEARCH

The Center conducts basic and applied research on factors influencing consumer decision making and behavior. It provides an organization through which faculty members from a number of disciplines may effectively work together to study the interface between consumers, various institutions, activities of governmental and private organizations and policy alternatives. The needs and behavior of special consumer groups (e.g., the elderly, children) and the impact of particular consumer attitudes and choice behavior in relation to their own and societal goals are of particular interest. For information, write the Director, Center for Consumer Research, 207 Matherly Hall, University of Florida.

INSTITUTE FOR DEVELOPMENT OF HUMAN RESOURCES

The Institute is an interdepartmental research and demonstration activity of the College of Education. Membership is open to all faculty in the University. Organized in 1966 to foster research into factors influencing learning and development from cradle to grave, the Institute for Development of Human Resources has received grant funds from state, federal, and private sources to foster both research and its dissemination to school systems and other educational agencies.

The major programmatic efforts have been (1) Parent education (for parents of toddlers and infants and parents of kindergarten through third grade children); (2) Systematic observation of teacher-pupil classroom behavior in elementary and secondary schools; (3) Studies of learning from the viewpoint of aptitude treatment interaction; (4) Studies of parent-child interaction; and (5) Studies of curriculum efforts which relate to the learner's self-development. The focus of these efforts is on research which leads to the improvement of educational practice.

INSTITUTE OF HIGHER EDUCATION

The Institute of Higher Educaton is an agency within the College of Education, responsible at the same time to the Vice President for Academic Affairs, and is defined as a research and service agency of the University focused upon higher education. Operating under the Institute are several organizational structures: The Florida Community College Interinstitutional Research Council, a consortium of community colleges in Florida with focus upon institutional and system-wide research; the Center for Allied Health Instructional Personnel, with emphasis upon developing allied health faculty for community colleges and universities; the Southeastern Community College Leadership Program, with a focus on developing and improving administrative leadership in community colleges; the State and Regional Leadership Program in Higher Education, a partnership program with Florida State University, for preparing and improving state agency staff personnel; and special projects of both research and service orientation which are assigned from time to time, often on a contract basis.

Many advanced graduate students find research projects of their own interests among the many activities of the IHE. For information, write the Director, Institute of Higher Education, University of Florida.

CENTER FOR DYNAMIC PLASTICITY

The Center conducts research and educational programs and disseminates information on the behavior of materials at high rates of deformation. In addition to structural materials (such as metals, polymers, and composites), the Center is concerned with biological materials (bones and soft tissues) and with dynamic soil mechanics. The Center has established a cooperative arrangement with the University of Bucharest to enhance international cooperation and exchange of information and personnel. For information, address the Director, Center for Dynamic Plasticity, 231 Aero Bldg., University of Florida.

BUREAU OF ECONOMIC AND BUSINESS RESEARCH

The Bureau is the research division of the College of Business Administration. A part of the Bureau's work is designed to further understanding of the economy of Florida and the Southeast. Economic, business, and related research supported by grant and the contract funds is undertaken in subject areas of interest to the faculty. Graduate students are involved also in these projects.

The Bureau publishes three periodicals, *Dimensions, Economic Leaflets,* and *Florida Economic Indicators,* an annual publication, *Florida Statistical Abstract,* and an irregular publication, *Population Studies.* Through these publications and through monographs, the Bureau disseminates the results of research and statistical studies on population, personal income, employment, building construction, and other subjects. For information, write the Director, Bureau of Economic and Business Research, 221 Matherly Hall, University of Florida.

CENTER FOR GERONTOLOGICAL STUDIES AND PROGRAMS

The Center provides an organization through which faculty members from many disciplines may work effectively both within and outside the University to study the problems of aging, to develop programs of benefit to the aged and to disseminate information derived from research in health care, housing, transportation, and other areas. The Southern Conference on Gerontology is held annually; the *Proceedings* are published by the University of Florida Press. For information, write the Director, Center for Gerontological Studies and Programs, 221 Matherly Hall, University of Florida.

HEALTH SYSTEMS RESEARCH DIVISION

The Division is an interdisciplinary activity organized within the Office of the Vice President for Health Affairs, J. Hillis Miller Health Center. Its function is to conduct research to improve the effectiveness and efficiency of the health services delivery system and of the health manpower education and training system and to develop methods for the optimal allocation of health care resources. Research projects are carried out for the academic units of the health center, the Shands Teaching Hospital and Clinics, and other health care facilities within the University and community. In addition, research is conducted through contracts and grants for health organizations and agencies at the state and national level.

The staff of the Division consists of faculty, students, and career service employees representing a diversity of backgrounds and disciplines. Among these are operations research, industrial and systems engineering, health and hospital administration, computer science, economics, medicine, dentistry and health related professions. Student support is provided through assistantships and fellowships. For information, write the Director, Health Systems Research Division, Box 210, J. Hillis Miller Health Center, University of Florida, Gainesville 32610.

CENTER FOR INFORMATION RESEARCH

The Center (CIR) is responsible for directing, coordinating and conducting advanced study and research activity in computers, information systems, software engineering, and their applications to multiple disciplines. As an interdisciplinary center, CIR creates a stimulating environment for basic and applied research to seek new insights in, and optimal solutions to, engineering, physical, biological, medical, management, environmental, and social problems. The Center staff is concerned with solving problems in various disciplines by using modern computing machines, recent communication sciences, and latest information technology.

The primary functions of CIR are (1) to conduct research in developing the theory and techniques for the design of computer systems and software for solving problems of our society; (2) to develop advanced technology for the design of new information systems for various disciplines; (3) to provide coordination and initiation of interdisciplinary attack on the complex techno-socio-economic, environmental as well as health, problems by the systems approach; (4) to provide internship opportunities for graduate students in information science and related areas; and (5) to assist industry and government in finding practical and efficient solutions to information-processing problems.

The research laboratories are equipped with a PDP-11/40 computer system, a Graphic-1 system, a PIDAC (Pictorial Data Acquisition Computer), a PDP-5 computer, a high-performance drum scanner. The Center sponsors the International Symposia on Computer and Information Science (COINS Symposia), cooperates with other University units in organizing and conducting conferences, seminars, short courses, and developmental programs in information science, and supports publication of scholarly books, monograph series, and an international journal on computer and information science.

Inquiries about the various programs and activities of the Center should be addressed to the Director, Center for Information Research, 339 Larsen Hall, University of Florida, Gainesville 32611.

CENTER FOR MACROMOLECULAR SCIENCE

The Center is developing a unified research and teaching faculty, drawing its members from the fields of chemical engineering, chemistry, biochemistry, microbiology, and environmental engineering. Current research in synthetic polymer chemistry includes originating and reducing to practice the synthesis of new materials, conducting scale-up operations, and evaluating such materials for a wide variety of applications. For information, write the Director, Center for Macromolecular Science, 420 Space Sciences Research Building, University of Florida.

MANAGEMENT CENTER

The Center develops continuing education programs for various groups of businessmen. Inquiries may be addressed to the Director, Management Center, 224 Matherly Hall, University of Florida.

CENTER FOR MATHEMATICAL SYSTEM THEORY

The Center was established in 1972 to advance research in all areas of system theory dependent on mathematical methodology. Both pure and applied problems are emphasized. The Center is operated on an interdisciplinary basis in cooperation with the Departments of Mathematics, Electrical Engineering, Systems Engineering, Statistics, and Engineering Sciences.

The permanent faculty of the Center presently includes Professors R. E. Kalman *(Director)*, V. M. Popov, and M. E. Warren. There are numerous affiliated faculty members and many visitors of international stature. An active research seminar is conducted throughout the year on recent developments in system theory, as well as certain aspects of computer science and biology.

Principal interest is currently in algebraic methods in system theory, such as theory of linear systems over a ring; algebraic-geometric structure of classes of linear systems; algebraic theory of infinite-dimensional continuous-time systems; classical theory of invariants as related to decoupling and other structural problems. Recent work has also been directed toward the identification of dynamical systems and fundamental aspects of decentralized and hierarchical control.

CENTER FOR NEUROBIOLOGICAL SCIENCES

The Center is the focus for several disciplines desiring a comprehensive view of the nervous system. The program is conducted through formal courses, seminars, colloquia, and laboratory research in the neurobiological sciences. Normally trainees may be affiliated with the Center through a basic science or clinical department. For information, write the Director, Center for Neurobiological Sciences, M-242, Medical Sciences Building, University of Florida.

PUBLIC ADMINISTRATION CLEARING SERVICES

The Clearing Service is a research and service adjunct of the Department of Political Science in the College of Arts and Sciences. It carries on a continuous program of research in public administration, political behavior, and public policy in Florida; publishes research studies and surveys of administrative and political problems in both scientific and popular monograph form; and publishes a *Civic Information Series* annually for assistance to citizen groups in their study of current issues in the state. For information, write the Director, Public Administration Clearing Services, 8 Peabody Hall, University of Florida.

BUREAU OF RESEARCH

The Bureau is one of the activities of the Colleges of Architecture and Fine Arts. It fosters and encourages research in all areas of the building arts and fine arts. It also provides an opportunity for graduate students and faculty members to engage in research and cooperate effectively in research with other departments and institutions. For information, write the Director, Bureau of Research, 102 Architecture and Fine Arts Bldg., University of Florida.

CENTER FOR RESEARCH ON HUMAN PROSTHESIS

The Center fosters interchange between the biomedical and engineering sciences in research on the development of prosthetic devices for neurosensory organs and limbs, particularly for visual prosthesis. For information, write the Director, Center for Research on Human Prosthesis, Visual Science Laboratory Annex, Dormitory O.

SOCIAL SCIENCES INSTITUTE

The Institute seeks to develop the research capability and productivity of younger faculty at the University of Florida by granting funds for research expenses through competitive awards in all fields of social science. For information, write the Director, Social Sciences Institute, 107 Peabody Hall, University of Florida.

University Counseling Center

The Center, 311 Little Hall, provides psychological services to the members of the student body and consultative services for the University staff members who counsel students. It also provides a practicum for graduate students in the Departments of Psychology and Counselor Education. It engages in institutional as well as basic research in the problems of counseling. Specific services include vocational, personal, marriage, and academic counseling. In these functions the University Counseling Center works closely with staff in the residence halls and with the academic advisers in the University College and upper-division colleges. The Center works with the University Mental Health Service on a referral basis and with the director of the early registration program in the orientation of prospective students to the University.

Florida Water Resources Research Center

The Center, funded by the Department of the Interior, was established in 1964 as a result of the passage of P. L. 88-379—The Water Resources Research Act of 1964—"to stimulate, sponsor, provide for, and supplement present programs for conduct of research, investigation, experiments, and the training of scientists in the fields of water and of resources which affect water."

Under the administration of the Center, current water research projects pertaining to the achievement of adequate statewide water resource management, and water quality and quantity are being conducted by staff members in various departments at the University of Florida and at four other colleges and universities in the state. For information, write the Director, Florida Water Resources Research Center, 220 A. P. Black Hall, University of Florida

Center for Wetlands

The Center for Wetlands is an intercollege research division dedicated to wetlands, their ecology, problems, management, and effective land use. The Center advances knowledge through special research approaches as systems ecological modelling and simulation, energy cost benefit analysis and planning, and field experiments on vegetation response to water control.

The Center fosters campus and statewide communication through a central workshop activity, organized research projects of county and state concern, wetlands publications, conferences and short courses, research data collections, and proposals for curricula. Support of faculty and graduate students is provided by active projects.

Representative research projects are "Cypress Wetlands for Water Management, Recycling, and Conservation," funded by The Rockefeller Foundation and the RANN Division of National Science Foundation, and "Models for Optimization of Land and Water Use in South Florida," funded by the United States Department of the Interior with an Interagency agreement with Florida State Division of State Planning in Tallahassee.

Interested persons should contact the Director, Center for Wetlands, Phelps Lab., University of Florida.

STUDENT SERVICES

Adviser to Foreign Students

The office of the adviser is the center for services performed in behalf of foreign students from their initial inquiries until their return home. The office coordinates with other University agencies and is charged with responsibilites involving admissions, reception, orientation, housing finances, health, immigration, academic counseling, petitions, practical training, employment, embassy and foundation reports, correspondence, legal problems, life counseling, and community relations. The adviser also serves as Fulbright Program Adviser and assists foreign faculty members.

CAREER PLANNING AND PLACEMENT CENTER

The Center, G-22 J. Wayne Reitz Union, functions as the central placement agency for the campus, with services available to all students and alumni of the University, and it works in conjunction with those schools and colleges that give direct employment assistance to their graduates.

In cooperation with educational and administrative units, counseling and testing services, and other related functions, the Placement Center makes its contribution to the development of the whole individual. Its primary aim is to offer assistance to students, from the time they enter school until they graduate, in the development of vocational goals and the attainment of their first career position. Assistance is also offered to alumni who have attended graduate school elsewhere, who are returning to civilian life from the military, or who desire to make changes in employment.

Functions include (1) serving as liaison between students and business, industrial, governmental, and educational organizations that seek college-trained personnel for permanent employment; (2) establishing and maintaining records on registrants, employment opportunities, and placement results; (3) conducting studies on the employment outlook, salary trends, progress of graduates in the working world, and related matters; (4) assisting students who leave school before graduation or who want summer jobs that relate to their fields of study and employment goals; (5) serving in a public relations capacity in dealing with employers and the public.

Specific services include career planning and guidance, counseling on the tools and techniques of the job search, arranging interviews between employers and students, providing personnel records and faculty ratings on students to employers, preparing and mailing lists of job opportunities to registrants, distributing recruitment booklets and materials, and administering tests for employers.

STUDENT HEALTH SERVICE

The Health Service provides a spectrum of medical services which includes primary medical care, preventive medicine, health screening programs and mental health consultation and counseling. These services are available to all full-time students in the University.

The service consists of an out-patient clinic and a 30-bed in-patient unit staffed by physicians, nurses, psychologists, laboratory and x-ray technicians and supporting personnel. It is housed in the Infirmary, which is centrally located on the campus.

The service is a unit of the J. Hillis Miller Health Center with its Colleges of Medicine, Nursing, and Health Related Professions. The facilities of the Health Center are available by consultation and referral through the Student Health Service. Specialty clinics are available in the Infirmary in some fields.

The health fee is a part of the tuition fee paid by all students. This fee covers ordinary out-patient visits, many laboratory tests and some medications. When more complicated diagnostic study or hospitalization is required, additional charges are made. For this reason, a supplemental health insurance plan is recommended.

A medical history and physical examination and certain immunizations are required before registration at the University.

Speech and Hearing Clinic

The Clinic, Room 436, Arts and Sciences Building, offers services without charge to any University student who has a speech or hearing disorder. This assistance is available at any time during the year and therapy sessions are adjusted to individual schedules. The student is encouraged to visit the Clinic and to use this service.

Editorial Assistance and Information

The Graduate School Editorial Office provides a *Guide for Preparing Theses and Dissertations* to assist the student in the preparation of the manuscript, and offers suggestions and advice on such matters as the preparation and reproduction of illustrative materials, the treatment of special problems, the use of copyrighted material, and how to secure copyright for a dissertation. The following procedures apply to the Graduate School's editorial services to students.

1. The responsibility for acceptable English in a thesis or dissertation, as well as the originality and acceptable quality of the content, lies with the student and the supervisory committee.

2. The Graduate School editorial staff acts only in an advisory capacity, but will be glad to answer questions regarding correct grammar, sentence structure, and acceptable forms of presentation.

3. If the student will bring his final rough draft to the Editorial Office of the Graduate School, the staff will examine a limited portion and make recommendations concerning the form of the thesis or dissertation before the final typing.

4. After the first submission of the dissertation in final form, the Editorial Office staff checks the format, paper stock, and pagination and scans portions of the text for general usage, references, and bibliographical form. Master's theses are checked for paper stock, format, and pagination.

5. Upon final submission, the signature pages and Final Examination forms for all theses and dissertations are checked against the Admission to Candidacy forms for the signatures of the college dean (except for the Colleges of Arts & Sciences and Business Administration *which require a special statement on the signature page)* and all members of the supervisory committee. **It is the responsibility of the student and the supervisory chairman to notify the Graduate School in writing of any changes which have been made in the structure of the supervisory committee.**

6. The Editorial Office maintains a file of experienced thesis typists, manuscript editors, and draftsmen which the student may examine to find assistance in the mechanical preparation of the manuscript.

Fields of Instruction

COLLEGES AND AREAS OF INSTRUCTION

AGRICULTURE
Agricultural & Extension
 Education, 74
Agronomy, 75
Animal Science, 77
Dairy Science, 113
Entomology & Nematology, 134
Food & Resource
 Economics, 140
Food Science, 143
Forest Resources & Conservation
 School of, 144
Horticultural Science, 159
Plant Pathology, 215
Poultry Science, 220
Soil Science, 234
Veterinary Science, 252

ARCHITECTURE
Architecture, 83
Building Construction, School of, 95
Urban & Regional Planning, 86

ARTS & SCIENCES
General, 88
Anthropology, 78
Astronomy, 88
Biochemistry & Molecular Biology, 90
Botany, 92
Chemistry, 101
Classics 101
 Latin, 109
Clinical Psychology, 109
Communicative Disorders, 111
English, 132
Geography, 150
Geology, 152
Germanic & Slavic Languages &
 Literatures, 154
History, 158
Latin American Studies,
 Center for, 45
Linguistics, 174
Mathematics, 181
Microbiology, 189
Philosophy, 207
Physics, 210
Political Science, 217
Psychology, 221

Religion, 229
Romance Languages &
 Literatures, 230
 French. 230
 Portuguese, 231
 Spanish, 231
Sociology, 232
Speech, 238
Statistics, 242
Zoology, 253

BUSINESS ADMINISTRATION
General, 96
Accounting, 71
Economics, 114
Finance & Insurance, 139
Health & Hospital
 Administration, 156
Management, 176
Marketing, 178
Real Estate &
 Urban Land Studies, 227

EDUCATION
Counselor Education, 111
Curriculum & Instruction,
 Division of, 113
 General Teacher Education, 148
 Instructional Leadership &
  Support, 167
 Subject Specialization Teacher
  Education, 124
Educational Administration
 & Supervision, 119
Foundations of Education, 146
Special Education, 235

ENGINEERING
General, 125
Agricultural Engineering, 73
Chemical Engineering, 98
Civil Engineering, 105
Electrical Engineering, 121
Engineering Sciences, 127
 Aerospace Engineering, 127
 Coastal & Oceanographic
  Engineering, 128
 Engineering Science &
  Mechanics, 130

COURSE DESIGNATORS

ADP Animal Science—General
AE Architecture
AED Agricultural & Extension Education
AGE Agricultural Engineering
AL Animal Science
APY Anthropology
ART Art
ASC Arts & Sciences—General
ASE Aerospace Engineering
ATG Accounting
ATY Astronomy
AY Agronomy
BA Business Administration—General
BCH Biochemistry & Molecular Biology
BCN Building Construction
BTY Botany
CE Civil Engineering
CHE Chemical Engineering
CLP Clinical Psychology
COE Coastal & Oceanographic Engineering
COM Journalism & Communications
CY Chemistry
DY Dairy Science
ED General Teacher Education; Instructional Leadership & Support; Subject Specialization Teacher Education
EDA Educational Administration & Supervision
EDC Counselor Education
EDE Childhood Education (see Curriculum & Instruction)
EDF Foundations of Education
EDH Special Education
EDS Secondary Education (see Curriculum & Instruction)
EDV Vocational, Technical, & Adult Education (see Curriculum & Instruction)
EE Electrical Engineering
EGC Engineering—General
EH English
ENV Environmental Engineering Sciences
ES Economics
ESM Engineering Science & Mechanics
EY Entomology & Nematology
FH French (see Romance Languages & Literatures)
FI Finance & Insurance
FLE Romance Languages & Literatures
FRE Food & Resource Economics
FS Food Science

FRC Forest Resources & Conservation
GN German (see Germanic & Slavic Languages & Literatures)
GPY Geography
GY Geology
HA Health & Hospital Administration
HRP Communicative Disorders; Health Related Professions—General
HSC Horticultural Science—Fruit Crops, Ornamental Horticulture; Vegetable Crops
HY History
ISE Industrial & Systems Engineering
LA Latin American Studies
LIN Linguistics
LN Latin (see Classics)
LW Law (see Health & Hospital Administration; Latin American Studies)
LWT Law—Taxation
MCY Microbiology
ME Mechanical Engineering
MED Medical Sciences—General; Anatomical Sciences; Immunology & Medical Microbiology; Neuroscience; Pathology; Pharmacology & Therapeutics; Physiology
MGT Management
MKG Marketing
MS Mathematics
MSC Music
MSE Materials Science & Engineering
NES Nuclear Engineering Sciences
NSG Nursing
OCT Occupational Therapy
PCL Political Science
PCY Pharmaceutical Chemistry
PE Portuguese (see Romance Languages & Literatures)
PHR Physical Education, Health, & Recreation
PHY Pharmacy
PPY Philosophy
PS Physics
PSY Psychology
PT Plant Pathology
PY Poultry Science
RC Rehabilitation Counseling
RE Real Estate & Urban Land Studies
RSN Russian (see Germanic & Slavic Languages & Literatures)

69

SCH Speech
SH Spanish (*see* Romance Languages & Literatures)
SLS Soil Science
STA Statistics
SY Sociology
THE Theatre
URP Urban & Regional Planning (*see* Architecture)
US Urban & Regional Research
VY Veterinary Science
ZY Zoology

Key to Abbreviations in Course Listings

Numbers within parentheses following course titles indicate hours of credit for the course: (4) = four credit hours.

For courses which may be repeated with change of content, the maximum allowable credit is indicated after the unit value: (3-6; max: 12).

S/U indicates a grade of Satisfactory or Unsatisfactory—the only grades awarded in courses numbered 697, 698, 699, and 799, which may be repeated as necessary. Other courses graded as S/U are noted in the departmental listings. Students using any of these courses to meet departmental language requirements should request the traditional letter grade.

H indicates a deferred grade assigned to a unit of work which requires more than one term to complete.

The Graduate Faculty listing for each department is for the academic year 1975-76.

Course offerings are subject to change. A *Schedule of Courses*, listing credit hours and section numbers, is published prior to each registration period.

ACCOUNTING

(College of Business Administration)

Chairman: J. K. SIMMONS
Graduate Coordinator: C. L. McDONALD

GRADUATE FACULTY 1975-76

Professors: L. J. BENNINGER; D. D. RAY; J. K. SIMMONS; W. E. STONE; S. C. YU
Associate Professors: I. N. GLEIM; G. L. HOLSTRUM
Assistant Professors: J. R. HASSELBACK; C. L. McDONALD; E. D. SMITH; D. A. SNOWBALL

Graduate Programs.—The Department of Accounting offers graduate work leading to the degrees Master of Business Administration (with an accounting concentration); Master of Arts in accounting; and Ph.D. in business administration with accounting major. The M.B.A. offers a broad business education with some accounting specialization. It is generally appropriate for students with undergraduate majors other than accounting. The M.A. is a specialist accounting degree and can be tailored to the student's career objective: public accounting, taxation, management accounting, or continuation in the Ph.D. program. The Ph.D. accounting major is designed to prepare students for a career in teaching and research at the university or college level or for research-oriented careers in business and government. Specific details for all programs will be supplied by the Graduate Coordinator upon request.

Admission: Students must have been admitted to the Graduate School of the University of Florida. M.B.A. students with accounting concentrations must meet the minimal standards of the University of Florida. The M.A. and Ph.D. accounting programs require admission standards of at least the following: For the M.A. program, a combined verbal and quantitative score of at least 1100 on the Graduate Record Examination (GRE); a combined Graduate Record Examination score of at least 1260 for the Ph.D. program; or a score of at least 500 for the M.A. and 550 for the Ph.D. program on the Graduate Management Admission Test (GMAT). Either the GRE or the GMAT scores are acceptable; but admission to the M.A. or Ph.D. accounting graduate programs cannot be granted until scores are received. Foreign students must submit a TOEFL test score of at least 500 and a satisfactory GMAT or GRE score.

M.B.A. (accounting concentration): Eighteen quarter hours of accounting subjects are required, with a minimum of 9 hours in courses approved for graduate credit. Undergraduate accounting courses (400 or above) may be taken with the approval of the graduate coordinator. Students without an undergraduate accounting degree must take approximately 22 quarter hours of accounting foundation courses prior to commencing the accounting concentration courses. Accounting courses taken prior to admission to the M.B.A. program may count towards satisfying the accounting foundation course requirements.

Master of Arts with accounting major: Admission to advanced courses in accounting requires that students have, or complete without graduate credit, approximately the courses required of an undergraduate accounting major. With this background the M.A. degree can normally be earned in four quarters.

THESIS OPTION. Requirements include 18 to 20 quarter hours of advanced accounting courses and the balance of a total of 36 hours in one or two minor fields (finance, operations research, management, etc.). A thesis on an accounting-related topic is required.

71

NONTHESIS OPTION. Fifty-four credits of course work are required. Six courses must be in accounting. Four courses must be selected in at least two of the following underlying disciplines: behavioral science, microeconomic theory, operations research, statistics.

Ph.D. in business administration with accounting major: Requirements include a core of courses in operations research, statistics, the behavioral sciences, and economic theory; two minor fields selected by the student and major field of accounting. Fulfillment of a research skill and a dissertation on an accounting-related topic are also required.

GRADUATE COURSES

ATG 504—Federal Income Taxation of Business Organizations (3) Applications of federal income tax concepts to formation, operation, liquidation, and reorganization of partnerships and corporations.

ATG 505—Federal Income Tax Planning (3) Federal income tax planning for the individual, partnership, estate, trust, and corporation.

ATG 507—Advanced Accounting Topics (4) Special topics in financial accounting and current reporting problems facing the accounting profession. Review of current authoritative pronouncements.

ATG 508—Management Information Systems Theory (4) *Prereq: BA 540. May not be taken by students who have completed ATG 418.* Examination of systems theory in relation to the accountant's function of providing information for management.

ATG 509—Accounting Problems (4) (Not offered 1976-77)

ATG 510—Financial Accounting (5) *May not be taken by students who have completed 201 and 203. Designed primarily for MBA candidates and other graduate students. Not open to accounting majors.* Functions and underlying principles of accounting stressed. Emphasis on analysis of financial conditions and business operations through an understanding of accounting statements.

ATG 517—Public Administration Accounting (4) Critical analysis of fund accounting, reporting practices, and accounting implications of budgeting processes for public and quasi-public organizations.

ATG 600—Accounting Theory (4) Current developments in accounting concepts and principles and their relevance to the status of current accounting practices.

ATG 603—Social and Economic Accounting (5) (Not offered 1976-77)

ATG 604—Accounting and Analytical Methods (5) Utilization of logic, including mathematics, in formulation of alternative accounting valuation models and in clarification of accounting concepts.

ATG 605—Federal Income Tax: Functional Analysis (5) Critical analysis of federal income tax provisions, especially as related to use of income concepts. Major emphasis on business-tax component of the federal income tax system.

ATG 606—Advanced Auditing (4) Role of the attest function in society and recent developments in the practice of auditing.

ATG 608—Interdisciplinary Considerations in Accounting Theory Development (5) Developments in related disciplines, such as economics, law, and behavioral sciences, analyzed for their contribution to accounting thought.

ATG 611—Cost Accounting Theory and Applications (4) *Prereq: BA 610 or permission of adviser.* Advanced problem solving covering various phases of cost accounting. Introduction to cost accounting literature.

ATG 691—Accounting Research and Reports (2) *Prereq: BA 690. Required of all candidates for the M.B.A. with an accounting concentration.* Supervised preparation of report on an accounting topic of current interest.

ATG 696—Individual Work in Accounting (1-5; max: 10) *Prereq: permission of department and approval of Director of Graduate Studies.* Reading and research in areas of accounting.

ATG 697—Supervised Research (1-5)

ATG 698—Supervised Teaching (1-5)

ATG 699—Master's Research (1-15)

ATG 701—Development of Thought in Accounting Theory (5) Inquiry into criteria for choice among income-determination and asset-valuation rules in context of public reporting.

ATG 702—Accounting Information for External Users (5) Generation of accounting data for nonmanagement evaluation and control of processes through which economic resources are administered.

ATG 707—Accounting Theory as Related to Managerial Decision Making (5) Theoretical framework of accounting related to decision-making processes of management.

ATG 790—Accounting Research Workshop (4; max: 12) In-depth analysis of current research topics in accounting. Paper presentation and critiques by visiting scholars, faculty, and doctoral students.

ATG 799—Doctoral Research (1-15)

AGRICULTURAL ENGINEERING
(College of Engineering)

Chairman: G. L. ZACHARIAH
Graduate Coordinator: R. C. FLUCK

GRADUATE FACULTY 1975-76

Professors: R. E. CHOATE; D. S. HARRISON; J. M. MYERS; T. C. SKINNER; G. L. ZACHARIAH
Associate Professors: L. O. BAGNALL; R. C. FLUCK; A. R. OVERMAN; L. N. SHAW; J. D. WHITNEY
Assistant Professors: C. D. BAIRD; D. E. BUFFINGTON; K. L. CAMPBELL; J. J. GAFFNEY; D. T. HILL; R. A. NORDSTEDT

The degrees Master of Science, Master of Engineering, and Engineer are offered students with graduate programs in agricultural engineering.

The Master of Science and Master of Engineering degrees are offered in the following areas of research: soil and water conservation engineering, waste management, power and machinery, structures and environment, and electric power and processing. The Master of Science degree is also offered in the area of mechanized agriculture.

A student with a degree in a related field may enter the graduate program if adequate articulation courses are included in his program. A normal master's program may be completed in 5 or 6 quarters. Students interested in graduate work in agricultural engineering should consult departmental advisers.

Candidates for an engineering master's degree are normally required to take AGE 601, 602, 603, and at least one of the following: AGE 670, 671, 672, 673, and 674. Other course work is taken in applicable basic and applied sciences to meet educational objectives and to comprise an integrated program as approved by the student's supervisory committee. Courses from other disciplines may be approved for graduate major credit.

Prerequisite for admission to any agricultural engineering graduate course is the approval of the instructor.

GRADUATE COURSES

AGE 601—Seminar (1) Discussions of research, current trends, and practices in agricultural engineering. S/U.

AGE 602—Research Methods in Agricultural Engineering (3) Approaches to scientific research, scientific method, design of experiments, research practices and techniques, and presentation of results.

AGE 603—Instrumentation in Agricultural Engineering Research (4) Principles and application of measuring instruments and devices for obtaining experimental data in agricultural engineering research.

AGE 671—Advanced Soil and Water Management Engineering (4) Physical and mathematical analysis of problems in infiltration, drainage, and groundwater hydraulics.

AGE 672—Advanced Farm Machinery (4) Machines and mechanized systems used in agriculture and related fields, with emphasis on functional design requirements, design procedures, and performance evaluation.

AGE 673—Advanced Agricultural Structures (4). Design criteria for agricultural structures including structural strength, steady and unsteady heat transfer analysis, environmental modification, plant and animal environmental physiology, and structural systems analysis.

AGE 674—Advanced Agricultural Process Engineering (4) Engineering problems in handling and processing agricultural products.

AGE 691—Special Topics in Agricultural Engineering (1-6; max: 10) Lectures, laboratory and/or special projects covering special topics in agricultural engineering.

AGE 696—Nonthesis Research in Agricultural Engineering (1-5; max: 10) Special problems in agricultural engineering.

AGE 697—Supervised Research (1-5)

AGE 698—Supervised Teaching (1-5)

AGE 699—Master's Research (1-15)

AGRICULTURAL & EXTENSION EDUCATION
(College of Agriculture)

Chairman & Graduate Coordinator: C. E. BEEMAN

GRADUATE FACULTY 1975-76

Associate Professor: C. E. BEEMAN
Assistant Professors: J. G. CHEEK; W. S. FARRINGTON; M. B. MCGHEE

The Department of Agricultural and Extension Education offers major work for the degrees of Master of Science and Master of Agriculture. The Master of Science, primarily for those interested in research, requires a thesis, while the Master of Agriculture does not (see requirements for master's degrees). The master's program in Agricultural and Extension Education is designed for those persons engaged in teaching agriculture (at all levels) in the public schools of Florida, those in the Cooperative Extension Service, and others in educational and leadership positions in agriculture who desire additional professional training.

A prospective graduate student need not have majored in Agricultural and Extension Education as an undergraduate. However, students with an insufficient background in either Agricultural and Extension Education or technical agriculture will need to include some basic courses in these areas in their program.

GRADUATE COURSES

AED 601—Advanced Agricultural Leadership (4) Training in leadership opportunities and responsibilities in agriculture, including small group leadership, program planning, community organization and development, human relationships, public affairs, and public policy.

AED 604—Agricultural and Extension Education Through Group Action (4) Advanced techniques in developing programs of agricultural and extension education through group action.

AED 605—Methodology of Planned Change in Agribusiness (4) Examination of processes by which professional change agents influence the introduction, adoption and diffusion of technological change in agriculture. Applicable to those who work closely with people.

AED 620—History and Philosophy of Agricultural Education (4) Historical development of agricultural education from its beginning in other countries to the present program in the United States, with attention to changing philosophies.

AED 621—Developing Community Programs in Agriculture (4) Application of basic principles and practices in developing community programs in agriculture at high school and post high school levels.

AED 622—Developing Curricular Materials for Programs in Agriculture (4) Development of appropriate curricular materials for high school and post high school programs in agriculture; preparation of materials by class members.

AED 624—Supervised Occupational Experiences in Agricultural Education (4) Basic problems in planning and supervising programs of occupational experiences in view of changes occurring in agricultural occupations.

AED 625—Adult Education in Agriculture (4) Establishment, organization of classes, use of appropriate teaching procedures, and evaluation of programs of adult education in agriculture.

AED 626—Seminar in Agricultural and Extension Education (1; max: 3)

AED 627—Nonthesis Research in Agricultural and Extension Education (1-5; max: 9) Library and workshop related to methods in agricultural and extension education, including study of research work, review of publications, and development of written reports.

AED 696—Problems in Agricultural and Extension Education (1-12; max: 12) For students qualified to select and pursue advanced research problems.

AED 697—Supervised Research (1-5)

AED 698—Supervised Teaching (1-5)

AED 699—Master's Research (1-15)

AGRONOMY

(College of Agriculture)

Chairman: C. Y. WARD
Graduate Coordinator: E. G. RODGERS

GRADUATE FACULTY 1975-76

Professors: F. CLARK; C. E. DEAN; W. G. DUNCAN; J. R. EDWARDSON; M. H. GASKINS; V. E. GREEN, JR.; K. HINSON; E. S. HORNER; D. E. MCCLOUD; G. O. MOTT; A. J. NORDEN; J. R. ORSENIGO; P. L. PFAHLER; H. L. POPENOE; E. G. RODGERS; O. C. RUELKE; S. C. SCHANK; C. Y. WARD; H. E. WARMKE; S. H. WEST; M. WILCOX

Associate Professors: W. L. CURREY; A. E. DUDECK; G. J. FRITZ; G. J. GASCHO; R. E. GODDARD; F. LE GRAND; G. M. PRINE; V. N. SCHRODER; R. L. SMITH; D. L. SUTTON; E. B. WHITTY

Assistant Professors: K. J. BOOTE; C. A. HOLLIS; P. M. LYRENE; P. MISLEVY III

Associate in Agronomy: L. A. GARRARD

The Department of Agronomy offers the Doctor of Philosophy and the Master of Science degrees, with specialization in crop ecology and climatology, crop nutrition and physiology, crop production, weed science, genetics, cytogenetics, or plant breeding. Specializations for the Doctor of Philosophy degree also include forest genetics and physiology. A nonthesis degree, Master of Agriculture, is offered with a major in agronomy.

Graduate programs emphasize the development and subsequent application of basic principles in each specialization to agronomic plants in Florida and throughout the tropics. The continuing need for increased food supplies is reflected in departmental research efforts. Some thesis and dissertation research may be conducted wholly or in part in one or more of several tropical countries.

A science background with basic courses in mathematics, chemistry, botany, microbiology, and physics is required of new graduate students. In addition to graduate courses in agronomy, the following courses in related areas are acceptable for graduate credit as part of the student's major: AL 602—Quantitative Genetics;

AL 656—Ruminant Physiology and Metabolism; BTY 604—Vegetation of the Tropics; BTY 615—Plant Growth and Development; FC 621—Environmental Measurements; SLS 626—Soil Fertility; STA 605—Advanced Methods of Statistics.

GRADUATE COURSES

AY 605—Rice (5) *Prereq: AY 311 and BTY 310, or equivalent.* Characteristics, production practices, pest control, physiological development, processing, and utilization of world rice crop.

AY 609—Sugarcane (4) *Prereq: AY 311 and BTY 310.* Morphology and anatomy of sugarcane. Role of plant nutrients and cultural practices. Diagnostic techniques. Principal diseases and pests affecting yield.

AY 611—Sugarcane Processing Technology (4) Same as FS 611. *Prereq: CY 362, 363.* Chemical and physical processes required for crystallization and refining of sugar.

AY 613—Oilseed Crops (4) *Prereq: AY 311, BTY 370, or equivalent.* Economically important oilseed plants, with emphasis on characteristics, production practices, physiological and biochemical development, processing, and utilization.

AY 614—Fiber Crops (4) *Prereq: AY 311, BTY 310, or equivalent.* Characteristics, production practices, physiological development, processing, and utilization of plant fibers having commercial importance in their natural or modified form.

AY 636—Tropical Pasture and Forage Science (5) *Prereq: AY 432 and AL 527, or consent of instructor.* Potential of natural grasslands of tropical and subtropical regions. Development of improved pastures and forages and their utilization in livestock production.

AY 641—Crop Nutrition (4) *Prereq: BTY 310.* Nutritional influences on differentiation, composition, growth, and yield of agronomic plants.

AY 642—Biochemistry of Herbicides (3) *Prereq: CY 565.* Metabolism, mechanism of action, and structure-activity relationships of herbicides.

AY 644—Physiology of Agronomic Plants (4) *Prereq: BTY 515.* Yield potentials of crops as influenced by photosynthetic efficiencies, respiration, translocation, drought, and canopy architecture.

AY 646—Crop Ecology (5) *Prereq: AY 311, BTY 301, and 310 or equivalent.* Relationships of ecological factors and climatic classification to agroecosystems, and crop modeling of the major crops.

AY 647—Crop Plants in Tropical Environments (12) *Prereq: approval by Organization for Tropical Studies.* Factors determining growth, development, and production of crop plants in tropical environments.

AY 658—Population Genetics (3) *Prereq: AY 362, STA 602.* Application of statistical principles to biological populations in relation to gene frequency, zygotic frequency, mating systems, and the effects of selection, mutation, and migration on equilibrium populations.

AY 660—Cytogenetics (5) *Prereq: basic courses in genetics and cytology.* Genetic variability with emphasis on interrelationships of cytologic and genetic concepts. Chromosome structure and number, chromosomal aberrations, apomixis, and application of cytogenetic principles.

AY 662—Advanced Genetics (4) *Prereq: AY 362; AY 465 or ADP 322.* Advanced genetic concepts and modern genetic theory.

AY 664—Topics in Genetics (2-4; max: 12) Same as AL 664. BTY 664, DY 664, PY 664, ZY 664. *Prereq: AY 362 or ZY 325.* Biochemical, bacterial, viral, statistical, radiation, serological, and human genetics; speciation, history of genetics, genetics of higher plants and animals.

AY 665—Advanced Plant Breeding (4) *Prereq: AY 362, 465, 658, STA 603.* Genetic basis for plant-breeding procedures.

AY 682—Genetics Seminar (1; max: 3) Current literature and developments in genetics.

AY 684—Graduate Agronomy Seminar (1; max: 3) *Required of all graduate students in agronomy.* Current literature and agronomic developments.

AY 688—Topics in Agronomy (2-4; max: 12) Critical review of selected topics in specific agronomic areas.

AY 696—Agronomic Problems (1-6; max: 12) *Prereq: minimum of one undergraduate course in agronomy or plant science.* Special topics for classroom, library, laboratory or field studies of agronomic plants.

AY 697—Supervised Research (1-5)
AY 698—Supervised Teaching (1-5)
AY 699—Master's Research (1-15)
AY 799—Doctoral Research (1-15)

ANIMAL SCIENCE—GENERAL
(College of Agriculture)

The Departments of Animal, Poultry, and Dairy Science have combined their curricula into an animal science curriculum. ADP 535 is a cross-departmental course taught by the faculty of the three departments.

GRADUATE COURSE

ADP 535—Animal Production in the Tropics (4) *Prereq: AL 411, 413, DY 301 or permission of instructor.* Management and environment factors which affect animal production in the tropics.

ANIMAL SCIENCE
(College of Agriculture)

Chairman: H. D. WALLACE
Graduate Coordinator: G. E. COMBS, JR.

GRADUATE FACULTY 1975-76

Professors: C. B. AMMERMAN; L. R. ARRINGTON; D. W. BEARDSLEY; E. L. BESCH; R. E. BRADLEY, SR.; C. B. BROWNING; J. W. CARPENTER; H. L. CHAPMAN, JR.; G. E. COMBS, JR.; J. H. CONRAD; G. K. DAVIS; G. T. EDDS; J. P. FEASTER; J. L. FRY; R. H. HARMS; J. F. HENTGES, JR.; M. KOGER; P. E. LOGGINS; J. K. LOOSLI; J. H. MANER; S. P. MARSHALL; J. E. MOORE; A. Z. PALMER; R. L. SHIRLEY; C. F. SIMPSON; H. H. VAN HORN, JR.; D. L. WAKEMAN; H. D. WALLACE; A. C. WARNICK; F. H. WHITE; C. J. WILCOX; H. R. WILSON; J. M. WING
Associate Professors: F. W. BAZER; J. E. BERTRAND; P. T. CARDEILHAC; J. R. CROCKETT; B. L. DAMRON; C. R. DOUGLAS; D. E. FRANKE; H. H. HEAD; J. A. HIMES; E. A. OTT; K. L. SMITH; W. W. THATCHER; R. A. VOITLE
Assistant Professors: S. W. COLEMAN; B. H. CRAWFORD; M. J. FIELDS; D. D. HARGROVE; S. LIEB; L. R. MCDOWELL; D. C. SHARP III; R. L. WEST

The Department of Animal Science offers the degrees of Master of Agriculture, Master of Science, and Doctor of Philosophy in the following areas: (1) animal nutrition, (2) meats, (3) animal breeding and genetics, and (4) animal physiology. A student may work on a problem covering more than one area of study. Large animals (beef cattle, dairy cattle, swine, poultry, and sheep) and laboratory animals are available for various research problems. Adequate nutrition and meats laboratories are available for detailed chemical and carcass quality evaluations. Special arrangements can be made to conduct research problems at the various branch agricultural experiment stations throughout Florida. A Ph.D. degree may be obtained in animal science, with dissertation research under the direction of members of the Departments of Dairy Science, Poultry Science, Veterinary Science, and Animal Science.

Departmental prerequisites for admission to graduate study include a sound science background, with basic courses in bacteriology, biology, mathematics, botany, and chemistry.

GRADUATE COURSES

AL 527—Animal Nutrition (5) *Prereq: ADP 312, BTY 370 or permission of instructor.* Carbohydrates, fats, proteins, minerals and vitamins and their function in the animal body.

AL 601—Topics in Animal Science (4) New developments in animal nutrition and livestock feeding, animal genetics, animal physiology, and livestock management.

AL 602—Quantitative Genetics (5) *Prereq: STA 320, AY 362.* Genetic and biometric principles underlying genetic characters that exhibit continuous variation.

AL 604—Meat Technology (4) Chemistry, physics, histology, bacteriology, and engineering involved in the handling, processing, manufacturing, preservation, storage, distribution, and utilization of meat.

AL 605—Experimental Technics and Analytical Procedures in Meat Research (4) Experimental design, analytical procedures; technics; carcass measurements and analyses as related to livestock production and meat studies.

AL 607—Physiology of Reproduction (5) *Prereq: VY 622, 623, ADP 407.* The interactions between the hypothalamus, pituitary gland and reproductive organs during the estrous cycle and pregnancy in the female and sperm production in the male. Embryonic and placental development from fertilization through parturition and factors affecting reproductive efficiency.

AL 650—Advanced Methods in Nutrition Technology (4) *Prereq: CY 204.* For graduate students but open to seniors by special permission. Demonstrations and limited performance of procedures used in nutrition research.

AL 651—Advanced Animal Nutrition (4) *Prereq: CY 381.* Proteins, carbohydrates, lipids, vitamins, and minerals related to enzyme activity and energy.

AL 652—Advanced Animal Nutrition Laboratory (3) *Prereq: CY 381.* Accompanying laboratory course for AL 651.

AL 653—Vitamins (4) *Prereq: organic chemistry.* Historical development, properties, assays, and physiological effects.

AL 654—Laboratory in Vitamins (2) Chemical determination and assay procedures. Accompanying laboratory course for AL 653.

AL 655—Mineral Nutrition and Metabolism (4) Physiological effect of macro- and micro-elements, mineral interrelationships.

AL 656—Ruminant Physiology and Metabolism (3) *Prereq: AL 527.* Review and correlation of the fundamental biochemical, physiological, and bacteriological research upon which the feeding of ruminants is based. Experimental methodology of rumen physiology and metabolism.

AL 657—Non-Ruminant Metabolism (3) *Prereq: AL 527.* Basic principles affecting absorption and assimilation of nutrients required for growth, reproduction, and lactation of swine and small laboratory animals.

AL 658—Equine Nutrition and Physiology (4) *Prereq: AL 527.* Principles affecting absorption and assimilation of nutrients and basic physiology of growth, reproduction, and exercise of the horse.

AL 659—Genetics of Animal Improvement (4) *Prereq: AL 602.* Continuation of AL 602. Application of statistical techniques and design in animal breeding research.

AL 660—Graduate Seminar in Animal Science (1)

AL 664—Topics in Genetics (2-4; max: 12) Same as AY 664, BTY 664, DY 664, PY 664, ZY 664.

AL 696—Problems in Animal Science (1-6; max: 12)

AL 697—Supervised Research (1-5)

AL 698—Supervised Teaching (1-5)

AL 699—Master's Research (1-15)

AL 799—Doctoral Research (1-15)

ANTHROPOLOGY
(College of Arts and Sciences)

Chairman: P. L. DOUGHTY
Graduate Coordinator: T. A. NUNEZ, JR.

GRADUATE FACULTY 1975-76

Graduate Research Professors: S. KIMBALL; C. WAGLEY
Distinguished Service Professor: C. H. FAIRBANKS
Professors: W. E. CARTER; P. L. DOUGHTY; B. M. duTOIT; E. M. EDDY; M. J. HARDMAN-DE-BAUTISTA; N. N. MARKEL; W. H. SEARS;* H. G. SMITH;* O. von MERING
Associate Professors: M. C. DOUGHERTY; J. D. EARLY;† T. HO;* W. R. MAPLES; M. L. MARGOLIS; G. A. MOORE, JR.; T. A. NUNEZ, JR.; J. A. PAREDES;* A. J. SUBLETT;† G. WEISS;† E. S. WING
Assistant Professors: K. A. DEAGAN;* R. GONZALO;* B. T. GRINDAL;* W. J. KENNEDY,† J. T. MILANICH; G. M. MILTON;* A. R. OLIVER-SMITH; B. A. PURDY; C. E. TAYLOR; S. J. WILKERSON

These members of the faculty of The Florida State University (*) and Florida Atlantic University (†) are also members of the graduate faculty of the University of Florida and participate in the doctoral degree program in the University of Florida Department of Anthropology.

Graduate work leading to the Master of Arts, Master of Arts in Teaching, the nonthesis Master of Arts, and the Doctor of Philosophy degrees is offered in social and cultural anthropology, archeology, physical anthropology, and anthropological linguistics.

In addition to the above tracks, the departmental faculty members have particular specialization and experience in Latin American and African area studies, urban and regional planning, peasantries, southeastern U.S. and Caribbean archeology and ethnohistory, historical archeology, anthropology and education, health, agriculture, and studies of social and cultural change and development.

Individual programs composed from these areas can be used to prepare students for careers in teaching, research, and community and governmental service. In cooperation with the Urban and Regional Development Center, the Center for Latin American Studies, the Center for African Studies, the Center for Tropical Agriculture, the J. Hillis Miller Health Center, and the College of Education, the department offers specialized preparation for careers in urban affairs, the health related professions, education, community development, and international programs.

The Master of Arts degree with thesis program provides the student with training in all subfields of anthropology. Normal distribution of work includes: (1) APY 600; (2) A minimum of two courses dealing with two different areas (North America, South America, Africa, etc.); (3) A minimum of one theory course each in social/cultural anthropology, physical anthropology, archeology, and linguistics; (4) Written departmental comprehensive examination in the subfields of anthropology; (5) Satisfactory completion of a thesis based on library or field research. Normally requires no more than one full quarter to complete.

The Master of Arts in Teaching is designed for students intending to teach in junior or four year colleges. The required distribution of work leading to this degree includes: (1) APY 600; (2) Satisfactory completion of at least 54 graduate quarter credit hours. These hours must include at least 9 credits in a departmental internship in teaching and 8 credits in a minor. At least three courses (which may be used as the minor) are required in educational psychology, sociology, and curriculum dealing with the junior college; (3) Written departmental comprehensive examination in the subfields of anthropology and in the minor field.

The nonthesis Master of Arts degree program prepares students for nonacademic positions in business and education, and in public and private service agencies where anthropological training in combination with other skills will be of practical use.

Students entering the program must have a general understanding of the perspectives and concepts of the various subfields within anthropology. The general requirements for this degree include: (1) APY 600; (2) Satisfactory.completion of 60 graduate quarter hours, of which 6 credits may be earned for the supervised internship course; (3) Comprehensive examination, either oral or written or both, in the student's field of concentration and his minor if he selects one; (4) Completion of a supervised internship, equivalent to a minimum of one-quarter duration, working with some public or private agency or on some appropriate project in the area of specialization. Students must submit an acceptable interpretive report based on the work experience at the end of the intern period.

A foreign language may be required in any master's degree program when the student's supervisory committee considers either a reading or a functional knowledge to be an appropriate professional skill in his field of interest.

The master's degree normally requires a minimum of 3 to 4 quarters of full-time course work in residence, depending upon the program selected.

Students are admitted to a doctoral program upon faculty recommendation after completing the master's comprehensive examinations. New intermediate-level students (more than one year of graduate work) coming from other universities will be evaluated and recommended for doctoral work by a faculty committee at the beginning of their period of residence. This program includes the distribution of work required for the master's programs. In addition, a doctoral student must work closely with a supervisory committee, which advises him on the choice of fields of specialization, around which further course work, reading, qualifying examinations, and doctoral research are arranged. The student must satisfy the language requirement and pass a written and oral qualifying examination administered by his supervisory committee. Ordinarily, at least a year of doctoral research and field work is required to produce a satisfactory dissertation.

Study for the Ph.D. degree in anthropology at the University of Florida by qualified master's degree recipients at Florida Atlantic University and Florida State University is facilitated by a cooperative arrangement in which appropriate members of these universities are members of the graduate faculty of the University of Florida.

Nonanthropology majors are requested to secure permission from the course instructor before enrolling in graduate level courses.

GRADUATE COURSES

APY 502—Kinship and Descent (4) Systematic and analytical treatment of marriage, descent, and alliances on a cross-cultural basis. Examination of social behavior and terminologies related to kinship systems drawn from traditional and modern societies.

APY 505—Principles of Anthropological Linguistics (5) Linguistics for anthropology majors. Detailed review of basic concepts and problems.

APY 506—Language and Culture (5) Principles and problems of anthropological linguistics. The cross-cultural and comparative study of language. Primarily concerned with the study of non-Indo-European linguistic problems.

APY 511—Phonology (5) Phonetics and phonemics, phonemic analysis, phonological theory, transcription, primary interest on non-Indo-European systems. Informants are used.

APY 512—Economic Anthropology (5) Concept of surplus. Classics of economic anthropology. Controversies between substantivists and formalists. Theoretical assumptions of contemporary case studies.

APY 513—Ritual and Symbolic Systems (5) Explores the various approaches to the understanding of symbolism through an examination of the structures, properties, and functions of myth and ritual. Systems of thought as described in the anthropological studies of traditional African, Oceanian, Australian, and American societies provide the data.

APY 517—Cultural Dynamics (4) Study of the background, conditions and nature of cultural change and stability; cultural change theories and processes such as diffusion, acculturation, modernization, and revitalization.

APY 518—Human Organization and Change (5) *Prereq: APY 517 or consent of instructor.* Theory and practice in applied anthropology. A case study approach to innovation and change in social institutions and cultural practices, with emphasis upon problems of planning and administration.

APY 520—Regional Cultures of Oceania (4) Peoples and cultures of Oceania, history, social structure, kinship system, land tenure, religion, arts and crafts, reaction to modernization, ecological adaptation. Regional focus in terms of Polynesia, Micronesia, or Melanesia may vary depending on demand.

APY 531—Laboratory Work in Anthropological Linguistics (1-5; max: 15)

APY 540—The Tribal Peoples of Lowland South America (4) Survey of marginal and tropical forest hunters and gatherers and horticulturalists of the Amazon Basin, Central Brazil, Paraguay, Argentina, and other areas of South America. Social organization, subsistence activities, ecological adaptations, and other aspects of tribal life will be covered.

APY 542—The Peoples of Brazil (4) Ethnology of Brazil. Historical, geographic, and socioeconomic material will be covered and representative monographs from the various regions of Brazil will be read. The contribution of the Indian, Portuguese, and African to modern Brazilian culture.

APY 543—Peoples of the Andes (4) The area-cotradition. The Spanish Conquest. The shaping and persistence of colonial culture. Twentieth-century communities—their social, land tenure, religious, and value systems. Modernization, cultural pluralism, and problems of integration.

APY 544—The Anthropology of Modern Africa (4) Study of continuity and change in contemporary African societies, with special reference to cultural and ethnic factors in modern nations.

APY 545—Caribbean Cultural Patterns (4) Investigation into cultural contact that has taken place in the Caribbean and results of that contact in terms of peoples and sociocultural units produced and processes of culture change involved.

APY 550—Seminar: Biological Basis of Social Behavior (4) *Prereq: consent of instructor.* Social behavior among animals from the ethological-biological viewpoint; the evolution of animal societies; the relevance of the ethological approach for the study of human development.

APY 563—Methodological Foundation for Anthropology (4) Examination of empirical and logical basis of anthropological inquiry; analysis of theory construction, research design, problems of data collection, processing, and evaluation.

APY 564—Quantitative Methods for Anthropology (4) *Prereq: APY 563 or consent of instructor.* Introductory survey of relevant quantitative procedures for collecting, analyzing, and interpreting anthropological data.

APY 574—Zooarchaeology (4) *Prereq: consent of instructor.* Human use of animal resources, with emphasis on prehistoric hunting and fishing practices. Origins of animal domestication.

APY 579—Introduction to Linguistic Field Methods (5) *Prereq: APY 505 or equivalent.* Field procedures, collections, and processing of language data.

APY 585—Bio-Behavioral Perspective on Human Character Structure (5) Application of ethological and psychodynamic concepts to the evolution of human psyche and character.

APY 590—The Culture of Planned Social Systems (4) *Prereq: consent of instructor.* Structure, function, and culture of non-kin social units within society. Planning, creation and perpetuation of specialized social groups such as revitalization movements, bureaucracies, and neoteric societies, such as planned cities and communes seen in cross-cultural perspective.

APY 595—Nonverbal Communication (5) Same as SCH 595. Theory and method in the experimental study of nonverbal communication. Nonlinguistic aspects of speech; interpersonal distance; physical appearance; body movements; body posture; facial expression; eye behavior; touching.

APY 600—The Profession of Anthropology (2) *Required of all graduate students.* Organization of the anthropological profession in teaching and research. Relationship between subfields and related disciplines; the anthropological experience; ethics.

APY 601—Seminar in Anthropological History and Theory (4) Theoretical principles and background of anthropology and its subfields.

APY 602—Principles of Cultural Anthropology (5) Nature of culture, social organization, and culture and personality. Theoretical orientations in topical and area studies, with emphasis on cultural dynamics.

APY 604—Principles of Political Anthropology (5) Problems of identifying political behavior. Natural leadership in tribal societies. Acephalous societies and republican structures. Kingship and early despotic states. Theories of bureaucracy.

APY 608—Psychological Anthropology (5) Recent and contemporary theoretical and methodological developments in the cultural aspects of cognitive and perceptual socio- and psycholinguistic interactional and transactional processes. Ordinary and abnormal developmental experiences in different cultural contexts related to personal character and social identity formation.

APY 609—Cultural Pluralism (4) *Prereq: consent of instructor.* Comparative anthropological perspectives on the geographic-ecological context and culture-historical main currents of North American and Latin American ethnic groups. Pluralistic basis of contemporary community systems and socioeconomic and political consequences of multiculturalism examined. Problems of multiethnic stratification within national cultures stressed.

APY 610—Medical Anthropology (5) *Prereq: consent of instructor.* Theory of anthropology as applied to nursing, medicine, hospital organization, and the therapeutic environment. Course includes instrument design and techniques of material collection.

APY 611—Advanced Archeological Field Methods (9) *Prereq: consent of instructor.* Planning, directing, and reporting archeological excavations. Students encouraged to prepare publishable papers.

APY 612—Ethnographic Field Methods (5) Methods for collecting ethnographic data. Entry into the field; role and image conflict. Participant observation, interviewing, content analysis, photography and documents, data retrieval, analysis of data.

APY 615—Problems of National Integration in Latin America (5) Conceptual problems of the society and culture of selected nation-states: nationalism, urbanization, peasant revitalization movements as integrative or divisive forces. Vertical institutions: church, school, markets, plantation, in particular communities.

APY 616—African Urbanization (4) Current conditions and problems flowing from detribalization, acculturation, and urbanization. Changes in values, attitudes, and institutions, as well as the reaction among the peoples of Africa in the form of traditional survivals, cultural revivals, and innovations.

APY 617—Seminar in Cross-Cultural Epidemiology (5) *Prereq: consent of instructor.* Disease patterns; health and well-being examined on a comparative cultural basis.

APY 620—Directed Culture Change in Latin America (5) Utopias in Latin American culture history. The Spanish Conquest as a social experiment. The post-Independence Liberal Reforms and social revolutions, compared with contemporary attempts at community development.

APY 621—Seminar in Archeology (5; max: 15) Selected topic.

APY 622—Seminar in Ethnology (5; max: 15) Areas treated are North America, Central America, South America, Africa, Oceania.

APY 623—Seminar in Physical Anthropology (5; max: 15) Selected topic.

APY 624—Seminar in Linguistic Field Methods (5; max: 15) Same as LIN 624. Analysis of a particular language through an informant.

APY 625—Man and Culture in Southern Africa (5) Prehistoric times through first contacts by explorers to settlers; the contact situation between European, Khoisan, and Bantu-speaking; empirical data dealing with present political, economic, social, and religious conditions.

APY 626—Seminar in Language and Culture (5; max: 15) *Prereq: APY 506.* Selected topic.

APY 640—Seminar on the Anthropology of Latin America (5; max: 15) *Prereq: reading knowledge of Spanish or Portuguese and consent of instructional staff.* Materials from the major branches of anthropology.

APY 645—Evolution of Culture (5) *Prereq: APY 300.* Theories of culture growth and evolution from cultural beginnings to dawn of history. Major inventions of man and their significance.

APY 661—Anthropology and Education (5) Comparative study of teaching and learning processes in societies of differing complexity and cultural variability. Empirical data examined from an anthropological perspective and in the context of theories about culture and perception, world view, rites of passage, culture and personality, and change.

APY 662—Culture and Learning (5) *Prereq: APY 661, or 15 credits in social sciences.* Cultural learning as a function of social environment based on studies of socialization practices in primate and human societies.

APY 667—Culture and Community (5) *Prereq: 15 to 20 credits in social sciences.* Examination of the method and theory of the empirical, inductive, natural history approach in the study of communities. Existing community studies are utilized to provide comparative analyses of social structure, culture patterns, and process of change.

APY 668—Seminar in Structure and Process in the Urban Environment (5) *Prereq: consent of instructor.* Anthropological view of the city through interaction of spatial and temporal behavior, ecology, culture institutions, and urban morphology.

APY 670—Comparative Structure and Process of Natural Groups (5) *Prereq: 15 to 20 credits in social sciences.* Comparative analysis of structure and process of natural groups in animal and human societies based on empirical studies of nonhuman primates, hunting bands, simple agriculturists, and natural groups in complex societies.

APY 675—Pattern, Structure, and Process (5) *Prereq: 15 to 20 credits in social sciences.* Advanced seminar in the theory of social anthropology.

APY 690—Special Topics in Anthropology (5; max: 15) *Prereq: consent of instructor.*

APY 696—Individual Work (1-5; max: 15) Guided readings on research in anthropology based on library, laboratory or field work.

APY 697—Supervised Research (1-5)

APY 698—Supervised Teaching (1-5)

APY 699—Master's Research (1-15)

APY 799—Doctoral Research (1-15)

ARCHITECTURE
(College of Architecture)

Dean: M. T. JAROSZEWICZ

Graduate Coordinator: H. B. HAMACHER

GRADUATE FACULTY 1975-76

Professors: A. F. BUTT; C. FEISS; B. Y. KINZEY, JR.; H. C. MERRITT, JR.; F. B. REEVES; H. H. SMITH; E. M. STARNES; W. G. WAGNER; W. L. WEISMANTEL

Associate Professors: J. F. ALEXANDER, JR.; E. E. CRAIN; A. J. DASTA; E. M. FEARNEY; H. B. HAMACHER; H. W. KEMP; F. F. LISLE, JR.; J. M. McRAE; J. A. SANDERSON; L. G. SHAW; M. M. SOLIS; O. F. WETTERQVIST

Assistant Professors: D. W. DONELIN; M. T. FOSTER; L. J. HAWKINSON; V. N. NERIKAR; G. RIDGDILL; G. SCHEFFER; T. R. WHITE; I. H. WINARSKY; G. A. YAGER

The Department of Architecture offers graduate work leading to the degrees of Master of Arts in Architecture and Master of Arts in Urban and Regional Planning (M.A.U.R.P.). Students are encouraged to enter the program in the fall quarter. They should not plan to take more than three consecutive quarters without a one-quarter interruption. Two years in residence are normally required for completion.

PROGRAM IN ARCHITECTURE

Prerequisite to admission to the Master of Arts in Architecture program is the degree Bachelor of Design, with appropriate studies in architecture or a degree determined by the department to be equivalent. Graduation from an accredited school of architecture having a five-year course of study is acceptable. In addition to satisfying University requirements for admission, applicants may be required to submit to the Department of Architecture supplementary material as evidence of an active interest in architectural work. The applicant should request detailed instructions from the department regarding such submission.

The student is expected to pursue studies related to his special field of interest in architectural design, architectural history, architectural structures, environmental technology, or architectural preservation. Additional information concerning programs for each of these areas is available from the department.

The student's overall college experience, including undergraduate programs in architecture and the two-year graduate program, is intended to be a complete unit of professional training leading toward practice in architecture or related professions. Concentration in this special field of interest should prepare the student for architectural practice with special emphasis upon his role as a member of a professional team.

Under special circumstances, the graduate faculty of the department may elect to admit students who have a Bachelor of Architecture degree from a five-year program for a one-year graduate program leading to the Master of Arts in Architecture. In these cases, the minimum registration required is 45 credits, including 9 credits in AE 699 or 629.

The department reserves the right to retain student work for the purposes of record, exhibition, or instruction.

GRADUATE COURSES

AE 552—Architectural Structures (5) *Prereq: AE 456.*

AE 561—Architectural Acoustics (4) *Prereq: AE 364.*

AE 571—Problems in Architectural History (4) *Prereq: AE 476.*

AE 572—Studies in Architectural Theory (4) *Prereq: AE 475.*

AE 581—Survey of Architectural Preservation, Restoration, and Reconstruction (4)

AE 582—Techniques of Architectural Documentation (4)

AE 583—Historic Preservation and Restoration: Interiors (4)

AE 584—Historic Preservation and Restoration: Landscape Architecture (4)

AE 601—Graduate Seminar (3-5; max: 9) *Required of all graduate students.*

AE 621—Architectural Research I (1-9) Special studies adjusted to individual needs. H.

AE 622—Architectural Research II (1-9) Special studies adjusted to individual needs. H.

AE 623—Architectural Research III (1-9) Special studies adjusted to individual needs. H.

AE 628—Professional Practice (2) *Prereq: sixth-year standing. Required for all AE graduate students.*

AE 629—Terminal Project (1-15) Course work in lieu of thesis, subject to approval of the supervisory committee. If work is a team project, the individual student must show evidence of his portion of the work accomplished. H.

AE 631—Architectural Design I (5) *Required of all graduate students.* Design of buildings, limitations of site topography, utilities, and relationship to other structures.

AE 632—Architectural Design II (8) *Prereq: AE 631.* Design of buildings within an urban complex. Forces of physical and social planning which influence the design.

AE 633—Architectural Design III (8) *Prereq: AE 632.* Design of buildings within an architectural complex of established character in collaboration with students in master's history program.

AE 634—Architectural Design IV (8) *Prereq: AE 633.* Design in detail of an individual building. H.

AE 635—Architectural Design V (8) *Prereq: AE 634.* Collaboration with students in the architectural structures and environmental technology options. H.

AE 651—Advanced Architectural Structures I (4) *Coreq: AE 552. MS 306.* Principles and applications of timber construction to architectural design problems.

AE 652—Advanced Architectural Structures II (4) *Coreq: AE 651, 552.* Theory and behavior of structural steel systems, and their responses to the solution of architectural problems.

AE 653—Advanced Architectural Structures III (6) *Prereq: AE 652.* Applications of structural steel systems to selected architectural problems.

AE 654—Advanced Architectural Structures IV (4) *Coreq: A E 552.* Theory and behavior of reinforced concrete systems and their responses to the solution of architectural problems.

AE 655—Advanced Architectural Structures V (6) *Prereq: A E 654.* Applications of reinforced concrete systems to selected architectural problems.

AE 656—Advanced Architectural Structures VI (4) *Coreq: A E 655.* Design and applications of precast and/or prestressed concrete elements in architecture.

AE 657—Advanced Architectural Structures VII (4) *Prereq: A E 552, 654.* Study of various soil properties and their applications in solving architectural design problems.

AE 658—Advanced Architectural Structures VIII (4) *Prereq: AE 552, 652, 654, and 657.* Investigation of selected problems in the field of architectural structures. Emphasis on student special interests.

AE 659—Advanced Architectural Structures IX (4) Directed studies and problems in collaboration with a team of students involving a coordinated building design. Architectural, structural and environmental aspects of a problem.

AE 660—Environmental Systems Design Laboratory I (4) *Prereq: A E 561. Coreq: A E 661.* Problems in acoustics analysis and design.

AE 661—Environmental Systems Design I (4) *Prereq: A E 561. Coreq: A E 660.* Applications of sound control in buildings, auditorium design, and noise control.

AE 662—Environmental Systems Design Laboratory II (4) *Coreq: A E 663.* Applied design of lighting, electric power distribution, and plumbing system for buildings.

AE 663—Environmental Systems Design II (4) *Coreq: A E 662.* Lecture portion of AE 662.

AE 664—Environmental Systems Design Laboratory III (4) *Coreq: A E 665.* Applied design of heating and air-conditioning systems for buildings.

AE 665—Environmental Systems Design III (4) *Coreq: A E 664.* Lecture portion of AE 664.

AE 666—Environmental Systems Design Laboratory IV (4) *Prereq: AE 664, 665. Coreq: A E 667.* Special studies in environmental systems related to current developments. Total energy systems, solar energy, heat conservation, and similar contemporary problems and trends.

AE 667—Environmental Systems Design IV (4) *Prereq: A E 664, 665. Coreq: A E 666.* Lecture portion of AE 666.

AE 668—Environmental Systems Design Laboratory V (4) *Prereq: AE 660, 661, 662, 663, 664, 665, 666, 667.* Directed studies and problems, in collaboration with a team of students, involving a coordinated building design. Architectural, structural, and environmental aspects of a problem developed as a total, compatible concept.

AE 669—Environmental Systems Design Laboratory VI (4) May be taken concurrently with or as a continuation of AE 668 to adjust to the breadth or length of the design problem assigned.

AE 671—Architectural History I (5) *Prereq: 9 credits of architectural history.* History of western civilization, with emphasis on architectural developments in their historical, physical, ideological, artistic, and social context.

AE 672—Architectural History II (5) *Prereq: A E 671.*

AE 673—Architectural History III (5) *Prereq: A E 672.*

AE 674—Architectural History: Area Concentration (5; max: 15) *Prereq: A E 673.* Development of techniques for research in architectural history.

AE 675—Architectural History: American I (5) *Prereq: 9 credits of architectural history.* Development of American architecture and the determinants affecting its function, form and expression.

AE 676—Architectural History: American II (5) *Prereq: A E 675.*

AE 677—Architectural History: Literature and Criticism (5; max: 15) *Prereq: A E 671.* Individual research with concentration on writing and architectural criticism.

AE 678—Architectural History: Regional (5) *Prereq: A E 676.* Group and individual studies of architecture unique to specific geographic regions.

AE 681—Technology of Preservation: Materials and Methods I (4) *Prereq: A E 581.* Materials, elements, tools and personnel of traditional building.

AE 682—Technology of Preservation: Materials and Methods II (4) *Prereq: A E 681.*

AE 683—Technology of Preservation: Problems and Processes (4)

AE 684—Technology of Preservation: Programming and Design I (4) *Prereq: A E 681.*

AE 685—Technology of Preservation: Programming and Design II (4) *Prereq: AE 681.*
AE 686—Techniques of Preservation: Legal and Economic Processes (4)
AE 697—Supervised Research (1-5)
AE 698—Supervised Teaching (1-5)
AE 699—Master's Research (1-15)

PROGRAM IN URBAN AND REGIONAL PLANNING

Prerequisite to admission to the Master of Arts in Urban and Regional Planning program is a baccalaureate degree in architecture, engineering, landscape architecture, or planning. Students with other degrees who show evidence of education and experience in planning and policy sciences may be admitted with approval of the faculty.

The program is designed to meet the criteria for recognition by the American Institute of Planners, the highest applicable standards for a graduate planning program. It provides a comprehensive planning education which includes nine fields of concentration as follows: history, theory and practice, systems, research methods, government regulations, infrastructure and circulation, urban and regional form, evaluation and studio.

Graduates of the program will have sufficient education for full professional standing according to the standards of the American Institute of Planners. This degree does not qualify the graduate for registration as an architect.

The department reserves the right to retain student work for the purposes of record, exhibition, or instruction.

GRADUATE COURSES

URP 601—Graduate Seminar (3-5; max: 9)
URP 602—Planning Design Theory and Practice (4)
URP 603—Design Fundamentals (4) Graphic, notation systems, creative methods by the planner.
URP 621—Planning and Design Research (1-9; max: 9) Supervised individual or group research projects. H.
URP 622—Government Regulations I (3) Principles of planning law and land use control regulations. The police power and regulation. The role of law in land use regulation. Early land use controls and zoning.
URP 623—Government Regulations II (3) *Prereq: URP 622.* Continuation of URP 622. Subdivision regulation, eminent domain, convenants and easements. Environmental regulations.
URP 624—Social Objectives in Urban and Regional Form (4) Societal objectives including housing and delivery of urban services.
URP 626—Planning Quantitative Methods (4) *Coreq: STA 602.* A survey of methods commonly used in urban planning with applied exercises.
URP 628—Professional Administration (4) Ethical, legal and administrative responsibilities of the planner.
URP 629—Terminal Project (1-15) Course work, in lieu of thesis, subject to approval of the supervisory committee. If the work is a team project, each individual must show evidence of his portion of the work accomplished. H.
URP 631—Planning Design Studio I. Project Level (4) Planning and design of development and redevelopment projects at the scale of groups, neighborhoods, and small urban areas. H.
URP 632—Planning Design Studio II. Urban Level (4) Solution of planning and design problems at urban scale including new communities planning. H.
URP 633—Planning Design Studio III. Regional Level (4) Federal and state planning exercises including case studies. H.
URP 634—Planning Design Studio IV. Super Regional Scale (4) Course addressing very large environmental systems. H.

URP 641—Planning of Urban/Regional Network Infrastructure (4) Visual and functional form, design quantification (cost effectiveness), and policy context of utility and circulation systems.

URP 661—Urban and Regional Systems (4) Holistic studies with fundamental systems modeling.

URP 662—City Models (4) *Prereq: ISE 453.* Simulation of urban systems.

URP 671—Planning History, Part I (4) An introduction to the nature of cities in history and to the public and private planning history. The history of urban design and planning for urban, metropolitan, regional and natural areas. International in scope. Deals with planning from antiquity to modern times.

URP 672—Planning History, Part II (4) *Prereq: URP 671.* Emphasis on the changing nature of urbanization and international experiments in planning solutions. Includes new towns and contemporary planning elements.

URP 681—Qualitative Evaluation of Place and Plan (4) Humanistic evaluation skills.

URP 682—Administration of Environmental Impact Statements (4) Management and decision-making aspects of EIS under U. S. Environmental Policy Act and Florida's Land and Water Management Act of 1972.

URP 697—Supervised Research (1-5)

URP 698—Supervised Teaching (1-5)

URP 699—Master's Research (1-15)

ART

(College of Fine Arts)

Chairman & Graduate Coordinator: E. E. GRISSOM

GRADUATE FACULTY 1975-76

Graduate Research Professor: J. N. UELSMANN

Professors: R. C. CRAVEN, JR.; E. E. GRISSOM; K. A. KERSLAKE; S. R. PURSER; J. J. SABATELLA; H. D. WILLIAMS

Associate Professors: J. G. NAYLOR; J. A. O'CONNOR; P. A. WARD

Master of Fine Arts Degree: An undergraduate major in art with adequate preparation in studio courses in fine arts and/or in the history, theory, and criticism of art is prerequisite to admission. Graduate study is divided between studio courses in ceramics, creative photography, drawing, painting, printmaking, sculpture, and advanced study in the history of art. Applicants for admission to a studio major must submit a portfolio. Two years of residence are normally required for completion of the requirements for this degree.

ART 500, 611, and 621 are required of all graduate majors. All other graduate courses may be repeated for credit with change of content. Some of the courses listed are offered regularly, while others are offered only as needed.

Graduate minors in the history of art: The graduate seminars are open to students minoring in the history of art, provided that suitable prerequisites have been completed. Courses in history, philosophy, or literature may often be substituted for prerequisites in art.

The department reserves the right to retain student work for the purposes of record, exhibition, or instruction.

GRADUATE COURSES

ART 500—Methods of Research and Bibliography (4)

ART 596—Individual Study (4 or 6) May be repeated with change of content.

ART 611—Seminar: Problems in the History, Theory, and Criticism of Art I (4)

ART 621—Seminar: Problems in the History, Theory, and Criticism of Art II (4)

ART 622—Seminar: Problems in the History, Theory, and Criticism of Art III (4)

ART 650—Advanced Drawing (4) *Prerea: ART 450.* May be repeated with change of content.
ART 651—Advanced Study (4 or 6) *Prereq: major in fine arts.* Art history, ceramics, drawing, painting, printmaking, creative photography, or sculpture. May be repeated with change of content.
ART 655—Research in Methods and Materials of the Artist (4 or 6) May be repeated with change of content.
ART 697—Supervised Research (1-5)
ART 698—Supervised Teaching (1-5)
ART 699—Master's Research (1-15)

ARTS AND SCIENCES—GENERAL

(College of Arts and Sciences)

GRADUATE COURSES

ASC 600—Scientist-in-the-Sea Training Program (12) *Prereq: consent of steering committee.* Blend of theoretical content and technical method to prepare advanced marine science students for underwater research. Includes topics in hyperbaric physiology and medicine, hyperbaric habitats and submersible vehicles, marine physical sciences, marine life sciences, psychological aspects of men-in-the-sea, underwater communication and navigation, diver technology, physical fitness and diving, and experimental application of course techniques.
ASC 641—Internship in College Teaching (3) *Prereq: permission of graduate major department. Required of all candidates for the Master of Arts in Teaching and the Master of Science in Teaching degrees.*
ASC 642—Internship in College Teaching (3) May be taken concurrently with ASC 641. *Required of all candidates for the Master of Arts in Teaching and the Master of Science in Teaching degrees.*
ASC 643—Internship in College Teaching (3) May be taken concurrently with ASC 642. *Required of all candidates for the Master of Arts in Teaching and the Master of Science in Teaching degrees.*

ASTRONOMY

(College of Arts and Sciences)

Chairman: F. B. WOOD
Graduate Coordinator: G. R. LEBO

GRADUATE FACULTY 1975-76

Professors: T. D. CARR; H. K. EICHHORN-VON WURMB;* A. E. S. GREEN; J. H. HUNTER, JR.;* G. C. OMER, JR.; A. G. SMITH; S. SOFIA;* R. E. WILSON;* F. B. WOOD
Associate Professors: J. R. BUCHLER; K.-Y. CHEN; H. L. COHEN; E. J. J. DEVINNEY, JR;* C. N. OLSSON; C. A. WILLIAMS*
Assistant Professors: F. F. DONIVAN, JR.; S. T. GOTTESMAN; G. R. LEBO; M. A. LYNCH; J. P. OLIVER; H. C. SMITH, JR.*

These members of the faculty of the University of South Florida are also members of the graduate faculty of the University of Florida and participate in the doctoral degree program in the University of Florida Department of Astronomy.

The Department of Astronomy offers graduate work in astrophysics or aeronomy leading to the degrees Master of Science and Doctor of Philosophy. Current research fields include radio astronomy, cosmology, photoelectric photometry of close double stars and intrinsic variables, photographic photometry of quasars, spectroscopy, certain fields of astrophysical theory, and aeronomy.

For unqualified admission to the program, a student should have an acceptable undergraduate degree in physics or astronomy. Students with degrees in related fields, such as engineering or mathematics, may be admitted with the understanding that certain foundation courses will have to be taken. If he so desires, an individual with a strong background in physics may perform the graduate research work in astronomy or aeronomy, but take the qualifying examination and degree in physics, rather than astronomy. Complete details of the program and research facilities are included in an illustrated booklet obtained by writing the Chairman for Astronomy, Room 231, Space Sciences Research Building.

Study for the Ph.D. degree in astronomy at the University of Florida by qualified master's degree recipients at the University of South Florida is facilitated by a cooperative arrangement in which appropriate members of the faculty of USF are members of the graduate faculty of the University of Florida.

GRADUATE COURSES

ATY 503—History of Astronomy (3) *Prereq: ATY 141 or 316-317.* A general survey of the history of astronomy from the earliest times down to the present day.

ATY 510—Solar System Astrophysics I (3) *Prereq: two years of college physics.* Survey of the solar system, including its origin and the laws of planetary motion. The earth as a planet: geophysics, aeronomy, geomagnetism, and the radiation belts. Solar physics and the influence of the sun on the earth.

ATY 511—Solar System Astrophysics II (3) *Prereq: ATY 510.* The moon and planets: exploration by ground-based and spacecraft techniques. The lesser bodies of the solar system, including satellites, asteroids, meteoroids, comets; the interplanetary medium.

ATY 601—Celestial Mechanics I (3) *Prereq: ATY 317, PS 500.* Analytical and numerical computation of orbits.

ATY 602—Celestial Mechanics II (3) *Prereq: ATY 601.*

ATY 603—Special Relativity (3) Same as PS 603. Introduction to Einstein's special theory of relativity employing tensor analysis, general invariance and the background of the general theory of relativity.

ATY 604—General Relativity (3) Same as PS 604. Einstein's general theory of relativity and relativistic cosmology.

ATY 605—Stellar Astrophysics I (3) *Prereq: ATY 316, 317.* Theoretical and observational approach to evolution, dynamics, and equilibria of stars and star systems.

ATY 606—Stellar Astrophysics II (3) *Prereq: ATY 605.*

ATY 607—Stellar Astrophysics III (3) *Prereq: ATY 606.*

ATY 608—Galactic Structure (3) Kinematics and dynamics of the galaxy.

ATY 611—Radio Astronomy I (3) *Prereq: ATY 316, 317. Coreq: PS 510, 515.* Measurement parameters; instrumentation of radio and radar astronomy; emission mechanism theories; radio propagation in plasmas; observational results of radio and radar astronomy and their interpretation.

ATY 612—Radio Astronomy II (3) *Prereq: ATY 611.*

ATY 613—Radio Astronomy III (3) *Prereq: ATY 612.*

ATY 617—Positional Astronomy I (3) Numerical methods (interpolation, errors, least squares) used in astronomy, especially positional astronomy; coordinate systems and their conversion, reduction of observations (especially reduction to apparent place), time systems, and the determination of proper motion and parallax.

ATY 618—Positional Astronomy II (3)

ATY 621—Astronomical Techniques I (3) *Prereq: ATY 317.* Theory and practice in the design and use of astronomical instruments; observation and reduction procedures used in applications such as astronomical photography, spectroscopy, and photo-electric photometry.

ATY 622—Astronomical Techniques II (3) *Prereq: ATY 621.*

ATY 623—Astronomical Techniques III (3) *Prereq: PS 410 or equivalent.* Theory and practice in design, construction, and use of radio astronomical instruments. Emphasis on design and construction of special radio astronomy receiving and antenna systems. Measurement techniques necessary for construction and use of systems are presented.

ATY 624—Astronomical Techniques IV (3) *Prereq: ATY 623.*

ATY 631—Extragalactic Astronomy and Cosmology (3) Interpretations of observational results and current theories concerning galaxies, clusters of galaxies, quasars, and cosmological evolution.

ATY 633—Radiopropagation and Ionospheric Physics I (3) Same as PS 633. *Prereq: PS 410 or equivalent.* Propagation of electromagnetic waves in magneto-ionic media, with emphasis on the terrestrial ionosphere, and cosmic conditions such as solar corona, interstellar media. Propagation of pulse signals; non-linear effects in the radio-wave propagation in the ionosphere; plasma resonances as observed from topside sounders; whistler propagation.

ATY 634—Radiopropagation and Ionospheric Physics II (3) Same as PS 634. *Prereq: ATY 633.* Ionospheric electron density and ion composition profiles; diurnal, seasonal, and global variations; pre-sunrise effects; electron and ion temperatures; traveling disturbances; solar flare and magnetic storm effects.

ATY 636—Atomic Physics of Planetary Atmospheres (3) Same as PS 636. *Prereq: basic courses in physics and mathematics through integral calculus.* Atomic and quantum theory, quantum mechanics and the central field problem, atomic and molecular spectroscopy, collisional cross sections for aeronomy.

ATY 637—Physics of the Earth's Upper Atmosphere (3) Same as PS 637. *Prereq: ATY 636.* Solar-terrestrial relations, aurora, airglow, and ionospheric phenomena. Remote sensing of atmospheric emissions and scattered solar radiation.

ATY 638—Physics of Planetary Atmospheres (3) Same as PS 638. *Prereq: ATY 637.* Radiative transfer in planetary atmospheres, from the x-ray to radio regions. Discussion of recent studies of the atmospheres of Venus, Mars, Jupiter, and other planets.

ATY 643—Visual and Spectroscopic Binary Stars I (3) *Prereq: ATY 605, 622.* Theoretical studies and analyses of observations of both visual and spectroscopic binaries.

ATY 644—Visual and Spectroscopic Binary Stars II (3) *Prereq: ATY 643.*

ATY 645—Eclipsing Binary Stars I (3) *Prereq: ATY 605, 622.* Theoretical studies and analyses of observations of eclipsing variables.

ATY 646—Eclipsing Binary Stars II (3) *Prereq: ATY 645.*

ATY 651—Variable Stars (3) *Prereq: ATY 317.* An overall picture of the different types of variable stars. Classification, light and spectral changes, population distribution, physical processes causing variability, the place of variables in stellar evolution. Use of variable stars in galactic and extragalactic studies.

ATY 680—Seminar in Modern Astronomy (1; max: 9) Recent developments in theoretical and observational astronomy and astrophysics. S/U.

ATY 696—Individual Work (1-5; max: 10) Supervised study or research in areas not covered by other courses.

ATY 697—Supervised Research (1-5)

ATY 698—Supervised Teaching (1-5)

ATY 699—Master's Research (1-15)

ATY 741—Close Binary Stars (3) *Prereq: ATY 646.* Role of close binaries in stellar evolution. Nonperiodic phenomena, mass loss and exchange, novae and nova-like variables, period changes.

ATY 799—Doctoral Research (1-15)

BIOCHEMISTRY AND MOLECULAR BIOLOGY
(College of Arts and Sciences)

Chairman: P. A. CERUTTI
Graduate Coordinator: T. W. O'BRIEN

GRADUATE FACULTY 1975-76

Professors: R. P. BOYCE; P. A. CERUTTI; M. FRIED; E. J. GABBAY; R. J. MANS; O. M. RENNERT; E. G. SANDER

Associate Professors: C. M. ALLEN, JR.; P. W. CHUN; C. M. FELDHERR; W. R. FISHER; A. S. LARKIN; T. W. O'BRIEN; R. M. ROBERTS; G. S. STEIN

Assistant Professors: R. J. COHEN; B. M. DUNN; P. J. LAIPIS; K. D. NOONAN; J. C. M. TSIBRIS

The Department of Biochemistry and Molecular Biology offers the Master of Science and Doctor of Philosophy degrees with specialization in physical biochemistry, molecular biology, and medical biochemistry.

Specific areas of study include structure and function of cellular and nuclear membranes in mammalian cells; regulation of cell division and gene expression; biochemistry of differentiation; biochemical genetics, inborn errors of metabolism; molecular biology of DNA replication and repair in bacterial and eukaryotic cells; biosynthesis of RNA, protein, polysaccharides, lipoproteins; isoprenoid metabolism; physical biochemistry of nucleic acids and proteins; mechanism of enzyme action; and marine biochemistry.

New graduate students should have adequate training in general, organic, quantitative, and physical chemistry as well as in physics and biology. Calculus is recommended. (See descriptions listed under Program in Medical Biochemistry at the end of this section for requirements of students wishing to specialize in this area.) Minor deficiencies may be made up immediately after entering Graduate School.

Doctoral candidates are required to take a core of biochemistry courses which include BCH 601, 602, 603, 606, 615, 616, and 617. Depending upon interests and background of the student, additional courses are recommended from the following list: BCH 578, 612, 614, 722, 723, and 724. The course of graduate study for doctoral candidates also includes advanced organic and physical chemistry, physiology, microbiology, and genetics.

GRADUATE COURSES

BCH 511—Physical Biochemistry and Molecular Biology (5) *Prereq: organic chemistry.* Structure, function and metabolism of cellular components. Topics include structure, biosynthesis, and function of macromolecules; bioenergetics; enzyme mechanisms.

BCH 512—Intermediary Metabolism (5) Intermediary metabolism; transport processes; biological control mechanisms.

BCH 513—Biochemistry Laboratory (2) *Coreq: BCH 511, 512.*

BCH 521—Current Trends in Biochemistry I (2) *Coreq: BCH 511.*

BCH 522—Current Trends in Biochemistry II (2) *Coreq: BCH 512.*

BCH 578—Chemistry of Biological Molecules (4) Same as CY 578. Mechanistic organic biochemistry. Emphasis on model systems, enzyme active sites, and physical and organic chemistry of biomacromolecules.

BCH 579—Biochemical Genetics (4) *Prereq: BCH 511, 512, 521, 522, or consent of instructor.* Presentation of classic and contemporary experiments in bacterial, plant, and mammalian systems.

BCH 601—Biochemical Structure and Function (4) *Prereq: organic chemistry. Coreq: physical chemistry.*

BCH 602—Metabolism (4)

BCH 603—Principles of Molecular Biology and Genetics (4)

BCH 606—Recent Advances in Biochemistry (2) *Prereq: BCH 601 or equivalent.* Areas of biochemistry and molecular biology selected by the faculty discussed critically and in depth. Emphasis on current controversy and theory, data interpretations, and scientific writing. Classes held informally in small groups during each quarter, involving all biochemistry faculty on a rotating basis.

BCH 612—Physical Biochemistry (4) *Prereq: general course in biochemistry (BCH 601 or 511) and in physical chemistry.* Physical chemistry and molecular structures of proteins, enzymes, and nucleic acids. Fundamentals of physical biochemistry techniques.

BCH 614—Bioenergetics and Enzyme Mechanisms (4) *Prereq: BCH 601, 602, 603.* Mechanisms of enzyme action and the energy transformations occurring in biological systems.

BCH 615—Research Methods in Biochemistry (2-6; max: 12) Same as MED 615. *Prereq: BCH 601, 602, 603.* Only by special arrangement. Biochemical research in which the student refines his research techniques in physical biochemistry, intermediary metabolism, and radio-isotopes under supervision of a staff member.

BCH 616—Biochemistry Seminar (1) Same as MED 616. *Required of graduate students in biochemistry; open to others by special arrangement.* Research reports and discussions of current research literature given by the departmental staff, invited speakers, and graduate students. S/U.

BCH 617—Special Topics in Biochemistry (2; max: 12) Same as MED 617. *Prereq or coreq: BCH 601, 602, or 603.* Supervised study in publications in specific areas of biochemistry, with informal weekly conferences, reports and lectures; individual faculty in charge of the course on a rotating basis.

BCH 697—Supervised Research (1-5)

BCH 698—Supervised Teaching (1-5)

BCH 699—Master's Research (1-15)

BCH 721—Biochemistry of Disease (3) Same as MED 721. *Prereq: general courses in bio-chemistry.* The molecular basis of human pathobiology. Biochemical mechanisms underlying selected disease states.

BCH 722—Molecular Biology I (4) Same as MED 722. *Prereq: general course in biochemistry* Chemical and physicochemical characteristics of the molecules concerned with heredity gene replication, and mutation, and of their biosynthesis and function.

BCH 723—Molecular Biology II (4) Same as MED 723. *Prereq: general course in bio-chemistry.* Biochemistry of nuclei, ribosomes, mitochondria, chloroplasts, Golgi bodies, lysosomes, cell walls and membranes; compartmentation and integrated cellular function.

BCH 724—Molecular Biology III (4) Same as MED 724. *Prereq: general course in bio-chemistry.* Molecular virology: growth and replication of animal viruses; organization and structure of viral and cellular chromosomes; RNA synthesis translation and transcription; mechanism of regulation of cellular metabolism.

BCH 799—Doctoral Research (1-15)

PROGRAM IN MEDICAL BIOCHEMISTRY

GRADUATE FACULTY 1975-76

P. A. CERUTTI, *Director;* R. P. BOYCE; W. R. FISHER; M. FRIED; P. J. LAIPIS; A. S. LARKIN; K. D. NOONAN; O. M. RENNERT; R. M. ROBERTS; E. G. SANDER; G. S. STEIN

A program in medical biochemistry is offered through the Department of Bio-chemistry leading to the M.S. and Ph.D. degrees in biochemistry.

The Ph.D. degree may also be earned as part of the special M.D.-Ph.D. program. This program is open only to medical students enrolled in the College of Medicine at the University of Florida. It is designed to make graduate-level education in biochemistry leading to the M.S. or Ph.D. degree available to specially selected students who are in the process of completing or who have already completed the M.D. degree.

Minimum requirements are a bachelor's degree and, in the case of students enrolled in the M.D.-Ph.D. program, those courses leading toward the M.D. degree. A supervisory committee will be appointed during the first year and will determine, in conjunction with the student, an appropriate curriculum. Besides the core of biochemistry required of all Ph.D. candidates in biochemistry, candidates specializing in medical biochemistry are required to take MED 596, 599, 615, 616, 617, 721, 722, 723, 724, and either BCH 699 or 799.

BOTANY

(College of Arts and Sciences)

Chairman: W. W. PAYNE
Graduate Coordinator: J. T. MULLINS

GRADUATE FACULTY 1975-76

Professors: D. S. ANTHONY; M. M. GRIFFITH; T. E. HUMPHREYS; J. T. MULLINS; W. W. PAYNE; L. SHANOR; I. K. VASIL; D. B. WARD
Associate Professors: H. C. ALDRICH; J. S. DAVIS; D. G. GRIFFIN III; J. W. KIMBROUGH; R. C. SMITH
Assistant Professors: G. E. BOWES; J. J. EWEL; T. W. LUCANSKY; A. E. LUGO

The Department of Botany offers graduate work leading to the degrees of Master of Science, Master of Agriculture, Master of Science in Teaching, and Doctor of Philosophy.

Specific areas of specialization in botany include ecology, physiology and biochemistry, cryptogamic botany, morphology and anatomy of vascular plants, systematics, cytology and ultrastructure.

For admission to graduate standing a student should present credits equivalent to those required of undergraduate majors in the department. Undergraduate major requirements include 36 credits in botany, a course with laboratory in genetics, mathematics through differential calculus, one year of college physics, and chemistry through organic. Those admitted without full equivalents of an undergraduate major will be required to make up the deficiencies by passing appropriate courses early in their graduate programs. A reading knowledge of a foreign language and credit for basic courses in zoology and bacteriology are desirable. The program of graduate study for each student will be determined by a supervisory committee. No more than 10 credits of BTY 696 may be used to satisfy the credit requirements for a master's degree. Each student pursuing the Ph.D. degree will be required to pass a written departmental examination on designated major areas of botany prior to the qualifying examination.

There are, in addition to the facilities of the department for graduate work, the following special resources that may be utilized in support of graduate student training and research: (1) the Florida Agricultural Experiment Stations, (2) the Marine Sciences Center on the Gulf of Mexico for studies in estuarine and marine habitats, (3) the resources of the Welaka Conservation Reserve, and (4) the Center for Tropical Agriculture, which can support studies in tropical and subtropical areas.

GRADUATE COURSES

BTY 500—Plant Geography (4) *Prereq: BTY 203 or 342 or 380.* Geography of the floras and types of vegetation throughout the world, with emphasis on problems of the distribution of taxa, and the main factors influencing types of vegetation.

BTY 501—Advanced Ecology (5) *Prereq: BTY 301 or equivalent, one course in physiology or consent of instructor. College physics, chemistry, and calculus are desirable.* Diversity measures, population dynamics, ecosystem classification, quantitative plant sociology, nutrient cycles, energy flow, productivity, modeling and computer simulation, and budgets at the ecosystem level.

BTY 502—Ecosystems of Florida (5) *Prereq: BTY 301 or equivalent.* Major ecosystems of Florida in relation to environmental factors and man's relationships to them. Phytotechniques of vegetation analysis applied during visits to selected ecosystems.

BTY 515—Intermediate Plant Physiology (5) *Prereq: BTY 310, and CY 362, 363, or 381, 382, 384, 385.* Fundamental physical and chemical processes underlying the water relations, nutrition, metabolism, growth, and reproduction of higher plants.

BTY 521—Introductory Mycology (5) *Prereq: BTY 203 or 380.* Fungi, with emphasis on comparative morphology.

BTY 522—Phycology (5) *Prereq: BTY 203 or 380 or consent of instructor.* Algae, especially their structure, reproduction, growth, classification, and evolution.

BTY 523—Mosses and Liverworts (5) *Prereq: BTY 203 or 380.* Morphology of the major groups of bryophytes, with emphasis on collection, identification, and ecology of these plants in Florida.

BTY 524—Lower Vascular Plants (5) *Prereq: BTY 532, and 342 or 542 or consent of instructor.* Living and fossil representatives of ferns and other vascular cryptograms, with emphasis on their structure, evolution, and classification.

BTY 532—Plant Anatomy (5) *Prereq: BTY 203 or 380 or consent of instructor.* Origin, structure, and function of principal tissues and organs of seed plants.

BTY 542—Taxonomy of Seed Plants (5) *Prereq: BTY 203 or 380 or equivalent.* Seed plants, their classification, gross morphology, and evolutionary relationships.

BTY 551—Cytology (5) Same as ZY 551. *Prereq: one year of general biology or equivalent, and consent of instructor.* Microscopic components of plant and animal cells. Structure, chemical constitution and function of the cell wall, protoplasm, cytoplasmic constituents and nucleus.

BTY 565—Radioisotope Theory and Techniques (5) *Prereq: CY 331 or consent of instructor.* Theory of radioactivity, of interaction with matter, radioactive decay, etc., given in sufficient detail to make the laboratory techniques and practices thoroughly understood.

BTY 602—Ecology of Aquatic Plants (5) *Prereq: BTY 501.* Role of plants in aquatic ecosystems. Field trips emphasize the flow of energy and systems structure.

BTY 604—Ecosystems of the Tropics (5) *Prereq: BTY 301:* Natural and man-dominated tropical ecosystems, their structure, function, and relation to man.

BTY 605—Tropical Biology: An Ecological Approach (12) Same as ZY 605. Intensive field study of ecological concepts in tropical environments. Eight weeks in different principal kinds of tropical environments. Offered Summer Quarter in Costa Rica as part of the program of the Organization for Tropical Studies.

BTY 607—Advanced Tropical Botany (12) *Prereq: BTY 310; BTY 501 or 542.* Limit: 10 participants. Offered Summer Quarter in Costa Rica as part of the program of the Organization for Tropical Studies. Topics are changed each year.

BTY 611—Biochemistry of Trees (3) Same as FRC 621. *Prereq: BCH 403.* Metabolic processes and constituents associated with tree growth, reproduction, formation of wood, terpene, and other natural products. Formation of important forest tree chemicals.

BTY 615—Plant Growth and Development (3) *Prereq: BTY 515.* Ways in which environmental factors influence plant growth and development.

BTY 616—Plant Nutrition (3) *Prereq: BTY 515.* Plant nutrition, including essentiality of elements, absorption of ions, utilization and role of nutrients, redistribution of minerals in plants, and water metabolism.

BTY 617—Plant Metabolism (3) *Prereq: BTY 515, BCH 402.* Metabolism of carbohydrates, fats, and nitrogen compounds in higher plants; cell structure as related to metabolism; metabolic control mechanisms.

BTY 618—Photophysiology of Plant Growth (4) *Prereq: BTY 515.* Effects of light on the physiology and biochemistry of plants. Photosynthesis and photorespiration emphasized. Properties of light, light sources, photochemistry, phytochrome action, photomorphogenesis, photoperiodism, and phototropism examined.

BTY 621—Biology and Taxonomy of the Basidiomycetes (5) *Prereq: BTY 521.* Isolating, collecting, and identification of field material required.

BTY 622—Biology and Taxonomy of Myxomycetes and Phycomycetes (5) *Prereq: BTY 521.* Morphology, development, and taxonomy of slime molds, water molds, and allied taxa emphasized.

BTY 623—Biology and Taxonomy of Ascomycetes and Their Imperfect Stages (5) *Prereq: BTY 521.* Morphology, development, and taxonomy of the Ascomycetes and Fungi Imperfecti emphasized. Field work required.

BTY 624—Fungal Genetics (5) Comparative genetics of mating type and sexual development, chromosome mapping, polyploidy, gene structure and function, and pathogenicity of selected fungi.

BTY 625—Fungal Physiology (5) Comparative physiology of growth, development, metabolism, and reproduction of selected fungi.

BTY 626—Lichenology (5) *Prereq: BTY 203 or equivalent.* The morphology and taxonomy of the lichens, with emphasis on their identification. Field trips to nearby areas of interest.

BTY 631—Developmental Morphology of Flowering Plants (5) *Prereq: BTY 380.* Developmental morphology of the vegetative and reproductive organs of flowering plants, with particular emphasis on form and function as revealed by recent experimental techniques.
BTY 632—Methods and Applications of Plant Cell and Tissue Culture (5) *Prereq: BTY 631.* Laboratory techniques for the culture of plant protoplasts, cells, tissues, and organs, and their applications in the study of cellular differentiation, development, genetics, and agriculture.
BTY 642—Advanced Taxonomy (3) *Prereq: BTY 542.* Problems in the classification of vascular plants. Published taxonomic studies reviewed as demonstration of techniques and principles involved in classification; intensive individual work required in field and herbarium application of procedures.
BTY 653—Electron Microscopy of Biological Materials (2) *Prereq: BTY 551 or ZY 551.* Use of the electron microscope, including fixation, embedding, sectioning, freeze-etching, negative staining, and use of the vacuum evaporator.
BTY 654—Laboratory in Electron Microscopy (2) *Prereq: BTY 551 or ZY 551; BTY 653 or concurrent registration in BTY 653.* Laboratory training in use of electron microscopes, ultramicrotomes, vacuum evaporators, and freeze-etch machines.
BTY 655—Plant Cytology (5) *Prereq: BTY 551.* Fundamental structures of plant cells, their functions, reproduction and relation to inheritance; recent research and techniques.
BTY 656—Cytochemistry (4) Cellular organization, cell function, and cytochemical technique.
BTY 664—Topics in Genetics (2-4; max: 12) Same as AL 664, AY 664, DY 664, PY 664, ZY 664. See AY 664.
BTY 692—Graduate Student Seminar (1; max: 3) Readings and oral presentation on general topics in botany.
BTY 695—Topics in Botany (2) Topics include plant biophysics, growth regulators, chromatography, water relations, ultrastructure cytology, plant morphogenesis, and biosystematics.
BTY 696—Individual Studies in Botany (1-5; max: 10) *Prereq: approval of department chairman and consent of instructor.* Individual, nonthesis, research problem in one or more of the following areas of botany: ecology, physiology and biochemistry, cryptogamic botany, morphology and anatomy of vascular plants, systematics, cytology and ultrastructure. Work selected to meet the interests and needs of the student.
BTY 697—Supervised Research (1-5)
BTY 698—Supervised Teaching (1-5)
BTY 699—Master's Research (1-15)
BTY 799—Doctoral Research (1-15)

SCHOOL OF BUILDING CONSTRUCTION
(College of Architecture)

Chairman: D. A. HALPERIN
Graduate Coordinator: B. H. BROWN, JR.

GRADUATE FACULTY 1975-76

Professors: B. G. EPPES; D. A. HALPERIN; L. A. JOHNSON
Associate Professors: B. H. BROWN, JR.; H. F. HOLLAND

Courses are offered leading to the degrees of Master of Science in Building Construction (thesis) and Master of Building Construction (nonthesis). Specialization may be in the areas related to construction such as materials, techniques, industrialized building and systems, management and the construction manager concept, research, and structural concepts.

There is no foreign language requirement. The objectives of this graduate program are to (1) provide advanced construction courses, (2) provide opportunity for study of construction problems and subjects in depth, (3) broaden the student's base of knowledge and understanding in the construction areas, (4) prepare for teaching, and (5) prepare for research.

Holders of the four-year undergraduate degree in building construction or its equivalent in related fields may normally complete the requirement for the master's degree in one academic year (three quarters) as full-time students. "Equivalent in related fields" should include studies in construction materials and methods, structures, and management. Students with undergraduate degrees but with deficiencies in these related fields may need longer residence for the master's degree, as they will be required to take specified basic courses to provide foundation for advanced courses.

The department reserves the right to retain student work for purposes of record, exhibition, or instruction.

GRADUATE COURSES

BCN 501—Advanced Construction Structures (4) *Prereq: BCN 323, 313.* Advanced topics in design of construction structures.

BCN 502—Advanced Construction Planning and Control (4) *Prereq: CIS 302 and BCN 432.* Time-cost relationships for various construction operations.

BCN 503—Advanced Construction Techniques (4) *Prereq: BCN 323.* Advanced continuation of BCN 323.

BCN 504—Construction Cost Analysis (4) *Prereq: ATG 201, BCN 432.* Comparative analysis of actual and estimated costs as used for project control.

BCN 505—Special Studies in Construction (3; max: 15) Special studies provide requirements of students desiring supplemental work in the building construction area.

BCN 506—Systems of Architectural Construction (4) *Prereq: BCN 322.* Study of industrialized construction techniques, designs, and costs for American and foreign systems.

BCN 520—Survey of Construction Techniques (5) Survey of work methods, materials and equipment employed on residental, commercial and industrial construction projects.

BCN 601—Building Construction (5-10; max: 10) Studies in building technology and construction management or in specialized areas of the building construction field.

BCN 602—Building Construction (5-10; max: 10)

BCN 603—Building Research (5-10; max: 10) Studies and investigations of selected problems in the building construction field.

BCN 604—Building Research (1-10; max: 10) H.

BCN 697—Supervised Research (1-5)

BCN 698—Supervised Teaching (1-5)

BCN 699—Master's Research (1-15)

BUSINESS ADMINISTRATION—GENERAL
(College of Business Administration)

Graduate programs offered by the College of Business Administration are the Doctor of Philosophy with a major in economics or with a major in business administration, Master of Arts in each of the departments of the college (accounting; economics; finance, insurance, and real estate; management; marketing), and the Master of Business Administration. Fields of concentration and requirements for the M.B.A. are given under *Requirements for Master's Degrees* in the front section of the *Catalog*.

Requirements for the Ph.D. in economics and for all M.A. degrees may be found under the description for the respective department.

The Ph.D. in business administration requires a principal or major field in one of the following: accounting, finance, insurance, management, marketing, or real estate and urban land studies. Requirements of the specific departments and specialities within the departments are stated in the departmental descriptions in this *Catalog*. All candidates for the Ph.D. in business administration must satisfy the following core requirements.

BA 591—Mathematical Methods and Their Application to Business and Economics Analysis (5)

STA 602—Statistical Methods in Research I (4)

STA 603—Statistical Methods in Research II (4)

BA 673—Concepts and Methods in the Behavioral Sciences (5)

ES 601—Macro Economic Theory (5)

ES 602—Price Theory (5)

Procedures for waiving these core requicements have been established. Additionally, the candidate must meet requirements for one or two minors. More detailed information may be obtained from the Associate Dean, College of Business Administration, Matherly Hall.

Admission Requirements: Applicants for all graduate programs in the College of Business Administration must meet the Graduate School's admission standards. These applicants may, however, use the Graduate Management Admission Test (GMAT) rather than the Graduate Record Examination Aptitude Test. While either test may be used, candidates for admission to the M.B.A. program are advised to take the GMAT.

GRADUATE COURSES

BA 540—Computer-Based Business Management (4) *Prereq: CIS 302, or consent of instructor.* Principles of data-processing management and the application of computers in solving business problems.

BA 560—Computer Concepts in Business (3) *Designed for MBA candidates who lack adequate preparation for utilizing computer hardware and software systems in managerial problem solving.* Mechanics and functioning of computer systems emphazing applications of software packages in managerial decision making and problem solving.

BA 564—Introduction to Managerial Statistics (4) *Designed for MBA candidates. Prereq: BA 591.* Basic concepts and methods of probability and statistics stressing applications in analyzing and solving business problems.

BA 591—Mathematical Methods and Their Application to Business and Economic Analysis (5) *Required of MBA candidates who have not had mathematics through calculus.* Matrix algebra and calculus applied to business and economic analysis.

BA 610—Managerial Accounting (4) *Designed for MBA candidates. Prereq: ATG 510, ES 502, BA 665.* Periodic income measurement; relation of accounting techniques to control of business operations; effects of federal income taxes on management decisions.

BA 620—Advanced Finance Topics (4) *Designed for MBA candidates. Prereq: all MBA foundation sequence courses.* Analysis of organizational problems from financial perspective integrating concepts from various organizational functions such as production, marketing, and personnel.

BA 630—Problems and Methods of Marketing Management (4) *Designed for MBA candidates. Prereq: MKG 531.* Concepts and techniques for resolving marketing management problems with students gaining experience in making applications.

BA 661—Managerial Quantitative Analysis (5) *Designed for MBA candidates. Prereq: BA 560, 564, 591.* Mathematical approaches and techniques applicable to the analysis and solution of managerial problems, with careful attention to problem formulation, mathematical analysis, and solution procedures. Involves substantial case work.

BA 664—Analysis of Decisions Under Uncertainty (3) *Designed for MBA candidates. Prereq: BA 560, 564, 591.* Statistical methodology for managerial decision making, analysis of decision trees, measurement of risk preferences, use of probability and utility assessment routines in decision analysis. Involves substantial case work.

BA 665—Statistical Analysis for Managerial Decisions (3) *Designed for MBA candidates. Prereq: BA 560, 564, 591.* Data analysis techniques useful for managerial problems with emphasis on difficulties in application and in interpretation of results. Includes experience in using computerized analytical procedures involving substantial case work.

BA 671—Human Behavior in Organizations (4) *Designed for MBA candidates. Prereq: MGT 510.* Relationship between the individual administrator and his supervisors, the employees whom he supervises, and his associates at his own level in the organization. .

BA 673—Concepts and Methods in the Behavioral Sciences (5) *Prereq: MGT 355.* Application of methodology and empirical findings from the behavioral sciences to business policies and practices.

BA 679—Business Policy (4) *Designed for MBA candidates and taken last quarter before graduation. Prereq: all MBA foundation and advanced graduate sequence required courses.* Cutting across the whole field of business administration, this course approaches business policy making and administration from the top management point of view.

BA 690—Seminar in Business Research and Reports (2) Discovery and utilization of available information relating to individual business problems. Several reports required for development of skills in presentation and interpretation of research findings. S/U.

CHEMICAL ENGINEERING
(College of Engineering)

Chairman: J. C. BIERY
Graduate Coordinator: R. W. FAHIEN

GRADUATE FACULTY 1975-76

Professors: R. B. BENNETT; J. C. BIERY; S. S. BLOCK; H. C. BROWN; R. W. FAHIEN; K. E. GUBBINS; F. P. MAY; W. J. NOLAN; J. P. O'CONNELL; H. E. SCHWEYER; D. O. SHAH; M. SMUTZ; M. TYNER; R. D. WALKER, JR.; A. W. WESTERBERG
Associate Professors: R. J. GORDON; L. E. JOHNS, JR.
Assistant Professor: D. W. KIRMSE

Graduate work for the Ph.D., M.E., and M.S. degrees in chemical engineering emphasizes these areas: (1) chemical engineering science—transport phenomena, fluid dynamics, thermodynamics, kinetics, statistical mechanics, microstructure of matter, and materials science; (2) chemical engineering systems—chemical reaction engineering, process control, process dynamics, optimization, separations processes; and (3) interdisciplinary chemical engineering—energy conversion and fuel cells, polymer science, microelectronics, process economics, biofluid mechanics, and bio-engineering.

Beyond the Graduate School requirements, admission to graduate work in chemical engineering depends upon the qualifications of the student, whose record and recommendations are carefully and individually studied. During registration week each graduate student registering for the first time is counseled to develop an initial study program best suited for his needs. The results of a brief examination covering the field of chemical engineering are also utilized by the graduate committee to guide the student. As a consequence, a program may include some undergraduate courses, if needed, to prepare for graduate course work.

The program of all students will involve research experience through the courses CHE 696, 699, or 799. All new graduate students are expected to become proficient in computer programming during their first quarter on campus.

GRADUATE COURSES

CHE 512—Process Systems Laboratory (3) *Prereq: CHE 411.* Measuring instruments, analog data manipulation and signal transmission in chemical process systems.

CHE 546—The Physics and Physical Chemistry of Polymers (3) Same as CY 546 and MSE 546.

CHE 561—The Organic Chemistry of Polymers (3) Same as CY 561 and MSE 561. Classification of polymerization types and mechanisms from a mechanistic, organic point of view.

Structure of synthetic and natural polymers and polyelectrolytes. Reactions of polymers. Practical synthetic methods of polymer preparation.

CHE 577—Disinfection, Sterilization, and Preservation (3) Description of problems and need for these treatments; causative agents and their nature; nature and use of chemical and physical antimicrobial agents; specific problems and solutions.

CHE 601—Graduate Seminar (1; max: 16)

CHE 602—Chemical Engineering Calculations (2) Calculation techniques used in advanced engineering problems.

CHE 603—Models and Methods (3) *Prereq: CHE 602.* Mathematical modeling and application to engineering problems of ordinary and partial differential equations, operational calculus, digital and analog computation techniques, complex variables, and integral equations.

CHE 604—Multidimensional and Discrete Systems (3) Applications of the mathematics of multidimensional and discrete systems to engineering problems. Matrix methods. Calculus of finite differences. Linear programming.

CHE 605—Applied Field Theory (3) Field equations of heat, mass, and momentum transport, and electromagnetic theory in orthogonal and nonorthogonal Euclidean and nonEuclidean geometries. Covariant and convective differentiation of tensors. Surface geometries. Applications of Laplace, Hemholtz, diffusion, and wave equations.

CHE 606—Applied Statistics and Probabilistic Systems (3) *Prereq: CHE 603.* Applications of random variables and probability distributions; stochastic models, Monte Carlo techniques; statistical inference, sampling distributions, tests of significance, and experimental design.

CHE 610—Process Dynamics I (3) Dynamics and control of chemical processing systems, with emphasis on the dynamics of the unit operations and chemical reactions. Analog simulation of chemical processing systems.

CHE 611—Process Dynamics II (3)

CHE 614—Computer Control of Processes (3) *Prereq: CHE 616.* Application of computers to control of chemical processes, including the practical work involved in planning, organizing, managing, and executing a computer control project.

CHE 615—Optimization Techniques (3) *Prereq: CHE 402 or 603.* Introduction to optimization techniques used in chemical process operations, process control, and systems engineering.

CHE 616—Process Systems Optimization (3) Optimization of chemical processes and systems, with particular emphasis on dynamic programming and the maximum principle.

CHE 617—Design Techniques for Process Systems (3) Computer-aided process simulation and design. Decomposition techniques for system synthesis, analysis and optimization.

CHE 621—Chemical Engineering Kinetics (3) Chemical kinetics useful in the design of chemical reactors; molecular collision theory, transition theory, homogeneous and heterogeneous reaction in gas, liquid, and solid phase with energy and mass transfer.

CHE 622—Reactor Design and Optimization (3) Application of the principles of chemical kinetics to the design of batch, tubular flow, and tank flow reactors for optimum conditions.

CHE 626—Transport Properties and Irreversible Thermodynamics (3) *Prereq: CHE 631; CHE 632 or 633.* Molecular models and statistical mechanical methods useful in the prediction and correlation of viscosity, diffusivity and thermal conductivity of fluids. Boltzmann equation, radial distribution function, cell models, absolute rate theory, corresponding states principle.

CHE 631—Thermodynamics of Reaction and Phase Equilibria (3) Methods for treating chemical and phase equilibria in multicomponent systems through the application of thermodynamics and molecular theory.

CHE 632—Applied Statistical Mechanics (3) Methods of wave mechanics and statistical mechanics in engineering problems.

CHE 633—Statistical Thermodynamics (3) Use of statistical mechanics to describe, predict, and correlate thermodynamic properties of compounds and mixtures.

CHE 640—Introduction to Transport Phenomena (3) *Prereq: MS 305.* Basic equations of change for heat, mass, and momentum. Applications of conservation and flux equations for laminar and turbulent flow. Radiation, transfer coefficients, macroscopic balances.

CHE 641—Transport Phenomena (3) *Prereq: CHE 442 or 640.* Rigorous development of differential conservation equations and macroscopic balances. Non-Newtonian fluid dynamics, turbulence, boundary layer theory, transfer coefficients. Applications.

CHE 642—Interfacial Transport Phenomena (3) *Prereq: CHE 641.* Transport of heat, mass, and momentum at interfaces. Heat and mass transfer coefficients, drag coefficient, and friction factor. Boundary layer theory.

CHE 643—Turbulent Transport Phenomena (3) *Prereq: CHE 641.* Statistical theory of turbulence; correlation coefficients, energy spectra, isotropy and homogeneity, eddy diffusivity, and viscosity tensors. Boundary layer theory.

CHE 644—Advanced Transport Phenomena (3) *Prereq: CHE 641.*

CHE 645—Rheology (3) Analysis and characterization of rheological systems.

CHE 646—Non-Newtonian Fluid Dynamics (3) Constitutive equations for non-Newtonian fluids (including viscoelastic substances) such as polymers, plastics, paints, and slurries.

CHE 647—Chemical Energy Conversion (3) *Prereq: CHE 442 or 640.* Principles of thermodynamics and transport phenomena applied to the analysis and design of chemical energy conversion devices.

CHE 648—Particulate Systems (3) Dynamics of fluid-solid , fluid-fluid, and biological systems; generalized population balances, macroscopic particle balance, kinetics of particle growth, birth and death functions, particle size determination. Crystallization, filtration, aerosols, entrainment, free molecule flow, and fluidized reactors.

CHE 650—Engineering Properties of Organic Materials (3) Theoretical studies in molecular science. Correlation of composition, microstructure, and morphology of organic materials with macroscopic engineering properties.

CHE 651—Macromolecular Materials (3) Formation, structure, and physical and chemical properties of macromolecules. Polymerization and processing methods. Commercial techniques in forming. Applications.

CHE 662—Mass Transfer Operations (3) Process design of equipment for mass transfer operations based on performance and economic optima.

CHE 663—Heat Transfer Operations (3) Process design of equipment for heat transfer operations based on performance and economic optima.

CHE 665—Stagewise Separations Processes (3) Theory, design, and evaluation of separation processes such as distillation columns, extractors, and absorbers. Multicomponent-multistage distributions using rigorous digital computer computational methods. Real-time modeling for process automation.

CHE 671—Process Engineering (3) Application of chemical engineering operations and processing to industrial operations, such as petroleum refinery, manufacture of phosphates and fertilizers, and paper pulp processing.

CHE 672—Process Equipment Design (3) Unit operations, with emphasis on design of equipment to perform the service required, considering capacity, materials, equipment, and economics.

CHE 673—Process and Plant Design (3) Techniques in the design of various complex chemical processes and plants.

CHE 676—Process Economy Analysis (3) Economics in design and operation of chemical engineering equipment. Analysis for decision under conditions of certainty and uncertainty with applications of queuing, Monte Carlo, Markov processes, and geometric and dynamic programming.

CHE 677—Biochemical Engineering (3) Physical and chemical peculiarities of living organisms and their products. Material and energy transfer in living systems, unit operations in biological processes, and industrial biochemical engineering processes.

CHE 678—Interfacial Phenomena I (3) *Prereq: CY 204, PS 213.* Air-liquid and liquid-liquid interfaces; surface-active molecules, adsorption at interfaces, foams, micro-and macroemulsions, retardation of evaporation and damping of waves by films, surface chemistry of biological systems.

CHE 679—Interfacial Phenomena II (3) *Prereq: CY 204, PS 213.* Solid-gas, solid-liquid, solid-solid interfaces. Adsorption of gases and surface-active molecules on metal surfaces, contact angle and spreading of liquids, wetting and dewetting, lubrication, biolubrication, flotation, adhesion, biological applications of surfaces.

CHE 680—Advanced Seminar in Chemical Engineering (2; max: 12) Research and current literature.

CHE 681—Advanced Seminar in Process Control (2; max: 12) *Prereq: CHE 610, 611.* Research and current problems.

CHE 682—Advanced Seminar in Transport Phenomena (2; max: 12) *Prereq: CHE 641.* Research and current literature.

CHE 683—Advanced Seminar in Thermodynamics (2; max: 12) *Prereq: CHE 631; CHE 632 or 633.* Research and current literature.

CHE 685—Advances in Separations Processes (3) *Prereq: CHE 665.* Separations processes such as thermal diffusion, molecular distillation, fractional crystallization, adsorption fractionation, and zone refining.

CHE 686—Advances in Process Systems Engineering (3) *Prereq: CHE 617.*

CHE 687—Advances in Numerical and Analytical Computation (3) *Prereq: CHE 603, 604.* Numerical and analytical techniques such as iterative matrix methods, hybrid computation, direct vector methods, functional analysis, and adaptive models.

CHE 690—Special Topics in Chemical Engineering I (1-6; max: 12) Separations processes, reactor design, applied molecular and kinetic theory, thermodynamics, particulate systems. Properties of chemical substances, transport phenomena, non-Newtonian fluid dynamics, turbulence, applied mathematics, computer science, biochemical and electrochemical engineering.

CHE 692—Special Topics in Chemical Engineering III (1-6; max: 12)

CHE 696—Individual Work (1-9) Individual engineering projects suitable for a nonthesis Master of Engineering degree.

CHE 697—Supervised Research (1-5)

CHE 698—Supervised Teaching (1-5)

CHE 699—Master's Research (1-15)

CHE 799—Doctoral Research (1-15)

CHEMISTRY
(College of Arts and Sciences)

Chairman: E. E. MUSCHLITZ, JR.
Graduate Coordinator: W. S. BREY, JR.

GRADUATE FACULTY 1975-76

Graduate Research Professors: H. A. LAITINEN; P. O. LÖWDIN; J. D. WINEFORDNER

Professors: R. G. BATES; M. A. BATTISTE; J. F. BAXTER; W. S. BREY, JR.; H. C. BROWN; G. B. BUTLER; J. A. DEYRUP; W. R. DOLBIER, JR.; R. D. DRESDNER; E. J. GABBAY; R. J. HANRAHAN; W. M. JONES; D. A. MICHA; E. E. MUSCHLITZ, JR.; N. Y. ÖHRN; G. J. PALENIK; W. B. PERSON; G. E. RYSCHKEWITSCH; H. H. SISLER; J. C. SLATER; P. TARRANT; C. A. VANDERWERF; W. WELTNER, JR.; J. A. ZOLTEWICZ

Associate Professors: S. O. COLGATE; J. F. HELLING; T. E. HOGEN ESCH; M. L. MUGA; G. H. MYERS; C. E. REID; G. M. SCHMID; R. C. STOUFER; M. T. VALA, JR.

Assistant Professors: J. R. EYLER; K. P. LI

The Department of Chemistry offers the Master of Science and the Doctor of Philosophy degrees with specialization in analytical, organic, inorganic, or physical chemistry. The nonthesis degree Master of Science in Teaching is also offered with a major in chemistry.

New graduate students should have adequate undergraduate training in inorganic, analytical, organic, and physical chemistry. Normally this will include as a minimum a year of general chemistry which may include qualitative analysis, one quarter of quantitative analysis, one year of organic chemistry, one year of physical chemistry, and one quarter of advanced inorganic chemistry. Additional courses in instrumental analysis, advanced physical and organic chemistry are desirable. Deficiencies in any of these areas may be corrected during the first year of graduate study. Such deficiencies are determined by a series of placement tests given prior to registration, and the results of these tests are used in planning the student's program.

The offerings CY 601, 602, 606, 607, 608, 612, 633, and 578 constitute a series of core courses designed to provide graduate students with a well-rounded background in the broad area of chemistry. Doctoral candidates, except those taking the chemical-physics option, are required to complete CY 601 and 2 hours of CY 602 plus 9 additional hours from the core courses. Additional courses are taken upon recommendation of the student's supervisory committee or his major professor, so that the total number of credits in courses acceptable for graduate credit is at least 42 hours. At least 24 quarter hours of these courses must be in 600-level or higher courses in chemistry.

A chemical-physics option is offered for students who will be doing research in areas of physical chemistry which require a strong background in physics. For this option, the requirement in chemistry is CY 601, 2 hours of CY 602, plus 6 additional hours from the core courses. In addition, a minimum of 22 credits in 400-level or higher physics courses, or a minimum of 12 such credits in physics and 12 in 400-level or higher mathematics courses, is required.

Candidates for the master's degree are required to complete CY 601, and any 6 hours of the other core courses. The Master of Science degree in chemistry requires a thesis. The nonthesis degree Master of Science in Teaching is offered with a major in chemistry.

GRADUATE COURSES

CY 543—Advanced Physical Chemistry Laboratory (3) *Prereq: CY 455.* Laboratory techniques used in experimental research; techniques of design and fabrication of scientific apparatus. Advanced experiments involving optical, electronic, and high vacuum equipment.

CY 545—Chemical Computations (3) *Prereq: CY 453 and knowledge of FORTRAN programming.* Solution of difficult chemical problems in equilibrium, kinetics, and spectroscopy. Applications of computers to chemical research—control of experimental procedures and data reduction.

CY 546—The Physics and Physical Chemistry of Polymers (3) Same as CHE 546 and MSE 546. *Prereq: CY 452 or equivalent.* Structure, configuration, conformation and thermodynamics of polymer solutions, gels, and solids. Thermal, mechanical, optical and rheological properties of plastics and rubbers, including demonstrations of experimental methods.

CY 550—Radiochemistry (3) *Prereq: CY 342 or 453 or consent of instructor.* Properties of radioactive nuclei, nature of radioactivity, nuclear structure, nuclear reactions, interaction of radiation with matter, chemical aspects of radioactivity, and applications of nucleonics to chemistry.

CY 551—Radiochemistry Laboratory (2) *Prereq: CY 331 and 342, or 453, or consent of instructor.* Radioactivity detection, radiochemical separations and analyses, radiochemistry laboratory techniques, the practice of radiological safety, and tracer applications of radioisotopes in chemistry and other fields.

CY 561—The Organic Chemistry of Polymers (3) Same as CHE 561 and MSE 561. *Prereq: CY 381, 362, or equivalent.* Classification of polymerization types and mechanisms from a mechanistic organic point of view. The structure of synthetic and natural polymers and polyelectrolytes. Reaction of polymers. Practical synthetic methods of polymer preparation.

CY 565—Organic Spectroscopy (2-3) *Prereq: CY 382.* Advanced study of characterization and structure proof of organic compounds by spectral methods, including IR, UV, NMR and mass spectrometry.

CY 578—Chemistry of Biological Molecules (4) Same as BCH 578. *Prereq: CY 382 or 388 and 453 or 342 or consent of instructor.* Mechanistic organic biochemistry. Emphasis on model systems, enzyme active sites, and physical and organic chemistry of biomacromolecules.

CY 596—Individual Problems, Advanced (3-5; max: 15) *Prereq: consent of faculty member supervising the work.* Double registration permitted. Assigned reading program or development of assigned experimental problem.

CY 601—Chemical Bonding and Spectra I (4) Basic methods and applications of quantum chemistry; atomic structure; chemical bonding in diatomic and polyatomic molecules. Brief introduction to molecular spectroscopy.

CY 602—Chemical Bonding and Spectra II (2; max: 4) *Prereq: CY 601.* Theory of symmetry and its chemical applications; semiempirical molecular orbital treatment of simple inorganic and organic molecules; further applications to inorganic and organic chemistry.

CY 604—Advanced Research Techniques in Chemistry (2-5; max: 12) A special topics course in advanced techniques employed in chemical research.

CY 605—Chemistry Colloquium (1-2; max: 7) Topics presented by visiting scientists and local staff members. Only beginning graduate students during the fall quarter are permitted to register for 2 credit hours one time only. S/U.

CY 606—Applied Molecular Spectroscopy (4) Applications and comparison of methods in analysis and molecular structure determination.

CY 607—Chemical Transformations (4) Important types of chemical reactions and their application to organic and inorganic synthesis.

CY 608—Chemical Dynamics (4) Basic concepts of rate laws, collision theory and transition state theory; an introduction to reaction dynamics, structural dynamics, and quantitative structure-reactivity correlations.

CY 610—Inorganic Preparations (5) Lectures and laboratory experiments showing the reactions and techniques used in the synthesis of inorganic compounds.

CY 612—Advanced Inorganic Chemistry (3) The crystalline state, acid-base, nonaqueous solvent, inorganic mechanisms.

CY 615—Chemistry of the Nonmetals (3) *Prereq: CY 607.* Relation of properties to atomic, molecular and crystal structures.

CY 616—Chemistry of the Metals (3) *Prereq: CY 602, 607.* Relation of properties to atomic, molecular, and crystal structures.

CY 617—Special Topics in Inorganic Chemistry (1-3; max: 15) Lectures or conferences on selected topics of current research interest in inorganic chemistry.

CY 618—Inorganic Chemistry Seminar (1) *Attendance required of graduate majors in inorganic chemistry. Prereq: graduate course in inorganic chemistry.* Presentation of one seminar. May be repeated for credit. S/U option.

CY 629—Chemical Physics (3) Same as PS 629. Interatomic and intermolecular forces. Energy transfer and reaction in molecular collision processes. Computational aspects of scattering theory.

CY 631—Spectrochemical and Separation Methods (1-5) Principles of atomic and molecular, spectrochemical and separation methods of analysis.

CY 632—Electrochemical Processes (1-5) Principles of electrochemical methods, ionic solutions, and electrochemical kinetics.

CY 633—Advanced Instrumental Analysis Laboratory (4) Principles of operation of instruments, optimization of instrumental conditions, and interpretation of instrumental data for qualitative and quantitative analysis.

CY 638—Analytical Chemistry Seminar (1) *Attendance required of graduate majors in the analytical area. Prereq: graduate course in analytical chemistry.* Presentation of one seminar. May be repeated for credit. S/U option.

CY 639—Special Topics in Analytical Chemistry (2; max: 12) *Prereq: two quarters of the CY 630 series.* Lectures or conferences covering selected topics of current interest in analytical chemistry.

CY 640—Physical Chemistry Seminar (1) *Attendance required of graduate majors in physical chemistry. Prereq: graduate course in physical chemistry.* Presentation of one seminar. S/U option.

CY 641—Chemical Thermodynamics (3) Energetics, properties of ideal and nonideal systems primarily from the standpoint of classical thermodynamics.

CY 642—Kinetic Theory (3) *Prereq: CY 641.* Classical statistics, the Maxwell-Boltzmann distribution, molecular collision dynamics, elements of transport theory, virial theorem, intermolecular forces.

CY 643—Statistical Thermodynamics (3) *Prereq: CY 642.* Fundamental principles of statistical thermodynamics with applications to systems of chemical interest.

CY 644—Advanced Chemical Kinetics (3) *Prereq: CY 608 or equivalent.* Rates and mechanisms of chemical reaction.

CY 645—Introduction to Molecular Spectroscopy (3) *Prereq: CY 602.* Molecular energy levels, spectroscopic selection rules; rotational, vibrational, electronic and magnetic resonance spectra of diatomic and polyatomic molecules.

CY 647—Quantum Theory of Matter I (3) Same as PS 647. *Prereq: CY 601 or PS 541.* Quantum mechanics of atoms; Hartree-Fock theory; interaction of radiation and matter; relativistic theory.

CY 648—Quantum Theory of Matter II (3) Same as PS 648. *Prereq: CY 647.* Diatomic and polyatomic molecules; symmetry properties and group theory.

CY 649—Quantum Theory of Matter III (3) Same as PS 649. *Prereq: CY 648.* Special topics in the quantum theory of atoms, molecules, and solids.

CY 650—Special Topics in Physical Chemistry (1-3; max: 15) Lectures or conferences covering selected topics of current interest in physical chemistry.

CY 652—The Physical Chemistry of Polymers (3) *Prereq: CY 382, 451, 452, and calculus through differential equations.* Configuration of polymer chains; solution properties of polymers and polyelectrolytes; solid state properties of polymers.

CY 653—Physical Chemistry of Surfaces (3) Liquid-gas and solid-gas interface; adsorption and heterogeneous catalysis.

CY 654—Colloids (2) Methods of preparation and characteristics of colloidal dispersions; optical, kinetic, electrokinetic, and rheological properties of colloidal and macromolecular systems.

CY 655—Elements of Quantum Chemistry (3) *Prereq: CY 602.* Brief treatment of the Schrödinger equation, followed by a survey of applications to chemical problems.

CY 657—Nuclear Chemistry (3) *Prereq: CY 550.* Radioactivity, nuclear structure, decay processes, nuclear reactions.

CY 658—Radiation Chemistry (2) *Prereq: CY 644 or 608.* Chemical and physical effects caused by ionizing radiations. Kinetics and mechanism of radiation-induced reactions.

CY 659—Photochemistry (2) *Prereq: CY 644 or 608.* Experimental and theoretical aspects of chemical reactions induced by visible and ultraviolet radiation. Fluorescence and chemiluminescence.

CY 661—Advanced Organic Chemistry (3) *Prereq: CY 382, 565.* Advanced organic chemistry intended to present a useful interpretation of descriptive fact and unifying theory.

CY 662—Advanced Organic Chemistry (3)

CY 663—Advanced Organic Chemistry (3) *Prereq: CY 662.* Synthesis of complex organic molecules, with emphasis on recent developments in approaches and methods.

CY 668—Chemistry of High Polymers (2) Fundamental approach to the chemistry of high polymers, with emphasis on the mechanisms of polymerization reactions and the relationship of physical properties to chemical constitution.

CY 669—High Polymer Chemistry Laboratory (2) *Prereq. or coreq: CY 668.* Two three-hour laboratories per week or their equivalent. Preparation of representative members of the high polymer family and determination of their physical properties, methods of polymerization, and determination of fundamental polymer properties.

CY 670—Organic Chemistry Seminar (1) *Attendance required of graduate majors in the organic area. Prereq: CY 661, 662, 663.* Presentation of one seminar. May be repeated for credit.

CY 671—Physical-Organic Chemistry (2) Theory and application of physical methods in the study of the behavior of organic compounds.

CY 673—Organometallic Compounds (3) *Prereq: CY 607.* Properties of organometallic compounds, the nature of the carbon-metal bond, compounds of metals in groups 1, 2, 3, and 4, and transition metals.

CY 674—Free Radical Reactions (2) *Prereq: CY 661, 662, 663.* Development and correlation of experimental methods, fact and theory of reactions involving organic free radicals.

CY 675—The Chemistry of Heterocyclic Compounds (2) *Prereq: CY 661, 662, 663.*

CY 677—Special Topics in Organic Chemistry (2) *Prereq: CY 661, 662.* Chemistry of selected types of organic compounds, such as alkaloids, carbohydrates, natural products, steroids.

CY 697—Supervised Research (1-5)

CY 698—Supervised Teaching (1-5)

CY 699—Master's Research (1-15)

CY 756—Special Topics in Theory of Atomic and Molecular Structure (3; max: 12) Same as PS 756. *Prereq: CY 649 or PS 649, or equivalent.* Mathematical techniques used in atomic, molecular, and solid-state theory. The one-electron approximation and the general quantum-mechanical many-body problem. Selected advanced topics.

CY 757—Theory of Atomic and Molecular Structure (3) Same as PS 757.

CY 799—Doctoral Research (1-15)

CIVIL ENGINEERING
(College of Engineering)

Chairman & Graduate Coordinator: J. H. SCHAUB

GRADUATE FACULTY 1975-76

Professors: B. A. CHRISTENSEN; L. E. GRINTER; J. A. PURPURA; H. S. SAWYER; J. H. SCHAUB; J. H. SCHMERTMANN; M. W. SELF; B. D. SPANGLER; J. A. WATTLEWORTH

Associate Professors: J. D. RUMBLE; B. E. RUTH; W. H. ZIMPFER

Assistant Professors: C. A. COLLIER; K. G. COURAGE; J. L. DAVIDSON; C. O. HAYS; R. L. SIEGEL

The following graduate degrees are offered to prepare qualified students for the professional practice of civil engineering: Master of Engineering, Master of Science, Engineer, and Doctor of Philosophy. All degree programs include areas of concentration in the specialties of construction, hydraulics, soil mechanics and foundations, structures, and transportation engineering. All degrees except the Ph.D. are available in a thesis or nonthesis program.

Programs designed to meet specific needs in civil engineering management and public works engineering are available within the various areas of concentration.

Resident graduate students are required to register for a minimum of 3 credits at 1 credit per quarter for CE 691. This credit is not applicable to the requirement for any degree. Nonthesis degree students must successfully complete a report of substantial engineering content for a minimum of 3 hours' credit in CE 694. Minor or supporting work is encouraged from a variety of related or allied fields of study.

GRADUATE COURSES

CE 501—Construction Equipment: and Procedures (3) *Prereq: CE 401 or consent of instructor.* Studies in equipment resource utilization in heavy construction. Theory and practice of mechanized construction procedures. Cost analysis. Optimizing crew and equipment.

CE 502—Construction Planning and Scheduling (3) *Prereq: CE 401.* Principles of planning, scheduling, organizing, and controlling construction projects. Studies in Critical Path Method and PERT, with resource leveling and financial scheduling. Linear programming applications in construction.

CE 505—Legal Aspects of Civil Engineering (3) Legal considerations encountered in professional practice, with particular emphasis on design and construction problems. Case studies.

CE 510—Highway Design (3) *Prereq: CE 410 or consent of instructor.* Design of flexible and concrete pavements.

CE 512—Transportation Engineering (4) *Prereq: consent of instructor.* Review of transportation engineering including systems, studies, and plans.

CE 513—Traffic Engineering Characteristics (4) *Prereq: consent of instructor.* Characteristics of drivers, vehicles, stream flow; volume, accident and speed studies; traffic flow theories, intersection capacities.

CE 514—Geometric Design of Transportation Facilities (4) *Prereq: CE 410 or consent of instructor.* Philosophical considerations in planning and design; design controls and criteria; elements of design; cross section elements; intersection design; freeway design; interchange design. Design projects.

CE 515—Traffic Control Systems (4) *Prereq: CE 513 or consent of instructor.* Pretimed signal systems. Traffic-actuated controllers. Traffic responsive systems. Electronic traffic detectors. Computer control of traffic. Automated traffic data collection techniques.

CE 520—Problems in Hydraulics (3) *Prereq. or coreq: CE 420 or consent of instructor.* Problem course covering application of methods presented in CE 320 and 420. Emphasis on numerical methods and computer application.

CE 521—Geohydrology (3) *Prereq: CE 420 or consent of instructor.* Elements of surface and subsurface hydrology. Darcy's law. Permeability and its determination in laboratory and field. Capillary forces. One-dimensional flow. Flow nets. Well hydraulics. Theis' recovery method. Numerical and experimental methods.

CE 522—Open-Channel Hydraulics I (3) *Prereq: CE 420 or consent of instructor.* Classification of flow. Specific energy, critical depth, and hydraulic jump. Velocity and bed shear stress distributions. Backwater curves. Channel transitions. Spatially varied channel flow. Design of channel systems. Emphasis on steady flow.

CE 523—Advanced Water Resources Engineering (3) *Prereq: CE 522 or consent of instructor.* The hydrological cycle. Hydrographs. Stormwater management in urban areas. Flow analysis and design principles for hydraulic structures and systems. Optimum design and operation of hydraulic structures and systems.

CE 525—Hydraulic Motors and Pumps (3) *Prereq: CE 420 or consent of instructor.* Introduction to the theory of hydraulic motors, turbines, pumps, and transmissions.

CE 530—Public Works Planning (3) Engineering planning for public need, priority analysis, methods of financing, growth capital vs. maintenance. Location analysis.

CE 560—Stress-Deformation Analysis of Soil Media (3) *Prereq: CE 461 or consent of instructor.* Nature of soil-water systems; analysis of stress, strains, equations of states; viscoelastic behavior of soils; failure in soil media.

CE 561—Soil Exploration for Engineering Design (3) *Prereq: CE 460 or equivalent.* Methods of soil exploration; techniques of soil sampling and in situ testing; field measurement of soil deformations and pressures; load tests (emphasis on field work and demonstrations).

CE 562—Foundation Design II (3) *Prereq: CE 461, 472.* Pile foundation design and installation, group capacity, drilled pier foundations, stability of excavations for deep foundations, braced cuts, and anchored bulkheads.

CE 570—Design in Prestressed Concrete (3) *Prereq: CE 574.* Principles of prestressed concrete, materials used in prestressed concrete, design of posttensioned and pretensioned beams for bending, bond and diagonal tension, review of existing specifications.

CE 572—Design of Highway Bridges (3) *Prereq: CE 574, 575.* Design of highway bridges of reinforced and prestressed concrete and of steel; study of highway specifications; details of design, study of types and economics.

CE 573—Design of Structural Systems (3) *Prereq: CE 574, 575.* Introduction to planning and design of structural systems, including building frames, bridge systems, space structures. Economic considerations in selection.

CE 574—Design of Concrete Systems (3) *Prereq: CE 472.* Ultimate strength analysis and design involving torsion with diagonal tension, members of irregular section, slabs, walls and footings. Building and bridge design. Introduction to prestressed concrete.

CE 575—Design in Steel and Timber (3) *Prereq: CE 470.* Continuation of CE 470. Advanced design of connections. Theory and design of built-up members and plate girders. Design of timber members and connections.

CE 590—Numerical and Computer Methods in Civil Engineering (3-6) *Prereq: ISE 350.* Practice in machine solution of civil engineering problems, with emphasis on matrix algebra and numerical methods. Solutions of nonlinear systems of algebraic and differential equations.

CE 591—Civil Engineering Systems (4) Civil engineering applications of systems engineering and operations research techniques including models of scheduling, linear programming, queueing theory, and simulation.

CE 602—Civil Engineering Practice (3) Advanced studies in the problems of civil engineering practice including social, legal, and environmental considerations as well as technical aspects. Case histories of civil engineering projects.

CE 603—Civil Engineering Operations (3) *Prereq: CE 502, 591.* Applications of quantitative methods of decision making to major civil engineering problem areas.

CE 610—Advanced Highway Engineering (3) *Prereq: CE 410.* Highway soil stabilization, behavior of granular and stabilized highway materials.

CE 611—Mass Transportation Systems (4) *Prereq: CE 512.* Capacity, speed, and cost of public mass transportation systems, analysis and simulation of alternate transportation systems; new systems.

CE 612—Urban Transportation Methods (4) *Prereq: CE 512.* Current mathematical models of traffic planning and urban activity. Trip generation, distribution and assignment. Modal split.

CE 613—Traffic Engineering Operations and Analysis (4) *Prereq: CE 513.* Operational techniques used to optimize traffic flow including control systems. Maintenance operations. Freeway operations and control. Intersection channelization.

CE 614—Highway Planning Decisions (3) Finance and administration, highway needs analysis, economics of location, highway planning studies.

CE 616—Highway Safety Analysis (3) *Prereq: CE 513.* Accident-reporting systems, statistics and characteristics of accidents, accident reconstruction and investigation procedures, factors involved in highway accidents, accident reduction and effects minimization.

CE 617—Airport Planning and Operations (3) *Prereq: CE 515.* Configuration, ground movements, baggage movements, parking, aircraft delay analysis, airport access, simulation of airport operations.

CE 618—Freeway Design and Operations (4) *Prereq: CE 513.* Operational characteristics of freeway systems. Geometric design configurations and effect on operation. Advanced analysis techniques. Freeway surveillance and control.

CE 619—Traffic Flow Theory (4) *Prereq: CE 513.* Macroscopic and microscopic traffic flow models, simulation, traffic system and network models, freeway corridor models.

CE 620—Groundwater Hydraulics (3) *Prereq: CE 521.* Laminar flow through porous isotropic and anisotropic media. Two-dimensional flow problems and potential theory methods. Three-dimensional flow. Multiple phase flow. Salt water intrusion. Dispersion. Turbulent groundwater flow. Transient flow.

CE 622—Open-Channel Hydraulics II (3) *Prereq: CE 522.* Unsteady open-channel flow. Equation of motion. Method of characteristics. Surge formation. Dam-break problem. Flood waves. Rating curves and expressions for discharge.

CE 623—Sediment Transport (3) *Prereq: CE 522.* Alluvial water courses. Critical shear stress and stable channels. Modes of sediment motion and bed formation. Suspended load. Bedload formulas and entrainment at the bed. Transport in closed conduits. Natural rivers. Meanders.

CE 624—Hydraulic Models and Analogs (3) *Prereq: CE 420.* Principles of hydraulic similitude. Special model laws and their limitations. Dimensional analysis. Distorted models with fixed or movable bed. Calibration of models; interpretation of model results. Electrical and laminar flow analogs. Applications.

CE 625—Hydraulic Measurements in Laboratory and Field (3) *Prereq: CE 420.* Modern hydraulic laboratory. Flumes and test rigs. Advanced methods for measurement of head, velocity, discharge, sediment transport. Auxiliary electronic equipment.

CE 627—Hydraulic Transients (3) *Prereq: CE 420.* Unsteady pipe flow. The surge tank. Waterhammer analysis. Numerical and graphical methods. Digital programming of unsteady flow situations.

CE 628—Hydraulics of Stratified Flow (3) *Prereq: CE 420, 522.* Uniform and nonuniform flow in multilayered systems, including hydraulic jumps and saline wedges. Oscillatory motion and interfacial mixing. Continuous-density gradients. Diffusion.

CE 640—Bituminous Materials (3 or 6) *Prereq: CE 410.* Engineering analysis of strength and deformation mechanisms for asphalt and asphalt-aggregate systems; sampling and testing.

CE 641—Advanced Metal Structures (3) Behavior of structural materials under static, dynamic, and repeated loads. Effects of temperature. Materials problems in structural design.

CE 642—Properties, Design and Control of Concrete (3) *Prereq: CE 340.* Portland cement and aggregate properties relating to design, control, and performance of concrete.

CE 660—Advanced Soil Mechanics (3-9; max: 9) *Prereq: CE 460.* Application of soil mechanics to the design and construction of buildings, foundations, earth structures, and highways.

CE 661—Advanced Foundations (3 or 6; max: 6) *Prereq: CE 461, 672, 660.* Special foundations using most recent information from soil mechanics and structural analysis. Pile foundations, mats, retaining walls and structures such as piers.

CE 662—Structure and Engineering Properties of Soils (3-9; max: 9) Factors influencing mechanical properties of soils; effective stress, cohesion and friction, shear-consolidation interaction, pore pressures, creep and dynamic effects. Research and laboratory instruction.

CE 663—Soil Dynamics (3-6) Dynamic principles; lumped systems; phase plane solution; elastic half-space theory; soil behavior under dynamic loading; foundation design problems under impulse, earthquake, pavement and steady-state vibrations.

CE 665—Theory and Practice of Soil Compaction (3) *Prereq: CE 460, 461.* Theories of compaction as applied to laboratory and field compaction. Properties of compacted soils. Factors influencing field compaction. Compaction control.

CE 670—Topics in Structural Dynamics (3-6) *Prereq: CE 674.* Analysis and design studies in selected topics such as dynamic response of structures, design for blast loads, and design for seismic forces.

CE 671—Advanced Reinforced Concrete (3-6; max: 6) *Prereq: CE 474.* Research in reinforced concrete and development of building code requirements; ultimate load theories and their application to design; special design problems.

CE 672—Analysis of Statically Indeterminate Structures (1-6; max: 6) *Prereq: CE 371, 472.* Frames with variable moment of inertia; arch and ring analysis by elastic center and column analogy; matrix solutions; redundant trusses; moment and shear distribution.

CE 673—Advanced Structural Laboratory (3) *Prereq: CE 371, 472.* Model studies and analysis. Applications to static and dynamic loadings. Mechanics of similitude and dimensional analysis. Vibration of beams; research studies.

CE 674—Advanced Structural Analysis (3-6; max: 6) *Prereq: CE 371, 472, ESM 302.* Approximate methods of analysis for structural members of variable section modulus, including problems on vibrations, column buckling, beam-columns, beams on elastic supports.

CE 676—Design of Framed Structures (3-6; max: 6) *Prereq: CE 671, 672.* Design of continuous trusses; secondary stresses; design of rigid frames; multistory frames, and arches.

CE 677—Design of Folded Plates and Shells (3-6; max: 6) *Prereq: CE 671, 672.* Analysis and design of folded plate, shell, tank, and cable-supported structures.

CE 679—Nonlinear Structural Analysis and Design (3-9; max: 9) *Prereq: CE 672.* Rigid-plastic and multilinear analysis and design of beams and frames. Yield line theory of slabs. Deflection analyses of columns, frames, curved compression members and suspension systems, with design applications.

CE 680—Advanced Prestressed Concrete Design (3) *Prereq: CE 474, 570.* Design and limit analysis of prestressed concrete structural systems. Continuous beams, slabs, frames, composite members. Prestressed concrete reservoirs, structural systems in building construction, foundations, harbors.

CE 681—Air Photo Interpretation: Engineering Applications (3) *Prereq: CE 512 or 561.* Interpretation of aerial photography for the evaluation and planning of transportation systems and selection of desirable sites for construction of civil engineering projects.

CE 682—Air Photo Interpretation: Terrain Analysis (4) *Prereq: CE 681.* Interpretive techniques used to identify soils, rocks, and engineering problems from aerial photography.

CE 690—Matrix Methods in Structural Analysis (3-6; max: 6) Matrix algebra relating to structural analysis. Development of matrix-method solutions for trusses and rigid frames. Problems programmed for the digital computer.

CE 691—Graduate Civil Engineering Seminar (1; max: 3)

CE 694—Master of Engineering or Engineer Degree Report (1-9) Individual work culminating in a professional practice-oriented report suitable for the requirements of the Master of Engineering or Engineer degree. Three credits only are applicable toward the requirements of each degree.

CE 696—Special Problems in Civil Engineering (1-9; max: 9) Studies in areas not covered by other graduate courses.

CE 697—Supervised Research (1-5; max: 5)

CE 698—Supervised Teaching (1-5; max: 5)

CE 699—Master's Research (1-15)

CE 799—Doctoral Research (1-15)

CLASSICS
(College of Arts and Sciences)

Chairman: G. L. SCHMELING

GRADUATE FACULTY 1975-76

Professor: G. L. SCHMELING
Associate Professors: K. V. HARTIGAN; D. G. MILLER
Assistant Professor: E. RUTLEDGE

The department offers a program leading to the Master of Arts with a major in Latin, which may be combined with a minor in Greek, history, or philosophy.

LATIN

GRADUATE COURSES

LN 599—Special Study in Latin (4)
LN 600—Special Study in Latin Literature (5; max: 15) Sample topics: Horace. Juvenal, Roman comedy, Roman historians.
LN 620—History of the Latin Language (5)
LN 630—Individual Work (3-5; max: i5) Readings, conferences, and reports. Subjects in language, literature, and civilization for which there are no special course offerings.
LN 697—Supervised Research (1-5)
LN 698—Supervised Teaching (1-15)
LN 699—Master's Research (1-15)

CLINICAL PSYCHOLOGY
(Colleges of Health Related Professions & Arts and Sciences)

Chairman: L. D. COHEN
Graduate Coordinator: V. D. VAN DE RIET

GRADUATE FACULTY 1975-76

Professors: B. BARGER; L. D. COHEN; H C. DAVIS, JR.; M. HARROWER (*emeritus*); .R. K. MCGEE; M. E. MEYER; N. W. PERRY, JR.; P. SATZ; A. S. SCHUMACHER
Associate Professors: E. COHEN; J. R. GOLDMAN; K. M. HEILMAN; V. D. VAN DE REIT
Assistant Professors: M. K. GOLDSTEIN; R. H. HORNBERGER; M. H. MCCAULLEY; W. C. RASBURY; W. J. RICE; R. M. SWANSON

The Department of Clinical Psychology, in collaboration with the Department of Psychology and a number of University and community agencies, conducts a professional program at the doctoral level in clinical psychology. This program is accredited by the American Psychological Association. Instruction and program activities are also offered in the emerging speciality of community psychology.

Courses and individual instruction under the sponsorship of the Department of Clinical Psychology are listed below. Other courses are listed with the Department of Psychology. In both departments, courses listed under the same number are identical.

Admission to the clinical psychology program and the awarding of master's and doctor's degrees appropriate to clinical psychology are administered through the Department of Psychology.

Students registering for these courses must secure permission of the instructor if they are not enrolled in the clinical psychology program.

GRADUATE COURSES

CLP 651—Practicum in Professional Psychology I (5; max: 20) *Prereq: CLP 658, 665, admission to program in clinical psychology.* Supervised training in appropriate work settings relating theoretical understanding of personality to case handling and consultation through a variety of psychological assessment and treatment procedures. Designed as a sequence of 4 quarters paralleling academic course work. Each succeeding registration requires increasing levels of competence and responsibility.

CLP 652—Practicum in Professional Psychology II (5; max: 20) *Prereq: CLP 651.*

CLP 653—Introduction to Clinical Psychology (3-5; max: 10) Seminar on issues and concepts in clinical psychology. Concurrent with field observation and participation.

CLP 656—Personality Assessment I (4) Basic procedures in assessing personality structure and dynamics, including diagnostic interview, case history, objective and projective tests.

CLP 657—Personality Assessment II (4) *Prereq: PSY 681, 682, 683, 684, 685, 686.* Advanced procedures, including diagnostic interview, case history, objective tests.

CLP 658—Personality Assessment III (4) *Prereq: CLP 657.*

CLP 659—Personality Assessment IV (4) *Prereq: CLP 658.* Advanced techniques in assessment and prediction.

CLP 664—Development and Appraisal of Vocational Choice (4) *Prereq: PSY 547.* Theories of vocational development and methods of appraisal.

CLP 665—Personal Counseling (4) Current theories and practices; role of the counselor and nature of the relationship.

CLP 696—Individual Work (1-5; max: 15) Reading or research in areas of clinical psychology.

CLP 697—Supervised Research (1-5)

CLP 698—Supervised Teaching (1-5)

CLP 751—Seminar: Current Clinical Literature (4; max: 20) Reading on selected topics in clinical psychology.

CLP 752—Issues in Psychological Treatment (4; max: 12) *Prereq: CLP 651, 665.* Seminar and case discussion based on critical issues in psychological treatment.

CLP 756—Seminar: Theory and Research Methods in Community Psychology (4) Principles, including those related to community and program evaluation, consultation, mental health education, early identification, and intervention. Research methods and current literature.

CLP 757—Theory and Practice of Psychological Consultation (4) Concepts and practices, including multiple roles and intervention strategies utilized by consultants as agents of organizational and social system change. Field experience in actual consultation settings in the community.

CLP 758—Seminar: Advanced Research Methods in Community Psychology (4) *Prereq: CLP 756.* Analysis of a community through methods of epidemiological and demographic data collection. Design of research for program evaluation and planning.

CLP 760—Current Methods of Psychological Treatment (5; max: 20) Seminar on integration of theory and methods in treatment of individuals and groups. Emphasis on contemporary psychotherapies.

CLP 761—Advanced Current Methods of Psychological Treatment (5; max: 20) Emphasis on practical experience and techniques in applying current methods of psychological treatment.

CLP 762—Psychological Treatment Through Community Intervention (4; max: 8) Theory and strategy of psychological treatment methods developed specifically for utilization in the practice of community psychology. Required client contact in an appropriate community agency.

CLP 763—Psychological Treatment of Children's Behavior Disturbances (4) *Prereq: PSY 681, 682, 683, 684, 685, 686.* Theories and practices.

CLP 764—Psychological Treatment of Adolescent Behavior Problems (4) *Prereq: PSY 681, 682, 683, 684, 685, 686.* Behavior problems in adolescents and young adults examined with regard to developmental theories and in terms of psychopathology. Emphasis on theory, research, and clinical treatment.

CLP 765—Psychological Treatment with Groups (4) Current theories and practices in group therapy as a form of psychological treatment. Exploration of group therapy intervention techniques.

CLP 766—Psychodiagnostic Appraisal and Assessment (4) *Prereq: CLP 685.* Synthesis of theory and practice of psychodiagnosis. Utilization of personality test batteries and other data oriented toward individual case study and group assignment.

CLP 769—Internship (5) *Required of all doctoral students in clinical psychology. Prereq: CLP 651.* Students in applied specializations placed in approved intern settings. Designed as a sequence of 3 quarters which must include a minimum of 1500 work hours. Reading assignments and conferences.

COMMUNICATIVE DISORDERS
(Colleges of Health Related Professions & Arts and Sciences)

Chairman & Graduate Coordinator: K. R. Bzoch

GRADUATE FACULTY 1975-76

Professors: K. R. Bzoch; L. C. Hammer
Assistant Professors: W. H. Cutler; L. L. LaPointe; E. Scroggie, Jr.; D. E. Sellers; W. N. Williams

The faculty of communicative disorders is primarily responsible for inter-disciplinary clinical teaching and research for the Colleges of Health Related Professions, Medicine, Dentistry, and Nursing in aspects of speech pathology and audiology related to the professional degree programs of these colleges.

Courses and degrees in speech pathology and audiology are offered by the Department of Speech in the College of Arts and Sciences. The descriptive listings of courses in speech pathology and audiology may be found under Department of Speech in the undergraduate and graduate catalogs. The following courses are customarily taught by faculty of the College of Health Related Professions who also hold appointments in the Department of Speech.

GRADUATE COURSES

HRP 551—Laboratory Study of Emergent Language Behavior (4)
HRP 696—Individual Study in Health Related Professions (4)
SCH 655—Seminar in Speech Pathology and Audiology: Cerebral Palsy (2)
SCH 657—Seminar in Speech Pathology and Audiology: Cleft Palate (2)
SCH 660—Seminar in Audiology: Diagnostic Procedures for Peripheral Hearing Disorders (2)
SCH 661—Seminar in Audiology: Hearing Aids (2)
SCH 749—Practicum in Speech Pathology in a Medical-Dental Setting (3-10; max: 10)
SCH 769—Practicum in Audiology in a Medical Setting (3-10; max: 10)

COUNSELOR EDUCATION
(College of Education)

Chairman: P. J. Wittmer
Graduate Coordinator: L. C. Loesch

GRADUATE FACULTY 1975-76

Professors: P. W. Fitzgerald; T. Landsman; D. Lane; R. D. Myrick; H. C. Riker; B. L. Sharp; R. O. Stripling; P. J. Wittmer
Associate Professors: A. G. Cranney; T. Goodale; W. D. Kline; P. G. Schauble; E. L. Tolbert
Assistant Professors: E. S. Amatea; L. C. Loesch; R. McDavis; M. R. McMillan; G. D. Seiler; T. M. Skovholt

Programs leading to the degrees Master of Education (awarded only upon completion of Specialist in Education degree), Specialist in Education, Doctor of Education, and Doctor of Philosophy degrees are offered through this department. Areas of specialization include school counseling, guidance, and psychology for positions in elementary, middle and secondary schools; student personnel in higher education for positions in community colleges, vocational-technical schools, colleges, universities, and other post-secondary school settings; correctional, developmental, and agency counseling for positions in community, state or federal settings. Emphasis on career counseling is a part of the preparation in all areas listed above. In cooperation with the Department of Psychology, the Doctor of Philosophy degree in counseling psychology is offered, with coursework being taken through both departments.

Candidates for admission are urged to complete a course equivalent to STA 310 before entering the program. In any event, this requirement must be met during the first quarter of graduate work.

GRADUATE COURSES

EDC 610—Principles of Guidance: The Helping Relationship (4) *Prereq. or coreq: EDF 641 or PSY 549.*

EDC 611—Vocational Development (4) *Coreq: EDC 710.*

EDC 612—Modern Counseling and Personnel Work (4) *Not open to majors in counselor education.*

EDC 613—Personnel Testing (4) *Prereq: STA 310.*

EDC 614—Counseling Theory (5) *Prereq: EDC 610. Coreq: EDC 620.* Major theories and orientations for counseling and personnel work.

EDC 618—Organization and Administration of Guidance and Personnel Programs (4) *Prereq. or coreq: EDC 614.*

EDC 620—Laboratory in Counseling (1) *Coreq: EDC 614.*

EDC 621—Sensitivity Exploration Laboratory (1) *Prereq. or coreq: EDC 610.*

EDC 622—Counseling with Children (4) *Prereq: EDC 614, 620, EDF 640 or equivalent.*

EDC 623—Group Procedures in Guidance and Personnel Work (4) *Prereq: EDC 614, 620.*

EDC 624—Group Counseling (4) *Prereq. or coreq: EDC 623, 710.*

EDC 626—Play Counseling and Play Process with Children (4) *Prereq: EDC 622.*

EDC 627—Counseling Older Persons, Theories and Techniques (4) *Prereq: EDC 614, 620.*

EDC 628—Counseling with Drug Abuse Cases (4)

EDC 629—Counseling Ethnic Minorities (4) *Prereq: EDC 614, 620.*

EDC 640—Student Personnel Services in Higher Education (4) *Prereq: EDC 641, 610.*

EDC 641—The College Community and the Student (4) *Prereq. or coreq: EDC 610.*

EDC 658—Counseling in Community Settings (4) *Prereq: EDC 614, 620, 710. Coreq: current enrollment in a community agency practicum or internship.*

EDC 659—Seminar for Counseling in Specialized Settings (4; max: 8)

EDC 660—Problems in Personnel Work (3-6; max: 10) Seminar in special problems in personnel work arranged by the department.

EDC 690—Special Topics (2-5; max: 15) *Prereq: consent of department chairman.*

EDC 696—Individual Work (2-5; max: 15) *Prereq: consent of staff members and department chairman; approval of proposed project.*

EDC 697—Supervised Research (1-5)

EDC 698—Supervised Teaching (1-5)

EDC 701—Seminar in Career Development (4) Advanced course on career development.

EDC 710—Practicum in Counseling (5; max: 25) *Prereq: EDC 614, 620 and written application to the practicum coordinator at least six weeks in advance of registration.*

EDC 711—Practicum in Group Counseling (5; max: 15) *Prereq: EDC 624. 10 credits in EDC 710, and written application to the practicum coordinator at least six weeks in advance of registration.*

EDC 712—Practicum in Student Personnel Work (5; max: 15) *Prereq: 10 credits in EDC 710 and written application to the practicum coordinator at least six weeks in advance of registration.*

EDC 713—Laboratory in Career Development (5)
EDC 714—Practicum in Counseling Older Persons (5; max: 10) *Prereq: EDC 614, 620, 627, and written application to the practicum coordinator at least six weeks in advance of registration.* Supervised experiences in settings appropriate to the student's professional goals. Audiotaping and videotaping utilized.
EDC 715—Seminar in Personnel Work (5) *Admission limited to graduate students in the Advanced School who are near completion of course work for a degree.*
EDC 716—Internship in Personnel Work I (5) *Prereq: completion of all practicum required for the Ed.S., Ph.D., or Ed.D. degree and written application to the internship coordinator at least six weeks before registration.* Ordinarily involves a full-time, supervised assignment to the staff of an educational or allied institution.
EDC 717—Internship in Personnel Work II (5)
EDC 718—Internship in Personnel Work III (5)
EDC 721—Consultation Procedures (4) *Admission limited to students in the Advanced School. Prereq: two quarters' credit of EDC 710.*
EDC 722—Evaluative Research in Counseling, Guidance, and Personnel Work (5) *Prereq: EDC 613.*
EDC 723—Seminar in Counseling Research (4) *Admission limited to doctoral candidates in counselor education.* Identification of specific problems, formation of theoretical foundations, and determination of appropriate research procedures.
EDC 740—Seminar in Higher Education Student Personnel (1-2; max: 6) *Prereq: EDC 640, 641.*
EDC 799—Doctoral Research (1-15)

DIVISION OF CURRICULUM AND INSTRUCTION
(College of Education)

Director & Graduate Coordinator: A. J. LEWIS

GRADUATE FACULTY 1975-76

(See the Departments of General Teacher Education, Instructional Leadership and Support, and Subject Specialization Teacher Education.)

The Division of Curriculum and Instruction consists of three departments: General Teacher Education, Instructional Leadership and Support, and Subject Specialization Teacher Education. Through these departments the following degrees are granted: Master of Education (nonthesis), Master of Arts in Education (thesis), Specialist in Education, Doctor of Education, Doctor of Philosophy. Degrees are offered in the following specializations:

General Teacher Education: Early Childhood; Elementary; Middle School; Secondary.

Instructional Leadership and Support: Educational Media and Instructional Design; Post-Secondary; Reading; Supervision and Curriculum Development; Vocational, Technical and Adult Education.

Subject Specialization Teacher Education: Arts; Business; Foreign Language; Language Arts; Mathematics; Music; Science; Social Studies.

DAIRY SCIENCE
(College of Agriculture)

Chairman: H. H. VAN HORN, JR.
Graduate Coordinator: H. H. HEAD

GRADUATE FACULTY 1975-76

Professors: C. B. BROWNING; B. HARRIS, JR.; S. P. MARSHALL; L. E. MULL; H. H. VAN HORN, JR.; C. J. WILCOX; J. M. WING

Associate Professors: H. H. HEAD; K. L. SMITH; W. W. THATCHER
Assistant Professor: K. C. BACHMAN

The Dairy Science Department offers the Master of Science in agriculture and the Master of Agriculture degrees (specialization in dairy production and dairy foods and products) and, in collaboration with the Departments of Animal Science and Microbiology, the Doctor of Philosophy degree (specialization in animal physiology, food science, genetics and nutrition).

Areas of interest include quantitative genetics, ruminant nutrition, reproductive and lactational physiology, endocrinology, biochemistry, management, microbiology, milk chemistry, and the processing of milk and milk products.

A departmental prerequisite for admission to graduate study in dairy science is a strong undergraduate background in the physical or biological sciences. A prospective graduate student need not have majored in dairy science as an undergraduate.

The following courses in related areas will be acceptable for graduate credit as part of the candidate's major: AL 602—Quantitative Genetics; AL 607—Physiology of Reproduction; AL 651—Advanced Animal Nutrition; AL 655—Mineral Nutrition and Metabolism; AL 656—Ruminant Physiology and Metabolism; STA 605 Advanced Methods of Statistics.

GRADUATE COURSES

DY 601—Dairy Science Research Techniques (4) *Prereq: STA 605.* Methods employed in research in specialized dairy fields; genetics, nutrition, physiology, microbiology, chemistry, or dairy technology.

DY 603—Graduate Seminar in Dairy Science (1)

DY 604—Endocrinology (5) *Prereq: BCH 511, 512, VY 623.* The endocrine system including anatomy of the brain, neuroendocrine control, gland function, hormone structure and biosynthesis, and relationship to reproduction, lactation, growth, and metabolism.

DY 605—Advanced Dairy Cattle Management (4) Modern scientific basis for management of Florida dairy cattle, including nutrition, physiology, and genetics. Group feeding, reproduction, and management under semitropical conditions.

DY 606—Energy Metabolism (4) Relationship of anatomy, physiology, and biochemistry to transformation of feed energy to free energy; energy utilization at levels of the cells, the organism, and the organism in relation to its environment.

DY 607—Advanced Physiology of Lactation (3) *Prereq: VY 623.* Anatomy and development of the mammary gland; endocrine regulation of mammary growth and milk secretion; the physiology and biochemistry of milk secretion; factors affecting milk yield and composition.

DY 610—Advanced Dairy Technology (5) Theories associated with chemical and physical changes of milk constituents during processing and storage of dairy products. Special tests and quality measurements essential in identifying and measuring degrees of these changes.

DY 664—Topics in Genetics (2-4; max: 12) Same as AL 664, AY 664, BTY 664, PY 664, ZY 664.

DY 696—Problems in Dairy Science (1-5; max: 12) Research problems in dairy husbandry or dairy manufacturing.

DY 697—Supervised Research (1-5)

DY 698—Supervised Teaching (1-5)

DY 699—Master's Research (1-15)

ECONOMICS
(College of Business Administration)

Chairman: I. J. GOFFMAN
Graduate Coordinator: R. D. BLAIR

GRADUATE FACULTY 1975-76

Graduate Research Professor: G. S. MADDALA
Professors: F. D. ARDITTI; R. H. BLODGETT; R. W. BRADBURY *(emeritus)*; J. R. DAVIS; C. H. DONOVAN; W. J. FRAZER; I. J. GOFFMAN; E. L. JACKSON *(emeritus)*; M. Z. KAFOGLIS; P. E. KOEFOD; M. R. LANGHAM; R. F. LANZILLOTTI; M. M. LOCKHART; J. W. MILLIMAN; J. R. VERNON; W. WOODRUFF
Associate Professors: R. D. BLAIR; M. B. CONNOLLY; D. A. DENSLOW; C. W. FRISTOE; F. O. GODDARD; A. R. HOROWITZ; N. G. KEIG; R. B. ROBERTS; F. A. SLOAN; W. G. TYLER
Assistant Professors: S. V. BERG; H. A. BLACK; H. H. FISHKIND; P. FRIEDMAN; A. A. HEGGESTAD; R. LUSKY; Y. TODA

The Department of Economics offers the Master of Arts (thesis and nonthesis options) and Doctor of Philosophy degrees, with specializations in business economics and forecasting, economic history, economic theory and quantitative analysis, human resource economics (including health care economics), industrial organization and social control, international economics and development, labor economics, Latin American area studies, monetary and fiscal economics, transportation and public utilities, and urban studies. The Master of Business Administration degree is also offered with a concentration in economics.

Specific areas of specialization include econometrics and mathematical economics, economic thought, economic development, economic history, labor and human resource economics, health care economics, industrial organization and social control, international trade, monetary economics, public finance, and urban-regional economics.

M.A. Core: ES 561, BA 591 or equivalent, ES 601, 602, 605. **Ph.D. Core:** ES 561, 562, BA 591 or equivalent, ES 601, 602, 605, 635, 701, 702.

GRADUATE COURSES

ES 501—Macroeconomic Theory (5) *Designed for MBA candidates.* Macroeconomic theory with respect to determinants of national employment, aggregate income, economic fluctuations, inflation, and the price level.
ES 502—Microeconomic Theory (5) *Designed for MBA candidates.* Determination of prices in a market economy; their role in allocating consumer and producer goods, in distributing incomes, and in effecting efficient combinations of resources in production.
ES 513—Economic and Social History of Russia (3) *Prereq: HY 331 or 332 or equivalent.* Survey from Tripolye to the Soviet Union. Development of agriculture, industry, and trade and their institutional manifestations; growth theory and conditions of economic growth.
ES 521—Central Banking and Monetary Policy (5) *Prereq: ES 321 or equivalent.* Critical study of the relationship between the Federal Reserve System, the money market, governmental finance, business fluctuations, and the internal and external value of money in the United States.
ES 531—Central Government Finance (5) *Prereq: ES 201-202.* Economic effects of public expenditures; war finance; personal income and estate taxes; corporate income and profit taxes; excise taxes; debt problems.
ES 535—State and Local Finance (5) *Prereq: ES 201-202.* Allocation of government functions and resources; property taxation, sales taxes, highway finance, business taxation; debt financing and control. Emphasis on Florida problems.
ES 536—Government Budgeting and Financial Administration (3) *Prereq: permission of department.* Budget process at various levels. Analysis of the operating behavior of governments in managing expenditure, debt, budgets, records, and reports.
ES 543—Foreign Exchange and International Financial Institutions (3) *Prereq: permission of department.* Study of the theoretical and practical aspects of foreign exchange.

ES 545—Financial Institutions and Fiscal Policies of Selected Latin American Countries (3) Public finances, money systems, and banking policies of representative countries of Latin America.

ES 547—Contemporary Economic Problems in Sub-Sahara Africa (3) Current developments in production, trade, and transportation, with emphasis on development plans in various countries.

ES 549—Comparative Analysis of Economic Systems (4) *Prereq: permission of department.* Theoretical and empirical study of contemporary societal economic systems.

ES 561—Econometric Models and Methods I (5) Introduction to econometrics, including a survey of the classical econometric models as well as the scope and method of econometrics. Emphasis on techniques and their uses.

ES 562—Econometric Models and Methods II (5)

ES 572—Economics of the Labor Market (5) *Prereq: ES 372.* Intensive analysis of the economics of the labor market; theoretical and practical aspects of wage determination; impact of collective bargaining on wages, employment, and prices; economic effects of legislation dealing with the operating of the labor market.

ES 581—Urban Economics (5) *Prereq: ES 201-202 and permission of department.* Economic analysis of urbanization and regional interdependence. Applicability of location theory and other economic analysis. Criteria for determining public expenditures and allocating costs in urban areas.

ES 585—Economics of Human Resource Development (3) *Prereq: ES 302 or equivalent.* The capital concept applied to human resources. Effects of education, health, population policies, and discrimination on the stock of human capital. Role of human capital in economic development.

ES 601—Macroeconomic Theory (5) Classical, Keynesian, and post-Keynesian aggregate income and employment analysis. Determination of price level and interest rate.

ES 602—Price Theory (5) *Prereq: BA 591 or equivalent.* Analysis, criticism, and restatement of neoclassical price and production theories. Demand, supply, cost of production, and price determination under various conditions of the market.

ES 603—Social and Economic Accounting (5) Same as ATG 603. Social accounts and comparative economic accounting systems. Emphasis on national income accounting, the national balance sheet, sector accounts, and flow of funds analysis.

ES 604—Capital Theory, Production, and Growth (5) *Prereq: ES 601.* Capital theory from the Austrian school to current developments. Production, distribution, and economic growth within the framework of capital theory. Empirical and statistical studies of important variables.

ES 605—The Development of Economic Thought I (5) Economic thought chronologically from Greek to contemporary times—including the chief schools in Great Britain, the Continent, and the United States. Marx and the socialists, nonorthodox thinkers, and critics of the classical school are treated equally with the main tradition.

ES 606—The Development of Economic Thought II (5) The two chief approaches in economic thought. Emphasis on philosophical outlook and methodology. Analytical approach and role of mathematics; calculus surveyed and related to the neoclassical theory. Relates the institutional approach to history and other social sciences; cultural theory of capitalist evolution.

ES 608—Present-Day Schools of Economic Thought (5) Contemporary American and English economic thinking with particular reference to developments occurring between the two World Wars. The writings of Hansen, Mitchell, Clark, and Commons in the United States, and of Keynes, Cole, Robinson, and Hobson in England.

ES 610—The American Economy to 1860 (5) A functional approach. World economic conditions that led to the settlement of America; the colonial period; the period of economic transition; the westward movement and the rise of a national economy; economic causes of the Civil War.

ES 611—The American Economy Since 1860 (5) The closing of the economic frontier. The development of a capitalistic economy and the trend toward economic and financial imperialism. Economic problems of the wars of 1914-18 and 1939-45, and postwar economic adjustments, domestic and foreign.

ES 614—The United States in the World Economy (1783-1970) (5) Same as HY 614. The interrelatedness of the United States' economy with other lands.

ES 615—Economics of Business Decisions (5) *Designed primarily for MBA candidates. Prereq: ES 502, BA 610, 661, 664, 665, MKG 531, FI 590.* Synthesis and application of microeconomic theory and related business administration principles to managerial decision making through a problem-solving orientation.

ES 616—Macroeconomic Models and the Firm (5) *Designed primarily for MBA candidates. Prereq: ES 501, 502, BA 661, 665.* Synthesis and application of macroeconomic theory and economic forecasting models to managerial decision making, with emphasis on understanding effects on the firm of economic actions taken by foreign and domestic governments.

ES 617—Theory of Economic Development (5) Broad analytical, nonhistorical framework for examining economic underdevelopment and possible escape therefrom. Transition to secular economic growth and principles by which an underdeveloped country can achieve development objectives.

ES 618—Economic Development Seminar (5) Theory and problems of economic development pertinent to market and nonmarket economies. Emphasis on the relationship between economic system development and economic growth.

ES 621—Monetary Economics I (5) Evolutionary and contemporary aspects of monetary theory. Qualities and characteristics of money, rate of interest, effectiveness of monetary policy, flow of funds between various sectors of the economy and financial markets; relationships between saving, investment, employment, price-level changes, and capital formation.

ES 622—Monetary Economics II (5) Economic instabilities in capitalistic society. Emphasis on forces operating to bring about changes in the general level of prices, including prices of productive agents, employment, and income.

ES 625—Seminar in Monetary Economics (5) Current topics of research in the journals, studies by government agencies, and other published and unpublished materials.

ES 632—Public Revenue and Distribution (5) *Prereq: ES 602.* Classical and modern theories of taxation; tax incidence and allocative and distributive effects of income, excise, sales, death, and other forms of revenue including user charges, debt and intergovernmental grants.

ES 633—Stabilization Policy (5) Tools for promoting economic stabilization and growth. Opposing viewpoints as to proper scope and relation of monetary and fiscal controls.

ES 634—Public Expenditures and Collective Decisions (5) *Prereq: ES 601, 602.* Theories of public expenditure, including public goods theory and associated systems of collective decision making. Criteria for the development of optimal fiscal systems and decision processes.

ES 635—Welfare Economics (5) A survey of welfare economics. Technical welfare formulation related to organic concepts of welfare and to political action in a democracy. Possibilities of normative economics evaluated.

ES 641—Theory of International Trade (5) Historical and economic background of foreign trade; theory of international trade; fundamentals of international exchange; international commercial policies and international trade; exchange fluctuations and their control; international monetary institutions.

ES 644—International Economic Relations (5) Capital formation in the underdeveloped countries, economic integration, balance of payments and international monetary reform, the economic consequences of population pressures and economic relations between the advanced and other nations.

ES 645—The Economy of Spanish Latin America (5) Contemporary economic and commercial problems in Spanish Latin America; current developments in production, transportation, and trade of the various countries.

ES 646—The Economy of Brazil (5) Economic development and contemporary economic and commercial problems of Brazil; production, transportation, and trade from both a national and a regional point of view.

ES 647—Financial and Fiscal Institutions of Selected Sub-Saharan Countries (5) Public finances and the money and banking policies of representative countries of Africa.

ES 649—Economic Systems Seminar (5) Market and nonmarket types of economies, their characteristics and economics, and their different significance for systems of government and general social orders, legal and juridical systems, and for business and public policy.

ES 654—Economics of Regulated Industries (5) Types and techniques of public control. Economic analysis and evaluation of regulatory and promotional policies. Administrative and legal aspects of the regulatory process. Special problems in particular industries.

ES 655—Industrial Organization and Social Control (5) Economic and other characteristics of modern industrial structures. Relationships between industrial structure, business conduct, and economic performance. Measurement of concentration and evaluation of performance. Public policies toward monopoly, conspiracy, and competition.

ES 657—Problems in Social Control (5) Nature and causes of market failure. Problems in developing and applying concepts of public interest in a market economy. Institutional restraints to economic solutions; coordination of political and market decisions concerning the allocation of resources.

ES 660—Nonstochastic Models (5) Same as FRE 660. *Prereq: MS 324 or ISE 401.* General linear programming model and its basic theorems, integer and nonlinear programming. Spatial equilibrium, input-output, and game theory models.

ES 661—Econometric Methods I (5) Same as FRE 661. *Prereq: STA 441 and MS 324 or ISE 401.* Stochastic models. The general linear model and problems associated with its use in econometric research. Theory of the simultaneous equation approach, model construction, and estimation techniques.

ES 662—Econometric Methods II (4) Same as FRE 662. *Prereq: ES 661 or FRE 661.* Single equation topics, errors in variables, nonspherical disturbances, and lagged variables. Dynamic simultaneous equation models and miscellaneous topics in multivariate analysis. Spectral and cross-spectral analysis.

ES 663—Research Seminar in Econometrics (1-3) Same as FRE 663. *Prereq: ES 661.* Empirical measurement in applied economics. Empirical problem requiring the construction, estimation, and defense of a quantitative economic model.

ES 665—Mathematical Economics I (5) *Prereq: BA 591 or equivalent.* Mathematical approach to microeconomic theory, including theory of the firm, theory of consumer behavior, and selected topics in market conditions.

ES 666—Mathematical Economics II (5) *Prereq: ES 665.* Probability and simulation models of economic behavior; mathematical models from monetary economics.

ES 669—Problems in Statistics and Business Forecasting (5) Problems of linear operation regression analysis which may be used by managers as a basis for decision making. It will add to the student's knowledge of sophisticated statistical methods to aid in the analysis of current business problems.

ES 672—Organized Labor in the United States (5) Problems connected with the relationship of organized labor with itself, management, government, and the public; labor policy and public welfare.

ES 673—Labor Markets, Manpower, and Public Policy (5) *Prereq: ES 672.* Labor markets and the role of unions as collective decision organizations; theories of collective choice. Unemployment as an economic and social problem. Analysis of various public and private labor-oriented programs, including social insurance, manpower training, poverty and others.

ES 674—Labor Economics (5) Wage determination and the role of wages in the economy; the effects of collective bargaining on wages, prices, and employment.

ES 675—Health Care Economics I (5) *Prereq: ES 602.* Fundamental economic relations governing the production, consumption and financing of health care services. Characteristics of demand and production relationships; response of supply, "shortages," and possibilities for factor substitution; insurance and organizational alternatives.

ES 676—Health Care Economics II (5) *Prereq: ES 602.* Theoretical and empirical evaluations relating to the economic performance of the health care sector. Optimal price and output policy including distributional considerations; cost-benefit analysis, public production, research and centralized vs. decentralized control.

ES 680—Regional Economics (5) Same as FRE 680. *Prereq: ES 401 and 402 or equivalent.* Definition of regions and elements of regional economic analysis. Location theory, regional interdependence and spatial equilibrium. Regional economic change, including economic accounts and other measures of activity; cycles, growth, and planned development.

ES 681—Urban Economics (5) *Prereq: ES 401 and 402 or equivalent.* Salient aspects of urban phenomena including theoretical explanations of the process of urbanization; city structures and models. Urban problems including poverty and race, housing, transportation and environment. The urban public economy, and urban public services.

ES 692—Neoclassical Economics (5) Analysis, criticism and restatement of neoclassical theories concerning distribution of income. Rent, interest, wages, profits, personal distribution.

supplementary distribution and noncapitalistic distribution. The writings of Marshall, Hicks, Cassel, Boulding, Pigou, Fisher, Douglas, Knight, Stigler, and Schumpeter provide background for the discussion.

ES 696—Individual Work in Economics (1-5; max: 10) Reading and/or research in the several areas of economics.

ES 697—Supervised Research (1-5)

ES 698—Supervised Teaching (1-5)

ES 699—Master's Research (1-15)

ES 701—Advanced Macroeconomic Theory (5) *Prereq: ES 601.* Advanced topics in macroeconomic theory, including wealth effects and money illusion, the homogeneity postulate and exceptions to classical doctrine. The role of expectations and stability analysis.

ES 702—Advanced Microeconomic Theory (5) *Prereq: ES 602.* Advanced topics in microeconomic theory. Axiomatic development of utility functions, stochastic and nonstochastic utility models. Static and dynamic production functions and investment criteria. General equilibrium and stability conditions.

ES 730—Advanced Economics Seminar (1-5; max: 10) *For advanced graduate students in economics. Prereq: student must have completed graduate core program and have preliminary dissertation topic.* Special topics.

ES 799—Doctoral Research (1-15)

EDUCATIONAL ADMINISTRATION & SUPERVISION
(College of Education)

Chairman & Graduate Coordinator: J. L. WATTENBARGER

GRADUATE FACULTY 1975-76

Professors: S. K. ALEXANDER, JR.; T. W. COLE, SR.; K. F. JORDAN; R. B. KIMBROUGH; R. B. MYERS; M. Y. NUNNERY; E. A. TODD; J. L. WATTENBARGER
Associate Professors: P. A. CLARK; C. A. SANDEEN
Assistant Professors: H. FRANKLIN; J. M. NICKENS

Programs leading to the degrees Master of Arts in Education, Master of Education, Specialist in Education, Doctor of Education, and Doctor of Philosophy are offered through the Department of Educational Administration and Supervision.

Areas of specialization include general administration, with emphasis on elementary and secondary administration, higher education administration with specialization in community college leadership as well as university leadership, vocational-technical administration, and administrative theory. A special program in the administration of allied health programs in higher education is also available.

The Institute of Higher Education provides advanced graduate students many opportunities for research and study in all areas of post high school education. Similarly, the Center for Community Education, the Center for Educational Facilities, and the Institute for Educational Finance provide opportunities with special emphasis in those areas.

A candidate for admission to the department will be judged not only on the basis of quantitative criteria (listed elsewhere in this *Catalog*) but also in relation to prior experience, especially as it relates to future career goals.

GRADUATE COURSES

EDA 600—Educational Organization and Administration (4) Foundation course in school administration. Basic concepts, principles, and practices in local, state, and federal organization and administration.

EDA 601—Organization and Administration of Elementary Schools (4) Organization and administration of elementary schools in terms of purposes and functions. Emphasis on skills and competencies desirable for leadership at a school center.

EDA 602—Organization and Administration of Secondary Schools (4) Duties and responsibilities of the school principal; competencies necessary for leadership in organizing, administering, supervising, and evaluating the secondary school center.

EDA 603—Public School Finance (4) State, local, and federal financing of education; the foundation program of school financing; principles and criteria of taxation for education; education and the national economy.

EDA 604—Public School Law (4) Legal status of schools in the United States; emphasis on Florida conditions, school laws, constitutional provisions, judicial decisions, Attorney General's rulings, and regulations of the State Board of Education.

EDA 605—Business Affairs in Education (4) Role and function of the business office and a review of current research and administrative procedures related to purchasing and supply management, school food service, transportation, insurance, indebtedness, and office management.

EDA 606—Supervised Practice in School Administration (4; max: 8) *Only advanced graduate students are permitted to enroll.* Students are given an opportunity to perform administrative duties under supervision. S/U.

EDA 607—Administration of School Personnel (4) Problems of the professional school staff and administration of staff personnel in public schools.

EDA 608—Educational Budgeting and Accounting Systems (4) Contemporary theory and research in fiscal budgeting and accounting processes in colleges and universities, elementary and secondary schools, with simulated practical application through case studies and problems dealing with annual budgets and cost effectiveness.

EDA 609—Problems in School Administration and Supervision (4; max: 8) In-service training course through regularly scheduled on-campus work conferences open only to superintendents and supervisors; or a problems course, offered through extension or on campus, for superintendents, supervisors, principals, junior college administrators, and trainees for such positions.

EDA 610—Organization and Administration of Adult Education (4) Overview of adult education in the United States; the role of administration in adult education; the job of the local director of adult education; Florida law and regulations relating to adult education in the public schools.

EDA 615—Principles of Community Education Administration (4) The developing concept and application of basic principles to administration of educational institutions and community agencies.

EDA 616—Theories and Practices of Community Education Administration (4) *Prereq: EDA 615.* Contemporary theories and practices, with emphasis on interagency coordination and cooperation, programming for lifelong learning and community member involvement in educational decision making.

EDA 617—Labor Relations in Public Education (4) Introduction to problems and issues. Emphasis on various aspects of employee, union, and management relationships in the public sector, including elementary, secondary, and higher education.

EDA 620—Administration in Special Education (4) *Prereq: EDH 300 or 600.* Local, state, and federal organization and administration, with emphasis on the administration of services to handicapped children.

EDA 631—Educational Leadership I (4) Basic course on the nature of educational leadership. Emphasis on the role of official leadership in group development, improving group structure, and program improvements.

EDA 632—Educational Leadership II (4) Contemporary research on diffusion of innovations, planning of change, organizational theory and political power in policy decision making. Role of administrators and instructional leaders in establishing educational policies.

EDA 640—Utilization of Computers in Educational Administration (4) *Prereq: EDA 600.* Man-machine systems in educational administration. Electronic data processing and the school administrator, educational information systems, and other computer applications.

EDA 641—Operations Research in Educational Administration (4) *Prereq: EDA 640 and statistics course.* Application of select quantitative systems techniques from management and operations research to educational administration: utilities, queuing theory, graph theory, decision theory, game theory, simulation, and modeling.

EDA 690—Special Topics (2-5; max: 15)

EDA 696—Individual Work (2-5; max: 15) For advanced students who wish to undertake an individual research project directly related to administration and supervision.

EDA 697—Supervised Research (1-5)

EDA 698—Supervised Teaching (1-5)

EDA 700—Educational Planning (4) Cooperative planning of educational programs. Skills and methodologies associated with developing annual and long-range comprehensive plans for meeting educational needs of school districts, colleges, and universities.

EDA 702—Planning Educational Facilities (4) School plant survey methods and planning of educational facilities. Field experience available.

EDA 703—The Financing of Higher Education (4) Financing of higher education, junior college through university. Economics of higher education, application of the planning, programming, budgeting system to higher education. Evaluation of various models of financing education from federal, state, and private sources, and student fees.

EDA 704—Higher Education Administration (4) Educational policies, functions, and practices.

EDA 705—The Law and Higher Education (4) Legal framework of colleges and universities; relationship between private and public institutions; federal and state statutory and constitutional provisions bearing on higher education; legal implications involved in administrative relationships with faculty and students.

EDA 706—Seminar: Theories of Educational Administration (4) *Prereq: year of graduate study.* Basic theories of the organization and administration of public education; historical origins of theories; assumptions underlying current concepts of administration and theory development.

EDA 707—Research Design in Educational Administration (3) *Open only to students in the Advanced School. Prereq: EDF 760.* Individually identified problems in administration conceptualized in theoretical terms and appropriate research procedures determined.

EDA 710—Coordination of State Systems of Higher Education (4) Organizational structure and the basic principles of coordination and control of higher education at state and regional levels. Principles of leadership expressed through controlling and coordinating boards; role of boards and staff in planning development and operation; state, regional, and national accrediting agencies.

EDA 720—Seminar in Administration and Supervision of Special Education (4; max: 12) *Prereq: EDA 600, 620.* Current problems in the provision of special education services in local, state, and federal programs.

EDA 721—Practicum: Special Education Administration (4-12; max: 12) *Prereq: EDA 720, 8 credits of special education, 8 credits of educational administration and written request to enroll six weeks prior to registration.*

EDA 730—Practicum in Supervision and Administration (3; max: 15) A seminar and an internship in administration and supervision. S/U.

EDA 799—Doctoral Research (1-15)

ELECTRICAL ENGINEERING
(College of Engineering)

Chairman & Graduate Coordinator: E. R. CHENETTE

GRADUATE FACULTY 1975-76

Graduate Research Professors: A. E. S. GREEN; R. E. KALMAN; J. T. TOU; A. VAN DER ZIEL

Professors: T. L. BAILEY III; T. E. BULLOCK; W. H. CHEN (*Dean, College of Engineering*); E. R. CHENETTE; D. G. CHILDERS; S. W. DIRECTOR; D. B. DOVE; A. E. DURLING; O. I. ELGERD; G. E. HAYNAM; R. C. JOHNSON, JR.; D. P. KENNEDY; F. A. LINDHOLM; A. H. NEVIS; J. R. O'MALLEY; R. PEPINSKY; V. M. POPOV; R. A. RAMEY, JR.; C. V. SHAFFER; J. R. SMITH; A. D. SUTHERLAND; D. C. TEAS; M. A. UMAN; A. H. WING; R. YII

Associate Professors: R. L. BAILEY; W. H. BOYKIN, JR.; L. W. COUCH II; K. E. DOMINIAK; K. L. DOTY; M. H. LATOUR; S. S. LI; A. PAIGE; S. Y. W. SU; R. L. SULLIVAN; G. D. WARD; J. K. WATSON; M. ZAHN
Assistant Professor: M. E. WARREN

The Department of Electrical Engineering offers the Master of Engineering, Master of Science, Engineer, and Doctor of Philosophy degrees. The department offers graduate study and research in biomedical engineering, computer and information science, communication science, system science, electronics, and electric energy science. The department also has interdisciplinary programs with medicine, sciences, and other engineering disciplines.

Study for the Ph.D. degree in electrical engineering at the University of Florida by qualified master's degree recipients at Florida Technological University is facilitated by a cooperative arrangement in which appropriate members of the faculty of FTU are members of the graduate faculty of the University of Florida.

Graduate students in the Department of Electrical Engineering have bachelor's degrees from many areas—electrical engineering, other engineering disciplines, mathematics, physics, chemistry, and other technical fields.

A thesis is required for all master's degree candidates. The minimum course work required for the master's degree is 49 credits, including no less than 40 credits of regular course work and up to 9 credits of the research course numbered EE 699.

The Ph.D. entrance exam will be given only once each year during the winter quarter and will consist of both a written and oral examination which all prospective Ph.D. students must take at the earliest opportunity.

The following course listing indicates the major areas of faculty interest. Special topics courses, EE 592, 596, 692, and 696, cover a variety of subjects for which there are no present courses.

GRADUATE COURSES

EE 514—Automatic Speech Processing (3) *Prereq: EE 333.* Various models of speech production and perception. Operation of mechanical speech synthesizers and a discussion of automatic speech recognition. Introduction to various measuring devices commonly used in speech laboratories.

EE 516—Cybernetics (5) *Not for electrical engineering majors.* Topics in communication, control, information processing and intelligence in man and machines, man-machine and machine-machine interactions.

EE 526—Applied Electronics (4) Application of electronic circuits to system design. Laboratory.

EE 533—Computational Techniques for Circuit Analysis (4) *Prereq: EE 333 or consent of instructor.* Numerical techniques as applied to simulation of circuit behavior.

EE 541—Computer Communications (3) *Prereq: EE 441.* Design of data communication networks; modems, terminals, error control, multiplexing, message switching, and data concentration.

EE 549—Digital Filtering (5) Analysis and design of digital filters for discrete signal processing; spectral analysis; fast Fourier transform.

EE 558—Applications of Magnetism (4) Properties and processes in magnetic materials introduced through examples such as inductors, pulse transformers, memory elements, microwave components, domain devices.

EE 562—Principles of Computer Interfacing (3) *Prereq: EE 462.* Functional, logical, and timing requirements in the control of peripheral equipment. Peripheral-processor communication and protocol.

EE 564—Hardware-Software Interactions: Time Sharing System (4) *Prereq: EE 463.* Input-output control and interface, resource sharing and allocation. Software (hardware) extensions of hardware (software) functions. Digital system evaluation.

EE 565—Principles of Information Science (3) *Prereq: EE 463.* Languages and models for structures of information, search and matching techniques, equipment technology, retrieval systems, structure and file evaluation.

EE 566—Hardware-Software Interactions: Nonnumeric Processing (3) *Prereq: EE 565 or consent of instructor.* Information representations; content and context search methods; associative memories; retrieval language mapping; parallel processing; hardware and software garbage collection.

EE 567—Modular Design of Digital Processors (3) *Prereq: EE 461.* Application of a modular design language to designing digital systems. Hardware constraints. Behavior and use of medium and large-scale integrated circuits.

EE 568—Pictorial Information Processing Principles (3) Pictorial data representation; feature encoding; special filtering; image enhancement; symbol manipulation; pictorial data storage; retrieval and display; interactive graphics; pattern classification.

EE 570—State Variable Methods in Linear Systems (4) *Prereq: EE 333.* Linear algebra and state variable methods for design and analysis of discrete and continuous linear systems.

EE 571—Analysis of Non-linear Systems (3) *Prereq: EE 570.* Analysis of nonlinear systems by Liapunov theory, perturbation, and describing functions.

EE 592—Special Topics in Electrical Engineering II (1-4; max: 12)

EE 596—Individual Work (1-6; max: 12) *Prereq: consent of department chairman.* Selected problems or projects.

EE 600—Elements of Linear Systems (3) *Prereq: MS 503 or consent of instructor.* Properties of systems. Convolution and transform theory for continuous and discrete-time signals in linear systems.

EE 601—Advanced System Theory I (4) Matrix theory required for the study of complex linearized dynamic systems and electric networks; stability theory; illustrative examples.

EE 602—Advanced System Theory II (3) *Prereq: EE 601.* Further application of matrix methods to dynamic systems and electric networks; extension to discrete, nonlinear, and nonstationary systems. Markov processes.

EE 611—Physical Optics for Engineers (3) Physical optics, spread and transfer functions, effects of spectrum limitations, noise, lens design specifications, optimization of lens systems.

EE 613—Electro-Optics I (3) *Prereq: undergraduate courses in fields and waves and in modern physics.* Gaseous, liquid, solid, and semiconductor lasers.

EE 614—Electro-Optics II (3) *Prereq: undergraduate courses in fields and waves and in modern physics.* Crystal optics; nonlinear optics, second harmonic generation and parametric oscillation; integrated optics; new devices.

EE 615—Electrical Activity of the Nervous System (3) Same as PS 615. *Prereq: MS 305; EE 333 or PS 415. Coreq: ME 360 or PS 420.* Analysis of the electrical signals of peripheral nerve and brain, with application of systems engineering techniques.

EE 616—Biophysical Models of Nerve Impulse Propagation (3) Same as PS 616. *Prereq: EE 615.* Analysis of chemical, electrical, hydrodynamic, and solid-state models of axonic and synaptic nerve transmission.

EE 617—Semiconductor Physical Electronics I (3) *Prereq: EE 325 or consent of instructor.* Crystal structures in semiconductors; imperfections; diffusion processes; lattice vibration spectra. Equilibrium properties of electrons and holes. One-electron energy band model.

EE 618—Semiconductor Physical Electronics II (3) *Prereq: EE 617.* Electronic transport phenomena. Boltzmann's equation and the relaxation-time approximation. Transport coefficients in semiconductors. Scattering mechanisms. Recombination-generation and trapping processes.

EE 619—Semiconductor Physical Electronics III (3) *Prereq: EE 618.* Excess carrier phenomena. Photoelectric effects in semiconductors. Optoelectronic devices. Metal-semiconductor devices. Metal-insulator-semiconductor (MIS) diodes. Thin-film devices.

EE 620—Semiconductor Junction Devices I (3) *Prereq: EE 427 or consent of instructor.* Semiconductor materials properties, equilibrium and nonequilibrium processes. Semiconductor junctions.

EE 621—Semiconductor Junction Devices II (3) *Prereq: EE 620.* Fundamental principles of bipolar transistors, junction field effect transistors, and metal oxide semiconductor field effect transistors.

EE 622—Electronic Circuits I (3) *Prereq: required undergraduate electronics sequence.* Linear circuit models of transistors; properties of linear active circuits, gain bandwidth limitations and optimum performance of amplifiers; theory and design of feedback amplifiers; applications to transistor and integrated circuits.

EE 623—Electronic Circuits II (3) *Prereq: EE 622.* Analysis and design of frequency-selective amplifiers; active RC circuits; harmonic and relaxation oscillators; applications to integrated circuits.

EE 624—Electronic Circuits III (3) *Prereq: EE 623.* Piecewise linear analysis techniques in the determination of optimum or limiting performance of transistor switching, sweep, and discrete-state circuits, large signal transistor circuit models; applications to discrete and integrated digital circuits.

EE 625—Network Representation of Solid-State Devices I (3) *Prereq: EE 325 or consent of instructor.* Relationship between equivalent-circuit models and the physical mechanisms governing device operation. Special attention given to approximations and methods of reasoning. Emphasis on large-signal, dynamic models for MOS transistors and related devices.

EE 626—Network Representation of Solid-State Devices II (3) Same as EE 625 except emphasis on bipolar transistors and related devices. EE 625 not a prerequisite.

EE 628—Fluctuation Phenomena I (3) *Prereq: EE 640.* Theory with applications to electrical engineering. Sources of noise in devices; influence upon performance of circuits and systems; limitation of detectors and sensitive measuring instruments.

EE 629—Fluctuation Phenomena II (3) *Prereq: EE 628.*

EE 630—Advanced Circuit Analysis (3) Advanced techniques of circuit analysis.

EE 631—Generalized Network Theory (3) *Prereq: EE 630 or 634.* Networks which are not necessarily linear, lumped, passive and reciprocal. The gyrator. Extensions of classical methods to more general networks.

EE 633—Computer-Aided Circuit Design (4) *Prereq: EE 533.* Design objectives, performance functions, optimization techniques as applied to circuit design; other state-of-the-art topics.

EE 640—Noise in Linear Systems (5) Passage of electrical noise and signals through linear systems. Statistical representation of random signals, electrical noise, and spectra.

EE 641—Theory of Communication I (5) *Prereq: EE 640.* Filtering, modulation, and demodulation of signals corrupted by noise; passage of electrical noise and signals through nonlinear filters and systems.

EE 642—Theory of Communication II (5) *Prereq: EE 641.* Optimum receiver principles; analysis of digital and analog communication systems in the presence of noise; modeling of communication channels.

EE 644—Signal Representation and Design (5) *Prereq: EE 443 or equivalent.* Representation of signals and noise by sampling, Fourier and other transform methods, complex variable techniques. Criteria of optimality in communication and ranging systems. Analytical signal theory; digital signal design.

EE 645—Statistical Decision Theory (5) *Prereq: EE 640.* Hypothesis testing of signals in the presence of noise by Bayes, Neyman-Pearson, minimax criteria; estimation of signal parameters.

EE 646—Space Communications (5) *Prereq: EE 641.* Telemetering systems, space communication links, satellite communications systems, space tracking, and navigation systems.

EE 649—Digital Signal Processing (5) *Prereq: EE 640.* Measurement and analysis of signals and noise. Digital filtering and spectral analysis; fast Fourier transform.

EE 651—Electromagnetic Field Theory and Applications I (3) *Prereq: undergraduate course in fields and waves.* Advanced electrostatics, magnetostatics, and time-varying electromagnetic fields.

EE 652—Electromagnetic Field Theory and Applications II (3) *Prereq: EE 651.* Wave propagation, waveguides, radiation, antennas.

EE 653—Wave Propagation in Anisotropic Media (3) *Prereq: EE 652.* Electrical properties of solids, liquids, and gases. Propagation of fields in anisotropic media.

EE 660—Foundations of Information Science (3) *Prereq: EE 461, 562.* Problems in information science; regular expressions; push-down automata; context-free languages; theory of algorithms; symbol manipulation; stochastic automata; associative memories; information storage and retrieval.

EE 661—Analysis and Synthesis of Switching Circuits (3) *Prereq: EE 461, 660.* Boolean algebra; switching circuits; topics in analysis and design of combinational and sequential digital circuits. Applications to cellular systems design.

EE 662—Computing Machine Theory (3) *Prereq: EE 562. Coreq: EE 660 or consent of instructor.* Evaluation, study and comparison of computer systems. Development of formal and informal models of computer architectures. Topics of current interest in computer organization.

EE 663—Applications of Automata Theory (3) *Prereq: EE 461, 660.* Introduction to regular expressions, push-down automata, context-free languages, formal grammars, Turing machines and their applications to computer organization and compiler design.

EE 664—Pattern Recognition Theory and Applications I (3) Decision functions; optimum decision criteria; distance functions; training algorithms; cluster seeking; unsupervised learning; piecewise linear machine; applications. H—changed after completion of EE 669.

EE 667—Microprocessors: Architectures and Applications, Laboratory (4) *Prereq: EE 462, 463.*

EE 669—Pattern Recognition Theory and Applications II (3) *Prereq: EE 664.* Feature extraction; data reduction; entropy functions; potential functions; classification algorithms; syntactic pattern description; recognition grammars; applications.

EE 670—Modern Control Theory I (3) *Prereq: EE 570, 601.* Optimization of systems using calculus of variations, dynamic programming, and the maximum principle. Extensive study of the linear plant quadratic loss case.

EE 671—Modern Control Theory II (3) *Prereq: EE 670 or CHE 616, and EE 640.* Optimization in the presence of noise. State observers, dynamic compensators, and Kalman-Bucy filters.

EE 672—Modern Control Theory III (3) *Prereq: EE 671.* Advanced and specialized topics of current interest in modern systems theory, with emphasis on computational methods.

EE 679—Nonlinear Control Systems (3) Same as ESM 679. *Prereq: EE 570.* Stability of nonlinear systems using Liapunov's second method, the Popov and other frequency domain criteria.

EE 680—Advanced Electric Energy Systems I (3) *Prereq: EE 485 or consent of instructor.* Energy systems in steady state; advanced analysis methods.

EE 681—Advanced Electric Energy Systems II (3) *Prereq: EE 680.* Optimum control strategies for energy systems under normal operating conditions.

EE 682—Advanced Electric Energy Systems III (3) *Prereq: EE 681.* Energy systems under faulted conditions; security considerations.

EE 685—Advanced Electromechanical Energy Conversion (3) Electromechanical energy conversion processes from a field theory point of view. Dynamics of media in the presence of electric and magnetic fields.

EE 692—Special Topics in Electrical Engineering (1-6; max: 18, including EE 696)

EE 695—Graduate Seminar (1; max: 4) Discussion of topics in fields of graduate study and research. S/U.

EE 696—Individual Work (1-6; max: 12) *Prereq: consent of department chairman.* Selected problems or projects.

EE 697—Supervised Research (1-5)

EE 698—Supervised Teaching (1-5)

EE 699—Master's Research (1-15)

EE 764—Topics in Information Storage and Retrieval (3) *Prereq: EE 565.* Data manipulation and description languages, information network, system evaluation, question-answering and man-machine communication.

EE 799—Doctoral Research (1-15)

ENGINEERING—GENERAL
(College of Engineering)
GRADUATE COURSES

EGC 541—Intermediate Fluid Dynamics (3) *Prereq: MS 305 and consent of instructor.* Vector calculus applied to the basic equations of fluid dynamics and transport phenomena.

EGC 601—Theory of Fluid Flow I (4) *Prereq: EGC 541.* Concepts of velocity potential, differential equations of motions, continuity, and state. Practical solutions of two- and three-dimensional flow.

EGC 602—Theory of Fluid Flow II (3) *Prereq: EGC 601.* Concepts of velocity potential, stream function, and irrotational flow. Application of conformal transformations to two-dimensional flow.

EGC 603—Theory of Fluid Flow III (4) *Prereq: EGC 601.* Differential equations of constant density viscous fluid flow and their exact and approximate solutions. Laminar and turbulent boundary layers. Magnetohydrodynamic effects.

EGC 604—Boundary Layer Theory (4) *Prereq: EGC 603.* Variable density laminar and turbulent boundary layers. Transformations to constant density flow. Integral methods. Mass transfer, diffusion, chemical reactions, extraneous effects.

EGC 605—Theories of Turbulent Flows (4) *Prereq: EGC 601, EE 640.* Mathematical theory of the turbulent motion of fluids. History and introduction to contemporary research in the statistical theory of turbulence.

EGC 621—Surface Hydrology (4) *Prereq: MS 305, ESM 311.* Mechanics of the occurrence and distribution of water by natural processes including the global energy balance, geophysical fluid motions, precipitation, run-off, infiltration, and water losses. Catchment characteristics and hydrograph analysis.

EGC 622—Operational Hydrology I (4) *Prereq: EGC 621.* Frequency analysis of hydrologic events. Hydrologic probability distributions. Analysis and synthesis of hydrologic data. Linear and nonlinear regression. Multivariate analysis of hydrologic signals.

EGC 623—Operational Hydrology II (4) *Prereq: EGC 622.* Correlation and spectral analysis of hydrologic signals and systems. Application of linear systems theory to components of hydrologic cycle and total rainfall-runoff process. Criteria for hydrologic instruments and networks.

EGC 633—Principles of Engineering Analysis I (3) *Prereq: MS 501.* Solution of ordinary differential equations with variable coefficients. Method of Frobenius, classification of singularities, integral representations of solutions. Treatment of classical equations of Bessel, Legendre, Hermite and Mathieu. Asymptotic solutions using the WBK method and saddle-point technique.

EGC 634—Principles of Engineering Analysis II (3) *Prereq: MS 501.* General methods for solving partial differential equations of first and second order. Classification into hyperbolic, elliptic, and parabolic types. Reduction to canonical form. Equations of wave propagation, heat conduction, and Laplace. Treatment of initial and boundary value problems.

EGC 635—Principles of Engineering Analysis III (3) *Prereq: EGC 634.* Dirichlet and Neumann boundary value problems. Green's function for Laplace's equation, conformal mapping spherical harmonics. Solution of the Helmholtz, Poisson, and biharmonic equations. Application to inviscid hydrodynamics, optical diffraction and gravitational potential theory.

EGC 636—Principles of Engineering Analysis IV (3) *Prereq: MS 501.* Solution of Volterra and Fredholm integral equations of the first and second kind. Inversion of self-adjoint operators via Green's function, properties of symmetric kernels, Hilbert-Schmidt theory and the bilinear formula. Treatment of the singular integral equations of Abel and Carleman. Iteration and approximation techniques.

EGC 637—Principles of Engineering Analysis V (3) *Prereq: EGC 633.* Solution techniques for nonlinear differential and integral equations. Equations of Riccati, van der Pol, and Hammerstein. Elliptic functions and Painlevé transcendents. Phase plane, singular points, limit cycles and stability of autonomous systems. Similarity transforms and singular perturbation theory applied to nonlinear partial differential equations arising in hydrodynamics.

EGC 640—Theoretical Acoustics (3) *Prereq: basic course in vibrations and some background with partial differential equations.* Fundamentals of wave phenomena in vibrating solid and fluid media. Analytical methods of attacking acoustical problems.

EGC 671—Introduction to Plasmas (3) *Prereq: PS 300, MS 505.* Nomenclature, materials, and plasma devices, fundamentals of plasma kinetic theory, low and high pressure discharges, technical applications.

EGC 672—Plasma Theory (4) *Prereq: EGC 671.* Microscopic and macroscopic foundations of plasma theory. Individual motion of charged particles and macroscopic plasma motion in an electromagnetic field. Nonequilibrium states and relaxation processes. Waves and in-stabilities.

EGC 675—Plasma Laboratory (4) Laboratory practice in use of equipment and determination of basic parameters of plasmas.

EGC 677—Gas Lasers and Their Engineering Applications (4) *Prereq: PS 340, NES 470.* Introduction to theory of gas lasers. Laser design; extensive coverage of applications of gas lasers.

ENGINEERING SCIENCES
(College of Engineering)

Chairman: K. T. MILLSAPS
Graduate Coordinator: B. M. LEADON

GRADUATE FACULTY 1975-76

Graduate Research Professors: N. CRISTESCU; A. E. S. GREEN; R. E. KALMAN
Professors: R. C. ANDERSON; W. H. BOYKIN, JR.; M. H. CLARKSON; I. K. EBCIOGLU;
  M. A. EISENBERG; C. S. HARTLEY; J. W. HOOVER; B. M. LEADON; E. R. LINDGREN;
  L. E. MALVERN; K. T. MILLSAPS; G. E. NEVILL, JR.; E. PARTHENIADES; J. A.
  PURPURA; O. H. SHEMDIN; R. L. SIERAKOWSKI; E. K. WALSH; D. T. WILLIAMS
Associate Professors: T.-Y. CHIU; C. G. EDSON; R. L. FEARN; G. W. HEMP; D.
  R. KEEFER; U. H. KURZWEG; S. Y. LU
Associate Engineers: J. E. MILTON; C. A. ROSS
Assistant Professors: D. M. SHEPPARD; U. A. UNLUATA; Y.-H. WANG

The Department of Engineering Sciences offers the Master of Engineering, Master of Science, and Engineer degrees in aerospace engineering, in coastal and oceanographic engineering, in engineering mechanics, and in engineering sciences. The Doctor of Philosophy degree is offered in aerospace engineering and in engineering mechanics, with specialized tracks in the latter discipline in coastal and oceanographic engineering, in engineering analysis and applied mathematics and in theoretical and applied mechanics.

Areas of specialization include aerodynamics, applied mathematics, applied optics, atmospheric science, biomechanics, coastal hydraulics and water quality control, coastal hydrodynamics and oceanography, coastal structures, control theory, creative design, fluid mechanics, solid mechanics, and structural mechanics.

AEROSPACE ENGINEERING

The following *Engineering Common Courses* are available for graduate major credit: EGC 541—Intermediate Fluid Dynamics; EGC 601—Theory of Fluid Flow I; EGC 602—Theory of Fluid Flow II; EGC 603—Theory of Fluid Flow III; EGC 604—Boundary Layer Theory; EGC 605—Theories of Turbulent Flows; EGC 611—High Speed Gas Dynamics I; EGC 612—High Speed Gas Dynamics II; EGC 613—High Speed Gas Dynamics III; EGC 633—Principles of Engineering Analysis I; EGC 634—Principles of Engineering Analysis II; EGC 635—Principles of Engineering Analysis III; EGC 636—Principles of Engineering Analysis IV; EGC 637—Principles of Engineering Analysis V; EGC 671—Introduction to Plasmas; EGC 672—Plasma Theory; EGC 675—Plasma Laboratory.

GRADUATE COURSES

ASE 501—Stability and Control of Aircraft (4) *Prereq: ESM 431, ASE 400.* Static stability and control; equations of motion; stability derivatives; stability of longitudinal and lateral motion of aircraft.

ASE 541—Aerospace Structural Composites I (3) *Prereq: MSE 300, ASE 441.* Various types and applications of structural composites used in flight structures. Introduction to analysis of structural composites.

ASE 570—Principles of Guidance and Control (3) *Prereq: ESM 330 or consent of instructor.* Review of current missile guidance systems. Relations between guidance and control. The control function: open and closed loop servo systems. Detection and information gathering as a factor in guidance precision.

ASE 601—Advanced Plasma Topics (3) Selected topics with application to aeronautics and astronautics.

ASE 602—Probe Techniques for Plasma Diagnostics (3) *Prereq: EGC 671.* Basic theory of electric and magnetic probes for plasma diagnostics; practical application to laboratory plasmas.

ASE 611—The Dynamics of Real Gases I (3) Introductory kinetic theory of gases including dynamics of binary collisions, conservation laws, velocity distribution functions, Boltzmann equation, equation of change, chemical equilibrium, and law of mass action. Rarefied and slip flow.

ASE 612—The Dynamics of Real Gases II (3) *Prereq: undergraduate thermodynamics and fluid mechanics.* Chemical thermodynamics and · statistical thermodynamics of real gas mixtures in flowing systems. Ionization, relaxation and nonequilibrium.

ASE 613—The Dynamics of Real Gases III (3) Radiative energy transfer in gases. Radiation gas dynamics including effects of line shapes, scattering, optically thick and thin systems, and gray approximations.

ASE 631—Advanced Aerospace Structures I (3) Steady state aeroelastic and structural problems. Flutter analysis. Transient loads, nonstationary and oscillating airfoil theory.

ASE 632—Advanced Aerospace Structures II (3)

ASE 633—Advanced Aerospace Structures III (3)

ASE 641—Aerospace Structural Composites II (3) *Prereq: ESM 652, ASE 541.* Analysis of fibrous reinforced structural composites for aerospace applications.

ASE 651—Near-Earth Space Operations (3) Technical problems associated with the manned orbiting laboratory.

ASE 662—Astronautical Mechanics I (3) *Prereq: ESM 644.* Small oscillations. Perturbation theory; methods of celestial mechanics. Numerical methods of orbit computation.

ASE 663—Astronautical Mechanics II (3) *Prereq: ASE 662.* Lunar theory; orbits about an oblate spheroid; tumbling of an orbiting vehicle. Atmospheric entry problem.

ASE 671—Advanced Space Instrumentation Laboratory (1-9; max: 9) Laboratory experiments relating to instrumentation of space vehicles. Scientific principles of instruments used or to be modified for space missions.

ASE 681—Advanced Aerospace Design (1-9; max: 15) Advanced aerospace design projects.

ASE 690—Graduate Seminar (1; max: 12) Discussion of topics in fields of graduate study and research. S/U.

ASE 691—Special Topics in Aerospace Engineering (1-9; max: 15) Laboratory, lectures, or conferences covering selected topics in aerospace engineering.

ASE 696—Aerospace Research (1-9; max: 15)

ASE 697—Supervised Research (1-5)

ASE 698—Supervised Teaching (1-5)

ASE 699—Master's Research (1-15)

ASE 799—Doctoral Research (1-15)

COASTAL AND OCEANOGRAPHIC ENGINEERING

The following *Engineering Common Courses* are available for graduate major credit: EGC 541—Intermediate Fluid Dynamics; EGC 601—Theory of Fluid Flow I; EGC 602—Theory of Fluid Flow II; EGC 603—Theory of Fluid Flow III; EGC 604—Boundary Layer Theory; EGC 605—Theories of Turbulent Flows; EGC 621—Surface Hydrology; EGC 633—Principles of Engineering Analysis I; EGC 634—Principles of Engineering Analysis II; EGC 635—Principles of Engineering Analysis III; EGC 636—Principles of Engineering Analysis IV; EGC 637—Principles of Engineering Analysis V.

GRADUATE COURSES

COE 550—Harbor Engineering (4) *Prereq: COE 400 or consent of instructor.* Principles of design in harbors; wave penetration, harbor oscillation; movement of sediments and pollutants; design in harbor structures; principles of harbor operations.

COE 560—Ocean Engineering (4) Basic oceanography; underwater instrumentation, floating platforms and buoys; fixed structures; submersibles; materials and testing; operations offshore.

COE 610—Ocean Waves I: Linear Theory (4) *Prereq: courses in calculus, differential equations, and fluid dynamics.* Ocean wave classification; solution of the linearized boundary value problem; simple harmonic waves; shoaling effects; internal waves.

COE 611—Ocean Waves II: Nonlinear Theory (4) *Prereq: COE 610.* Perturbation development of nonlinear water wave theories. Regions of validity of various theories. Dynamics and kinematics of nonlinear wave trains composed of single and multiple fundamental components.

COE 612—Ocean Wave Spectra (4) *Prereq: COE 610.* Ocean wave spectra: measurement, analysis, and application. Systems approaches to calculation of responses of linear and nonlinear coastal and oceanographic processes.

COE 613—Estuarial Hydromechanics and Engineering I (4) *Prereq: COE 610.* Tidal theory. Analytical and numerical methods for computation of one- and two-dimensional propagation of tides and storm surges in estuaries and bays; method of characteristics; hydraulic bore; seiches; solitary wave.

COE 614—Estuarial Hydromechanics and Engineering II (4) *Prereq: CE 628, COE 613.* Salinity intrusion in tidal estuaries; diffusion dispersion entrainment and mixing; analytical and numerical methods for predicting salinity intrusion and distribution of pollutants; laboratory exercises.

COE 615—Estuarial Hydromechanics and Engineering III (4) *Prereq: COE 614.* Estuary shoaling and dredging practices; tidal energy; model investigations and study of selected case histories.

COE 620—Coastal Structures I (4) *Prereq: COE 610.* Design principles for breakwaters, jetties and piers, shore protection, harbor design, offshore structures.

COE 621—Coastal Structures II (4) *Prereq: COE 610, 620.* Case studies in the design and performance of coastal and offshore engineering construction.

COE 630—Littoral Processes (4) *Prereq: COE 610.* Longshore currents and sediment transportation by waves and wind; effects of groins, jetties, and other coastal structures on littoral processes.

COE 631—Simulation Techniques (4) Similitude laws, analog and numerical modeling, studies of littoral drift, harbor resonance, wind-driven circulation, storm surge, wave generation.

COE 632—Selected Field and Laboratory Problems (3-8) Field investigations employing modern research techniques and instrumentation; correlation of measurements with predictions.

COE 640—Physical Oceanography (4) *Prereq: calculus and differential equations.* Historical introduction. Structure of the oceanic basins. Physical and chemical properties of sea water and property distributions. Heat budget, dynamics of ocean movement and oceanic waters.

COE 641—Air-Sea Interaction I: Microscale (4) *Prereq: COE 610.* Equations of motion and stresses at the air-sea interface; the classical instability theory; recent theories of energy transfer from air to water; thermodynamic considerations; the growth of waves; wave forecasting.

COE 642—Air-Sea Interaction II: Macroscale (4) *Prereq: basic courses in calculus and fluid mechanics.* Composition and properties of the marine atmosphere; air-sea fluxes and energy transfer; global heat and water budget; tropical disturbances; large-scale momentum exchange.

COE 643—Advanced Topics in Coastal and Oceanographic Engineering (1-6) Wave forces, internal waves; sediment transport; surges in basins; instrumentation; advanced data analysis techniques; nonlinear wave mechanics; ship waves.

COE 691—Graduate Seminar (1; max: 12) Discussions and presentations in graduate study and research. S/U.

COE 697—Supervised Research (1-5)

COE 698—Supervised Teaching (1-5)

COE 699—Master's Research (1-15)

ENGINEERING SCIENCE AND MECHANICS

Students taking 500-level courses for graduate major credit will be required to do additional reading, problems, and reports.

The following *Engineering Common Courses* are available for graduate major credit: EGC 541—Intermediate Fluid Dynamics; EGC 601—Theory of Fluid Flow I; EGC 602—Theory of Fluid Flow II; EGC 603—Theory of Fluid Flow III; EGC 604—Boundary Layer Theory; EGC 605—Theories of Turbulent Flows; EGC 611—High Speed Gas Dynamics I; EGC 612—High Speed Gas Dynamics II; EGC 613—High Speed Gas Dynamics III; EGC 630—Analytical Techniques for Engineers and Scientists I; EGC 631—Analytical Techniques for Engineers and Scientists II; EGC 632—Analytical Techniques for Engineers and Scientists III; EGC 633—Principles of Engineering Analysis I; EGC 634—Principles of Engineering Analysis II; EGC 635—Principles of Engineering Analysis III; EGC 636—Principles of Engineering Analysis IV; EGC 637—Principles of Engineering Analysis V; EGC 638—Approximation Techniques in Engineering and Science I; EGC 639—Approximation Techniques in Engineering and Science II.

GRADUATE COURSES

ESM 510—Laser Principles and Applications (4) *Prereq: consent of instructor.* Operating principles of solid, electric discharge, gasdynamic and chemical lasers. Application of lasers to lidar, aerodynamic and structural testing and for cutting and welding of materials.

ESM 527—Modern Techniques of Structural Dynamics I (3) *Prereq: ESM 302, 303, 330 and ISE 350.* Modern methods of elastomechanics applied to systematic analysis and automatic computation. Finite difference techniques, matrix force and displacement methods, finite element modeling. Application of digital computers.

ESM 533—Advanced Mechanics of Solids and Structures (3) *Prereq: ESM 303.* Analysis of stress and strain in deformable bodies. Elastic stress-strain relations. Theories of failure. Shear center. Unsymmetrical bending of beams. Curved beams. Beams on elastic foundations. Torsion of bars. Energy methods.

ESM 534—Elevated Temperature Stress Analysis (3) *Prereq: ME 430, ESM 303.* Sources of heat and heat transfer. Transient temperatures and stresses in tubes, rings, shafts, beams, and built up structures. Elementary problems of plates and shells. Material properties at elevated temperatures. Design procedures for elevated temperatures.

ESM 536—Intermediate Dynamics (3) *Prereq: ESM 302, 330.* Motion of particles and rigid bodies under constant and variable force fields. Introduction to Hamilton and Lagrange equations.

ESM 549—Experimental Stress Analysis I (3) *Prereq: ESM 303.* Introduction to techniques of experimental stress analysis in static systems. Lecture and laboratory include applications of electrical resistance strain gauges, photo elasticity, brittle coatings, moiré fringe analysis and x-ray stress analysis.

ESM 596—Individual Study (1-9; max: 9) *Prereq: ESM 302, MS 304.* Individual research projects in solid and fluid mechanics at an advanced undergraduate, and beginning graduate level.

ESM 601—Continuum Mechanics I (3) *Prereq: ESM 303.* Foundations of continuum mechanics. Analysis of motion and deformation. Conservation laws; tensor properties of stress and strain. Constitutive theory. Thermodynamics of continuous media.

ESM 602—Continuum Mechanics II (3) *Prereq: ESM 601.* Specific constitutive classes of continuous media; elastic solids, Newtonian and non-Newtonian fluids. Materials which exhibit plastic and viscoelastic behavior. Formulation of specific problems.

ESM 603—Advanced Continuum Mechanics (3) *Prereq: ESM 602.* Comprehensive, unified treatment of the mathematical theories of solid and fluid mechanics, including gases.

ESM 605—Principles of Mechanics in Biomedical Engineering (3) *Prereq: ESM 601.* Rheological behavior of biological materials subject to steady-state and dynamic loading. Mathematical models and analytical techniques used in the biosciences. Experimental techniques for material property investigation of representative body tissues.

ESM 621—Theory of Structural Vibrations I (4) *Prereq: ESM 420.* Lagrange's equations. Multiple degree of freedom systems. Free and forced motions. Normal coordinates. Effect of damping. Use of matrix methods, computers, Rayleigh-Ritz and other approximation techniques.

ESM 622—Theory of Structural Vibrations II (4) *Prereq: ESM 621.* Longitudinal and torsional vibrations of bars, lateral vibrations of bars, membranes, and plates. Normal mode, lumped parameter, and transformation methods. Transmission and reflection of stress waves in isotropic elastic media.

ESM 623—Nonlinear Vibrations I (4) *Prereq: ESM 420 or 621.* Phase plane and singular point methods. Limit cycles. Method of averaging. Application to one degree of freedom autonomous and nonautonomous systems. Nonlinear resonance. Stability of solutions. Parametrically excited systems. Method of perturbations.

ESM 624—Nonlinear Vibrations II (3) *Prereq: ESM 623.* Multiple degree of freedom systems. Averaging and perturbations. Systems with slowly varying parameters. Nonlinear continuous systems.

ESM 625—Random Vibrations (3) *Prereq: ESM 621.* Statistical analysis, response of discrete single and multiple degree of freedom dynamical systems to stationary random forces and parametric excitation. Extension to continuous systems and nonstationary excitation. Applications to engineering problems.

ESM 628—Modern Techniques of Structural Dynamics (3) *Prereq: ESM 527, 621.* Modeling of complex structural systems occurring in aeronautical, mechanical, and structural engineering. Response of such systems to impulse, shock, and random excitations, emphasizing computer techniques.

ESM 635—Introduction to Plates and Shells (3) *Prereq: ESM 303.* Small-deflection theory of plates. Boundary conditions. Rectangular and circular plates. Energy methods. Large deflections of plates. Orthogonal curvilinear coordinates. Surfaces of shells. Membrane theory of shells. Bending of shells of revolution.

ESM 636—Numerical Methods of Engineering Analysis I (3) *Prereq: ISE 351.* Variational principles. Minimum potential energy. Relaxation, Rayleigh-Ritz and Galerkin methods. Modern computer techniques.

ESM 637—Numerical Methods of Engineering Analysis II (3) *Prereq: ESM 636.* Trefftz's procedure. Prager's function space concept. Perturbation and collocation procedures. Use of computer.

ESM 638—Introduction to Finite Element Methods (4) *Prereq: ESM 601, 652, or consent of instructor.* Finite element idealization of plane, axisymmetric and three-dimensional elasticity problems. Variational formulation of continuum and plate bending problems. Isoparametric elements and computational techniques. Extension to inelastic time varying and nonlinear field problems.

ESM 644—Advanced Dynamics I (3) *Prereq: ESM 536.* Dynamics of particles and rigid bodies applied to advanced engineering problems utilizing variational and transformation principles.

ESM 645—Advanced Dynamics II (3) *Prereq: ESM 644.* Theory and application of Lagrangian equations to engineering problems. Hamilton-Jacobi theory and its applications.

ESM 646—Stability of Dynamical Systems (3) *Prereq: ESM 420 or 536.* Basic concepts of stability, stability and asymptotic behavior of motion. Forced oscillations of systems with nonlinear characteristics. Floquet theory, Mathieu and Hill equations, Liapunov's direct method, criterion of Routh-Hurwitz, Popov and others.

ESM 652—Introduction to Elasticity (3) *Prereq: ESM 303.* Analysis of stress. Analysis of strain. Stress-strain relations of elasticity. Compatibility equations. Plane elasticity in Cartesian and polar coordinates.

ESM 653—Theory of Elasticity I (3) *Prereq: ESM 652.* Solution of two-dimensional problems by means of complex variable methods. Energy principles and variational methods.

ESM 654—Theory of Elasticity II (3) *Prereq: ESM 653.* Three-dimensional problems including torsion, bending, stress concentration, thermal stress, and stress-wave propagation.

ESM 655—Introduction to Theory of Thermal Stresses (3) *Prereq: ESM 534.* Theory of thermal distortion and induced thermal stresses. Strain energy principles. Two- and three-dimensional problems. Creep. Thermal instability.

ESM 667—Theory of Elastic Stability (4) *Prereq: ESM 635 or 674.* Stability criteria. Elastic stability of bars, frames, plates; cylindrical, conical, spherical, and shallow shells. Postbuckling behavior of plates. Plates and shells under dynamic loading.

ESM 670—Introduction to Inelastic Behavior of Materials (3) *Prereq: ESM 303, MS 501.* Fundamental inelastic theory including plasticity and viscoelasticity. Applications to beams, bars, rings, and plates. Dynamic inelastic effects. Problems in creep and stress relaxation.

ESM 671—Theory of the Inelastic Continuum (3) *Prereq: ESM 601, 670.* Stress and strain in inelastic media. Flow, deformation, and incremental theories. Ideally plastic media.

ESM 673—Theory of Plates (3) *Prereq: ESM 601.* Fundamental equations for the bending and stretching of thin plates with small deformations. Large deformations of plates with nonlinear considerations. Energy methods applied to plate problems. Thermal stresses in plates.

ESM 674—Theory of Shells (3) *Prereq: ESM 673.* General theory of deformation of thin shells. Static analysis of shells, shells of revolution, dynamics of shells.

ESM 675—Methods of Analysis for Plates and Shells (3) *Prereq: ESM 674.* Application of various approximate shell theories to engineering problems and the methods of solution. Numerical analysis of shells.

ESM 676—Inertial Guidance and Control (3) Same as EE 676. *Prereq: EE 670.* Modern navigational and vehicle guidance and control techniques based on use of inertial reference.

ESM 679—Nonlinear Control Systems (3) Same as EE 679. *Prereq: EE 570.* Stability of nonlinear systems using Liapunov's second method, the Popov and other frequency domain criteria.

ESM 682—Theory of Viscoelasticity (3) *Prereq: ESM 601, 670.* Theories of solid and fluid materials which exhibit history dependence. Development from Boltzmann linear viscoelasticity to general thermodynamic theories of materials with memory.

ESM 683—Dynamic Plasticity (3) *Prereq: ESM 601, 670.* Analysis of propagation of impact-induced transient loading and unloading waves of uniaxial stress or strain in inelastic solids. Rate-dependent and rate-independent constitutive assumptions. Experimental verifications. Combined stress waves.

ESM 684—Special Topics in Dynamic Plasticity (1-4; max: 9) *Prereq: ESM 683.*

ESM 690—Graduate Seminar (1; max: 10) Discussions and presentations in the fields of graduate study and research. S/U.

ESM 692—Special Topics in Engineering Mechanics (1-9; max: 18)

ESM 696—Individual Study (1-9; max: 18)

ESM 697—Supervised Research (1-5)

ESM 698—Supervised Teaching (1-5)

ESM 699—Master's Research (1-15)

ESM 799—Doctoral Research (1-15)

ENGLISH
(College of Arts and Sciences)

Chairman: W. HELLSTROM
Graduate Coordinator: I. G. CLARK III

GRADUATE FACULTY 1975-76

Graduate Research Professor: A. L. WILLIAMS
Professors: G. E. BIGELOW; R. H. BOWERS, JR.; R. A. BRYAN; W. C. CHILDERS; R. H. GREEN; W. HELLSTROM; T. W. HERBERT; P. LISCA; J. F. NIMS; J. B. PICKARD; W. R. ROBINSON; H. M. STAHMER; D. STRYKER
Associate Professors: T. K. BEYETTE; R. E. BRANTLEY; C. S. CARNELL; I. G. CLARK III; H. E. CREWS; M. F. DEAKIN; A. M. DUCKWORTH; R. C. FOREMAN, JR.; W. L. FRAZER; S. H. GALE; S. R. HOMAN, JR.; M. S. KIRKPATRICK; J. LARSEN; K. M. McCARTHY; H. G. MOSS; A. A. MURPHREE; M. NEW; C. E. TILLMAN; J. F. VOGEL; T. R. WALDO

Assistant Professors: B. J. ANDERSON; A. C. BREDAHL, JR.; R. B. KERSHNER, JR.; M. NELSON; J. M. PERLETTE; C. G. SNODGRASS; R. S. THOMSON; J. B. TWITCHELL; G. L. ULMER

The Department of English offers the Master of Arts with specialization in literature, creative writing, community college teaching, and linguistics and the Doctor of Philosophy with specialization in literature and linguistics. A nonthesis Master of Arts is offered with specialization in literature and community college teaching as is a Master of Arts in Teaching with a major in English.

Specific areas of specialization for the Doctor of Philosophy include linguistics, Medieval, Renaissance, Restoration and 18th-century, 19th-century British, American literature to 1900, Contemporary British and American literature. Specialization in the literary study of film and folklore is also possible.

New graduate students should have completed an undergraduate English major of at least 36 quarter hours, while doctoral students should have a Master of Arts degree in English. All graduate students must take a course in bibliography and methods of research, and doctoral students must complete an internship in college teaching.

GRADUATE COURSES

EH 530—Individual Work in Creative Writing (4; max: 16)
EH 596—Special Study in English (1-5)
EH 600—Bibliography and Methods of Research (4)
EH 607—Practicum in the Teaching of College English (4)
EH 613—The Language of Film (4) Use of film in teaching English composition, literature, and the humanities.
EH 614—Communications and Popular Culture (4) Study of the origins and qualities of the popular arts in modern society.
EH 615—The Teaching of Business and Technical Writing (4)
EH 616—Principles of Community College and Adult Reading Instruction I (4) Study of the psychology of adult learners, diagnosis of reading problems, and teaching the skills of the reading process.
EH 617—Laboratory in Community College and Adult Reading Instruction II (4) *Prereq: EH 616.* Observation of and instruction by in-service community college teachers in diagnosis, materials, and study skills.
EH 618—Linguistics in the Community College (4)
EH 619—Studies in English Linguistics (4; max: 16)
EH 620—Studies in Old English (4; max: 16)
EH 626—Studies in Middle English (4; max: 16)
EH 630—Studies in Renaissance Literature (4; max: 16)
EH 633—Studies in Shakespeare (4; max: 16)
EH 640—Studies in Restoration and 18th-Century Literature (4; max: 16)
EH 646—Studies in 19th-Century British Literature (4; max: 16)
EH 650—Studies in 20th-Century British Literature (4; max: 16)
EH 655—Studies in American Literature Before 1900 (4; max: 16)
EH 660—Studies in 20th-Century American Literature (4; max: 16)
EH 665—Studies in Irish Literature (4; max: 16)
EH 666—Studies in Literary Criticism (4; max: 16)
EH 670—Studies in Folklore (4; max: 16)
EH 675—Studies in the Movies (4; max: 16)
EH 677—Studies in Fiction (4; max: 16)
EH 678—Studies in Verse (4; max: 16)
EH 679—Studies in Drama (4; max: 16)
EH 684—Stylistics (4)
EH 687—Variable Topics (1-5; max: 16)
EH 690—Fiction Writing (4; max: 16)

EH 691—Verse Writing (4; max: 16)
EH 692—Children's Literature (4; max: 16)
EH 696—Individual Work (1-4; max: 16)
EH 697—Supervised Research (1-5)
EH 698—Supervised Teaching (1-5)
EH 699—Master's Research (1-15)
EH 700—Seminar in Bibliography (4; max: 16)
EH 705—Seminar in Linguistics (4; max: 16)
EH 720—Seminar in Medieval Literature (4; max: 16)
EH 730—Seminar in Renaissance Literature (4; max: 16)
EH 735—Seminar in Shakespeare (4; max: 16)
EH 740—Seminar in Restoration and 18th-Century Literature (4; max: 16)
EH 745—Seminar in 19th-Century British Literature (4; max: 16)
EH 750—Seminar in 20th-Century British Literature (4; max: 16)
EH 755—Seminar in American Literature before 1900 (4; max: 16)
EH 760—Seminar in 20th-Century American Literature (4; max: 16)
EH 770—Seminar in Folklore (4; max: 16)
EH 775—Seminar in the Movies (4; max: 16)
EH 780—Seminar in Genres (4; max: 16)
EH 790—Seminar in Variable Topics (1-5; max: 16)
EH 799—Doctoral Research (1-15)

ENTOMOLOGY AND NEMATOLOGY
(College of Agriculture)

Chairman: F. G. MAXWELL
Graduate Coordinator: S. H. KERR

GRADUATE FACULTY 1975-76

Graduate Research Professor: R. I. SAILER

Professors: G. E. ALLEN; R. M. BARANOWSKI; L. BERNER; J. E. BROGDON; R. F. BROOKS; A. K. BURDITT; W. F. BUREN; H. L. CROMROY; A. G. B, FAIRCHILD; D. H. HABECK; S. H. KERR; L. C. KUITERT; G. C. LaBRECQUE; J. E. LLOYD; C. S. LOFGREN; F. G. MAXWELL; P. B. MORGAN; M. MURPHEY; J. L. NATION; V. G. PERRY; H. L. RHOADES; F. A. ROBINSON; G. C. SMART, JR.; B. J. SMITTLE; J. R. STRAYER; T. J. WALKER; D. E. WEIDHAAS; M. J. WESTFALL, JR.; W. H. WHITCOMB; R. C. WILKINSON, JR.

Associate Professors: J. F. BUTLER; D. W. DICKSON; G. L. GREENE; R. E. LOWE; C. W. McCOY, JR.; H. OBERLANDER; R. S. PATTERSON; S. L. POE; D. E. SHORT; D. SILHACEK; R. E. WAITES; B. R. WISEMAN; R. E. WOODRUFF; R. B. WORKMAN

Assistant Professors: D. W. HALL; F. A. JOHNSON; P. G. KOEHLER; J. R. Mc-LAUGHLIN; D. R. MINNICK; C. A. MUSGRAVE; D. E. STOKES; J. H. TSAI

The Department of Entomology and Nematology offers the Master of Agriculture, Master of Science, and Doctor of Philosophy degrees in entomology and nematology. Members of the graduate faculty include the departmental resident faculty, faculty located on University of Florida campuses away from Gainesville, scientists of the U. S. Department of Agriculture, and scientists with other State of Florida agencies such as the Division of Plant Industry, Florida State Department of Agriculture and Consumers Service. The graduate faculty is qualified to direct graduate students in all specialities of entomology, nematology, and acarology.

New graduate students should have background in biology, chemistry, physics, and mathematics and knowledge of basic entomology or nematology. Minor deficiencies may be made up after entering graduate school. Each new student is required to take diagnostic examinations in biology and either entomology or nematology. In addition each new student of entomology must either satisfactorily complete diagnostic tests in insect identification, insect ecology, insect physiology, and applied entomology or take specified courses in these areas.

General requirements for graduate degrees are established by the Graduate School and listed elsewhere in this *Catalog*. A specific program of study is prepared by the appointed supervisory committee for each student. Supervisory committees for students pursuing the Ph.D. will plan programs of study having at least 90 hours of graduate credit other than thesis or dissertation research. As many as 45 of these hours may be transferred from another graduate school. Ph.D. qualifying examinations are administered by the student's supervisory committee plus two other faculty members appointed by the chairman of the department.

GRADUATE COURSES

EY 518—Tropical Entomology (4) *Prereq: EY 301 or EY 318 or equivalent.* Biologies, life histories, and various approaches to control of major agricultural insect and arachnid pests encountered in the tropics.

EY 522—Tropical Nematology (5) *Prereq: EY 303 or equivalent.* Plant parasitic nematodes and the diseases they cause to plants of tropical and subtropical areas of the world. Offered in odd years only.

EY 601—Information Techniques in Entomology (1) Sources of entomological information and methods for acquiring, storing, and retrieving it.

EY 606—Insect Systematics (5) *Prereq: EY 460, knowledge of insect variety and classification.* Principles of systematics as they apply to insects. Nomenclature, phenetics, phyletics, evolution, and zoogeography.

EY 608—Comparative Anatomy of the Hexapoda (5) *Prereq: EY 410.* Includes comparative histology of selected species, with reference to the new electron microscopy findings; the laboratory will cover insect histological techniques.

EY 611—Special Topics in Entomology and Nematology (1-2; max: 6) Reports and discussions pertaining to selected topics announced in advance. S/U.

EY 612—Insect Physiology (5) *Prereq: EY 410, organic chemistry or equivalent.* Physiological study of the various organs and tissues of insects.

EY 613—Growth and Development in Insects (4) Analysis of insect development, with emphasis on determination, pattern formation, regeneration, and hormone action.

EY 615—Insect Behavior (5) Principles of animal behavior with an evolutionary perspective. Genetics, physiology, ecology and evolution of behavior; especially communication, reproduction, predator-prey interactions. Field and research work, critiques and discussion.

EY 616—Insect Ecology (5) *Prereq: EY 612.* Interrelations of insects and their physical and biotic environment. Population dynamics and control of population size. Field and laboratory techniques.

EY 618—Insect Toxicology (5) *Prereq: EY 301, organic chemistry or equivalent.* Insecticides and acaricides: structure, toxic action, metabolism, hazards, residues in relation to health. Acquired resistance to pesticides. Research methods in toxicology.

EY 620—Medical Entomology (5) *Prereq: EY 420.* Arthropods (except mosquitoes) parasitic on man: collection, identification, and bionomics of local species.

EY 621—Mosquitoes (5) *Prereq: EY 420.* Mosquitoes: collection, identification, bionomics, and relationship to the health of man.

EY 622—Biological Control of Insects (5) *Prereq: EY 301.* Principles involved in the natural and biological control of insects.

EY 623—Immature Insects (5) *Prereq: EY 460.* Structure and identification of immature forms of insects, especially the Holometabola.

EY 624—Acarology (5) *Prereq: EY 301.* Morphology, phylogeny, taxonomy, and economic importance of mites.

EY 625—Research Techniques in Entomology (5) Demonstration and use of modern techniques, equipment, and procedures in research on insects. Conducted principally in the U.S.D.A. Entomology Research Laboratory.

EY 626—Aquatic Insects (5) *Prereq: EY 460.* Life histories and ecologies of aquatic insects.

EY 630—Plant Parasitic Nematodes (5) *Prereq: EY 303.* Morphology, taxonomy, life cycles, pathogenicity, and control of the plant parasitic nematodes.

EY 631—Morphology and Physiology of Nematodes (5) *Prereq: EY 303.* Anatomical study of the organs of nematodes and their vital functions.

EY 632—Taxonomy of Nematodes (5) *Prereq: EY 631.* Taxonomy and identification of members of the Phylum Nemata.

EY 633—Marine Nematodes (3) *Prereq: consent of instructor.* Taxonomy, morphology, physiology, ecology, and life cycles of free living marine nematodes.

EY 634—Radiation in Insect Studies (5) *Prereq: consent of instructor.* Specialized topics and current research on radiation in entomology.

EY 635—Insect Resistance in Crop Plants I (4) Principles of plant resistance to insects.

EY 636—Insect Resistance in Crop Plants II (3) Methods of developing plant resistance to insects.

EY 637—Veterinary Entomology (5) *Prereq: EY 420.* Arthropods parasitic on animals: biology, control, and host arthropod interaction. Collection, identification, and bionomics of arthropods affecting animals other than man.

EY 640—Insect Pathology (5) *Prereq: MCY 302 or consent of instructor.* Interrelationship of insects and pathogenic microorganisms; history, classification, morphology, mode-of-action, and epidemiology of entomogenous bacteria, viruses, protozoa, and fungi.

EY 642—Microbial Control of Insects (5) Principles and concepts of the utilization of insect pathogens in arthropod control programs: mass production, safety, compatibility with other control methods, utilization of natural epizootics and the role of pathogens in pest management programs.

EY 696—Problems in Entomology and Nematology (1-6; max: 12) Individual study under faculty guidance. Student and instructor to agree on problem and credits prior to registration.

EY 697—Supervised Research (1-5)

EY 698—Supervised Teaching (1-5)

EY 699—Master's Research (1-15)

EY 799—Doctoral Research (1-15)

ENVIRONMENTAL ENGINEERING SCIENCES
(College of Engineering)

Chairman: E. E. PYATT
Graduate Coordinator: H. A. BEVIS

GRADUATE FACULTY 1975-76

Graduate Research Professors: H. A. LAITINEN; H. T. ODUM

Professors: H. A. BEVIS; B. G. DUNAVANT; T. DES. FURMAN; W. MAUDERLI; W. H. MORGAN; E. E. PYATT; J. E. SINGLEY; P. URONE

Associate Professors: W. E. BOLCH, JR.; P. L. BREZONIK; J. L. FOX; J. P. HEANEY; W. C. HUBER; C. D. KYLSTRA; D. A. LUNDGREN; C. E. ROESSLER

Assistant Professors: S. E. BAYLEY; G. BITTON; L. D. HARRIS; J. ZOLTEK, JR.

Graduate study is offered leading to the degrees of Master of Engineering, Master of Science, Engineer, and Doctor of Philosophy in the field of environmental engineering sciences. Areas in which the student may specialize include air resources, water supply and water pollution control, environmental resources management, environmental biology, water chemistry, radiological health, solid wastes, and systems ecology.

Both master's degrees are available in cooperation with the Department of Civil and Coastal Engineering with an area of concentration in public works engineering.

Direct admission into the Master of Science program requires a bachelor's degree in engineering or in a basic science such as chemistry, physics, biology, or mathematics. Persons with a degree in a nontechnical field may also be admitted into this program upon the completion of specified articulation.

Direct admission into the Master of Engineering program requires that the student be a graduate engineer. Other persons wishing to enter this program will be required to take articulation work sufficient to bring their backgrounds into substantial agreement with those with undergraduate engineering training. The Master of Engineering degree is accredited by the Engineers' Council for Professional Development (ECPD). The specific program of study for each student must be approved by his supervisory committee.

It normally requires one calendar year to complete the requirements for a master's degree. If articulation work is required, it may take longer, depending upon the extent of the student's deficiency.

The following *Engineering Common Courses* are available for graduate major credit: EGC 621—Surface Hydrology; EGC 622—Operational Hydrology I; EGC 623—Operational Hydrology II.

GRADUATE COURSES

ENV 500—Treatment of Wastewater (4) *Prereq: CE 451, ENV 531 or consent of instructor.* In-depth study of the physical, chemical, and biological processes utilized in the treatment of wastewater, with special emphasis on cause and effect of physical and biological actions.

ENV 520—Environmental Biology (4) *Prereq: consent of instructor.* Basic cellular organization and processes related to waste treatment. Role of environmental engineering in maintaining stability of fresh water, marine, and terrestrial ecosystems.

ENV 522—Environmental Health (4) Effects of environmental pollution upon health. Methods of evaluation, treatment, and prevention of pollutants of health significance.

ENV 531—Water and Wastewater Analysis (4) *Prereq: 3 quarters of general chemistry.* Principles of analytical chemistry and their application to determination of chemical composition of natural waters. Emphasis on methods used in routine determinations of water quality and wastewater strength.

ENV 540—Survey of Radiological Health (4) Oriented toward ENV majors not specializing in radiological health. Quantitative overview of radiation principles, sources, detection, measurement, and protection.

ENV 551—Introduction to Air Pollution (4) Principal types, sources, dispersion, effects, and physical, economic, and legal aspects of control of atmospheric pollutants.

ENV 560—Ecological and General Systems (4) *Prereq: MS 305 or consent of instructor.* Systems ecology, including examples, languages, theoretical formulations, and models for design, synthesis, and prediction of systems of man and nature.

ENV 561—Ecological Engineering Seminar (2) *Prereq: consent of instructor.* Principles of environmental design and means for guiding self-design of systems of nature and man, including review of manageable ecological systems, regional patterns, technological interfaces, new approaches, and literature.

ENV 580—Municipal Refuse Disposal (3) Quantities and characteristics of municipal refuse. Collection methods, transfer stations, equipment, and costs. Refuse disposal practices, regional planning, and equipment.

ENV 591—Special Topics in Environmental Engineering I (1-5; max: 12) *Prereq: consent of instructor.* Laboratory, lectures, or conferences covering specially selected topics.

ENV 600—Advanced Waste Treatment Operations (4) *Prereq: ENV 500.* Biological, physical, and chemical processes used in the treatment of domestic and industrial wastewater. Development of design parameters and operating procedures based on experimentally derived data.

ENV 601—Advanced Environmental Engineering Design I (5) *Prereq: ENV 600.* Layout and design of sanitary sewage systems, pumping stations, force mains, wastewater treatment plants, and methods of effluent disposal. Design parameters, cost, and financing.

ENV 602—Advanced Environmental Engineering Design II (5) Development of water supplies, layout and design of distribution systems, pumping and storage facilities, and water treatment plants. Design parameters, cost, and financing.

ENV 611—Water Quality Management (4) *Prereq: consent of instructor.* Water quality management applied to streams, lakes, and tidal estuaries and embayments. Influence and effects of municipal and industrial wastes on public water supplies, shellfish, storage, recreational uses, industrial uses, and wildlife.

ENV 613—Environmental Resource Systems (4) Standard and criteria for evaluation of environmental resources projects. Formulation of mathematical models and environmental problems. Application of systems engineering and operations research as aids in decision making.

ENV 616—Urban Environmental Problems (4) Overall problem of developing and maintaining a high quality physical environment in urban areas. Systems analysis approach to air, land, and water quality management problems.

ENV 617—Estuarine Systems (4) Coastal systems, their components, processes, systems, models, and management including tropical, arctic, and man-affected types, field trip, and literature review.

ENV 618—Pollution Transport Systems (4) *Prereq: MS 305, ESM 311.* Distribution of pollutants in natural waters and the atmosphere. Diffusive and advective transport phenomena. Analytical and numerical prediction methods.

ENV 624—Water Science Seminar (1-5; max: 9) Chemical, physical, and biological science of the behavior of natural waters presented by area specialists.

ENV 626—Aquatic Microbiology (4) Role of microorganisms in fresh and marine waters which receive waste effluents or are used as public water supplies. Emphasis on phytoplankton.

ENV 627—Biology of Aquatic Systems (4) Macroscopic plant and animal forms which may serve as indicators of water quality in streams and lakes.

ENV 628—Environmental Microbiology (4) Interaction between microbial populations. Behavior of microorganisms in fresh water, marine and soil environments. Stress of pollution on microbial communities.

ENV 630—Environmental Chemistry (1-5; max: 5) *Prereq: CY 204 or 213.* Water treatment, chemical composition of natural waters, and other phases of environmental chemistry. Applications of physical and organic chemistry to aqueous and gaseous systems.

ENV 631—Advanced Water Analysis (4) Advanced chemical procedures used in water chemistry research. Application of instrumental methods for determination of trace inorganic and organic natural water constituents.

ENV 632—Principles of Water Chemistry I (3) *Prereq: ENV 630.* Application of chemical principles to reactions and composition of natural waters; emphasis on equilibrium and thermodynamic concepts.

ENV 633—Principles of Water Chemistry II (3)

ENV 634—Advanced Water Treatment (5) *Prereq: ENV 431, 630 or consent of instructor.* Advanced concepts in chemical processes of examination and treatment of potable water.

ENV 641—Radiological Techniques (5) *Prereq: ENV 540.* Application of radiological techniques to environmental engineering. Theory and operation of advanced detection instrumentation. Laboratory experiments on measurement and control of radionuclides in the environment.

ENV 642—Radioactive Wastes (4) *Prereq: ENV 500, 540.* Source, treatment, and disposal of radioactive wastes. Emphasis on prevention of environmental contamination.

ENV 643—Electronic Product Radiation (4) *Prereq: undergraduate course in modern physics.* Evaluation of hazards, application of standards and engineering of controls for any electromagnetic or particulate radiation from an electronic device, especially microwave sources, lasers and all types of electronic components emitting x-rays.

ENV 644—Health Physics (4) *Prereq: NES 540.* Techniques of hazard evaluation and radiation control; monitoring methods; survey techniques; biological sampling; instrument calibration; exposure standards and radiation protection regulation; on-site radiation safety surveys and evaluation.

ENV 650—Occupational Health (4) Effects, assessment, and control of physical and chemical factors in man's working environment, including chemical agents, electromagnetic radiation, temperature, humidity, pressures, illumination, noise, and vibration.

ENV 652—Environmental Instrumentation (5) Basic instrumentation and instrumental techniques for the measurement of environmental parameters and pollutants.

ENV 653—Aerosol Mechanics (4) Generation, collection and measurement of aerosols. Theory of the fluid dynamic, optical, electrical and thermal behavior of gas-borne particles.

ENV 654—Air Pollution Sampling and Analysis (4) Determination of the concentration of normally encountered ambient pollutants. Methodology of source sampling. Practical experience in ambient and source sampling.

ENV 655—Air Pollution Control Measures (4) Design, analysis, operational limitations, cost and performance evaluation of control processes and equipment. Field visits to and inspection of industrial installations.

ENV 656—Environmental Meteorology (4) Dynamics and thermodynamics of the atmosphere related to environmental problems. Analysis of weather charts. Numerical weather prediction models.

ENV 657—Environmental Micrometeorology (4) Prediction of downwind pollutant concentrations from point, line, and area sources. Theory of turbulence and phenomena related to problems in diffusion and dispersion of contaminants in the lowest layer of the atmosphere.

ENV 668—Health Hazards of Man's Environment (4) *Prereq: basic biology.* Environmental factors which adversely affect man's well-being are related to epidemiology and human physiology.

ENV 670—Graduate Environmental Engineering Seminar (1-2) S/U.

ENV 671—Special Problems in Environmental Engineering (1-5; max: 12)

ENV 693—Nonthesis Project (1-3; max: 3) Individual project under faculty guidance to satisfy requirement for nonthesis master's degree.

ENV 696—Individual Work (1-5; max: 12) Faculty-supervised individual research or study of material not covered in formal courses.

ENV 697—Supervised Research (1-5)

ENV 698—Supervised Teaching (1-5)

ENV 699—Master's Research (1-15)

ENV 799—Doctoral Research (1-15)

FINANCE AND INSURANCE
(College of Business Administration)

Chairman & Graduate Coordinator: C. A. MATTHEWS

GRADUATE FACULTY 1975-76

Graduate Research Professor: E. F. BRIGHAM
Professors: F. D. ARDITTI; W. M. HOWARD; C. A. MATTHEWS; J. B. MCFERRIN
Associate Professors: L. A. GAITANIS; R. H. PETTWAY; J. G. RICHARDSON; M.S. TYSSELAND
Assistant Professors: D. R. KLOCK; W. A. MCCOLLOUGH; D. J. NYE; R. C. RADCLIFFE; D. G. TAYLOR

The Department of Finance, Insurance, Real Estate and Urban Land Studies offers the nonthesis degree, Master of Business Administration, and the thesis degree, Master of Arts, in finance with specializations in financial management, financial markets and institutions, and investments. It also offers a major and minor in the Doctor of Philosophy degree in business administration. Each of these degrees is also offered in risk and insurance.

New graduate students should have adequate undergraduate training in mathematics and statistics or be willing to devote sufficient time to acquire the necessary foundation in these areas. Though no graduate major may be completed without adequate course work on the 500 or higher level, certain undergraduate courses in finance and insurance are available for graduate credit as a part of a candidate's major. These include FI 462 and 486.

For admission to courses 500 level and above, the student must have been admitted to the Graduate School and normally should have undergraduate courses in fields pertinent to the graduate courses selected; or, where necessary, special arrangements may be made with the approval of the department chairman.

GRADUATE COURSES

FI 520—Financial Markets and Institutions (4) *Prereq: intermediate macroeconomics.* Interest rate theory and functions; the role of financial institutions.

FI 524—Security Markets and Pricing (4) *Prereq: FI 590 or consent of instructor.* An examination of security market structure and the theory of security selection and pricing.

FI 528—Corporation Finance (4) *Prereq: FI 427 or consent of instructor.* The application of business finance problems. Students prepare written solutions to case problems.

FI 590—Business Financial Management (4) *Required of all M.B.A. degree candidates who have had no basic business finance course. Prereq: ATG 510.* Analysis of business financing and investing decisions.

FI 620—Problems in Commercial Banking (5) *Prereq: FI 420.* Monopoly and competition as applied to banking; bank organization and structure, adequacy of bank capital, problems of asset management and of providing successor management.

FI 622—Seminar in Investments (5) *Prereq: FI 524.* Individual research and group discussion employing materials available from publications and reports by governmental agencies and groups in industry.

FI 625—Money and Capital Markets (5) *Prereq: FI 421, college-level mathematics, and statistics.* Financial markets, with emphasis on flow of funds, interest rate determination, and allocation of resources.

FI 627—Problems in Corporation Finance (5) *Prereq: FI 528 and MGT 570.* The firm's cost of capital and the utilization by firm of its cost of capital in its investing and financing decisions.

FI 629—International Finance: Monetary Systems (5) *Prereq: FI 421.* International monetary systems, post-World War II international monetary problems, and attempts at reconstruction.

FI 637—Quantitative Analysis of Financial Decisions (5) *Prereq: MGT 570 and FI 627.* Application of quantitative methods to the solution of specific financial problems with special reference to mathematical programming, simulation, and other methods of discrete optimization.

FI 662—Seminar in Life Insurance (5) *Prereq: FI 462.* Problems in life insurance and related fields.

FI 665—Seminar in Property and Liability Insurance (5) *Prereq: FI 365, 366.* Meaning, economic influences, social values, principles and practices of property and liability insurance.

FI 668—Problems in Risk Management (3) Insurance hazards of business concerns and governmental units, with consideration of insurance protection available.

FI 691—Finance Research and Reports (2) *Prereq: BA 690.* Supervised preparation of a report on a topic of current interest in finance. Required of all candidates for the M.B.A. with a finance concentration.

FI 696—Individual Work in Finance (1-5; max: 10) *Prereq: permission of department and Director of Graduate Studies.* Reading and/or research in finance as needed by graduate students.

FI 697—Supervised Research (1-5)

FI 698—Supervised Teaching (1-5)

FI 699—Master's Research (1-15)

FI 727—Theory of Finance I (5) Normative investment and financing criteria examined for the individual and the corporation when capital markets are imperfect and investment returns uncertain.

FI 728—Theory of Finance II (5) Mean-variance and state preference approaches to security market equilibrium; efficacy of stochastic dominance rules in ordering uncertain prospect and the multiperiod portfolio decision.

FI 790—Finance Research Workshop (4; max: 8) Analysis of current research topics. Paper presentation and critiques by doctoral students, faculty, and visiting scholars.

FI 799—Doctoral Research (1-15)

FOOD AND RESOURCE ECONOMICS
(College of Agriculture)

Chairman: L. POLOPOLUS
Graduate Coordinator: W. W. MCPHERSON

GRADUATE FACULTY 1975-76

Graduate Research Professor: W. W. McPHERSON
Professors: D. L. BROOKE; H. B. CLARK; C. D. COVEY; M. R. LANGHAM; L.
POLOPOLUS; C. N. SMITH; K. R. TEFERTILLER; M. L. UPCHURCH
Associate Professors: C. O. ANDREW; C. G. DAVIS; J. K. DOW; K. C. GIBBS; J.
HOLT; E. T. LOEHMAN; W. K. MATHIS; L. H. MYERS; F. J. PROCHASKA; J. E.
REYNOLDS; R. W. WARD; G. A. ZEPP
Assistant Professors: J. C. CATO; W. A. COLETTE; R. D. EMERSON; G. F. FAIRCHILD;
C. F. KIKER; G. D. LYNNE; J. A. NILES; D. S. TILLEY

Programs leading to the degrees of Master of Agricultural Management and
Resource Development (M.A.M.R.D.), Master of Science, and Doctor of Philosophy are offered with specializations in agricultural business management, economic
development, econometrics, food systems, and resource and environmental
economics. The department participates in the programs of the Center for Latin
American Studies, the Center for Tropical Agriculture, the Center for Rural
Development, the Center for Environmental Programs, and the University's program as a Sea Grant Institution.

Students who hold a bachelor's degree with their major field of study in an
area other than food and resource economics should consult with the graduate
coordinator concerning acceptance for graduate study.

In addition to the courses listed, there are seminars for organized discussion
of current topics and for review of graduate students' research.

GRADUATE COURSES

FRE 501—Special Topics in Food and Resource Economics (1-6; max: 6) *Prereq: consent
of department.* Lectures, conferences, or laboratory covering specially selected topics.
FRE 522—Firm Efficiency (3) *Prereq: ES 302.* Economic efficiency of plant operation,
synthetic cost analysis, systems planning, and optimum firm size and location.
FRE 531—Natural Resource Planning and Development (4) *Designed for majors
outside the department. Prereq: MS 302 and ES 301.* Theory applied to natural
resource development, criteria for evaluating natural resource planning and development.
FRE 541—Foreign Agricultural Development Planning (5) *Prereq: FRE 301.* Special reference
given to low-income countries.
FRE 603—Topics in Food and Resource Economics (1-6; max: 6) Current developments
in food and resource economics.
FRE 604—Intermediate Agricultural Production Economics (4) Basic concepts of producer
choice. Planning periods, information needs, and management strategies. Budgeting, linear
programming, and theory of the firm.
FRE 605—Intermediate Consumption Economics and Agricultural Marketing (4)
Theory of consumer choice and demand. Demand for agricultural products and
services, with implications for marketing and consumer welfare.
FRE 606—Rural Welfare and Development Policy (5) *Prereq: ES 401, 402, FRE
447, or consent of instructor.* Underdevelopment in the U.S. within a historical
framework. Nature and consequences of levels of human and nonhuman investment
in a dynamic setting.
FRE 607—Activity Analysis for Economic Decisions (4) *Prereq: FRE 301, 460, and
STA 320.* Maximization, minimization, and planning over time, space and form with
applications to agricultural and foresty firms. Computer routines. Introduction to
other research and systems techniques.

FRE 608—Elements of Econometrics (4) *Prereq: FRE 301, STA 320, FRE 460, or BA 591.* Econometric problem solving and determining quantitative relationships among economic variables in agriculture and related industries.

FRE 610—Economics of Agricultural Production I (5) *Prereq: FRE ˙460 or BA 591, FRE 604.* Producer decisions including theoretical and empirical problems of multifactor, multiproduct and polyperiod cases under different market structures. Input demand and product supply functions at the commodity and industry levels.

FRE 611—Economics of Agricultural Production II (5) *Prereq: FRE 610.* Firm growth, effects of risk and uncertainty on producer choice and an introduction to probabilistic theory of the firm. Relation between aggregate consequences of producer behavior and social welfare.

FRE 620—Consumption and Demand (4) *Prereq: FRE 460 or BA 591 and FRE 605 or ES 402.* Theories of consumer behavior in static and dynamic contexts; analysis of household expenditure and demand.

FRE 621—Industrial Organization of Agricultural Markets (4) *Prereq: ES 302 or 402.* Analysis of market structure, conduct, and performance. Evaluation of current public policy and institutional arrangements.

FRE 630—Natural Resource Economics (4) *Prereq: FRE 460 or BA 591; FRE 604, ES 401.* Natural resource development; economic objectives, criteria for evaluation; agency use of criteria for natural resource development.

FRE 631—Land Tenure and Taxation in Agriculture (4) *Prereq: FRE 430.* Philosophy and history of property rights and taxation. Effects of property rights and taxes on factor employment, land use, output, land values, income distribution, and social welfare.

FRE 632—Natural Resource Utilizations (4) *Prereq: FRE 604.* Resources as inputs and economic basis for resource use and development. Role of individuals, groups, and agencies in resolving conflicts and improving resource use.

FRE 640—Foundations of Agricultural Policies (3) *Prereq: ES 402.* Policy-making processes. Relationships among economic, political, and social goals and actions which shape the institutions of the agricultural economy and its relations with other sectors.

FRE 641—Agricultural Policies and Programs in the U.S. (3) *Prereq: FRE 440, ES 401.* Theoretical and empirical treatment of relations between goals and programs. Effects of policies on volume and location of output, prices and income in the U.S.

FRE 645—Economic Development and Agriculture (5) *Prereq: ES 301, 302, or FRE 301.* Relation of human, capital, and natural resources, technology, and institutions to income growth and distribution. Development planning in low-income countries.

FRE 646—Agriculture's Role in the Growth of Latin American Nations (4) Agricultural development in relation to facts and theories of national growth, international relations, and hemispheric understanding and cooperation.

FRE 650—International Agricultural Policy and Trade (5) *Prereq: FRE 460 or BA 591; ES 341.* Trade theory applied to international policies, agreements, and programs.

FRE 660—Nonstochastic Models (5) Same as ES 660. *Prereq: ISE 401.* General linear programming model and its basic theorems, integer and nonlinear programming. Spatial equilibrium, input-output, and game theory models.

FRE 661—Econometric Methods I (5) Same as ES 661. *Prereq: STA 441, ISE 401.* Stochastic models. General linear model and problems associated with its use in econometric research. Theory of the simultaneous equation approach, model construction, and estimation techniques.

FRE 662—Econometric Methods II (4) Same as ES 662. *Prereq: FRE 661 or ES 661.* Single equation topics; errors in variables, nonspherical disturbances, and lagged variables. Dynamic simultaneous equation models and topics in multivariate analysis.

FRE 663—Research Seminar in Econometrics (1-3) Same as ES 663. *Prereq: FRE 661 or ES 661.* Advanced topics and empirical measurement in applied economics.

FRE 680—Regional Economics (5) Same as ES 680. *Prereq: ES 401, 402.* Definitions of regions and elements of regional economic analysis. Location theory, regional interdependence and spatial equilibrium. Regional economic change, including economic accounts and other measures of activity; cycles, growth and planned development.

FRE 682—Regional Economic Planning (5) *Prereq: FRE 610 or 680.* Regional policy, objectives, and multiple goal decision making. Decision models for regional planning; input-output, linear programming, and simulation techniques.

FRE 690—Science and Research Methodology (3) Investigation of role of science, philosophy, and the scientific method in research. Emphasis on application of scientific methods to food and resource economics research.

FRE 691—Procedures in Planning and Conducting Research (3) Concepts of research and the application of scientific methods in planning and conducting research in food and resource economics.

FRE 696—Problems in Food and Resource Economics (1-9; max: 9) Individual study in selected areas. Problems of interest to the student and agreeable to the instructor.

FRE 697—Supervised Research (1-5)
FRE 698—Supervised Teaching (1-5)
FRE 699—Master's Research (1-15)
FRE 799—Doctoral Research (1-15)

FOOD SCIENCE
(College of Agriculture)

Chairman: R. A. DENNISON
Graduate Coordinator: F. W. KNAPP

GRADUATE FACULTY 1975-76

Professors: E. M. AHMED; R. A. DENNISON; J. W. KESTERSON; R. F. MATTHEWS
Associate Professors: H. APPLEDORF; R. P. BATES; R. J. BRADDOCK; F. W. KNAPP;
    J. A. KOBURGER; H. A. MOYE; R. C. ROBBINS; N. P. THOMPSON; W. B. WHEELER
Assistant Professors: J. DENG; J. L. OBLINGER

The Department of Food Science offers work leading to the degrees of Master of Science and Master of Agriculture. Programs leading to the Doctor of Philosophy degree with emphasis on problems related to food science may be obtained through the areas of microbiology and horticultural science, with faculty members from food science directing the program. Areas of specialization are nutrition, food product and process development, food chemistry, food microbiology, food quality, and food safety. In addition to studies with the conventional agricultural commodities, the department has research projects with seafood.

Prerequisite for admission to graduate study, in addition to the requirements of the Graduate School, is a good scientific background. Students with insufficient background in chemistry, physics, mathematics, or microbiology will be required to take these prerequisite subjects without graduate credit.

GRADUATE COURSES

FS 600—Research Planning (2) Food science investigations, identifying problems, planning and initiating research, experimental techniques, analysis of data, and reporting of results. Required of all first-year graduate students.

FS 601—Advanced Food Microbiology (4) *Prereq: FS 403.* Selection of media and laboratory methods, chemical and biological determinations, characterization of foodborne pathogens and spoilage organisms.

FS 602—Nutritional Aspects of Foods (4) *Prereq: BCH 511 and a course covering the principles of nutrition.* Nutrient needs of man, factors affecting the nutrient quality of foods and substances present in foods which may adversely affect the body.

FS 603—Instrumental Analysis and Separations (4) *Prereq: CY 331, FS 408.* Instrumental analysis and separations techniques in the analysis of foods; gas chromatography, infrared spectrophotometry, UV visible spectrophotometry, nuclear methods and chromatographic separations.

FS 604—Pesticide Analysis (4) Current pesticide analytical procedures. Sampling methods, extraction, clean up, and detection of pesticides in biological organisms and environments.

FS 605—Industrial Food Fermentations (4) *Prereq: FS 403.* Microbiological, chemical, and physical principles in controlled fermentations of foods and food constituents.

FS 606—Food Processing Systems (4) *Prereq: MS 302, FS 403.* Processing systems of current importance and those of future potential evaluated with emphasis on food engineering principles and the resulting biochemical, microbiological, and nutritional interactions.

FS 607—Food Chemistry (4) *Prereq: BCH 511, FS 408.* Functions of lipids, carbohydrates, proteins, enzymes, and other components in foods and their reactions and interactions during food processing and storage.

FS 608—Psychophysical Aspects of Foods (4) Physical and chemical stimuli controlling human sensory perception of texture, color, and flavor of foods. Methods of measurement and influence of processing methods on quality attributes of foods.

FS 611—Sugarcane Processing Technology (4) Same as AY 611. *Prereq: CY 362 and 363.* Chemical and physical processes required for crystallization and refining of sugar.

FS 621—Food Product Development (4) *Prereq: 8 credits in food science.* Theoretical and technological considerations of food product development.

FS 641—Advanced Human Nutrition (3) *Prereq: BCH 511 or AL 527.*

FS 642—Proteins and Amino Acids in Nutrition (3) *Prereq: BCH 512.* Nutritional aspects of proteins and amino acids, with emphasis on requirements, evaluation, and formulation of diets for various physiological functions.

FS 643—Nutritional Aspects of Carbohydrates and Lipids (3) *Prereq: BCH 512.* Role of carbohydrates and lipids in nutrition, with emphasis on energy metabolism.

FS 644—Current Topics in Human Nutrition (3) Critical reading of scientific literature in areas of current interest. Focus on those experimental results related to controversial areas of diet planning. Emphasis on analysis of experimental results and practical applications in a seminar format.

FS 651—Topics in Food Science (1-6; max: 12) Special aspects of food science studied in the classroom, laboratory, library, pilot plant, or the food industry.

FS 661—Food Science Seminar (1) Preparation and presentation of reports on specialized aspects of research in food science.

FS 697—Supervised Research (1-5)

FS 698—Supervised Teaching (1-5)

FS 699—Master's Research (1-15)

SCHOOL OF FOREST RESOURCES AND CONSERVATION

(College of Agriculture)

Director: J. L. GRAY
Graduate Coordinator: R. E. GODDARD

GRADUATE FACULTY 1975-76

Professors: J. L. GRAY; C. M. KAUFMAN; J. W. MILLER, JR.; W. L. PRITCHETT
Associate Professors: D. J. FORRESTER; R. E. GODDARD; J. B. HUFFMAN; R. A. SCHMIDT; W. H. SMITH; E. T. SULLIVAN
Assistant Professors: D. R. CROWE; K. C. EWEL; L. D. HARRIS; D. H. HIRTH; C. A. HOLLIS III; W. R. MARION; D. M. POST; J. V. SHIREMAN; L. D. WHITE

The School offers work leading to the degree of Master of Science, with specializations in forestry, forest products and technology, range ecology and wildlife ecology. The nonthesis degree Master of Forest Resources and Conservation is also offered with the same specializations. The Doctor of Philosophy degree may be earned in forest science through cooperation with the Departments of Agronomy, Botany, Entomology and Nematology, Plant Pathology, and Soil Science.

Specific areas of specialization include forest genetics, forest tree physiology, forest entomology, forest pathology, forest soils and nutrition, and forest recreation.

Graduate students should have adequate undergraduate training in biology, English, chemistry and mathematics, obtained by completing at least one year's work in each field. Students with inadequate background may be required to take undergraduate courses pertinent to their field of interest early in their graduate program. Such courses are considered foundation work and carry no graduate credit.

GRADUATE COURSES

FRC 601—Research Planning for Resource Decisions (4) *Prereq: consent of instructor.* Scientific methodology employed in natural resources research, including problem analyses and the selection, planning, conduct, and presentation of results of a research project.

FRC 605—Research Methods in Wildlife Ecology (4) Field and laboratory procedures used in wildlife research.

FRC 611—Seminar (1; max: 3) S/U.

FRC 612—Topics in Forestry (1-5; max: 9) Selected topics in forest sciences and multiple-use management of forest land for timber production, wildlife, and recreation.

FRC 615—Forest and Range Wildlife Ecology I (4) Major ecosystems in the U.S. for forest and range animals. Plant and animal components and their relation to reproductive patterns and factors controlling wild animal populations.

FRC 616—Forest and Range Ecology II (4)

FRC 618—Tropical Forestry (4) *Prereq: FRC 403.* Forests of the tropics, climatic influences, local laws and customs affecting forestry practice, multiple-use implications, wood properties and uses in relation to forest development, forest types and management; stress on American tropics.

FRC 620—Advanced Physiology of Forest Trees (3) *Prereq: BTY 515.* Factors influencing forest tree and stand energy balance, flowering, seed production, germination, water relations and growth; applications to forestry problems.

FRC 626—Forest Genetics I (4) *Prereq: an acceptable background in genetics.* Application of principles of genetics in the silvicultural handling of forest stands; selection, hybridization, and tree-breeding techniques.

FRC 627—Forest Genetics II (4)

FRC 630—Forest Soils (4) Same as SLS 630. *Prereq: SLS 421, 423, FRC 381.* Soil as a component of forest ecosystems. Soil chemical, physical, and biological properties influencing tree growth and biogeochemical cycles.

FRC 631—Advanced Wood Preservation (4) Relationships between wood and wood-deteriorating agencies; evaluation and analysis of preservatives; factors involved in treating wood; treatment and service evaluation.

FRC 636—Advanced Waterfowl Ecology (5) *Prereq: FRC 437 or consent of instructor.* Advanced theory and techniques in the management of waterfowl populations, including analyses of significant related research.

FRC 650—Methods in Natural Resource Interpretation (4) *Prereq: consent of instructor.* Interpreting natural resource information to the public, with emphasis on significant research pertaining to the effectiveness of various interpretive media.

FRC 652—Timber Physics (3) *Prereq: PS 215.* Physical nature and properties of wood in relation to moisture, heat, sound, electricity, and mechanical forces.

FRC 653—Wood Chemistry (3) *Prereq: organic chemistry.* Chemical nature and properties of wood and its constituents in relation to industrial processing.

FRC 680—Advanced Forest Economics (4) *Prereq: FRC 420.* Economics and economic problems of forestry and forest industries. Major emphasis on the forest economy of the United States.

FRC 696—Research Problems in Forest Resources and Conservation (3-9; max: 12)

FRC 697—Supervised Research (1-5)
FRC 698—Supervised Teaching (1-5)
FRC 699—Master's Research (1-15)

FOUNDATIONS OF EDUCATION
(College of Education)

Chairman: R. R. SHERMAN
Graduate Coordinator: D. L. AVILA

GRADUATE FACULTY 1975-76

Graduate Research Professor; I. J. GORDON

Professors: D. L. AVILA; M. C. BAKER; B. B. BROWN; R. L. CURRAN; W. H. GUERTIN; V. A. HINES; H. G. LEWIS, SR.; J. M. NEWELL; W. W. PURKEY, SR.; R. R. RENNER; B. L. SIEGEL; R. S. SOAR; H. L. WASS

Associate Professors: W. A. BUSBY; G. E. GREENWOOD; B. J. GUINAGH; R. E. JESTER; A. J. NEWMAN; R. R. SHERMAN; W. B. WARE; A. O. WHITE

Assistant Professors: S. D. ANDREWS; P. T. ASHTON; J. K. BENGSTON; L. M. CROCKER; S. B. DAMICO; R. B. WEBB

The Department of Foundations of Education offers the Master of Education, the Master of Arts in Education (with thesis), the Specialist in Education, the Doctor of Education, and the Doctor of Philosophy degrees with specialization in psychological foundations, research foundations, and social foundations of education.

Specific areas of specialization include human development, personality theory, learning theory, and general educational psychology within psychological foundations; research methodology, computer instruction, educational statistics, and measurement and evaluation within research foundations; and social, historical, and philosophical foundations and comparative and international education within social foundations. Special program opportunities are available through participation in the activities and research of the Institute for the Development of Human Resources.

GRADUATE COURSES

EDF 600—History of Education (5) Salient issues in education from the Reformation to the present.
EDF 601—Ancient and Medieval Education (5) Pedagogical practice and thought in China, India, Semitic nations, Greece, Rome, Islam, and Medieval and Renaissance Europe.
EDF 610—Philosophical Foundations of Education (5) Philosophical bases for democracy and education.
EDF 620—Socioeconomic Foundations of Education (4) Survey of the socioeconomic foundations of education.
EDF 625—Educational Sociology (5) Educational experiments with the social variables of decision-making systems, task, or curriculum, group size, and group social composition.
EDF 631—Comparative Education (4) Relationships of school and society in different cultural areas of the world.
EDF 632—Education in Latin America (4) Traditions and contemporary social, political, and cultural aspects.
EDF 640—Educational Psychology: Human Development (5) Current research and theories in the area of human development.
EDF 641—Educational Psychology: Personality Dynamics (5) Dynamics of behavior and their implications for education, counseling and guidance, administration, family relationships, and social action.

EDF 642—Educational Psychology: Problems (5) Individualized study of problems dealing with child development, adolescence, learning, and other areas of educational psychology.

EDF 643—Educational Psychology: Learning Theory (5) Logic and methodologies of theories of learning.

EDF 644—Laboratory in Human Development I (5) Supervised field and laboratory experiences in the observation, evaluation, and educational modification of human development. Contact with children of different ages and experience with learning, measurement, evaluation, and research.

EDF 645—Laboratory in Human Development II (5) *Prereq: EDF 644.*

EDF 646—Educational Psychology: General (5) *Not open to students majoring in psychology or psychological foundations of education.* Basic principles, techniques, and research in educational psychology; designed for graduate students preparing to teach who have a minimal background in psychology.

EDF 647—Educational Psychology: Aging and Education (5) Psychological and social processes in aging; education for aging and rehabilitation.

EDF 648—Educational Psychology: Death Education (4) Attitudes toward death, dying process, funeral practices, and grieving. Role of education for better understanding and coping with death.

EDF 649—Practicum in Educational Psychology (5) *Prereq: consent of instructor.* Supervised experience in a practical work situation dealing with problems and issues appropriate to psychological foundations, and their resolution.

EDF 650—Theory of Measurement (5) *Prereq: EDF 360, 450.* Introductory study of true score models, reliability, validity, norms, scaling, item analysis and basic elements of instrument selection.

EDF 660—Educational Statistics (4) *Prereq: EDF 360.* Statistical methods as applied to educational data and problems.

EDF 661—Computers in Educational Research (5) *Prereq: EDF 360, 450. Coreq: EDF 660.* Introduction to computer principles and programming, including practice problems on Computer Center equipment. Application to complex statistical analyses and educational research.

EDF 662—Practicum in Educational Research (3-12; max: 12) *Prereq: EDF 664; arrangements must be made with instructor prior to registration.* Experience in conducting various phases of quantitative educational research under individual supervision.

EDF 663—Research Methods in Education (5) *Prereq: EDF 360 or 450.* Research methods applicable to classroom practices. Cannot be used to meet the research preparation requirement for the Ed.D. degree.

EDF 664—Quantitative Foundations of Educational Research (10) *Prereq: STA 310, 320, or equivalent.* Integrated coverage of fundamentals in the general field of educational research. Includes statistics, experimental design, and data processing.

EDF 665—Assessment of Classroom Behavior (4) Instruction in at least four systems for measuring teacher-pupil behavior, representing the social-emotional and cognitive domains. Observation practiced in classrooms as well as with audio and video tape and film.

EDF 666—Seminar on Research on Effective Teaching (4) Systematic observation as a frame of reference for recording, analyzing, and conceptualizing teaching; research results; implications for teaching and learning.

EDF 690—Special Topics (2-5; max: 15) *Prereq: consent of department chairman.*

EDF 696—Individual Study (2-5; max: 15) For advanced students who wish to study individual problems in psychological, social, or philosophical foundations of education, or research or measurement under faculty guidance.

EDF 697—Supervised Research (1-5)

EDF 698—Supervised Teaching (1-5)

EDF 699—Master's Research (1-15)

EDF 701—Educational Classics (5; max: 10) Historical and philosophical examination of enduring writings on education from ancient to modern times.

EDF 710—Education and Moral and Spiritual Ideas (5) Moral ideas, the relation of moral values to school subjects, and the question of direction and systematic moral and spiritual instruction in the schools.

EDF 711—Theories of Mind (5) Mind and thinking processes, with implications for curriculum organization and classroom practice.

EDF 712—Contemporary Education Theories (5) *Seminar for post master's students.* Contemporary philosophical theories of education.

EDF 720—School and Society (5) *Open to students admitted to the Advanced School.* Provides a social and philosophic frame of reference for the society in which education occurs and its implications for the functioning of the school.

EDF 725—Research in Educational Sociology (5) Same as SY 725.

EDF 740—Educational Psychology: Cognition in the Educative Process (5) *Prereq: EDF 640.* Cognitive development as applied to curriculum development and teaching procedures.

EDF 741—Educational Implications of Perceptual Psychology (5) *Prereq: EDF 641.* Research literature on human behavior and its implications for educational theory and practice.

EDF 743—Advanced Educational Psychology: Learning (5) *Prereq: EDF 643.* Educational implications of contemporary approaches to learning. Relationship between topics in learning and their implications for instructional practices.

EDF 747—Advanced Educational Psychology: Seminar in Aging and Education (5) *Prereq: 647 or consent of instructor.* Research literature on aging process; implications for educational planning; critical examination of existing programs.

EDF 760—Methods of Educational Research (4) *Primarily for Ed.D. candidates. Prereq: EDF 360.* Examination of research methodologies. Problem identification as well as organization and presentation of data.

EDF 764—Advanced Quantitative Foundations of Educational Research (5; max: 10) *Prereq: EDF 664.* Integrated coverage, through team-teaching, of important approaches to educational research. Includes advanced statistics, design, computer applications, and analysis of selected research.

EDF 765—Seminar in Educational Research (4) *Prereq: EDF 664. Coreq: EDF 764.* Educational researches to develop appreciation of the investigations and understanding of the methodological techniques employed.

EDF 766—Analysis of Educational Research (4) *Prereq: EDF 664, 764. Coreq: EDF 765.* Educational researches to develop appreciation of important methodological techniques and newer approaches in educational research.

EDF 768—Evaluation of Educational Projects and Systems (5) *Prereq: EDF 450 (or equivalent) and at least one course in statistics or research methods.* Ways of evaluating special educational projects and continuously operating school systems.

EDF 780—Seminar in Educational Foundations (5; max: 15) Historical, philosophical, social, psychological, aesthetic, and comparative foundations of education.

EDF 799—Doctoral Research (1-15)

GENERAL TEACHER EDUCATION
(College of Education)

Chairman & Graduate Coordinator: R. B. MYERS

GRADUATE FACULTY 1975-76

Professors: F. P. HILLIARD; R. B. MYERS

Associate Professors: E. V. AMBROSE; R. A. BLUME; L. C. OBERLIN; A. B. PACKER; J. J. SHEA

Assistant Professors: M. L. HANES; S. O. JOHNSON; S. M. KINZER; L. L. LAMME; G. M. SCHUNCKE; J. P. TISON

The department offers programs leading to the Master of Education (nonthesis) or Master of Arts in Education (thesis) degrees with specialization in the following areas: elementary education, early childhood education, and middle school education. The department offers programs leading to the Specialist in Education, Doctor of Education, and Doctor of Philosophy degrees with specializations in elementary and early childhood education.

GRADUATE COURSES

EDE 500—Seminar in Elementary Education I (4) *Prereq: EDE 405 or teaching experience.*
EDE 503—Laboratory in Nursery-Kindergarten Teaching I (4) *Prereq. or coreq: EDF 341, or consent of instructor and teaching experience.*
EDE 504—Laboratory in Nursery-Kindergarten Teaching II (4) *Prereq. or coreq: EDE 503 and EDF 341, or consent of instructor and teaching experience.*
EDE 600—Elementary School Curriculum (4) *Prereq: ED 600 or a course in curriculum.* Content and methods. Primarily for students with no course background or teaching experience in elementary curriculum.
ED 601—The Emergent Middle School (4) Program, organization, and rationale of the newly emerging middle school in American school districts.
EDE 601—Practices in Childhood Education (4) *Prereq: course backround or teaching experience in the elementary curriculum.* Elementary school practices in relation to fundamental principles of curriculum development; selection, organization, and development of effective teaching-learning situations.
EDS 602—The Secondary School Curriculum (4) Scope, function, and types of secondary school curricula and ways of improving existing programs.
EDE 603—Early Childhood Education I (4) Trends in the teaching of nursery and kindergarten children as shown in past and current educational theory.
ED 604—Practicum in Middle School Education (4; max: 12) *Prereq: eligibility for regular rank III certificate in elementary, middle, or secondary school teaching; 27 credits in English language arts, mathematics, science, or social studies; course in the teaching of reading; ED 601 (may be corequisite).*
EDE 604—Early Childhood Education II (4) Current organization patterns and program models affecting nursery and kindergarten curriculum.
EDS 604—Curriculum Development Laboratory (2-5; max: 15) Guided experiences in developing resource units for teaching and in writing courses of study.
EDE 605—Resources for Early Childhood Education (4; max: 8) *Prereq: matriculation in an early childhood education graduate program.* Laboratory experiences in an array of community and institutional agencies.
EDE 608—Individualization of Instruction (4) School patterns as determiners of educational programs in childhood education. Innovative approaches in nursery, kindergarten, elementary and middle schools.
ED 620—The Education of Culturally Disadvantaged Children and Youth (4) Curriculum content and procedures pertinent to educational needs.
EDS 631—Secondary Education Lecture Series (1; max: 3) Current problems and issues presented by departmental faculty and visiting educators.
EDE 635—Supervision of Pre-Service Teachers (4) *Open to graduate students with certification and background in childhood education.*
EDS 635—Supervision of Pre-Service Teachers (2-5; max: 15) Functions of the directing teacher in the program, including problems and procedures of supervising the work of pre-service teachers.
ED 649—Subject-Area Planning for Elementary Teachers (3-6; max: 6) *Offered only by extension.* Workshop for the development of individual, city-wide, or county-wide plans for improving programs in language arts, social studies, mathematics, health, art, music, science, etc.
ED 660—Subject-Area Planning for Secondary Teachers (4) *Offered only by extension.* A workshop for the development of individual, city-wide, or county-wide plans for improving instruction in secondary school subjects.
ED 682—Field Laboratory for Faculty Study of Special Problems (3-9; max: 9) *Offered only by extension.* To assist teachers in single schools, groups of schools, or county systems in improving certain subject areas or in working on special problems within the system.
EDE 690—Special Topics (2-5; max: 15) *Prereq: permission of department chairman.*
EDE 696—Individual Work (2-5; max: 15) For advanced students who wish to study individual problems in childhood education and/or early childhood education under faculty guidance.
EDE 697—Supervised Research (1-5)
EDE 698—Supervised Teaching (1-5)

EDE 700—Problems in Childhood Education I (4) Advanced course in elementary school curriculum.

EDS 700—Seminar in Secondary Education (2-5; max: 15) *Open to advanced graduate students only upon consent of the staff of secondary education.* Current research and an overview of the total program in secondary education.

EDE 701—Problems in Childhood Education II (4)

ED 702—Seminar in Middle School Education (4) *Open to students in Advanced School. Prereq: approval of instructor.* Theory, research and practices in education, program development, in-service teacher training, and instruction strategies.

EDE 702—Evaluation in the Elementary School (4) Point of view, methods, and techniques used in appraising behavioral growth of pupils; evaluation of the objectives of the total program.

EDE 703—Seminar in Childhood Education II (4-8; max: 8) *Open to advanced graduate students.* Current research and an overview of the total program.

EDE 704—Seminar in Early Childhood Education (2-8; max: 8) *Open to advanced graduate students.* Problems and issues.

EDS 731—Secondary Education Colloquium (1; max: 6) Topics presented by departmental faculty, students, and visiting educators. S/U.

GEOGRAPHY
(College of Arts and Sciences)

Acting Chairman: C. I. CROSS
Graduate Coordinator: C. W. SPURLOCK

GRADUATE FACULTY 1975-76

Professors: J. R. ANDERSON; R. E. CRIST *(emeritus)*; J. R. DUNKLE; J. P. LATHAM;† R. B. MARCUS; H. MCCONNELL; * S. MCCUNE; W. H. MORGAN; D. L. NIDDRIE; D. J. PATTON;* H. L. POPENOE; R. J. TATA;† B. G. VANDERHILL*
Associate Professors: G. A. ANTONINI; A. K. CRAIG;† C. I. CROSS; D. DRYESON;* E. A. FERNALD;* G. W. SHANNON; N. D. WINSBERG*
Assistant Professors: T. D. BOSWELL; V. R. HETRICK; A. J. LAMME; D. R. LEE;† J. J. LOUVIERE;* L. A. PAGANINI; W. A. RABIEGA;* R. R. SCHULTZ;† C. W. SPURLOCK

These members of the faculty of The Florida State University (*) and Florida Atlantic University (†) are also members of the graduate faculty of the University of Florida and participate in the doctoral degree program in the University of Florida Department of Geography.

The Department of Geography offers work for the following graduate degrees: Master of Arts or Master of Science (thesis); Master of Arts in Teaching or Master of Science in Teaching (nonthesis but with required teaching experience); Doctor of Philosophy. A graduate student should have an undergraduate major in geography or in the social sciences with emphasis in geography. Deficiencies in undergraduate work in geography can be corrected concurrently with registration in graduate-level courses.

The department provides general work in geography at the master's level but specializes at the doctoral level in economic and cultural geography, particularly agricultural and urban geography, and in the regional geography of the United States, Latin America, and Africa south of the Sahara. The department maintains close ties with interdepartmental programs in tropical agriculture, urban and regional planning studies, Latin American studies and African studies; certificates in these fields may be obtained in addition to graduate degrees in geography.

Study for the Ph.D. degree in geography at the University of Florida by qualified master's degree recipients at FSU and at FAU is facilitated by a cooperative arrangement in which appropriate members of these two universities are members of the graduate faculty of the University of Florida.

GRADUATE COURSES

GPY 501—Advanced Air Photo Interpretation (3) *Prereq: GPY 300 or consent of instructor.* Uses of aerial photographs in geographical research.

GPY 502—Remote Sensing (3) *Prereq: GPY 501.* Uses of remote sensing imagery in geographical research.

GPY 505—Advanced Cartography (3) *Prereq: GPY 405; CIS 302, 405, or consent of instructor.* Advanced methods of cartography, including computer cartography and elements of cartographic reproduction.

GPY 508—Advanced Quantitative Analysis in Geography (3) *Prereq: GPY 408; STA 602 or equivalent.* Use of advanced quantitative techniques with geographic applications; development of research methods integrating quantitative analysis.

GPY 523—Geography of World Agriculture (5) World distribution of crops and livestock in relation to natural and cultural conditions; discussion of problems of agriculture in terms of products, economic organization, and agricultural regions; significance in world affairs.

GPY 526—Advanced Urban Geography (4) Empirical and theoretical spatial analysis of the various economic, demographic, and social facets within and between urban settlements.

GPY 527—Industrial Location (4) *Prereq: GPY 321 or consent of instructor.* Emphasis on location theory and its practical applications.

GPY 535—Land Tenure and Rural Settlement (5) Advanced study of systems of land tenure throughout the world, with special attention to geographical factors underlying their development.

GPY 538—Transportation Geography (4) *Prereq: GPY 200, 321, or consent of instructor.* Introduction to and assessment of current methods of describing, analyzing, and explaining spatial patterns of transport phenomena.

GPY 551—Research Methods in Population Geography (4) Most frequently used research methods.

GPY 596—Individual Study: Directed Readings (4; max: 16)

GPY 600—History of Geographical Thought (5) Development of knowledge illustrated by writings of representative geographers.

GPY 603—Introduction to Geographical Research (5) *Prereq: admission to graduate program in geography.* Geography as a science; problem formulation; research methods and design in geography.

GPY 605—Field Course in Geography (3) Methods of geographical field work. Observation, classification, interpretation, note-taking, traversing, and mapping of data. Areal analysis; land forms, climate, vegetation, soils, resources, settlement patterns, and land use.

GPY 606—Individual Field Work (3)

GPY 615—Cultural Plant Geography in the Tropics (3) Origin and dispersal of economic plants in the tropics. Their areal distribution under varying cultural and physical environments. Potential and limitations of technology in increasing food production.

GPY 621—Seminar: Economic Geography (4; max: 15) *Prereq: consent of instructor.* Selected problems in geography of economic activity.

GPY 625—Seminar: Developing Nations (4; max: 15) *Prereq: consent of instructor.* Selected problems in geography of developing nations.

GPY 635—Seminar: Land and Water Utilization (5; max: 15) *Prereq: consent of instructor.* Selected problems in utilization of land and water resources.

GPY 651—Seminar in Population (5) Same as SY 672. Combination lecture and seminar dealing with social and population problems from a spatial perspective. Major research project required.

GPY 661—Problems in Cultural Geography (5) Cultural problems pertaining to American social geography and to the impact of Western culture on aboriginal settlements.

GPY 681—Seminar: United States and Canada (5) Geography of the United States and Canada, with emphasis on patterns of settlement and distribution and development of economic activities.

GPY 685—Seminar: Middle America and the Caribbean (5) Cultural, economic, political, and resource characteristics and development of representative areas.

GPY 686—Seminar: South America (5) Cultural, economic, political, and resource characteristics and development of representative areas.

GPY 688—Resource Utilization and Conservation in Latin America (4) Regional appraisal of human and natural resources. Analysis of the role of resource utilization and conservation in the development of Latin American countries.

GPY 689—Seminar: Land, Man, and Migration in Latin America (4) Physical and cultural factors in population movements in Latin America, particularly from cold highlands to hot lowlands, and from rural sectors to metropolitan areas.

GPY 690—Tropical Lands and Their Utilization (12) *Prereq: GPY 501.* Field course emphasizing analytic inquiries into land use systems in Costa Rica. Special topics on land utilization types are environmental influences, settlement and field patterns, the market factor, labor supply, and transportation. Given in Costa Rica as part of the program of the Organization for Tropical Studies.

GPY 695—Selected Topics in Geography (1-6) *Prereq: baccalaureate degree in geography or a related field.* Seminar in modern geography.

GPY 696—Individual Work (1-5; max: 15)

GPY 697—Supervised Research (1-5)

GPY 698—Supervised Teaching (1-5)

GPY 699—Master's Research (1-15)

GPY 799—Doctoral Research (1-15)

GEOLOGY
(College of Arts and Sciences)

Chairman: J. L. EADES
Graduate Coordinator: A. F. RANDAZZO

GRADUATE FACULTY 1975-76

Graduate Research Professor: E. S. DEEVEY, JR.

Professors: H. K. BROOKS; G. M. GRIFFIN, JR.; D. NICOL; E. C. PIRKLE, JR; F. M. WAHL; S. D. WEBB

Associate Professors: F. N. BLANCHARD; J. L. EADES; T. H. PATTON; R. W. PIERCE, JR.; A. F. RANDAZZO

Assistant Professors: P. A. MUELLER; G. D. SHAAK; D. L. SMITH; D. P. SPANGLER

The Department of Geology offers a program leading to the Master of Science degree (thesis) and the Master of Science in Teaching (nonthesis) designed for those students interested in teaching earth science at community junior colleges. Areas of specialization include environmental geology, geochemistry, geomorphology, geophysics, marine geology, mineralogy-petrology, sedimentology and sedimentary petrology, and paleontology-stratigraphy.

For admission to graduate status in the Department of Geology a student must have a baccalaureate degree with a major in geology or a related field. A course in field methods or a summer field course is recommended. Deficiencies in undergraduate work in geology can be corrected with registration in graduate-level courses. Candidates for the master's degree in geology are advised to plan their work to secure a firm foundation in geology, mathematics, and chemistry, physics, or biology rather than to specialize too narrowly. Forty-five total quarter hours will be required for the Master of Science in Geology, of which at least 7 courses, totaling at least 28 hours, must be in *organized* geology courses (excluding research, special projects, teaching, etc.). A maximum of 9 hours of thesis research credit will be allowed. The remaining 8 hours can be either in additional geology hours *or* in a *declared* minor in another field.

During graduate residence, each student is required to take the Graduate Record Examination Advanced Test in Geology and score higher than the 50th percentile.

The score of this comprehensive examination must be reported to the candidate's supervisory committee before the final examination can be scheduled.

GRADUATE COURSES

GY 501—Geomorphology (4) *Prereq: G Y 409.* Application of the principles of geomorphology to the origin and evolution of landscapes.

GY 507—Vertebrate Paleontology (4) Same as ZY 407. *Prereq: ZY 309 or G Y 202.* Evolutionary history of major vertebrate groups, with emphasis on principles of prehistoric investigation.

GY 508—Geochemistry (4) *Prereq: G Y 202 and C Y 213.* The abundance and terrestrial distribution of the elements and their behavior during various geological processes.

GY 515—Mineralogical Analysis by X-Ray Methods (4) *Prereq: G Y 407 or consent of instructor.* Theory and practice of x-ray diffraction and emission, with emphasis on identification of crystalline materials.

GY 517—Marine Geology (4) *Prereq: G Y 202 or consent of instructor.* Principles and methods of submarine geology, with special reference to the submerged margins of the continents.

GY 518—Optical Crystallography (4) *Prereq: G Y 407 or consent of instructor.* Theory of crystal optics and the application of the polarizing microscope to optical properties of nonopaque substances.

GY 540—Geology Summer Field Camp (12) *Prereq: G Y 201 and 202 and consent of instructor.* Geological field procedures, techniques and instruments used in eight weeks of field work in Arizona, Utah, Nevada, and Colorado.

GY 550—Ground Water Geology (4) Principles of ground water geology, with special reference to the Coastal Plain and Florida.

GY 560—Sedimentology (4) *Prereq: G Y 418.* Analytical methods and geological interpretation of classic sediments.

GY 580—Development of the Geological Sciences (3) History of the development of human knowledge in the "Earth Sciences" from the early Grecian writers to the birth of modern geology.

GY 582—Introduction to Geophysics (4) *Prereq: G Y 201 and one year of college physics or consent of instructor.* Physics of the earth. Study of gravity and magnetic fields, seismic waves, thermal history, size and shape.

GY 584—Principles of Exploration Geophysics I (4) *Prereq: G Y 201 and one year of college physics or consent of instructor.* Reflection and refraction seismology; theory, interpretation, instruments.

GY 585—Principles of Exploration Geophysics II (4) *Prereq: G Y 201 and one year of college physics or consent of instructor.* Gravitational, magnetic, and electrical methods of exploration; instrumentation, surveying techniques, data reduction, interpretation.

GY 600—Tectonics (4) *Prereq: G Y 409.* Interrelationships of orogenic belts and plate tectonic theory of the crust and upper mantle.

GY 601—Geomorphology of Southeastern United States (4) *Prereq: G Y 501.* Geomorphology of the Atlantic and Gulf Coastal Plain, including the Mississippi Flood Plain and Delta, the Piedmont, Crystalline, and Folded Appalachians, and southern part of the Appalachian Plateau and adjacent areas.

GY 607—Ancient Vertebrate Faunas (4) Same as ZY 607. *Prereq: G Y 507 or Z Y 507.* Evolution, distribution, and extinction of vertebrate faunas, with emphasis on problems in paleoecology, paleogeography, and patterns of phylogeny.

GY 608—Seminar in Evolution (4) Same as ZY 608. Processes, mechanisms, patterns, and orientation of evolution.

GY 611—Mineralogy of Clays (4) *Prereq: G Y 518.* Structure, composition, properties, origin, and mode of occurrence of the clay minerals.

GY 612—Nonmetallic Geologic Materials (4) *Prereq: G Y 408.* The geologic occurrences, properties, and uses of limestone, shales, and other nonmetallic deposits.

GY 613—Seminar on Mineral Deposits and Conservation Geology (4) Study of exploration of mineral resources and environmental problems associated with their utilization.

GY 614—Isotope Geology (4) *Prereq: general inorganic chemistry, calculus and geochemistry or their equivalent, and consent of instructor.* Isotopes, stable and unstable, and discussion of geochronologic and tracer studies.

GY 616—Analytical Geochemistry (4) *Prereq: general inorganic chemistry, calculus and geochemistry or their equivalent, and consent of instructor.* Fundamentals of chemical analysis of geologic materials and training in common geochemical instrumental analytical methods.

GY 618—Petrographic Mineralogy (4) *Prereq: GY 518.* Application of optical crystallography to the study and identification of rock-forming minerals in thin section, including an introduction to petrography.

GY 619—Sedimentary Petrography (4) *Prereq: GY 518.* Sedimentary rocks in thin section, with emphasis on their genesis as determined from mineral composition, texture, and occurrence.

GY 623—Micropaleontology (4) *Prereq: GY 421.* Classification and identification of biostratigraphically important microfossil groups and their use in local and regional correlation.

GY 624—Paleoecology (4) *Prereq: GY 421 or ZY 308.* Paleoautecology, paleosynecology, historical biogeography of marine invertebrates, and ecological rules as applied to fossil invertebrates.

GY 625—Advanced Invertebrate Paleontology (4) *Prereq: GY 421.* Local field problems in paleoecology or biostratigraphy.

GY 640—Cenozoic and Mesozoic Stratigraphy (4) Cenozoic and Mesozoic stratigraphy, with emphasis on the stratigraphy of the Gulf and Atlantic Coastal Plain; American and European relationships.

GY 651—Hydrogeology (4) *Prereq: GY 550.* Principles and concepts of groundwater flow systems; techniques of flow system delineation; hydrogeologic problems common to water development.

GY 660—Seminar (1; max: 3) Reading in special topics.

GY 661—Sedimentary Petrology (4) *Prereq: GY 560 or consent of instructor.* Origin, composition, and structures of sedimentary rocks, including tectonic, paleogeographic, and environmental interpretation.

GY 662—Carbonate Sedimentology (4) *Prereq: GY 518.* Limestones and dolostones, their origin, occurrence, and significance; study of recent and ancient carbonate depositional regimes.

GY 664—Fluvial, Deltaic, and Transitional Environments of Sedimentation (4) *Prereq: GY 470; GY 560 or 661.* Environmental factors and sediment types accumulated in fluvial, deltaic, and other transitional environments; recognition of these environments in ancient rocks.

GY 668—Coastal and Estuarine Geology (4) *Prereq: GY 517, 560 or COE 610.* Origin and distribution of coastal and estuarine earth materials, evolution of morphological features and the dynamic changes that occur because of the interplay between terrestrial, marine, and atmospheric processes.

GY 675—Geological Oceanography (4) *Prereq: GY 470 or 517, and 560.* Structural development, sedimentation processes, and sediments of continental slope, rise, abyssal plain, and associated deep-sea environments.

GY 676—Offshore Oil, Gas, and Other Mineral Resources (4) Hydrocarbon and mineral resources of the offshore area.

GY 690—Special Topics in Geology (1-4; max: 12) Lectures, conferences, or laboratory sessions covering selected topics of current interest in modern geology.

GY 696—Individual Work (1-5; max: 15) For work beyond that offered in regular courses.

GY 697—Supervised Research (1-5; max: 5)

GY 698—Supervised Teaching (1-5; max: 5)

GY 699—Master's Research (1-15)

GERMANIC AND SLAVIC LANGUAGES AND LITERATURES

(College of Arts and Sciences)

Chairman: C. J. GELLINEK
Graduate Coordinator: E. I. SCHÜRER

GRADUATE FACULTY 1975-76

Professors: C. J. GELLINEK; E. I. SCHÜRER
Associate Professors: O. W. JOHNSTON; W. J. SULLIVAN III; M. E. VALK
Assistant Professors: E. C. BARKSDALE; G. BRINKER-GABLER; L. P. JOHNSON;
P. O. JUHL; H. W. KRAFT; D. M. POPP

The department offers programs of study leading to M.A. and M.A.T. degrees in German. Areas of specialization are German literature and Germanic philology and medieval literature. In addition, sufficient courses are available for a graduate minor in Russian. A Ph.D. program in German is currently under consideration. The graduate program is designed to prepare students for careers in teaching, business, research, journalism, and diplomacy.

The prerequisite for admission to graduate work is an undergraduate major in the field, including advanced courses in both literature and language. Qualified candidates with B.A. degrees in other disciplines will be considered. A good foundation in a second non-Germanic language is desirable.

GRADUATE COURSES

RSN 506—Grammar and Composition Exercises (4) Advanced work in the grammar of the clause, and practice in composition based on Russian readings.
RSN 512—The Development of the Russian Language (4) Phonological and morphological changes in the Russian language from late Indo-European times to the present.
RSN 513—Russian Syntax and Style (4) Linguistic studies of the grammar of Russian.
RSN 514—Studies in Old Church Slavonic (4) Outline of OCS grammar and readings in the monuments and liturgical writings.
RSN 527—Survey of Russian Literary History I (5) Tolstoy, Dostoevsky, and other major pre-twentieth-century figures studied in the context of Russian intellectual currents and the history of European literature.
RSN 528—Survey of Modern Russian Literature II (5) Soviet literature and the schools of the pre-Revolutionary literary milieu.
RSN 540—Studies in Russian Drama and Theatre (4)
RSN 551—Advanced Studies in Russian Literature (4)
RSN 596—Independent Studies (1-4) *Available only by special arrangement.*
GN 550—Philosophy & German Literature (4) Influence of famous German philosophers (from Leibniz, Kant and Hegel to Marx, Nietzsche and Heidegger) on the literature and culture of Germany.
GN 600—Special Study in Germanic Languages and Literatures (5; max: 15) Intensive study of a selected topic.
GN 602—Beginning German for Graduate Students I (4) For graduate students with no formal preparation who need to acquire a reading knowledge. S/U.
GN 603—Beginning German for Graduate Students II (4) *Prereq: GN 602 or the equivalent.* For graduate students working to acquire proficiency in reading, S/U option.
GN 604—The Genius of Goethe (5) Selected works of Goethe in the context of the artistic, social, and political conditions of his time.
GN 606—Advanced Speaking and Writing Exercises (4) Practice in structure and style of oral and written German.
GN 612—The Evolution of the German Language (4) Historical survey of the German language as a mirror of the cultural forces that shaped its development.
GN 613—Studies in German Poetry (4) Extensive and intense reading and interpretation of German lyrical poetry though the ages. Different styles and themes examined and analyzed.
GN 620—The Bible in Gothic (5)
GN 624—The Viking Sagas (4)
GN 625—Readings in Sagas and Scaldic Poetry (4)
GN 628—18th-Century German Literature (4) Major themes, forms and techniques in the literature of the Enlightenment or "Sturm und Drang" and its development in relation to the cultural, moral, and political problems of the times.

GN 629—Studies in German Classical Literature (4) Major literary achievements of the Weimar classic examined and interpreted. Readings include Goethe, Schiller, Hölderlin, and Kleist.

GN 630—Studies in Romantic or Post-Romantic Literature (4) Analysis of the uniquely German aspect of the Romantic movement in Europe. Major works of the German Romantics or "Junges Deutschland" examined in terms of themes, style, and common goals.

GN 640—Studies in German Drama and Theatre (4) Main tendencies in the development of German drama during different literary periods. Study of dramatic theory and analysis of masterpieces, set against the social and political background as interpreted by the playwrights.

GN 645—18th-Century German Literature (4) Lasting contributions of the great German poets and writers of the period, with reference to the prevailing social and historical conditions.

GN 650—Seminar in Germanic Studies (5; max: 15) *Required of all candidates for a master's degree in German.* Methodology and research problems.

GN 651—Middle High German Love Poetry (4) *Prereq: GN 455, 655, or equivalent.* Major works of Hartmann von Aue, Gottfried von Strassburg, Wolfram von Eschenbach, and Walther von der Vogelweide.

GN 652—Fate, Fortune, and Frivolity (5) Survey of 17th-century Baroque poetry, drama, and novel, with intensive reading and analysis of major works.

GN 653—Post-War Literature: East and West (5) Developments and trends in poetry, the novel, and the theatre after World War II in the Federal Republic of Germany, the German Democratic Republic, Austria, and Switzerland.

GN 655—Introduction to Middle High German Literature (4)

GN 660—Kafka, Hesse, Brecht, and Grass (4) Major trends and techniques in modern German writing. Close analysis of representative works as well as the historical and social background.

GN 696—Independent Studies (2-5; max: 16) *Available only by special arrangement.*

GN 697—Supervised Research (1-5)

GN 698—Supervised Teaching (1-5; max: 5)

GN 699—Master's Research (1-15)

HEALTH AND HOSPITAL ADMINISTRATION
(College of Health Related Professions)

Chairman & Graduate Coordinator: J. M. CHAMPION

GRADUATE FACULTY 1975-76

Professor: J. M. CHAMPION
Associate Professors: R. A. ELNICKI; K. E. KILPATRICK
Assistant Professor: N. D. RICHIE

The Program in Health and Hospital Administration offers the following courses as part of the major sequence leading to the degree Master of Business Administration with a concentration in health and hospital administration; the degree is offered by the College of Business Administration. Requirements for this degree are described more fully in the section of the *Catalog* dealing with requirements for the Master of Business Administration.

For admission to courses listed below, the student must have been admitted to the Graduate School, College of Business Administration, and to the program in health and hospital administration.

For listings of other courses required of students enrolled in the program in health and hospital administration, see the Departments of Business Administration (BA 610, 664, 671, 679, 690); Economics (ES 615, 616); Industrial and Systems Engineering (ISE 635).

GRADUATE COURSES

HA 600—**Perspectives in Health (4)** Factors operating in health and disease in an individual or a society. Historical and social background of disease, its etiology, and the organization of medical care.

HA 601—**Hospital Organization, the Community and Patient Care (3)** Hospital culture in relation to organizational philosophy and changing health patterns, with emphasis on the patient care process; concept and application of environmental therapy; current research in the hospital and health field.

HA 602—**Financial Administration of Health and Hospital Care (3)** Analysis of sources and uses of health care funds.

HA 610—**Seminar in Health and Hospital Administration (4)** Departmental organization of the general hospital, designed to help integrate course work with the administrative residency.

HA 611—**Seminar in Health and Hospital Administration (2)** Formal study, through readings, lectures, and case discussions, of major issues and problems in hospital organization and management.

HA 612—**Introduction to Rehabilitation Facility Administration (2)** Rehabilitation process as it relates to administration of rehabilitation facilities; history and philosophy of the rehabilitation movement; system of delivering rehabilitation services.

HA 640—**Research in Health and Hospital Administration (5).** Directed investigation of an administrative problem fundamental to health and hospital administration.

HA 641—**Practicum in Health and Hospital Administration (2; max: 7)** Application of management concepts and principles to voluntary and governmental health facilities, associations, and organizations.

HA 646—**Residency in Health and Hospital Administration (7; max: 14)** Supervised field work in an administrative setting. Designed as a sequence of two quarters. S/U.

HA 691—**Hospital Administration Research and Reports (2)** *Prereq: BA 690.* Supervised preparation of a report on a topic of current interest in hospital administration.

LW 686—**Hospital and Health Law Seminar (2)** Law relating to hospital and medical administration. Designed especially for students in the graduate program in hospital and health administration.

HA 696—**Individual Study in Hospital Administration (2)**

HEALTH RELATED PROFESSIONS—GENERAL
(College of Health Related Professions)

Dean: H. K. SUZUKI

The following courses are offered under the supervision of the office of the dean by an interdisciplinary faculty and deal with material of concern to two or more of the areas of specialty offered in the College of Health Related Professions. These courses are also open to students of other colleges, with the permission of the course instructor.

GRADUATE COURSES

HRP 551—**Laboratory Study of Emergent Language Behavior (4)**

HRP 600—**Perspectives in Health (4)** Same as HA 600. Health and disease in an individual or a society. Historical and social background of disease, its etiology, and the organization of medical care.

HRP 620—**Seminar: The Health Related Professions (4)** Trends affecting the health professions and the relations among these professions, the scientific disciplines, and the community. Required for allied health professions trainees.

HRP 690—**Special Topics (1-5; max: 10)**

HRP 696—**Individual Study in Health Related Professions (3-5; max: 10)**

HRP 697—**Supervised Research (1-5)**

HRP 698—**Supervised Teaching (1-5)**

HISTORY
(College of Arts and Sciences)

Chairman: A. L. FUNK
Graduate Coordinator: H. W. PAUL

GRADUATE FACULTY 1975-76

Graduate Research Professor: W. WOODRUFF
Professors: D. BUSHNELL; D. M. CHALMERS; R. T. CHANG; H. J. DOHERTY, JR.; A. L. FUNK; M. V. GANNON; C. GOSLINGA; E. A. HAMMOND; L. N. MCALISTER; N. W. MACAULAY, JR.; J. K. MAHON; H. W. PAUL; S. PROCTOR; A. SUAREZ
Associate Professors: M. L. ENTNER; M. H. KELE; C. C. STURGILL; N. M. WILENSKY; H. A. WILSON; G. D. WINIUS
Assistant Professors: D. R. COLBURN; R. H. DAVIS, JR.; G. S. HENRY; G. E. POZZETTA; C. J. SOMMERVILLE

The Department of History offers the degrees Master of Arts and Doctor of Philosophy. The nonthesis degree, Master of Arts in Teaching, is also offered with a major in history. The master's degree may be taken with specialization in Medieval, European, British, United States, Latin American, East Asian, or African history. The Doctor of Philosophy degree may be taken with specialization in United States, European, or Latin American history.

Applicants must provide the department with the following evidence of aptitude and interest: (1) completion of at least 40 quarter hours of history at the undergraduate or graduate level; (2) three references from persons competent to evaluate the applicant's potential for graduate work; (3) an essay of from three to five double-spaced typewritten pages identifying the applicant's career goals and particular regional, temporal, or topical interests within the general field of history and, if possible, thesis or dissertation interests.

In addition to meeting the requirements of the Graduate School, candidates must meet the following departmental requirements.

Master of Arts in Teaching: (1) at least 28 credits in history, including 5 in HY 602 or 603; (2) at least 8 credits in a minor outside history; (3) 9 credits in a departmental internship in teaching through registration in ASC 641, 642, and 643; (4) reading knowledge of one foreign language.

Master of Arts: (1) 20 credits in the field of specialization; 18 in other fields of history, including 5 in HY 602 or 603; 8 in a minor outside history; (2) a thesis in the field of specialization, with 9 credits given under HY 699; (3) reading knowledge of one foreign language.

Doctor of Philosophy: (1) Passing a preliminary examination in the major field to test a candidate's general knowledge and level of literacy; (2) passing qualifying examinations consisting of written examinations in the field of specialization and three minor fields, and a general oral. The minor fields may be selected from among the three fields of doctoral specialization named above and from those listed for the M.A. degree. With the permission of the supervisory committee, the student may substitute for one of the listed fields a minor which relates directly to primary teaching and research interests; (3) HY 602, 603, and 700; (4) reading knowledge of at least one foreign language; (5) a teaching internship of 6 credits through registration in ASC 641, 642, or 643; (6) a dissertation in the field of specialization for which credit is given under HY 799.

GRADUATE COURSES

Courses at the 400 level may be selected under the "Topics" sequence 501-506.

HY 501—Topics in European History (4; max: 16)
HY 502—Topics in United States History (4; max:16)
HY 503—Topics in Latin American History (4; max: 16)
HY 504—Topics in British History (4; max: 16)
HY 505—Topics in East Asian History (4; max: 16)
HY 506—Topics in African History (4; max: 16)
HY 596—Special Studies (4; max: 16)
HY 602—Theories and Methods I (5)
HY 603—Theories and Methods II (5)
HY 613—The Middle Ages (5; max: 15)
HY 614—The United States in the World Economy, 1783-1960 (5) Same as ES 614. Interrelatedness of the United States economy with the economies of other lands; circumstances which have enabled the American people to alter the course of world history.
HY 618—Europe, 1500-1763 (5)
HY 619—European Expansion (5)
HY 620—Seminar in the History of Modern European Thought (5; max: 15)
HY 623—Readings, Modern Europe (5; max: 15) Three sequences: 18th century, 19th century, 20th century.
HY 624—Central Europe (5)
HY 625—Western Europe Since 1763 (5)
HY 626—Eastern Europe (5)
HY 633—England (5; max: 15)
HY 640—Historians and American Society (5; max: 10) Historiography. Seminar in the analysis of works of important historians on the American people. Considerations of schools, theories, philosophies, and functions of history.
HY 641—Seminar in the History of American Military Policy (5; max: 10)
HY 642—Seminar in American Thought (5; max: 15)
HY 643—Seminar in United States Urban-Ethnic History (5; max: 10)
HY 646—Colonial America (5) English colonies from their origins to about 1781.
HY 647—United States, Early National (5) From 1781 to the end of the War of 1812.
HY 648—United States, the Middle Period (5) From 1815 to 1850.
HY 649—United States, Division and Reunion (5) From the War with Mexico to 1877.
HY 650—The Emergence of Modern America (5) From 1877 to the entrance of the U.S. into World War I.
HY 651—America Between the Wars (5) From U.S. entrance into World War I to U.S. entrance into World War II.
HY 652—Recent America, Since 1945 (5)
HY 660—Africa (5; max: 15)
HY 670—Historical Literature of Latin America I (5)
HY 671—Historical Literature of Latin America II (5)
HY 672—Seminar in Brazilian History (5) May be repeated.
HY 673—Seminar in Colonial Spanish America (5) May be repeated.
HY 674—Seminar in Independent Spanish America (5; max: 15)
HY 682—Readings in Japanese History (5; max: 15)
HY 696—Individual Study (5; max: 20)
HY 697—Supervised Research (1-5; max: 5)
HY 698—Supervised Teaching (1-5; max: 5)
HY 699—Master's Research (1-15) *Required of all candidates for the M.A. degree.*
HY 700—Comparative History (5; max: 15) *Required of all candidates for the Ph.D. degree.*
HY 799—Doctoral Research (1-15)

HORTICULTURAL SCIENCE
(College of Agriculture)

Chairman: J. F. KELLY

FRUIT CROPS

Chairman: R. H. BIGGS
Graduate Coordinator: J. SOULE

ORNAMENTAL HORTICULTURE

Chairman & Graduate Coordinator: W. J. CARPENTER

VEGETABLE CROPS

Chairman: J. F. KELLY
Graduate Coordinator: B. D. THOMPSON

GRADUATE FACULTY 1975-76

Professors: J. A. ATTAWAY; R. H. BIGGS; C. W. CAMPBELL; W. J. CARPENTER; C. A. CONOVER; H. W. FORD; J. F. GERBER; W. GRIERSON; C. B. HALL; J. N. JOINER; J. F. KELLY; R. C. J. KOO; A. H. KREZDORN; C. D. LEONARD; S. J. LOCASCIO; G. A. MARLOWE, JR.; J. MONTELARO; H. J. REITZ, JR.; T. J. SHEEHAN; J. W. SITES; J. SOULE; I. STEWART; B. D. THOMPSON
Associate Professors: L. G. ALBRIGO; C. E. ARNOLD; J. F. BARTHOLIC; D. W. BUCHANAN; A. E. DUDECK; D. D. GULL; L. H. HALSEY; S. E. MALO; D. B. MCCONNELL; R. L. PHILLIPS; R. T. POOLE; W. B. SHERMAN; G. J. WILFRET; W. J. WILTBANK
Assistant Professors: C. R. BARMORE; M. J. BASSETT; D. J. CANTLIFFE; W. S. CASTLE; D. F. HAMILTON; L. C. HANNAH; L. K. JACKSON; C. R. JOHNSON; S. R. KOSTEWICZ; G. S. SMITH, JR.; B. O. TJIA

The Departments of Fruit Crops, Ornamental Horticulture, and Vegetable Crops offer a joint program in horticultural science leading to the Master of Science and Doctor of Philosophy degrees with specialization in fruit crops, ornamental horticulture, or vegetable crops. The nonthesis degree Master of Agriculture is also offered with a major in fruit crops, ornamental horticulture, vegetable crops, or horticultural science.

Areas of emphasis include crop physiology and biochemistry, seed physiology, crop breeding and genetics, biochemical genetics, environmental science, crop production and management, landscape horticulture, and postharvest physiology, biochemistry, and handling.

New graduate students should have sound undergraduate training in horticulture or plant science which should include 18 to 24 undergraduate credits in fruit crops, ornamental horticulture, vegetable crops, or general horticulture and botany, mathematics, chemistry, soils, entomology, and plant pathology or equivalent. Student interest and available guidance and facilities will determine the area of emphasis within a given specialization for the thesis or dissertation problem. It is possible to conduct certain types of research for the Master of Science and Doctor of Philosophy degrees at one of the Agricultural Research and Education Centers or Agricultural Research Centers of the Institute of Food and Agricultural Sciences. Students in food science may receive the Doctor of Philosophy degree through the horticultural science program.

GRADUATE COURSES

HSC 601—Horticultural Science Seminar (1; max: 4) Oral presentation of material in one of the following areas: literature review related to the student's research, research results, or a published paper of relevance to horticulture. Subject matter will be determined by the instructor. S/U.

HSC 603—Morphology of Horticultural Crops (5) *Prereq: BTY 532.* Morphological features of tropical and temperate zone horticultural crops, their modification by environment, and their relation to cultural practices and production problems.

HSC 604—Taxonomy of Horticultural Crops (5) *Prereq: BTY 380.* Nomenclature, classification and identification of tropical and temperate zone horticultural crops, with emphasis on the scientific basis and utility of the various systems.

HSC 605—Perennial Horticultural Crop Breeding (5) *Prereq: A Y 362.* Principles of woody horticultural crop breeding and varietal improvement, including patterns of evolution, mechanisms of heredity, and genetic parameters. Specific breeding problems in tropical and deciduous fruit and ornamental crops.

HSC 606—Herbaceous Horticultural Crop Breeding (3) *Prereq: A Y 362.* Techniques in breeding herbaceous crops for horticultural qualities and for resistance to diseases and animal pests; methods of testing new introductions.

HSC 607—Biochemical Genetics of Higher Plants (4) *Prereq: A Y 362 or ZY 325 and BCH 579 or equivalents.* Discussion of current evidence bearing on gene function and regulation, examples of the use of plant mutants in the elucidation of biochemical pathways, and examination of somatic cell genetics in higher plants.

HSC 611—Seed Physiology (5) *Prereq: BTY 310.* Study of the dormancy, germination, growth and development of seeds and the life processes involved; methods of handling and processing.

HSC 612—Nutrition of Horticultural Crops (5) *Prereq: BTY 310 and OH 441 or FC 403 or equivalent.* Physiological, biochemical and environmental factors influencing nutritional status of horticultural plants and the resulting effects on growth, yield, and quality.

HSC 613—Environmental and Developmental Physiology of Horticultural Crops (5) *Prereq: BTY 310.* Physiology of growth and development of horticultural crops, with emphasis on interfacing plant responses to environmental factors.

HSC 614—Chemical Regulators of Horticultural Crops (4) *Prereq: HSC 613 or equivalent.* Physiology and biochemistry of chemical regulators as related to horticultural crops, with emphasis on manipulative practices.

HSC 615—Postharvest Physiology (5) *Prereq: BTY 310 and VC 451, OH 442 or FC 437 or equivalent.* Advances in plant physiology and other areas of science applied in quality maintenance and postharvest handling of fruit, vegetable, and ornamental crops.

HSC 620—Agricultural Meteorology (5) Climate and meteorology of the biosphere in relation to horticultural crops. Heat budget of the plant-soil surface, turbulent transport, evapotranspiration, frost protection, and agricultural climatology.

HSC 621—Environmental Measurements (3) *Prereq: consent of instructor.* Methods and techniques employed in the characterization of the biosphere. Sensor selection, measuring and recording equipment for light, wind, temperature, humidity, and heat flow.

HSC 626—Rootstock-Scion Relationships (4) Influence on disease susceptibilities, soil and climatic adaptations, bud-union incompatibilities and production.

HSC 627—Nursery Production and Management (4) *Prereq: BTY 310, PLS 301, 311 and OH 420, FC 442, HSC 632 or HSC 633 or equivalent.* Literature review and application of research results to problems of commercial production of woody ornamentals and fruit crops.

HSC 630—Citriculture (5) Citrus growing, emphasizing the problems offered by varying sites, soils, climates, rootstocks, and cultivars.

HSC 631—Citrus Production Management (5) Methods of tabulating and evaluating the functions of citrus trees in relation to fruit production. Actual field recognition of the various factors and the means of properly organizing field management.

HSC 632—Tropical Fruits (4) *Prereq: consent of instructor.* Botanical and horticultural characteristics and cultural problems of tropical fruits, with emphasis on those of major importance to Florida.

HSC 633—Tropical Beverage, Nut and Spice Crops (4) *Prereq: consent of instructor.* Botanical and horticultural characteristics and cultural problems of perennial tropical fruit crops which require processing before consumption or utilization.

HSC 634—Tropical Fruit Production and Research in Florida (5) A comprehensive study of tropical fruit production and research at the Agricultural Research and Education Center at Homestead and field locations in South Florida. (Students will be in residence for 4 weeks at the Center. Offered alternate years in SS.)

HSC 640—Orchidology (4) *Prereq: OH 441.* The principles and practices involved in the production of orchid plants and flowers, including nomenclature, breeding, seed culture, harvesting, and handling.

HSC 641—Research and Development in Turfgrass Science (4) *Prereq: OH 463.* Principles and practices of turfgrass improvement and management, including propagation, nutrition, physiology, soil management, and experimental methods applied to turf research.
HSC 650—Advanced Olericulture (5) *Prereq: BTY 310.* Survey of scientific knowledge related to production of vegetable crops.
HSC 691—Topics (2-5; max: 10) Study of contemporary research in horticultural science.
HSC 692—Practicum in Horticultural Science (2-5; max: 10) *Admission limited to graduate students majoring in horticultural science.* Supervised and individual work in professional areas of horticulture.
HSC 696—Nonthesis Research in Horticultural Science (1-5; max: 5)
HSC 697—Supervised Research (1-5)
HSC 698—Supervised Teaching (1-5)
HSC 699—Master's Research (1-15)
HSC 799—Doctoral Research (1-15)

IMMUNOLOGY AND MEDICAL MICROBIOLOGY
(College of Medicine)

Chairman: K. I. BERNS
Graduate Coordinator: G. E. GIFFORD

GRADUATE FACULTY 1975-76

Professors: E. M. AYOUB; L. W. CLEM; R. B. CRANDALL; G. E. GIFFORD; J. E. MCGUIGAN; J. W. SHANDS, JR.; P. A. SMALL, JR.; M. D. YOUNG
Associate Professors: H. BAER; Y. M. CENTIFANTO; E. M. HOFFMAN; R. H. WALDMAN
Assistant Professors: D. C. BIRDSELL; D. H. DUCKWORTH; J. M. GASKIN; L. O. INGRAM; K. D. LEY

The Department of Immunology and Medical Microbiology offers programs leading to the Master of Science and Doctor of Philosophy degrees in the medical sciences, with specialization in immunology and medical microbiology.

Specific areas of specialization include infectious diseases, cellular and humoral immunity, immunochemistry, microbial genetics, parasitology, dental microbiology, and bacterial and animal virology.

The undergraduate preparation for graduate study in microbiology should be wide in scope and should include general biology, physics, chemistry (2 to 3 years, including organic and physical chemistry), and preferably statistics, calculus, genetics, and bacteriology. A bachelor's degree in bacteriology or microbiology is not required. In graduate school the student will at first obtain a general background in microbiology as preparation for research and teaching. The remaining course work should be arranged according to the student's interests and competence. Through individual planning of course work, research, and teaching, the graduate student is offered an educational atmosphere to help him develop certain skills and gain intellectual independence and initiative.

GRADUATE COURSES

MED 551—Microbiology (7) Introduction to the study of microbiology.
MED 554—Medical Parasitology (2) Introduction to the major groups of animal parasites infecting man, with special emphasis on life history, epidemiology, and laboratory diagnosis.
MED 650—Public Health Microbiology (1-6; max: 18) Same as MCY 650. *Prereq: consent of director of laboratories.* Reference study, laboratory practice of diagnostic techniques in Microbiology Diagnostic Laboratories, Shands Teaching Hospital, University of Florida Health Center, or in residence at Bureau of Laboratories, State Department of Health, Jacksonville.

MED 651—Special Topics in Microbiology (1-6; max: 18) Same as MCY 651. Contemporary research in an aspect of general microbiology.

MED 652—Virology (5) Same as MCY 652. Nature of viruses and mechanisms of viral infection: animal, bacterial, and plant viruses.

MED 653—Virology Laboratory (3) Same as MCY 653. *Prereq. or coreq: MED 652.* Laboratory experiments on the nature of viruses and mechanisms of viral replication; other consequences of viral infections.

MED 654—Research Planning (5) Same as MCY 654. *Prereq: 20 credits in progressive study of microbiology.* Scientific research, including initiating a problem, experimental techniques, analysis and evaluation of data, reporting; illustrated by bacteriological examples.

MED 655—Experimental Microbiology (2-5; max: 8) Application of physical, chemical, and biological techniques to experimental problems in microbiology. Individual laboratory study under supervision.

MED 656—The Literature of Microbiology (3) Same as MCY 656. *Prereq: 12 credits of microbiology.* Bibliographic method in searching the literature of specified areas of the discipline.

MED 657—Microbial Metabolism (5) Same as MCY 657. *Prereq: BCH 603.* Intermediary metabolism of microorganisms; metabolic pathways that are unique or characteristic primarily of microorganisms.

MED 658—Microbial Physiology (5) Same as MCY 658. *Prereq: MED 657.* Structural and functional elements of microorganisms and mechanics of their regulatory systems. Mechanisms of control of microbial DNA replication, cell division, ribosome and cell-wall formation; kinetic studies of normal and abnormal growth.

MED 659—Principles of Immunology (5) Same as MCY 659. *Prereq: MCY 505 or MED 551.* Biological and biochemical aspects of host resistance and immunity; the chemical and physiochemical properties of the proteins of immune reactions.

MED 660—Immunology Laboratory (3) Same as MCY 660. *Coreq: MED 659; consent of staff.*

MED 661—Biology of Uncommon Microorganisms (5) Same as MCY 661. *Prereq: MCY 302.* Natural distribution, metabolic activities, isolation, and culture of selected groups of microorganisms.

MED 662—Microbial Genetics (5) Same as MCY 662. Microbial genetics, including mutation, selection, transformation, transduction, conjugation, and episomal factors; molecular structure and function of genes.

MED 663—Parasitic Diseases of the Tropics and Subtropics (5) Same as MCY 663, VY 663, ZY 663. See MCY 663.

MED 664—Viral Diseases (3) Same as MCY 664. *Prereq: MED (MCY) 652.* Pathogenesis of viral disease including cytopathic and oncogenic viruses. Diagnostic and preventive measures.

MED 665—Microbial Infections (5) Pathogenesis of selected bacterial and fungal diseases, emphasizing the clinical and pathological aspects of human infection.

MED 666—Microbiology I (6) Same as MCY 666. Intensive review of principles of immunity, physiology, and genetics of bacteria, virology, infection, and ecology.

MED 667—Microbiology II (3) Same as MCY 667.

MED 668—Regulation in Biological Systems (5) Same as MCY 668. *Prereq: MCY 520, 521, 657; BCH 601, 602.* Control of enzyme activity: kinetic, structural, inhibition (allosteric and non-allosteric), and energy level control; permeases; control of enzyme synthesis; positive and negative; repression, induction, catabolic repression, cyclic AMP; hormonal control.

MED 669—Seminar (1; max: 12) Same as MCY 669. *Attendance required of all graduate majors at one research presentation each week as scheduled.* S/U.

MED 750—Journal Colloquy (1; max: 12) Same as MCY 750. Critical presentation and discussion of recent original articles in the microbiological literature.

MED 751—Research Conference (1; max: 12) Same as MCY 751. Critical discussion and appraisal of research programs of faculty and students of the department. S/U.

MED 752—Clinical Immunology (2) Principles of basic immunology and immune reactions important in human disease, such as immediate and delayed hypersensitivity, immune complexes, the Arthus phenomenon, graft rejections.

INDUSTRIAL AND SYSTEMS ENGINEERING
(College of Engineering)

Chairman: M. E. THOMAS
Graduate Coordinator: H. D. RATLIFF

GRADUATE FACULTY 1975-76

Professors: J. F. BURNS; R. L. FRANCIS; R. E. KALMAN; E. P. MARTINSON *(emeritus)*; E. J. MUTH; J. A. NATTRESS; B. D. SIVAZLIAN; M. E. THOMAS; D. B. WILCOX *(emeritus)*
Associate Professors: M. ARIET; B. L. CAPEHART; K. E. DOMINIAK; T. J. HODGSON; K. E. KILPATRICK; R. S. LEAVENWORTH; J. F. MAHONEY; H. D. RATLIFF; P. E. VALISALO
Assistant Professors: D. W. HEARN; T. J. LOWE; L. W. SCHRUBEN

The Department of Industrial and Systems Engineering offers the Master of Engineering and the Master of Science, each with a thesis or nonthesis option, with specialization in computer science, industrial engineering, operations research, and systems engineering. In addition, the department offers the Engineer degree and the Doctor of Philosophy degree with specialization in industrial engineering, operations research, and systems engineering.

A degree in one of the engineering disciplines or in mathematics, statistics, or physics is prerequisite. Where the student's background is deficient, an articulation program of foundation courses will be required.

GRADUATE COURSES

ISE 540—Measurements in Bioengineering (3) Modern techniques for measurements and quantification of physical, physiological, and psychological responses of man to stimulus. Utilization of these measurements in industrial, medical, and sports fields.

ISE 551—Digital Computer Techniques (3) *Prereq: ISE 351, 401.* Numerical methods for dealing with linear and nonlinear algebraic systems, eigenvalue and eigenvector problems, optimum seeking problems, and ordinary differential equations, including error, stability, and efficiency analysis.

ISE 552—Digital Computer Techniques (3) *Prereq: ISE 551.* Sophisticated techniques for solving integrodifferential equations, boundary and characteristic value problems, and partial differential equations.

ISE 557—Analog Simulation Techniques (3) *Prereq: ISE 357.* Analog computer simulation techniques as applied to chemical processes, mechanical, and electromechanical systems, and random phenomena. Solutions to problems in optimization and economic systems. Methods of testing model accuracy.

ISE 558—Hybrid Computer Techniques (3) *Prereq: ISE 357 or 481.* Hybrid computer systems and their use in solution of problems in systems analysis. Special emphasis on software. Conversion techniques associated with digital-to-analog and analog-to-digital.

ISE 562—Reliability Engineering (3) *Prereq: STA 440.* Mathematical models and methods of reliability engineering. Typical component failure distributions from component failure to system failure. Reliability block diagrams and fault trees.

ISE 570—Operations Analysis I (3)

ISE 571—Operations Analysis II (3)

ISE 601—Introduction to Optimization Theory (3) *Prereq: linear algebra, advanced calculus.* Conditions for maxima and minima of differentiable functions; unconstrained, equality constrained, and inequality constrained functions.

ISE 602—Dynamic Programming (3) *Prereq: ISE 601.* Characterization of multistage decision problems as a sequence of single-stage problems. Functional equation of dynamic programming, composition, and Mitten's sufficiency condition. Markovian decision problems, state variable reduction techniques, and related approximation schemes.

ISE 603—Dynamic Optimization Theory (3) *Prereq: ISE 601, 602.* Dynamic programming approach to the necessary conditions of variational calculus. Pontryagin's maximum principle, continuous and discrete. Comparison of variational approach and dynamic programming from a computational point of view.

ISE 604—Linear Programming (3) *Prereq: matrix theory.* Theoretical and computational aspects of the simplex method. Duality theory, parametric analysis, sensitivity analysis, and selected topics.

ISE 605—Extensions of Linear Programming (3) *Prereq: ISE 601, 604.* Algorithmic extensions of the simplex method of linear programming. Large-scale linear programs. Extensions to nonlinear problems.

ISE 606—Nonlinear Programming (3) *Prereq: ISE 601, 605.* Optimization techniques for static and dynamic nonlinear systems subject to various constraints. Inequality theorems, geometric programming, convex programming, decomposition, and optimum seeking methods.

ISE 607—Flows in Networks (3) *Prereq: college algebra.* Mathematical formulations and solution techniques for general flow problems including the techniques of implicit enumeration. Applications to problems of scheduling, routing, and network design in industrial, environmental, and transportation contexts.

ISE 608—Discrete Optimization Theory (3) *Prereq: ISE 604, 607.* Modeling and theory associated with optimization problems where some variables are restricted to integer values. Relationships between network flow algorithms and linear programming. Matching and Chinese Postman problem. General integer programming algorithms.

ISE 609—Advanced Topics in Mathematical Programming (1-4) *Prereq: consent of instructor.* Lectures on selected topics of an advanced nature in mathematical optimization and its applications. Students give presentations on selected research papers. May be repeated with change of content.

ISE 610—Mathematical Theory of Inventory (3) *Prereq: ISE 671, STA 660.* Mathematical theory of inventory systems. Single- and multicommodity inventory problems analyzed as problems in dynamic programming and as Markov decision processes.

ISE 611—Industrial Dynamics I (3) *Prereq: computer programming and probability theory.* Dynamics of industrial systems, emphasizing models that incorporate decision making, its interactions with information, money, orders, material, personnel, and capital equipment, using theories of elementary feedback systems, difference equations, and probability.

ISE 612—Industrial Dynamics II (3) *Prereq: ISE 611.* Dynamic simulation models, improvement of system behavior through changes in system structure and decision policy, and the interpretation of simulation results relative to system objective.

ISE 620—Games and Gaming (3) *Prereq: matrix theory, probability theory.* Games in extensive and normal form. Two-person games. Formulation of two-person games as a linear programming problem. Cooperative and noncooperative games. Concepts and methods of gaming, including experimental management gaming.

ISE 621—Advanced Engineering Economy (3) *Prereq: STA 440, ISE 571.* Mathematical models for expenditure analysis under uncertainty. Relationship between investment decision criteria and microeconomic theory. Capital planning and budgeting. Decisions involving expansion, acquisitions, replacement, and disinvestment.

ISE 622—Decision Theory (3) *Prereq: ISE 621, 671.* Formulation of decision criteria and decision strategies in a probabilistic environment. Industrial applications of input-output analysis and von Neumann-Morgenstern utility theory. Statistical decision functions.

ISE 630—Advanced Production Control (3) *Prereq: ISE 571, 671.* Production planning and control; problem identification and formulation.

ISE 631—Work Measurement Theory (3) *Prereq: ISE 330, 470, STA 440.* Systems of work measurement and work methods. Comparisons of systems.

ISE 632—Facilities Systems Design (3) *Prereq: ISE 433, 671.* Facilities planning, including information analysis, man-machine requirements, facility location methodologies, material handling analysis, storage and warehousing, assembly line balancing, and physical distribution.

ISE 635—Health Systems Analysis I (4) Introduction to quantitative analysis, total value analysis, resource allocation techniques, stochastic service systems, simulation, quality of care audits and hospital control and management systems.

ISE 636—Health Systems Analysis II (4) *Prereq: ISE 635.* Stochastic aspects of hospital and health systems and the influence of variability and uncertainty in health management decisions.

ISE 640—Human Factors Engineering (3) *Prereq: a course in human engineering or perceptual psychology.* Effects of human factors on the performance of systems containing extensive man-machine interactions.

ISE 641—Behavior Systems Engineering (3) *Prereq: ISE 640.* Behavioral and engineering principles' underlying prediction and management of human behavior, design of organization systems, and development of synthetic behavior systems.

ISE 642—Man-Machine Systems Design (3) *Prereq: ISE 640 or instructor's approval.* Engineering design concepts of interfaces between man and machine.

ISE 651—Digital Simulation Techniques (3) Computer programming aspects of digital simulation. Use of simulation languages such as SIMSCRIPT or GPSS. Simulation of large-scale, mathematically indeterminate systems.

ISE 652—Dynamic Modeling and Simulation (3) *Prereq: STA 660.* Methods for input-output analysis of complex systems. Computational techniques.

ISE 653—Information Systems (3) Introduction to information theory and coding, document and reference retrieval, fact and information retrieval, measures of effectiveness, mathematical models of retrieval systems, and schemes for the storage of information.

ISE 654—Numerical Techniques for Linear Systems (3) *Prereq: linear algebra and calculus.* Intensive analysis of Gaussian elimination. LU decomposition, floating point round-off analysis, iterative improvement. Storage and manipulation of sparse matricies. Other topics in linear computation.

ISE 657—Analog Computer Techniques (3) *Prereq: ISE 557.* Analog computer techniques to study complex systems. Analog computer logic as an additional tool in problem solving. Boundary value problems and dynamic parameter optimization techniques.

ISE 658—Analog-Hybrid Systems (3) *Prereq: ISE 657.* Hybrid computer systems, both hardware and software. Sampling theory, quantizing theory, and error analysis. Hybrid computer techniques for solving partial differential equations and optimization problems. Examples of adaptive control systems.

ISE 659—Advanced Hybrid Computer Techniques (3) *Prereq: ISE 557.* Hybrid computer techniques superior to digital or analog techniques. Boundary value, dynamic parameter optimization, fluid network simulation, optimal control and techniques such as random search, steepest ascent, gradient methods, dynamic programming, and the maximum principle.

ISE 660—Statistical Quality Control (3) *Prereq: STA 440 or 607; ISE 571.* Theoretical basis for control charts on variables and attributes data. Cumulative sum control charts. Mathematics of sampling plans for attributes and variables. Bayesian decision rules. Evolutionary operation.

ISE 661—Statistical Forecasting Models (3) *Prereq: ISE 401; STA 441.* Classification of models for forecasting. Polynomial and autoregressive models. Estimation of model parameters. Analysis of industrial data.

ISE 662—Reliability Theory (3) *Prereq: matrix theory, STA 441, ISE 562.* Reliability models as a function of system configurations. Reliability prediction for various underlying component failure laws. Sensitivity analysis. Models of interdependent systems.

ISE 670—Mathematical Methods of Operations Research I (3) *Prereq: matrix theory, transform theory, probability theory.* Topics covered include theory of queues, classical optimization, and linear programming.

ISE 671—Mathematical Methods of Operations Research II (3) *Prereq: ISE 670.* Dynamic programming, nonlinear programming, the maximum principles, game theory, and decision theory.

ISE 672—Modeling Methods of Operations Research (3) *Prereq: ISE 350, 671.* Operations research modeling of large-scale problems, including dynamic models, stochastic models, waiting line models, and simulation methods.

ISE 676—Stochastic Systems Analysis I for Engineers and Scientists (3) Same as STA 676. *Prereq: STA 660.* Overview and classification of stochastic processes. Modeling of physical phenomena as stochastic processes. Methodology and applications from systems engineering and operations research.

ISE 677—Stochastic Systems Analysis II for Engineers and Scientists (3) *Prereq: STA 660, ISE 676 or consent of instructor.* Filtered Poisson process. Semi-Markov decision processes and optimal control. Models of traffic flow. Theory of storage.

ISE 678—Markov Decision Processes for Engineers (3) *Prereq: ISE 602, STA 660, ISE 604.* Markov and semi-Markov decision processes, dynamic programming solutions, fractional linear programming solutions, computational techniques, analysis of industrial and engineering data, applications.

ISE 679—Seminar in Applied Stochastic Processes (3) *Prereq: ISE 676 or 677 and consent of instructor.* Lectures on advanced topics. Student presentation and discussion of research papers. Development of research topics.

ISE 680—Queuing Theory (3) *Prereq: matrix theory, transform theory, STA 660.* Classification of queuing systems and waiting line problems. Model formulation. Analysis of selected systems. Applications to engineering systems.

ISE 681—Stochastic Service Systems (3) *Prereq: ISE 670.* Modeling of large-scale engineering systems. Input-output analysis. Methods of handling uncertainty. Optimum design.

ISE 684—Systems Analysis I (3) *Prereq: ISE 402, STA 440, EE 474.* Review of linear systems. State variable methods for systems analysis. Techniques of modeling. Computer methods. Application to control problems.

ISE 685—Systems Analysis II (3) *Prereq: ISE 684.* Optimal control theory and system optimization techniques. Statistical methods of data analysis. Estimation theory. Kalman filtering.

ISE 686—Advanced Systems Design (3) *Prereq: ISE 685, 671, EE 570.* Application of the techniques of operations research, control theory and systems analysis to the design of systems. Completion of a design project.

ISE 690—Graduate Seminar (1) May be repeated for additional credit. S/U.

ISE 696—Special Problems (1-9; max: 18) Laboratory, lecture, field work, or conferences.

ISE 697—Supervised Research (1-5)

ISE 698—Supervised Teaching (1-5)

ISE 699—Master's Research (1-15)

ISE 797—Special Problems (1-9; max: 18) Laboratory, lecture, field work, or conferences.

ISE 799—Doctoral Research (1-15)

INSTRUCTIONAL LEADERSHIP AND SUPPORT

(College of Education)

Chairman: W. M. ALEXANDER

GRADUATE FACULTY 1975-76

Professors: W. M. ALEXANDER; R. CREWS; W. H. DRUMMOND; H. T. FILLMER; C. G. HASS; W. D. HEDGES; J. W. HENSEL; A. J. LEWIS; W. R. POWELL; E. L. WENZEL; E. L. WILLIAMS
Associate Professors: G. D. LAWRENCE; A. B. SMITH III
Assistant Professors: P. S. GEORGE; M. K. MORGAN; L. L. SMITH

The Department of Instructional Leadership and Support offers graduate study in the following areas: educational media and instructional design; post-secondary education; reading; supervision and curriculum development; and vocational, technical and adult education. Courses are listed below under each of these specialization areas with an additional listing of general courses provided by the department.

Programs leading to the Master of Education and Master of Arts in Education degrees are offered with specializations in educational media and instructional design, reading, and vocational, technical and adult education. Specialized graduate study leading to the degrees of Specialist in Education, Doctor of Education, and Doctor of Philosophy is offered in these areas and also in post-secondary education and in supervision and curriculum development.

GRADUATE COURSES
GENERAL

ED 648—Problems in Curriculum and Instruction (3-15; max: 15) Covers topics not available in regularly listed courses. To be used for credit in institutes, workshops, and short credit courses.

ED 682—Field Laboratory for Faculty Study of Special Problems (3-9; max: 9) *Offered only by extension.* To assist teachers in single schools, groups of schools, or county systems in improving certain subject areas or in working on special problems within the system.

ED. 690—Special Topics (2-5; max: 15) *Prereq: consent of department chairman.*

ED 696—Individual Work (2-5; max: 15) *Student must have approval of proposed project prior to registration in course.* For advanced students who wish to study individual problems under faculty guidance.

ED 697—Supervised Research (1-5)

ED 698—Supervised Teaching (1-5)

ED 699—Master's Research (1-15)

ED 730—Field Experience in Curriculum and Instruction (1-5; max: 15) *Admission limited to graduate students in the Advanced School.* Supervised experiences appropriate to the student's professional goals.

ED 799—Doctoral Research (1-15)

Educational Media and Instructional Design

ED 611—Educational Technology Readings (4) Technology available today to aid the teacher in all aspects of the educational process, including an assessment of the strengths and weaknesses of the various components.

ED 612—Media Center Production Techniques (4) *Prereq: ED 419.* Designed to train media specialists, materials supervisors and audiovisual coordinators in the use of photographic processes, including portable televisions.

ED 613—Educational Technology Center Operation (4) *Prereq: ED 418 or 651.* Organization and operation of school, county, junior college, regional or college learning resource or education technology centers, including arrangement and evaluation of material and equipment.

ED 614—Programmed Instructional Materials (4) Evaluation and effective use of programmed instructional materials. Practice in construction of programmed materials provided in student's area of emphasis.

ED 615—Microteaching, Instructional Television and the Classroom (4) Planning, production, utilization, and evaluation of videotaped programs which demonstrate microteaching principles and practices. Portable videotape equipment utilized.

ED 616—Selection of Media Center Materials (4) Selection of print and non-print media center materials.

ED 617—Cataloging and Classification of Print and Non-Print Materials (4) Standard systems used in an educational setting.

ED 618—Production Graphics (4) Principles of layout and design, and their application to the production and evaluation of media graphics.

ED 619—Organization of Reference Sources and Services (4) Basic types of materials, with practice in their selection, use, and evaluation.

ED 621—Practicum in Educational Media and Instructional Design (4-12) Supervised experiences appropriate to the student's professional goals.

ED 622—Instructional Development (4) The instructional development (instructional systems design) process as a means toward precise communication and instructional improvement. Realities of application as well as theoretical constructs.

ED 623—Computer Applications in Education (4) Enables students to communicate with computer technologists and/or apply information about this technology to the solution of educational problems.

ED 711—Seminar in Educational Media and Instructional Design (4) Seminar for advanced graduate students.

Post-Secondary Education

ED 603—The Community Junior College in America (4) Programs, issues and problems.

ED 640—American Higher Education (4) History, philosophy, and policies, with emphasis on current practices and problems.

ED 641—Practicum in College Teaching I (4-8; max: 12) *Prior arrangements must be made with the coordinating professor of the College of Education.* Provision made for the student to teach under the supervision of a professor at either the community college, four-year college, or university level. Seminars cover topics related to improvement of college teaching.

ED 642—Practicum in College Teaching II (4) *Prior arrangements must be made with the coordinating professor of the College of Education.*

ED 643—The Principles and Practices of College Teaching (4) The nature of the teaching-learning process, with particular emphasis on undergraduate curriculum, course planning, educational technology, ways of evaluating the teaching process, and the contributions of psychology to college teaching.

ED 743—Seminar: Curriculum in Higher Education (4) *Prereq: ED 603 or 640.* Issues and problems in college and university curriculums. Emphasis on general education and curriculum evaluation.

Reading

ED 560—Reading in the Primary Grades (4) Basic course for teaching reading, with emphasis on materials and methods for use with young children at prereading and beginning reading levels.

ED 561—Reading in the Intermediate Grades (4) Basic course, with emphasis on materials and methods for teaching reading to students in upper elementary grades, middle and junior high schools.

ED 562—Reading in the Secondary School (4) Patterns of reading instruction in the secondary school; methods of teaching reading for teachers of all subject areas; preparation, selection, and use of instructional materials; selected field or microteaching experiences.

ED 680—Corrective Reading (4) *Prereq. or coreq: ED 683.* Diagnosis, correction, and prevention of reading difficulties in both elementary and secondary schools; work with children in the application of principles under study.

ED 681—Practicum in Corrective Reading (4) *Prereq. or coreq: ED 683.* Diagnosis, correction, and prevention of reading difficulties in both elementary and secondary schools; work with children in the application of principles under study.

ED 683—Trends in the Teaching of Reading (4) *Prereq: basic course in teaching reading.* Trends analyzed by study of research; consideration of controversial issues involving classroom organization, methods, and materials.

ED 684—Problems in Reading (4) *Prereq. or coreq: ED 683.* Specific reading problems, such as those encountered in the classroom situation, will be selected for exhaustive study by individuals or small groups; the teaching of reading on any grade level.

ED 685—Organization and Supervision of School Reading Programs (4) Procedures for planning, improving, and evaluating reading programs on a system-wide basis.

ED 686—Selection and Production of Reading Materials (4) Criteria for selection, the principles of production, and the creation and construction of reading materials.

ED 687—Technology in Reading Instruction (4) Operation and application of equipment, hardware, and systems used in reading instruction.

ED 688—Issues in High School and Adult Reading (4) Exploration of significant problems, points of view, and trends in high school and adult reading, with an emphasis on research.

ED 757—Theory of Clinical Procedures in Reading (4) *Prereq: ED 680, 681, and 8 other 600 level hours in reading.* Relationships involved in diagnosis, clinical thinking, and judgmental framework with an exploration of diagnostic systems in reading.

ED 758—Clinical Diagnosis in Reading (4) *Prereq: post-master's status; reading certification or equivalent.* Supervised experience in diagnosis and remedial techniques of severe reading disabilities. Primarily individual tutoring.

ED 759—Practicum in Clinical Diagnosis (4) *Prereq: post-master's status; reading certification or equivalent.* Supervised experience in diagnosis and remedial techniques of severe reading disabilities. Primarily individual tutoring.

ED 761—Seminar in Reading (4) *Prereq: ED 683 and 684; year of graduate study.* Contemporary issues and research in reading.

ED 762—Analysis of Theory and Research in Reading (4; max: 12) *Prereq: ED 757.* Detailed and critical study of outstanding theories and research contributions to the field of reading, with implications for education.

ED 763—Internship in Reading (4; max: 16) *Prereq: advanced graduate standing and prior arrangements made with coordinating professor in reading program area.* Provides for directed practice in the area of reading; students are placed in an approved and supervised field position for practical experience.

Supervision and Curriculum Development

ED 600—The School Curriculum (4) *Required in all graduate programs in curriculum and instruction.* Philosophic and research bases underlying the development of the total school program from kindergarten through community college. Basic curriculum course for graduate students.

ED 605—Contemporary Issues in Career Education (4) Examination of issues, analysis of problems and techniques for integrating career education into the total school curriculum, and evaluation of contemporary research.

ED 620—The Education of Culturally Disadvantaged Children and Youth (4) Curriculum content and procedures pertinent to educational needs.

ED 625—Alternative Models for Classroom Discipline (4) Examining the issues of discipline and management in the schools. Emphasis on increasing the classroom teacher's ability to apply alternative strategies for effective discipline.

ED 633—Supervision and the Change Process (4) *Prereq: EDA 631.* Review of theories of change applicable to education. Discussion of roles of instructional leaders using alternative models of change.

ED 634—Group Process in Education (4) Group organization and operation, with opportunity to develop skills in group leadership and interpretation of group interaction.

ED 635—Evaluation in the School Program (4) Procedures and techniques of evaluation in school programs, with particular emphasis on needs assessment, school self-study, and course evaluation.

ED 670—Workshop in Human Relations in Education (3-9; max: 9) Principles and practices in the field of human relations and their implications for interpersonal and intergroup problems in the family, school, and community.

ED 700—Instruction: Theory and Research (4) *Prereq: ED 600.* Theories of instruction and research in the learning process, mental health, creativity, the thought process, human relations, group dynamics, communication, and other fields contributing to a theory of instruction.

ED 701—Curriculum: Theory and Research (4) *Prereq: ED 600.* Theories of curriculum organization, and a survey of curriculum research and patterns of curriculum.

ED 720—Seminar in the Education of Disadvantaged Children and Youth (4) *Open to advanced graduate students.* Research and literature dealing with developing programs for culturally disadvantaged children and youth.

ED 731—Seminar on Instructional Leadership (4) Relates theory, research, and practice focused on ongoing roles and problems of instructional leaders in elementary, middle, and secondary schools.

ED 740—Programs of Teacher Education (4) Organization and problems of teacher education institutions; types of students, patterns of curricula, functions of staff, significant organizations and agencies, and special studies.

ED 741—Internship in Teacher Education I (4) Problems of pre-service teacher education and participation in the planning and teaching of pre-service courses.

ED 742—Internship in Teacher Education II (4)

ED 752—Bases of Curriculum and Instruction Theory I (4) *Alternates quarterly with ED 753. Prereq: ED 600 or equivalent.* Application of theory and research in the behavioral sciences to the development of curriculum and instruction theory. Topics include social forces, human development, learning, knowledge, and personality theories.

ED 753—Bases of Curriculum and Instruction Theory II (4) *Alternates quarterly with ED 752. Prereq: ED 600 or equivalent.* Application of theory and research in the behavioral sciences to the development of curriculum and instruction theory. Topics include intelligence, cognition, small group organization, motivation, and attitudes and values theories.

Vocational, Technical and Adult Education

EDV 560—Technical Education Program Development (4) Essentials of educational program planning and development. Objectives, organization, staffing, finances, facilities, surveys, advisory committees, occupational analysis; recruitment, selection, guidance, and placement of students in various occupational programs.

EDV 570—Education for Adults (4) Characteristics of the principal age groups in adult education (young, middle-aged, and older adults). Variations added by socioeconomic, other community conditions and implications for adult education programs explored.

EDV 571—Methods, Materials and Evaluation in Adult Education (4) Study and use of methods and materials most effective and appropriate for various adult groups. Applications of evaluative principles and procedures to the appraisal of adult education endeavors.

EDV 580—Curriculum and Organization in Vocational-Technical Health Occupations Education (4) Basic principles and practices in developing curriculums in vocational-technical health occupations. Emphasis on curriculum, planning and revision, factors influencing the curriculum, organization of the curriculum and means for evaluating the program.

EDV 600—Administration of Vocational Education (4) Basic principles of administering a program on national, state, and local levels.

EDV 601—Foundations of Program Planning for Vocational Education (4) Socioeconomic forces; school-community relationships; employee-employer relationships; principles, concepts, and practices affecting policy and program planning.

EDV 602—Supervision of Vocational Education (4) Concepts and supervisory procedures pertaining to supervision of different facets of local, state, and national programs.

EDV 660—Technical Education in Post High School Programs (4) Analysis of technical education in modern society, with emphasis on college and other post high school programs leading to the Associate of Science or similar degrees or certificates of competency in technical and semiprofessional occupations.

EDV 661—Teaching Technical Education (4) *Prereq: bachelor's degree in a technical area.* Objectives, content, resource materials, evaluation, and methods of teaching technical subjects at the post high school level.

EDV 670—Adult Education: Progress and Prospects (4) An overview of the historical development and current status of adult education in America; characteristics of the adult learner; trends in adult education.

EDV 671—Teaching in Adult Education (4) Settings, techniques, materials and methods for teaching adults; identification and examination of the problems of the adult learner; evaluation in adult education.

EDV 672—The Program Planning Process in Adult Education (4) Principles and processes involved in program planning in adult education, the theoretical foundations upon which the process is predicated and articulated, the institutional and community organization needed, and the program planning roles of professional and lay leaders.

EDV 690—Special Topics (2; max: 15) *Prereq: consent of department chairman.*

EDV 696—Individual Work in Vocational, Technical, and Adult Education (2-5; max: 15) *For advanced students wishing to study under faculty guidance. Before registering, a student must have approval of the proposed study.* Problems in vocational, technical, or adult education.

EDV 697—Supervised Research (1-5)

EDV 698—Supervised Teaching (1-5)

EDV 700—Seminar in Vocational and Technical Education (4) *Prereq: post-master's standing.* Current research and an overview of the total program in vocational, technical, and adult education.

EDV 760—Developing Technical Programs (4) Program planning and development for technical education, including determination of need, development of curriculum, establishment of advisory committees, selection of faculty and students, planning facilities, organizing staff, budgeting, evaluation of program effectiveness, and follow-up of graduates.

EDV 761—Contemporary Issues in Technical Education (4) Legislation, funding, accreditation, licensure, and other matters which are potentially problem areas in technical education.

EDV 770—Adult Education in the Community College (Junior College) (4) Types of community college programs in adult education. Methods of community survey and ways of identifying and defining educational needs of adults.

EDV 771—Contemporary Issues in Adult Education (4) Problems, emerging trends, legislation, funding and other contemporary issues in adult education.

JOURNALISM AND COMMUNICATIONS
(College of Journalism and Communications)

Dean: R. LOWENSTEIN
Graduate Coordinator: R. R. RUSH

GRADUATE FACULTY 1975-76

Professors: K. A. CHRISTIANSEN; M. N. EDWARDSON; H. H. GRIGGS; J. P. JONES; F. N. PIERCE
Associate Professors: G. A. BUTLER; J. S. DETWEILER; J. L. GRIFFITH; L. J. HOOPER, JR.; A. J. JACOBS; R. N. PIERCE; J. R. PISANI; R. R. RUSH; R. D. WHITTAKER
Assistant Professors: R. L. KENDALL; K. E. M. KENT

The degree of Master of Arts in Journalism and Communications is offered with a major in communication. Specialization may be in advertising, broadcasting, communication research, international communication, journalism, media management, or public relations.

Prerequisite to admission is a bachelor's degree in advertising, broadcasting, journalism, public relations, or some allied field. The student who does not hold a degree in one of these fields may be required to complete satisfactorily prerequisite undergraduate work.

Adequate preparation in the social sciences and humanities is required of each student. An introductory course in statistics is strongly recommended for all candidates as early as possible.

Forty-five credits are required for the degree, of which 9 are for the thesis. A minor field will be selected in consultation with the major adviser and will depend on the special needs of the student. Eight to 10 credits will qualify for the minor, although a minor of up to 18 credits will be permitted. COM 601, 606 and 660 are required of all candidates.

GRADUATE COURSES

BR 518—Teaching Through Television (5) Instructional television production and utilization; studio workshop, readings, and discussion sessions. Open to majors in media, College of Education, others by consent of instructor.

COM 601—Research Methods in Mass Communication (4) Introduction to experiments, surveys, content analysis; sampling and measurement. Laboratory applications.

COM 602—Advertising Research Problems (4) Testing advertising appeals and efficiency, market analysis, consumer analysis.

COM 603—Broadcast Station Management (4) Station organization, operational policies, market research, programming policy, network affiliation, federal and state regulations governing the broadcasting industry, FCC procedures.

COM 604—Newspaper Production and Management (4) Newspaper business management, good will, budgets, accounting, labor problems, taxes, legal questions, postal regulations, newspaper promotion, circulation, advertising problems, weekly and small daily publishing.

COM 605—Seminar in Mass Communication and Society (4) Rights, responsibilities, ethics of communication media; government and communication media; economic, political, social determinants of the character and content of mass communication.

COM 606—Mass Communication Theory (4) Structure, content, process, effects of communication; contributions of other disciplines to knowledge about the process, e.g., semantics, linguistics, learning theory; barriers to effective communication; use of research concepts.

COM 609—Seminar in Legal Problems of Mass Communication (4) Current problems confronting mass media in such areas as constitutional interpretation, conflicts between media and the rights of others, regulation, the nature of jurisprudence.

COM 611—Seminar in History of Mass Communication (4) Reading, critical study, and advanced investigative report on an approved research subject.

COM 614—Problems in Public Relations (4) Specialized areas in public relations, case studies, community relations, analysis of public relations problems in the light of public relations and other communication theory.

COM 615—Seminar in Problems of News Gathering and Presentation (4) Internal problems of news media operation. Status of personnel, effects of technological developments, news decision making, defining objectivity, improving news coverage.

COM 616—Seminar in Journalism Teaching (4) Research and training for journalism teaching and supervision of student publications.

COM 619—International Communication I (4) Analysis and comparison of print and electronic communication systems among nations and cultures, barriers and stimuli to international communication, mass media in national development.

COM 621—Advanced Research Methods (4) *Prereq: COM 601 and STA 602 or equivalent.* Scientific method, measurement, analysis.

COM 623—Broadcast Program and Production Problems (4) Lecture and laboratory in planning and production of complex programs.

COM 625—Advanced Radio, Television, and Film Writing (4) *Prereq: consent of instructor.* Forms, techniques, and types of writing as they apply to radio, television, and film.

COM 628—Radio and Television in Education (4) The broadcast media in public school education and adult education; current usages in direct and indirect teaching and continuing education.

COM 629—International Communication II (4) *Prereq: COM 619.* Specialized or regional aspects of international communication; in-depth investigation by students of particular concepts and research literature presented in COM 619.

COM 632—Creative Advertising Strategy and Consumer Behavior (4) Findings of the social sciences as guides for decisions in creative advertising planning; effects of consumer behavior concepts in shaping advertising message content and improving media selection.

COM 660—Communication Colloquium (1; max: 4) Research exchange, methodology, new techniques. S/U.

COM 690—Special Topics in Mass Communication (2-5; max: 12) *Prereq: consent of instructor or graduate adviser.*

COM 696—Individual Work (1-5; max: 10) Reading or research course in areas of mass communication needed by graduate students.

COM 697—Supervised Research (1-5; max: 5)
COM 698—Supervised Teaching (1-5; max: 5)
COM 699—Master's Research (1-15)

CENTER FOR LATIN AMERICAN STUDIES
(College of Arts and Sciences)

Director & Graduate Coordinator: W. E. CARTER

GRADUATE FACULTY 1975-76
Professors: W. E. CARTER; G. A. SOARES; A. SUAREZ
Associate Professor: G. A. ANTONINI

The Center for Latin American Studies offers the following programs in graduate studies: (1) an interdisciplinary Master of Arts with major in Latin American Studies, (2) a Certificate in Latin American Studies for master's and doctoral students in conjunction with disciplinary degrees in the graduate programs of the Departments of Anthropology, Business Administration, Economics, Education, Food and Resource Economics, Geography, History, Political Science, Romance

Languages (Spanish) and Sociology, (3) a Certificate in Latin American Demographic Studies, in a special program of Latin American Demography, for master's and doctoral students in conjunction with the Departments of Geography, Sociology, and Economics.

The graduate program of Latin American Studies consists of 165 courses with Latin American content taught in the above departments. In cooperation with the Center for Tropical Agriculture, 64 additional courses with Latin American content taught in the Institute of Food and Agricultural Sciences may be accepted for credit toward meeting certain requirements for graduate certificates in Latin American Studies.

A description of the several degree and certificate programs in Latin American Studies may be found in the section *Special Programs*. Listings of courses other than those enumerated below may be found in individual departmental descriptions and the *Bulletin* of the Center for Latin American Studies. Copies of the *Bulletin* may be obtained from the Director, 319-B Grinter Hall.

GRADUATE COURSES

LA 640—Latin American Area Seminar (5; max: 15) *Prereq: Latin American area concentration.*

LW 677—Latin American Legal Institutions Seminar (3) *Prereq: LW 694.* A general survey of the legal systems of the American Republics.

LW 678—Latin American Trade and Investment Seminar (3) *Prereq: LW 694.* Legal problems involved in trading with and formation and operation of business enterprises in Latin America.

LW 694—Law Seminar Preparation (1) *Prerequisite for each law seminar.*

LA 696—Individual Work (3-5; max: 15) Reading or research in topics focusing on a Latin American area, but cutting across disciplines.

LA 699—Master's Research (1-5; max: 15)

LINGUISTICS
(College of Arts and Sciences)

Director: J. CASAGRANDE
Graduate Coordinator: C. C. CHU

GRADUATE FACULTY 1975-76

Professors: C. J. GELLINEK; J. C. HARDER; M. J. HARDMAN-DE-BAUTISTA; P. J. JENSEN; I. R. WERSHOW

Associate Professors: J. CASAGRANDE; C. C. CHU; H. DER-HOUSSIKIAN; D. DEW; K. M. McCARTHY; B. SACIUK; R. J. SCHOLES; W. J. SULLIVAN III

Assistant Professors: P. A. KOTEY; D. G. MILLER; R. M. THOMPSON

Linguistics draws its faculty from seven participating departments: anthropology, classics, English, Germanic and Slavic languages and literatures, humanities, Romance languages and literatures, and speech. It offers a flexible program of study leading to the Ph.D. with a major in linguistics and three specializations at the M.A. level: (1) general linguistics, (2) teaching of the English language as a second language (TESL), and (3) the application of linguistics to the teaching of reading.

Individualized doctoral programs may emphasize syntax, phonology and linguistic change as either theoretical or descriptive constructs of one or more languages. A student may also work in any of the areas represented by the competence of the faculty.

For admission to graduate work in linguistics, the student should have an undergraduate major in a language or language-related subject such as anthropology, psychology, or speech. The student should also have done basic work in general linguistics, phonetics and phonemics, data gathering, and English structure. Deficiencies in undergraduate preparation must be satisfied before the student can proceed to full-time graduate work.

Master's candidates who opt for general linguistics are required to take LIN 605, 610, 620, 630, 640. Candidates for TESL must take LIN 602, 620, 650, EH 401, 619, and a course in English literature. Candidates for general linguistics and TESL must also have a structural knowledge of one foreign language. Students in the reading specialization are required to take LIN 594, 610, 620, 656, 665, EH 619, EDF 450, EH 492, ED 680, 681, 683, 684 and one of the following: ED 560, 561, 562. These requirements are adequate for reading certification if candidates hold a rank III Florida Teaching Certificate in any related area (or the equivalent from another state). No foreign language is required for the reading specialization.

Doctoral candidates are required to take LIN 605, 610, 611, 620, 621, 630, 640 and any other courses required by their supervisory committee. The Ph.D. also requires a working knowledge of one foreign language and a structural knowledge of two others. One of the required languages must be non-Western.

For further information write to the Director, Program in Linguistics, 162 Grinter Hall, University of Florida 32611.

GRADUATE COURSES

LIN 505—Principles of Anthropological Linguistics (4) Same as APY 505. *For anthropology majors.* Detailed review of basic concepts and problems.

LIN 594—Language Acquisition (5) Same as SCH 594. Critical review of relevant theoretical and research literature.

LIN 602—Principles of Linguistics (4) Basic theories of general linguistics, their methodologies, and their impact on current trends in linguistics.

LIN 610—Introduction to Phonological Studies (4) *Prereq: LIN 602.* Insights into the phonological levels of language. Features, contrast, markedness. Solving of problems from natural languages.

LIN 611—Phonological Theory I (4) *Prereq: LIN 610.* Phonological analysis and construction of theoretical arguments.

LIN 612—Phonological Theory II (4) *Prereq: LIN 611.* Recent issues in phonology.

LIN 618—Linguistics in the Community College (4) Same as EH 618. Designed to acquaint community college teachers with the fundamentals of linguistics and their use in the classroom.

LIN 620—Introduction to Syntactic Studies (4) *Prereq: LIN 602.* Insights into the grammatical level of language with problems from natural languages.

LIN 621—Syntactic Theory I (4) *Prereq: LIN 620.* Grammatical analysis and construction of theoretical arguments.

LIN 622—Syntactic Theory II (4) *Prereq: LIN 621.* Recent issues in syntax and semantics.

LIN 624—Seminar in Linguistic Field Methods (5; max: 15) *Prereq: APY 579.* Analysis of a particular language through an informant.

LIN 630—Historical Linguistics (4) *Prereq: LIN 610, 620.* Theory and methods of comparative historical linguistics.

LIN 631—Linguistic Change (4) *Prereq: LIN 612, 622.* Historical linguistics from the point of view of generative grammar.

LIN 640—History of Linguistics (4) *Prereq: LIN 610, 620.* Linguistic thought from pre-Socratic to the 20th century.

LIN 650—Materials and Techniques for TESL (4) Review of theories of TESL teaching methods and materials. Instruction in classroom materials.

LIN 652—TESL Observation and Analysis (2) *Prereq: LIN 650.* Classroom procedures in teaching English as a second language observed in the English Language Institute. Seminar once a week for analytical discussions of classes observed.

LIN 655—Sociolinguistics (4) *Prereq: LIN 610, 620.* Language in its social context.
LIN 656—American Social Dialects (4) *Prereq: introductory linguistics course.* Language variations, especially in relation to the ethnic and racial boundaries of American society.
LIN 657—Bilingualism in America (4) Psycholinguistic and sociolinguistic aspects of bilingualism, with implications for education.
LIN 661—Structure of a Specific Language (4) *Prereq: introductory linguistics course.* Linguistic examination of one of the following: Aymara, Arabic, Cakchiqual, Eskimo, Armenian, Chinese, Gã, Bulgarian, Polish, Swahili, Ukranian, Turkish, Twi.
LIN 665—Contrastive Analysis (4) Theory of contrastive analysis and its application to second language acquisition.
LIN 690—Special Topics (4; max: 36)
LIN 696—Individual Study (1-4; max: 30)
LIN 697—Supervised Research (1-5)
LIN 698—Supervised Teaching (1-5)
LIN 699—Master's Research (1-15)
LIN 799—Doctoral Research (1-15)

MANAGEMENT

(College of Business Administration)

Chairman: I. HOROWITZ
Graduate Coordinators: H. R. FOGLER; H. J. REITZ, JR.

GRADUATE FACULTY 1975-76

Professors: J. M. CHAMPION; W. M. FOX; I. HOROWITZ; J. B. RAY, JR.; J. W. WYATT
Associate Professors: R. A. ELNICKI; J. M. FELDMAN; H. R. FOGLER; J. H. JAMES; R. B. JENNINGS; A. MAJTHAY; H. J. REITZ, JR.
Assistant Professors: C. B. BARRY; L. M. DAVIDSON; R. R. JESSE, JR.; G. J. KOEHLER; J. W. YOUNG

The Department of Management offers the Master of Arts and the Doctor of Philosophy degrees with specialization in management science, personnel management and management. The Master of Business Administration degree is also offered with a major in management.

In general, graduate students can pursue either a quantitative or behaviorally oriented management program or some combination of the two. Each student's program is designed to reflect his or her individual needs and interests.

For admission to courses numbered 600 and above, the student must have been admitted to the Graduate School and normally should have had undergraduate courses in fields pertinent to the graduate courses selected; where necessary, special arrangements may be made with the approval of the department chairman.

GRADUATE COURSES

MGT 510—Foundations of Management and Organizational Behavior (4) Fundamentals of the managerial process and organizational behavior.
MGT 570—Production Management Problems (5) Problems in the management of industrial enterprise; management principles and mathematical analysis applied to manufacturing; product development and production; materials and production control; employee relations.
MGT 610—Managerial Planning (4) Managerial functions of planning. Requirements and complexities of corporate planning activity. Development of the theoretical basis of the planning process.
MGT 611—Organizational Behavior: Theory and Practice I (4) *Prereq: BA 673.* Consideration of method and theory in the study of human behavior in organizational contexts. Focuses on individual motivation and the organizational environment.
MGT 612—Organizational Behavior: Theory and Practice II (4) *Prereq: BA 673.*

MGT 614—Seminar in Management (4) *Prereq: MGT 610, 611.* Historical foundations and evolutionary development of management concepts; comparative analysis of management patterns; emerging problems of management interests.

MGT 615—Motivation in Organizational Settings (4) *Prereq: BA 673 or equivalent, and consent of instructor.* Theory and research on motivational processes relevant to, and applied to, individual human behavior in complex organizations.

MGT 616—Theory and Skills of Organization Development (4) *Prereq: BA 673 or equivalent, and consent of instructor.* Dual focus on (1) theory and research on the planning of change in complex organizations, and (2) laboratory practice in building intervention used by change agents.

MGT 650—Personnel Techniques and Administration (4) *Prereq: MGT 450.* Realistic cases which point up organizational, human relations, and administrative problems of the personnel administrator.

MGT 660—Problems in Collective Bargaining (4) History, present status, and trends of collective bargaining, with an analysis of its economic, social, and legal aspects.

MGT 670—Linear Programming for Management Scientists (3) *Prereq: MGT 570.* Solving a linear programming model; evaluation of the solution, and linear programming computer software and its use.

MGT 671—Decision Processes Under Uncertainty (5) *Prereq: STA 440, 441.* Introduction to statistical decision theory, including the vonNeumann-Morgenstern behavioral axioms, forms, techniques for assessing probabilities, and penalty functions, with managerial and economics applications.

MGT 672—Optimization in Simulation Modeling (3) *Prereq: MGT 472.* Use of simulation techniques in managerial decision problems, including random number generation, and search procedures for determining optimal policies.

MGT 673—Optimization in Static Managerial Models (4) *Prereq: MGT 570.* Introduction to the theory and application of unconstrained and constrained optimization in static managerial decision models.

MGT 674—Optimization in Dynamic Managerial Decision Models (4) *Prereq: MGT 673.* Introduction to the theory of dynamic optimization in discrete-time and continuous-time models, with managerial and economics applications.

MGT 675—Optimization in Discrete Managerial Decision (2) *Prereq: MGT 570.* Introduction to the theory of discrete optimization, and the basic ideas and tools of an exact solution method and successful heuristic methods, with managerial and economics applications.

MGT 676—Graphs and Networks in Managerial Decision Models (1) *Prereq: MGT 570.* Introduction to the theory of graphs and networks, computational aspects, and managerial and economics applications.

MGT 677—Markov Decision Processes (4) *Prereq: STA 440.* Application of Markov processes for managerial decisions, including probability estimation problems, and transition reward structures.

MGT 678—Decision Processes Under Conflict (3) *Prereq: MGT 570.* Managerial and economics applications of game theory models, including conflict resolution, bargaining, risk sharing, and group decision processes in a managerial context.

MGT 690—Special Topics in Management (4) *Prereq: consent of department well in advance of registration.* Topics more specialized or advanced than regularly listed courses.

MGT 691—Management Research and Reports (2) *Required of all candidates for the M.B.A. with a management concentration. Prereq: BA 690.* Supervised preparation of a report on a management topic of current interest.

MGT 696—Individual Work in Management (1-5; max: 10) *Prereq: consent of department and Director of Graduate Studies.* Reading and/or research in management.

MGT 697—Supervised Research (1-5)

MGT 698—Supervised Teaching (1-5)

MGT 699—Master's Research (1-15)

MGT 790—Workshop in Management (3; max: 12) *Required of all doctoral candidates in management. Prereq: MGT 510, 570, BA 673, 664 or equivalent.* Readings and research in management. Each student must present a research project for discussion and comment.

MGT 799—Doctoral Research (1-15)

MARKETING
(College of Business Administration)

Chairman: J. B. COHEN
Graduate Coordinator: A. R. WILDT

GRADUATE FACULTY 1975-76

Professors: G. G. BECHTEL; J. D. BUTTERWORTH; J. B. COHEN; R. B. THOMPSON
Associate Professors: J. H. FARICY; N. R. HESS; Z. V. LAMBERT; M. B. MAZIS; W. L. WILKIE
Assistant Professors: O. T. AHTOLA; A. A. ANDERSON; R. J. BOEWADT; A. R. WILDT

The Department of Marketing offers a specialization within the Master of Arts program in Business Administration, a concentration in the nonthesis Master of Business Administration degree program, and both a major and a minor field in the Doctor of Philosophy degree in business administration. No graduate major may be completed without adequate course work on the 600 or higher level.

For admission to courses listed below, the student must have been admitted to the Graduate School and normally should have had undergraduate courses in fields pertinent to the graduate courses selected; or, where necessary, special arrangements may be made with the approval of the department chairman.

GRADUATE COURSES

MKG 531—Marketing Principles and Institutions (3) *Primarily designed for M.B.A. candidates who lack adequate preparation in marketing.* Descriptive and analytical approach to the study of marketing institutions and functions.

MKG 621—International Marketing I (5) *Prereq: MKG 531.* Strategies leading to the penetration of foreign markets.

MKG 631—Seminar in Marketing Theory (5) *Prereq: MKG 531.* Advanced principles, theories, and problems in marketing. Functional, institutional, cost, and historical approaches from both the social and firm points of view.

MKG 639—Seminar in Marketing Management (5) *Prereq: MKG 531.* Advanced case course dealing with the wide range of operational problems faced by the marketing manager.

MKG 652—Consumer Behavior (5) Methodology and findings in the social sciences applied to individual and aggregate behavior of consumers.

MKG 665—Public Policy Research in Marketing (5) *Prereq: MKG 652 and 671 or equivalents, or consent of instructor.* Analysis of regulatory and other public policy programs involving marketing practices which impact on the consumer. Emphasis on role of consumer research in resolution of public policy issues.

MKG 671—Seminar in Marketing Research (5) *Prereq: MKG 531 and BA 664.* Advanced case course dealing with the wide range of operational problems faced by the marketing manager.

MKG 673—Quantitative Analysis for Marketing Decisions (5) *Prereq: MKG 531, MGT 570, BA 591, 664 or STA 603.* Application of quantitative concepts and techniques to the solution of marketing problems.

MKG 690—Special Topics in Marketing (5) *Prereq: consent of department.* Selected topics in marketing management, research, or theory.

MKG 691—Marketing Research and Reports (2) *Required of all candidates for the M.B.A. with a marketing concentration. Prereq: BA 690.* Supervised preparation of a report on a topic of current interest in marketing.

MKG 696—Individual Work (1-5; max: 10) *Prereq: consent of department.* Reading and/or research in marketing.

MKG 697—Supervised Research (1-5)

MKG 698—Supervised Teaching (1-5)

MKG 699—Master's Research (1-15)

MKG 752—Consumer Information Processing and Decision Making (5) *Prereq: STA 603 and four graduate credits in consumer behavior or social psychology.* Behavioral and statistical concepts applied to the study of consumer decision making and to the development of models of buyer behavior.

MKG 774—Multidimensional Scaling for Market and Societal Analysis (5) Same as PSY 718. *Prereq: STA 603 or equivalent and fundamentals of matrix algebra.* Derivation of utilities from preferential choices; measurement of spatial attributes underlying utility; principal components and distance decompositions; scaling categorical judgments in survey research.

MKG 790—Workshop in Marketing Research (4) *Prereq: MKG 671 or equivalent, or consent of instructor.* In-depth analysis of current research topics in marketing. Emphasis on research programs of leading scholars in the field. Students critically appraise the rationale, strengths and weaknesses of each study.

MKG 799—Doctoral Research (1-15)

MATERIALS SCIENCE AND ENGINEERING
(College of Engineering)

Chairman: E. D. VERINK, JR.
Graduate Coordinator: R. E. REED-HILL

GRADUATE FACULTY 1975-76

Professors: R. T. DeHOFF; D. B. DOVE; R. W. GOULD; A. G. GUY; C. S. HARTLEY; L. L. HENCH; J. J. HREN; R. E. HUMMEL; J. KRONSBEIN (*emeritus*); R. PEPINSKY; R. E. REED-HILL; F. N. RHINES; E. D. VERINK, JR.; E. D. WHITNEY
Associate Professors: R. E. LOEHMAN; G. Y. ONODA

The Department of Materials Science and Engineering offers the Master of Science, Master of Engineering, Doctor of Philosophy, and the Engineer degree. All degrees may be obtained with specialization in metallurgical or ceramic engineering.

Specific areas of concentration within the department include biomaterials, corrosion, diffusion, mechanical behavior, quantitative microscopy, reaction kinetics in the solid state, and structural analysis.

The minimum requirement for admission to the program is a bachelor's degree in materials science and engineering or in a related field. Graduate students who can present the prerequisites for graduate courses without having to take more than 18 credits in advanced undergraduate courses will be considered to have fulfilled this requirement.

GRADUATE COURSES

MSE 546—The Physics and Physical Chemistry of Polymers (3) Same as CHE 546 and CY 546. The structure, configuration, conformation and thermodynamics of polymer solutions, gels and solids. Mechanical, optical, and rheological properties of plastics and rubbers. Demonstrations of experimental methods.

MSE 561—The Organic Chemistry of Polymers (3) Same as CHE 561 and CY 561. Classification of polymerization types and mechanisms from a mechanistic, organic point of view. The structure of synthetic and natural polymers and polyelectrolytes. Reactions of polymers. Practical synthetic methods of polymer preparation.

MSE 601—Advanced Phase Diagrams I (3) Phase diagrams considering systems with as many as four components; emphasis on pressure-temperature-composition diagrams.

MSE 602—Advanced Phase Diagrams II (3) *Prereq: MSE 601.*

MSE 610—Electron Theory of Solids for Materials Scientists I (4) Wave equation and its application to free electrons, bound electrons and electrons in crystals. Electron-band theory and its applications. Electrical properties of metals, alloys and semiconductors, heat capacity, thermal properties.

MSE 611—Electron Theory of Solids for Materials Scientists II (4) Atomistic (classical) and electron theory of the optical properties of metals, alloys and dielectrics. Nonlinear optics, lasers, Raman-spectra.

MSE 612—Electron Theory of Solids for Materials Scientists III (4) Electron theory of magnetism, magnetic properties and their relationship to microstructure (para-, dia-, ferro-, antiferro-, ferri- and metamagnetism). Superconductors.

MSE 615—Optical Properties of Metals and Alloys (3) Optical properties by reflection, refraction, and absorption; methods for determining optical constants of metals; relation between optical and electric constants; atomistic theory of optical constants; optical properties in metal research.

MSE 617—Growth, Structure and Properties of Thin Films (3) Preparative techniques, structural characteristics and electronic properties of metallic, semiconducting, and dielectric films.

MSE 620—Advanced Physical Metallurgy I (4) *Prereq: MSE 421.* Energetics of phase transformations; spinodal decomposition, heterogeneous and homogeneous nucleation in solid state reactions.

MSE 621—Advanced Physical Metallurgy II (4) *Prereq: MSE 620.* Growth and dissolution of particles in solids; cellular growth; coarsening; martensite transformations; sintering and other solid state processes.

MSE 622—Advanced Physical Metallurgy III (4) *Prereq: MSE 421.* Annealing processes and their relation to the cold worked state, including recovery, recrystallization, and grain growth.

MSE 625—Diffusion in Solids (3) *Prereq: MSE 420.* Physical basis, equations, and theories of diffusion; tracer, chemical, multicomponent, and multiphase diffusion in general force fields.

MSE 630—Radiation Damage in Solids (3) Action of thermal neutrons and fast particles upon solids, property changes by irradiation in pure metals and alloys, irradiation effects in semiconductors and ionic crystals; radiation phenomena in quartz, insulators, electronic devices and fissionable materials.

MSE 640—Advanced Mechanical Metallurgy I (4) *Prereq: MSE 440.* Theory of elasticity; advanced theory of plasticity; theory and properties of dislocations; dislocation motion and interactions; application to deformation processes; survey of recent advances in the field.

MSE 641—Advanced Mechanical Metallurgy II (4) Continuum theory of dislocation. Stress fields, displacement fields, energies of simple shapes and finite arrays of dislocations. Continuous distributions of dislocations and their relationship to mechanical properties. Relation of the state of dislocation to the geometry of deformed lattices.

MSE 650—Metallurgical Thermodynamics (3) *Prereq: MSE 452.* Thermodynamics of metallurgical systems; surfaces in solids, irreversible processes.

MSE 651—Advanced Topics in Corrosion (3) *Prereq: MSE 453.* Theories and mechanisms of corrosion. Current literature on oxidation and corrosion.

MSE 660—Advanced X-Ray Diffraction I (4) *Prereq: MSE 461.* Kinematic x-ray diffraction theory and applications to materials analysis.

MSE 661—Advanced X-Ray Diffraction II (3) *Prereq: MSE 660.*

MSE 662—Transmission Electron Microscopy (4) *Prereq: MSE 461.* Kinematical and dynamical theory of contrast in thin crystals. Laboratory studies, defect structure, applications to electron diffraction. Laboratory included.

MSE 663—Specialized Research Techniques in Materials Science (1-3; max: 15) Specialized research techniques in materials science utilizing primarily STEM, TEM, SEM, EMP, FIM, and optical metallograph.

MSE 664—Scanning Electron Microscopy and Electron Probe Microanalysis (4) *Prereq: MSE 460.* Fundamentals of scanning electron microscopy and electron probe microanalysis. Laboratory.

MSE 665—X-Ray Spectrochemical Analysis (4) *Prereq: MSE 460 or consent of instructor.* Application of x-ray spectrochemical analysis to problems in metallurgy, ceramics and biomaterials.

MSE 667—Quantitative Microscopy (3) Fundamental relationships of quantitative microscopy and their application to microstructural characterization; designing and testing models for microstructural evolution.

MSE 670—Seminar in Metallurgy (1) S/U.

MSE 671—Seminar in Metallurgy and Ceramic Science (1-2)

MSE 680—Atomic Processes in Crystalline Ceramics (4) Processes leading to the control of thermal and mechanical properties of ceramics through microstructure. High temperature reactions involving solids, diffusion, grain growth, and phase transformations in ceramic systems. Sintering phenomena.

MSE 681—Electronic Processes in Crystalline Ceramics (4) *Prereq: MSE 483 or consent of instructor.* The defect solid state and its relation to electrical properties of ceramic materials. Ionic conductivity in ceramics. Solid electrolytes. Theory of electron transport in metallic, semiconducting and insulating ceramics.

MSE 682—Structure and Properties of Glasses (4) Theory of glass structure, phase separation, nucleation, crystallization, glass-ceramics. Influence of composition, structure, and environment on physical and surface properties.

MSE 683—Ceramic Processing (4) Introduction to the science of ceramic processing, with emphasis on theoretical fundamentals. Examples of state of the art industrial processes discussed.

MSE 685—Science of Biomaterials I (3) *Undergraduate chemistry essential.* Introduction to variables that control compatibility and performance of biomaterials, including physical and chemical properties, corrosion, fatigue, and interfacial histochemical changes.

MSE 686—Science of Biomaterials II (3) *Undergraduate chemistry essential.* Anatomical variables, stresses, materials selection, and selected literature readings.

MSE 696—Special Topics in Materials Science and Engineering (1-6; max: 9)

MSE 697—Supervised Research (1-5)

MSE 698—Supervised Teaching (1-5)

MSE 699—Master's Research (1-15)

MSE 701—Product Liability: Effective Use of Engineering Experts (3) Available for credit toward graduation in the College of Law. Basic engineering concepts underlying product failure and safety, causal relationships, proof of negligence and standards of care. No engineering background required.

MSE 799—Doctoral Research (1-15)

MATHEMATICS
(College of Arts and Sciences)

Chairman: A. R. BEDNAREK; *Associate Chairman:* Z. R. POP-STOJANOVIC
Graduate Coordinator: D. C. WILSON

GRADUATE FACULTY 1975-76

Graduate Research Professors: R. E. KALMAN; S. M. ULAM

Professors: A. R. BEDNAREK; J. K. BROOKS; N. DINCULEANU; J. E. KEESLING; C. W. NELSON; V. M. POPOV; Z. R. POP-STOJANOVIC; R. G. SELFRIDGE; A. K. VARMA

Associate Professors: P. BACON; B. L. BRECHNER; S. S. CHEN; D. A. DRAKE; R. R. KALLMAN; D. R. LEWIS; C. P. LUEHR; J. MARTINEZ; R. D. MAULDIN; T. O. MOORE; S. A. SAXON; M. L. TEPLY; T. WALSH; D. C. WILSON

Assistant Professors: D. K. BLEVINS; L. S. BLOCK; T. T. BOWMAN; D. A. CENZER; J. A. DRAPER; K. B. FARMER; M. P. HALE, JR.; J. A. LARSON; R. L. LONG; E. C. NUMMELA; G. X. RITTER; K. N. SIGMON; J. G. SLAGLE; N. L. WHITE; R. W. YOH; S. E. ZARANTONELLO

The Department of Mathematics offers the degrees of Doctor of Philosophy, the Master of Science and Master of Arts, and the Master of Arts in Teaching and Master of Science in Teaching, each with a major in mathematics.

There are opportunities for concentrated study in a number of specific areas at both the master's and doctoral levels. Competent faculty directs studies and research in algebra, number theory, analysis, geometry, topology, logic, differential equations, control theory, probability theory, mathematical systems theory, numerical analysis, approximation theory, combinatorial analysis, graph theory, computer applications, mathematical physics, and biomathematics.

In addition to the requirements of the Graduate School, the minimum prerequisite for admission to the program of graduate studies in mathematics is the completion, with an average grade of B or better, of at least 36 credits of undergraduate mathematics, including a full year of calculus and three quarters of appropriate work beyond the calculus. Students lacking part of the requirements will be required to make up the deficiency early in their graduate work.

Prerequisites to individual courses should be determined before registration by consultation with the instructor concerned through the departmental office.

Some of the courses listed are offered only as needed. Since times for offering courses are estimated a year in advance, certain changes may be made if needs are known by the department.

The courses MS 531, 532, 533, 541, 542, and 543 are required for all advanced degree programs in mathematics.

The requirements for the master's degree are 48 hours of course work, at least 27 hours of which are 600-level course work in mathematics. If a thesis is written, up to 9 hours of MS 699 may count toward these hour requirements. A comprehensive written examination is required of all master's students.

The requirement for a doctoral degree is at least 54 hours of 600-level course work in mathematics. No hours of teaching, colloquium, thesis, or individual work will count toward this requirement. In addition to the Graduate School requirements, the doctoral student must pass a written and oral comprehensive preliminary examination administered by the department to become a candidate for the degree. The doctoral student must pass reading knowledge examinations in two of the following foreign languages: French, German, or Russian.

The dissertation is an important requirement for the doctoral degree in mathematics. The topic for the dissertation may be chosen from a number of areas of current research in pure and applied mathematics.

Every graduate student is expected to attend the regular colloquium.

Details concerning all requirements for graduate degrees in mathematics can be obtained by writing the Mathematics Department Graduate Selection Committee.

GRADUATE COURSES

MS 501—Intermediate Differential Equations for Engineers and Physical Scientists (3)
MS 502—Vector Analysis (3)
MS 503—Introduction to Complex Variables for Engineers and Physical Scientists (4)
MS 504—Introduction to Operational Calculus (3)
MS 505—Introduction to Partial Differential Equations (3)
MS 509—Introduction to Functional Analysis I (4)
MS 510—Introduction to Functional Analysis II (4)
MS 517—Numerical Methods of Differential Equations (4) Discrete and variational methods (numerical) for the solution of ordinary and partial differential equations.
MS 529—Rings, Modules and Linear Algebra (4) *Prereq: undergraduate linear algebra.* Structure of principal ideal domains and their modules, with application to abelian groups and linear transformations.
MS 531—Introductory Algebra I (3) *Prereq: MS 432 or 427.* The basic algebraic systems: groups, rings, vector spaces and modules. Linear transformations, matrices, and determinants, the Galois theory.
MS 532—Introductory Algebra II (3) *Prereq: MS 531.*
MS 533—Introductory Algebra III (3) *Prereq: MS 532.*
MS 541—Modern Analysis I (3) *Prereq: MS 303.* Topology of metric spaces, numerical sequences and series, continuity, differentiation, the Riemann-Stieltjes integral, sequences and

series of functions, the Stone-Weierstrass theorem, functions of several variables, Stokes' theorem, the Lebesgue theory.

MS 542—Modern Analysis II (3) *Prereq: MS 541.*

MS 543—Modern Analysis III (3) *Prereq: MS 542.*

MS 547—Advanced Calculus I (3)

MS 548—Advanced Calculus II (3)

MS 549—Advanced Calculus III (3)

MS 551—Introduction to Set Theory (4) Basic axioms and concepts of set theory, axiom of choice, Zorn's lemma, Schröder-Bernstein theorem, cardinal numbers, ordinal numbers, and the continuum hypothesis.

MS 552—Introduction to Topology I (4) Basic axioms and concepts of point-set topology, compactness, connectedness, separation axioms, metric spaces, metrization, Tietze extension theorem, Urysohn lemma, Tychonoff theorem.

MS 553—Introduction to Topology II (4)

MS 566—Theory of Graphs I (4)

MS 567—Theory of Graphs II (4)

MS 601—Mathematical Methods of Physics and Engineering I (3) *Prereq: MS 501, 502, 503, 505, or equivalent.* Orthogonal functions; integral transforms; theory of distributions; integral equations; eigenfunctions and Green's functions; special functions; boundary and initial value problems, with emphasis on potential theory (Laplace and Poisson equations), the wave equation, and the diffusion equation.

MS 602—Mathematical Methods of Physics and Engineering II (3) *Prereq: MS 601.*

MS 603—Mathematical Methods of Physics and Engineering III (3)

MS 607—Fourier Series I (3) *Prereq: MS 601.* Fundamental theorems on convergence, differentiation, and integration. Applications to boundary value problems.

MS 608—Fourier Series II (3) *Prereq: MS 607.*

MS 609—Introduction to Calculus of Variations for Engineers and Physical Scientists (3) *Prereq: MS 601.* Extremals for integrals with fixed endpoints, effect of varying endpoints, transversality condition, direct methods.

MS 610—Tensor Analysis (3) *Prereq: MS 502, 601.* The calculus of tensors, with special attention to its application to differential geometry, problems from physics, and n-dimensional spaces.

MS 611—Applications of Group Theory in the Physical Sciences (3) *Prereq: PS 647.* Group theory, the theory of representations of groups and their relationship to the problems of physics.

MS 614—Numerical Analysis (4) *Prereq: MS 411; MS 543 or 446.* Designed to acquaint research students with numerical analysis, error analysis of differential equations, integral equations, eigenvalue, and matrix problems with study of errors.

MS 615—Partial Differential Equations I (3) *Prereq: MS 505; MS 543 or 603.* Cauchy-Kowalewski theorem, first order equations, classification of equations, hyberbolic equations, elliptic equations, parabolic equations, hyperbolic systems, nonlinear hyperbolic systems, existence theory based on functional analysis. Applications to partial differential equations arising from physical sciences.

MS 616—Partial Differential Equations II (3)

MS 617—Partial Differential Equations III (3)

MS 618—Stochastic Differential Equations and Filtering Theory I (3) Introduction to random functions; the Brownian motion process. Ito's stochastic integral; Ito's stochastic calculus; stochastical differential equations. Linear filtering; Kalman filtering; nonlinear filtering theory.

MS 619—Stochastic Differential Equations and Filtering Theory II (3) *Prereq: MS 618.*

MS 620—Stochastic Differential Equations and Filtering Theory III (3) *Prereq: MS 619.*

MS 621—Introduction to Commutative Algebra and Algebraic Geometry I (3)

MS 622—Introduction to Commutative Algebra and Algebraic Geometry II (3)

MS 623—Introduction to Commutative Algebra and Algebraic Geometry III (3)

MS 624—Mathematical Logic I (3) Languages, models, and theories; Gödel's completeness and incompleteness theorems; formal number theory and axiomatic set theory; applications to other areas of mathematics.

MS 625—Mathematical Logic II (3) *Prereq: MS 624.*

MS 626—Mathematical Logic III (3) *Prereq: MS 625.*

MS 631—Algebra I (3) *Prereq: MS 533.* Sylow theorems, solvable and nilpotent groups, Jordan-Holder theorem, abelian groups, Jacobson radical, Jacobson density theorem, Wedderburn-Artin theorem.

MS 632—Algebra II (3) *Prereq: MS 631.*

MS 633—Algebra III (3) *Prereq: MS 632.*

MS 635—Projective Geometry (3) Projective and affine planes, coordinatization theorems, central collineations, the Desarguesian configuration, K-arcs and ovals, translation planes, quasifields, (group) congruences, Moufang planes, isotopis, derivation.

MS 636—Incidence Geometry I (3) *Prereq: MS 635 or consent of instructor.* Latin squares, nets, designs, partial designs, Hjelmslev planes, Bruck-Ryser-Chowla theorem, Hall multiplier theorem, Bose-Shrikhande-Parker theorem.

MS 637—Incidence Geometry II (3) *Prereq: MS 636 or consent of instructor.*

MS 638—Differential Geometry I (3) *Prereq: MS 502, 601. Recommended: MS 610.* First part of a three-term sequence. Classical differential geometry of curves and surfaces, differentiable manifolds, tensor analysis, affine connection, Riemannian geometry, Lie groups, Lie algebras, applications to physics.

MS 639—Differential Geometry II (3) *Prereq: MS 638.*

MS 640—Differential Geometry III (3) *Prereq: MS 639.*

MS 641—General Theory of Measure and Integration I (3) *Prereq: MS 543.* The Daniell approach to integration, abstract measure theory, abstract Lebesgue integral, convergence theorems for integrals, Riesz representation theorem. L^p spaces, various modes of convergence. Banach spaces, Hahn-Banach theorem, open-mapping theorem, uniform-boundedness principle. Hilbert spaces, differentiation of functions of one real variable, Vitali's covering theorem, differentiability of monotone functions, absolutely continuous functions and indefinite integrals, the Lebesgue-Radon-Nikodym theorem.

MS 642—General Theory of Measure and Integration II (3) *Prereq: MS 641.*

MS 643—General Theory of Measure and Integration III (3) *Prereq: MS 642.*

MS 645—Advanced Topics in Integration I (3) *Prereq: MS 643 and 663.* Current topics in integration, reference to function spaces and to spaces provided with algebraic or topological structures.

MS 646—Advanced Topics in Integration II (3) *Prereq: MS 645.*

MS 647—Advanced Topics in Integration III (3) *Prereq: MS 646.*

MS 648—Mathematical Analysis for Statisticians (4) *Coreq: STA 610.* Set theory, cardinality, metric spaces, limits, continuity, differentiation, approximation of functions, series of functions. Applications to probability and statistics stressed.

MS 649—Mathematical Analysis for Statisticians (4) *Prereq: MS 648.* Measure and integration; additive set functions and measures; Lebesgue measure in R^n, Egorov's theorem, Lebesgue and Lebesgue-Stieltjes integrals, monotone convergence, dominated convergence. L^p spaces, Radon-Nikodym theorem, Fubini theorem, and Kolmogorov-Daniell theorems. Applications in probability and statistics.

MS 650—Mathematical Analysis for Statisticians (4) *Prereq: MS 649.* Matrix theory: algebraic requirements for experimental designs, distribution theory and Markov processes. Fourier series: convergence results, Gibbs phenomenon, relation to time series. Characteristic functions: continuity, differentiability conditions, Helley's theorems, examples.

MS 651—Complex Analysis I (3) *Prereq: MS 543.* Rapid survey of properties of complex numbers, linear transformations, geometric forms and necessary concepts from topology. Complex integration, Cauchy's theorem and its corollaries, Taylor's series and the implicit function theorem in complex form. Conformality and the Riemann-Caratheodory mapping theorem. Theorems of Bloch, Schottky and the big and little theorems of Picard, Harmonicity and Dirichlet's problem.

MS 652—Complex Analysis II (3) *Prereq: MS 651.*

MS 653—Complex Analysis III (3) *Prereq: MS 652.*

MS 656—Combinatorial Theory I (3) Matching theory, Ramsey's theorem, lattice theory, Möbius inversion, generating functions, Polya's theorem, combinatorial geometries (or matroids), applications.

MS 657—Combinatorial Theory II (3)

MS 658—Combinatorial Theory III (3)
MS 661—Topology I (4) *Prereq: MS 553.* A basic introduction to advanced topology. Topics covered include general topology, algebraic topology, homotopy theory and topology of manifolds.
MS 662—Topology II (4) *Prereq: MS 661.*
MS 663—Topology III (4) *Prereq: MS 662.*
MS 666—Theory of Convexity I (3) Affine sets, convex sets and cones, convex functions, closures of convex functions, continuity of convex functions, separation theorems, directional derivatives and subgradients, ordinary convex programs and Lagrange multipliers. Fenchel's duality theorem, saddle-functions.
MS 667—Theory of Convexity II (3)
MS 668—Theory of Convexity III (3)
MS 690—Special Topics in Mathematics (3) *Prereq: consent of graduate adviser, who should be consulted well in advance of registration.*
MS 696—Individual Work (3; max: 12)
MS 697—Supervised Research (1-5)
MS 698—Supervised Teaching (1-5)
MS 699—Master's Research (1-15)
MS 701—Advanced Topics in Topology I (3) *Prereq: MS 663.* Topics change yearly. The MS 701-702-703 sequence may be repeated once.
MS 702—Advanced Topics in Topology II (3)
MS 703—Advanced Topics in Topology III (3)
MS 711—Seminar in Mathematical System Theory (3) *Prereq: admission to doctoral study.* Critical review of current developments in system theory, with strong emphasis on (but not limited to) questions of mathematical interest. Presentations by invited speakers as well as by students and faculty affiliated with the Center for Mathematical System Theory. Intensive discussions by participants rather than ex cathedra lectures. May be repeated.
MS 712—Seminar in Applied Mathematics I (3) Various topics in applications of mathematics both classical and in areas of current research. May be repeated for credit.
MS 713—Seminar in Applied Mathematics II (3)
MS 714—Seminar in Applied Mathematics III (3)
MS 745—Theory of Numbers I (3) *Prereq: two of MS 633, 643, 653.* Introduction to the theory of numbers; theorems on divisibility; congruences, number-theoretic functions; primitive roots and indices; the quadratic reciprocity law; Diophantine equations and continued fractions.
MS 746—Theory of Numbers II (3) *Prereq: MS 745.*
MS 747—Theory of Numbers III (3) *Prereq: MS 746.*
MS 755—Advanced Topics in Functional Analysis I (3) *Prereq: MS 633, 643.* Algebraic and topological approach to material and methods current in analysis. May be repeated once.
MS 756—Advanced Topics in Functional Analysis II (3; max: 6) *Prereq: MS 755.*
MS 757—Advanced Topics in Functional Analysis III (3; max: 6) *Prereq: MS 756.*
MS 765—Advanced Topics in Algebra I (3; max: 6) *Prereq: MS 633; MS 643, 653, or 663.* Current topics in algebra.
MS 766—Advanced Topics in Algebra II (3; max: 6) *Prereq: MS 765.*
MS 767—Advanced Topics in Algebra III (3; max: 6) *Prereq: MS 766.*
MS 771—Introduction to Mathematical System Theory I (4; max: 8) *Required for doctoral work in system theory. Prereq: consent of instructor.* Fundamental mathematical structures in the description of dynamical systems, especially linear system and finite automata. Problems of controllability, observability, structure and identification. Topics change to reflect current developments. H.
MS 772—Introduction to Mathematical System Theory II (4)
MS 799—Doctoral Research (1-15)

MECHANICAL ENGINEERING
(College of Engineering)

Chairman: R. B. GAITHER
Graduate Coordinator: R. A. GATER

GRADUATE FACULTY 1975-76

Professors: E. A. FARBER; R. B. GAITHER; R. K. IREY; J. MAHIG; C. C. OLIVER; V. P. ROAN, JR.; D. TESAR
Associate Professors: W. C. ALLEN; R. A. GATER; C. K. HSIEH; J. M. VANCE
Assistant Professors: H. A. INGLEY, III; C. A. MORRISON; G. PIOTROWSKI

Programs are available leading to the degrees of Master of Science, Master of Engineering, Engineer, and Doctor of Philosophy. General areas or programs within which students may specialize are biomechanical systems, energy conversion systems, mechanical systems, and thermal systems.

Within the specializations noted above are unique opportunities to complete theoretical and experimental research investigations in a wide variety of subspecialties including acoustics, automatic controls, biomechanics, combustion, cryogenics, energy conversion, environmental control, fluid dynamics, gas dynamics, heat transfer, kinematic synthesis, machine dynamics, propulsion, solar energy, thermodynamics, and vibrations.

The following *Engineering Common Courses* are available for graduate major credit: EGC 541—Tensor Fields and Fluid Dynamics; EGC 601—Theory of Fluid Flow I; EGC 602—Theory of Fluid Flow II; EGC 603—Theory of Fluid Flow III; EGC 604—Boundary Layer Theory; EGC 611—High Speed Gas Dynamics I; EGC 671—Introduction to Plasmas; EGC 672—Plasma Theory.

GRADUATE COURSES

ME 520—Control System Theory (3)
ME 535—Biomechanics of Surgical Implants (3)
ME 540—Engineering Acoustics and Noise Control (3)
ME 550—Gas Dynamics of Internal Flow Systems (3)
ME 555—Intermediate Heat Transfer (3)
ME 560—Statistical Thermodynamics (3)
ME 561—Classical Thermodynamics (3)
ME 577—Advanced Refrigeration (3)
ME 580—Advanced Dynamics of Machinery (3)
ME 581—Design Synthesis in Vibrations (3)
ME 589—Similitude in Mechanical Engineering Design (3) Principles of similitude for model design, analysis, and design analogies. Similitude as a basis for design optimization.
ME 591—Gas Turbines and Jet Engines (3)
ME 593—Mechanical Design I (3)
ME 594—Mechanical Design II (3)
ME 620—Instrumentation and Measurements Laboratory (1) Methods of measuring properties most often encountered in modern research; emphasis on actual measurement rather than theory.
ME 621—Feedback Control System Design I (3) Design and compensation of linear feedback control systems. Mechanical, hydraulic, pneumatic, electromechanical systems.
ME 630—Sliding-Element Bearing Analysis and Design (3) *Prereq: ME 450, ESM 311 or ASE 402.* Theory and design analysis of hydrodynamic bearings, hydrostatic bearings, and solid lubricated sliding bearings.
ME 631—Rolling-Element Bearing Analysis and Design (3) *Prereq: ME 482 and 483, or ESM 533.* Theory and design analysis of ball bearings and roller bearings.
ME 639—Advanced Rotor Dynamics (3) *Prereq: ME 439 or 480 (or ESM 520) and consent of instructor.* Analysis of dynamic stability, critical speeds, and unbalance response of rotor-

bearing systems. Special problems encountered in modern applications operating through and above the critical speeds.

ME 641—Advanced Noise Control (3) *Prereq: ME 540 or consent of instructor.* Engineering approaches to control of noise associated with industrial operations and transportation systems. Community noise control.

ME 650—Special Topics in Fluid Dynamics (3) *Prereq: ME 450 or equivalent.* Advanced fluid dynamics topics for mechanical engineers.

ME 651—Special Topics in Heat Transfer (3) *Prereq: ME 430.* Theoretical evaluation of physical constants. Techniques needed for solution of heat transfer problems involving all three modes: conduction, convection, and radiation.

ME 652—Thermodynamics of Fluid Flow I (3) Laws of mechanics, thermodynamics, and heat transfer combined to give general relationships for solution and better understanding of flow phenomena.

ME 653—Thermodynamics of Fluid Flow II (3) *Prereq: ME 652.*

ME 654—Thermodynamics of Fluid Flow III (3) *Prereq: ME 653.*

ME 655—Conduction Heat Transfer (3) *Prereq: MS 305, ME 430.* Mathematical description of conduction. Solution of conduction problems by series, transform, and numerical methods in generalized unsteady systems with appropriate boundary conditions.

ME 656—Convective Heat Transfer I (3) Conservation equations for continuum fluids. Exact and approximate solutions for laminar flow.

ME.657—Radiation Heat Transfer (3) *Prereq: MS 305, ME 430.* Physics of radiation, general integral equations, simplified analyses for diffuse and gray surfaces. Equation of transfer and simplified participating gas analysis. Free molecule flow heat transfer.

ME 658—Convective Heat Transfer II (3) *Prereq: ME 656.* Heat transfer analysis of multiphase and multicomponent fluid systems. Consideration of mass transport. Radiation coupling. Analysis of turbulent flows.

ME 659—Advanced Heat Transfer (3) *Prereq: ME 657, 658.* Modern developments. Interaction phenomena.

ME 660—Advanced Statistical Mechanics and Kinetic Theory (3) *Prereq: ME 560.* Highly degenerate Bose and Fermi systems. Statistical mechanics of dependent particles. The Boltzmann transport equation and transport properties.

ME 661—Advanced Thermodynamics (3) Thermodynamics of nonsimple systems. Multicomponent and multiphase thermodynamic analysis.

ME 662—Irreversible Thermodynamics (3) *Prereq: ME 661, 656.* General equations of conservation for heterogeneous, nonsimple reacting continua. Constitutive equations in general. Onsager reciprocity theorem. Example applications in mixed potential systems.

ME 663—Energy Conversion (3; max: 6) Conversion of available forms of energy into mechanical and electrical forms; energy conversion schemes, including conventional cycles in unusual environments, MHD, solar cells, thermionic and photogalvanic conversion and fuel cells.

ME 664—Combustion I (3) *Prereq: ME 560, 561.* Chemical reactions in gases, reactive gas dynamics, and general combustion phenomena, including vessel explosions, gas-phase diffusion flames, and droplet and particle combustion.

ME 665—Combustion II (3) *Prereq: ME 664.* Premixed gas flames, aerodynamics of flames, detonation, heterogeneous combustion, supersonic combustion, and solid and liquid propellant combustion in rockets.

ME 666—Solar Energy Utilization (3; max: 6) Solar energy; its availability and characteristics; its conversion and utilization as heat for power, refrigeration, distillation, photochemical reactions; solar energy as a research tool.

ME 667—Special Topics in Solar Energy (3; max: 9) *Prereq: undergraduate course in thermodynamics and heat transfer.* Selective surfaces, solar traps, solar energy storage, solar fuel cells, direct conversion of solar radiation.

ME 668—Gas Turbine Design and Performance (3) *Prereq: ME 591.* Design of gas turbine components and advanced performance calculations based on best available gas properties and coordinated with actual data on large gas turbines, jets.

ME 675—Advanced Air Conditioning I (3) Air-conditioning system selection and system design; air handling techniques including noise control, cleaning, temperature and humidity control; modern technological development and economic analysis.

ME 676—Advanced Air Conditioning II (3) *Prereq: ME 675.* Industrial applications, special requirements for hospitals, schools; survival shelter criteria.

ME 678—Fluerics and Fluidics (3) Coanda effect, basic fluid control element, bi-stable and proportional fluid amplifiers, feedback fluid oscillators, fluid pulse counters, fluid inverters, and/or gates, fluidic and flueric control and interlock circuits.

ME 680—Dynamics of Mechanical Systems (3) *Prereq: ME 480.* Applications of the classical theory of dynamics to the analysis and mathematical simulation of systems in which dynamic loads predominate.

ME 681—Mechanical Vibrations I (3) Linear and torsional vibrations; systems of one or more degrees of freedom; vibrations absorbers and dampers.

ME 682—Mechanical Vibrations II (3) *Prereq: ME 681.* Vibration analysis of multicylinder engines, rotating machinery, and flexible members in linkages.

ME 683—Dynamic Synthesis of Direct Contact Mechanisms (3) *Prereq: ME 483.* The design of direct contact mechanisms by classical techniques of rigid body systems and finite differences applied to systems composed of elastic components.

ME 684—Coplanar Kinematic Synthesis I (3) *Prereq: ME 381.* Multiply separated position theory for 3, 4, and 5 positions of the moving system. Curvature transformation, circle point curves, and Burmester point theory. Treatment is analytical, with emphasis on the theory of algebraic curves.

ME 685—Coplanar Kinematic Synthesis II (3) *Prereq: ME 684.* Application of theory in ME 684. Point-path, coplanar, and function generation synthesis problems for linear, circular, or geared constraints. Reduction of parameters and optimization concepts.

ME 686—Spatial Kinematic Synthesis and Analysis (3) Geometry of motion in three dimensions. Single position design depending on orders of contact with spatial curves. Finitely separated position design by matrix methods. Synthesis and analysis of spatial motions.

ME 687—Computer-Aided Design: Optimization (3) *Prereq: ISE 470, ME 579.* Parameter optimization techniques in machine systems.

ME 690—Mechanical Research I (1-3; max: 6) Research projects in mechanical engineering.

ME 692—Advanced Mechanical Laboratory I (3) Experimental projects in mechanical engineering.

ME 695—Graduate Seminar (1; max: 9) S/U.

ME 696—Individual Projects in Mechanical Engineering (1-3; max: 12)

ME 697—Supervised Research (1-5)

ME 698—Supervised Teaching (1-5)

ME 699—Master's Research (1-15)

ME 799—Doctoral Research (1-15)

MEDICAL SCIENCES—GENERAL
(College of Medicine)

The College of Medicine offers a program leading to the Doctor of Philosophy and Master of Science degrees in the basic medical sciences, with specialization in immunology and medical microbiology, neuroscience, pathology (including anatomical sciences), pharmacology, and physiology. The Department of Biochemistry *(College of Arts and Sciences)* also offers Ph.D. and M.S. programs. Training in these scientific disciplines is planned to prepare the student for a career in research and teaching, rather than in clinical practice, for which the Doctor of Medicine degree program is designed.

The graduate faculty and the courses offered are listed under department headings in this *Catalog.* A minor is not required but may be chosen in another of the basic sciences listed below or elsewhere in the *Catalog.* All facilities of the College of Medicine are available to graduate students in this program. Though an undergraduate major in biological or physical science is desirable, concentration in mathematics or engineering is an appropriate foundation for the Ph.D. in medical sciences. Satisfactory completion of a thesis based on research is a requirement for a graduate degree in the medical sciences (see *College of Medicine Catalog*).

In addition, the College of Medicine offers a Medical Scientist Training Program (combined M.D.-Ph.D. degree) to highly qualified students. Candidates for this five-to-seven-year program must satisfy admission requirements of both the College of Medicine and the Graduate School. Applicants should specify the basic science department to which admission is sought; they will be admitted following independent approval by the Medical Admissions Committee, the departmental Graduate Selection Committee, and a Medical Scientist Training Program Board. Applications are coordinated through the Office of the Dean of the College of Medicine. Study and dissertation research in departments other than basic science departments in the College of Medicine may be included in this program.

GRADUATE COURSES

MED 565—Radioisotope Theory and Techniques (5) Same as BTY 565, ZY 565, and NES 585. *Prereq: CY 331 or consent of instructor.* Theory of radioactivity, interaction with matter, and radioactive decay given in sufficient detail to make the laboratory techniques and practices thoroughly understood.

MED 631—Clinical Rounds for Graduate Students (2-5; max:10) *Permission of coordinator and clinical instructor necessary.* Graduate students of the medical sciences disciplines will attend conferences and attend ward rounds with a clinical mentor on the service of their choice. May be repeated.

MED 696—Research in Medical Sciences (1-15; max: 15) Supervised research other than that for the thesis or dissertation in biochemistry, immunology and medical microbiology, neuroscience, pathology, physiology, and pharmacology.

MED 697—Supervised Research (1-5; max: 5)

MED 698—Supervised Teaching (1-5; max: 5)

MED 699—Master's Research (1-15)

MED 799—Doctoral Research (1-15)

MICROBIOLOGY

(College of Arts and Sciences)

Chairman: P. H. SMITH
Graduate Coordinator: D. E. DUGGAN

GRADUATE FACULTY 1975-76

Professors: J. W. BROOKBANK; L. W. CLEM; G. E. GIFFORD; P. H. SMITH; M. E. TYLER

Associate Professors: P. M. ACHEY; H. C. ALDRICH; A. S. BLEIWEIS; D. E. DUGGAN; E. H. HOFFMANN; D. H. HUBBELL; J. A. KOBURGER; J. F. PRESTON III; E. P. PREVIC; K. L. SMITH

Assistant Professors: G. BITTON; L. O. INGRAM; N. J. SCHNEIDER

Graduate study is offered leading to Master of Science and Doctor of Philosophy degrees in microbiology. Instruction and guidance are collaborative among faculty in the Colleges of Arts and Sciences, Agriculture, and Medicine, and the Florida Bureau of Laboratories.

Student research areas include anaerobic metabolism; marine ecology; cell wall chemistry and immunochemistry; complement immunochemistry; cytokinesis; RNA, DNA, protein synthesis; physiology of blue-green bacteria; bacterial genetics; dairy, soil, or food microbiology; or interdisciplinary cellular and developmental biology.

Prerequisites for admission to graduate study, in addition to those of the Graduate School, are a broad educational base including mathematics, physics, and chemistry through organic and analytical; basic courses in botany and zoology; and preferably at least one course in bacteriology. An undergraduate major in physical science, engineering, or general biology is usually acceptable. Reciept of an advanced degree requires detailed knowledge in biology, microbiology, and chemistry; undergraduate deficiencies may require additional study prior to completion of graduate work.

GRADUATE COURSES

MCY 505—Advanced General Immunology (5) *Prereq: MCY 302.* In-depth study of cellular and humoral systems involved in the response of vertebrates to foreign substances. Laboratory exercises in serological techniques.

MCY 506—Advanced Studies of Bacterial Pathogens (5) *Prereq: MCY 505.* In-depth study of host-parasite relationships in the diseases of man and animals. The characteristics of bacterial pathogens. Intensive laboratory study of techniques of isolation and identification of bacterial pathogens.

MCY 507—Microbial Ecology (5) *Prereq: consent of instructor.* Distinctive characters and ecology of major bacterial taxa, and contemporary nomenclature in Bergey's Manual.

MCY 510—Advanced Studies in General Virology (5) *Prereq: MCY 302; coreq: BCH 511.* In-depth study of viruses and mechanisms of infection and replication of bacterial, animal, and plant viruses.

MCY 519—Advanced Studies in Structure and Physiology of Microorganisms (5) *Prereq: MCY 302, CY 382; BCH 511 desirable.* In-depth physical and chemical approach to an understanding of microbial anatomy, including cell walls, membranes, capsules, mesosomes, flagella, ribosomes, and the nucleoid. Kinetics of normal and abnormal growth and cell division in microorganisms. Integration of macromolecular syntheses throughout the division cycle.

MCY 520—Advanced Study of Metabolism of Microorganisms (5) *Prereq: MCY 302, CY 382; BCH 511 desirable.* In-depth study of energy metabolism and metabolic pathways of microorganisms and quantitation of metabolic phenomena.

MCY 521—Advanced Genetics of Microorganisms (5) *Prereq: MCY 302 and CY 382.* In-depth studies of genetic systems in bacteriophage and microorganisms, with emphasis on mutation and recombination. Detailed consideration of control of metabolic pathways in bacteria at the level of the gene.

MCY 549—Radiation Effects and Radiation Biology (5) *Prereq: undergraduate major in science or bioengineering; calculus, organic chemistry, and biology; consent of instructor.* Physical and chemical background of radiation and effects, and survey of biological effects and mechanisms. Emphasis on events at the macromolecular and cellular level.

MCY 628—Environmental Microbiology (4) Same as ENV 628. Interaction between microbial populations. Behavior of microorganisms in fresh water, marine and soil environments. Stress due to pollution on microbial communities.

MCY 649—Special Topics in Radiation Biology (5) *Prereq: MCY 549; one year each of college physics, mathematics, and biology or botany; chemistry through organic.* Readings and research on the biological effects of radiation, with emphasis on cellular effects and mechanisms.

MCY 650—Public Health Microbiology (1-6; max: 18) Same as MED 650. *Prereq: consent of department chairman and director of laboratories.* Reference study and laboratory practice of diagnostic techniques in the Microbiological Diagnostic Laboratory, Shands Teaching Hospital, University of Florida Health Center or in residence at the Bureau of Laboratories, State Department of Health, Jacksonville, Florida.

MCY 651—Special Topics in Microbiology (1-6; max: 18) Same as MED 651. *Prereq: 6 credits in graduate major courses.* Contemporary research in a particular aspect of general microbiology.

MCY 652—Virology (5) Same as MED 652. Selected topics on modern concepts of the nature of viruses and mechanism of viral infection; animal, bacterial, and plant viruses.

MCY 653—Virology Laboratory (3) Same as MED 653. *Prereq. or coreq: MCY 652.* Selected laboratory experiments on the nature of viruses and mechanisms of viral replication; other consequences of viral infections.

MCY 654—Research Planning (5) Same as MED 654. *Prereq: 20 credits in progressive study of microbiology.* Processes involved in scientific research, including initiating a problem, experimental techniques, analyses and evaluation of data and reporting, illustrated by bacteriological examples.

MCY 656—The Literature of Microbiology (3) Same as MED 656. *Prereq: 12 credits of microbiology.* Bibliographic method in searching the literature. Literature of specified areas of the discipline.

MCY 657—Microbial Metabolism (5) Same as MED 657. *Prereq: BCH 603.* Intermediary metabolism of microorganisms; metabolic pathways that are unique or characteristic primarily of microorganisms.

MCY 658—Microbial Physiology (5) Same as MED 658. *Prereq: MCY 657.* Structural and functional elements of microorganisms and mechanics of their regulatory systems. Mechanisms of control of microbial DNA replication, cell division, ribosome and cell-wall formation, kinetic studies of normal and abnormal growth.

MCY 659—Principles of Immunology (5) Same as MED 659. *Prereq: MCY 505 or MED 551.* Biological and biochemical aspects of host resistance and immunity. Chemical and physiochemical properties of the proteins of immune reactions.

MCY 660—Immunology Laboratory (3) Same as MED 660. *Prereq: consent of staff. Coreq: MCY 659.*

MCY 661—Biology of Uncommon Microorganisms (5) Same as MED 661. *Prereq: MCY 302.* Natural distribution, metabolic activities, isolation, and culture of selected groups of microorganisms.

MCY 662—Microbial Genetics (5) Same as MED 662. *Prereq: MCY 521, general genetics.* Microbial genetics, including mutation, selection, transformation, transduction, conjugation, and episomal factors; molecular structure and function of genes.

MCY 663—Parasitic Diseases of the Tropics and Subtropics (5) Same as MED 663, VY 663, ZY 663. Animal parasitology covering mechanisms of parasitic infections, physiology of parasites, and immune responses of the host.

MCY 664—Viral Disease (3) Same as MED 664. *Prereq: MCY (MED) 652.* Pathogenesis of viral disease, including cytopathic and oncogenic viruses. Diagnostic and preventive measures.

MCY 666—Microbiology I (6) Same as MED 666. Intensive review of principles of immunity, physiology, and genetics of bacteria, virology, infection, and ecology.

MCY 667—Microbiology II (3) Same as MED 667.

MCY 668—Regulation in Biological Systems (5) Same as MED 668. *Prereq: MCY 520, 521, 657; BCH 601, 602.* Control of enzyme activity; kinetic, structural inhibition (allosteric and non-allosteric), and energy level control; permeases; control of enzyme synthesis: positive and negative; repression, induction, catabolic repression, cyclic AMP; hormonal control.

MCY 669—Seminar (1) Same as MED 669. *Attendance required of all graduate majors at one student and one nonstudent presentation each week as scheduled.* May be repeated with change of content.

MCY 696—Experimental Microbiology (1-12) *Prereq: 12 credits of microbiology.* Application of physical, chemical, and biological techniques to experimental problems in microbiology. Individual laboratory study.

MCY 697—Supervised Research (1-5)

MCY 698—Supervised Teaching (1-5)

MCY 699—Master's Research (1-15)

MCY 750—Journal Colloquy (1) Same as MED 750. Critical presentation and discussion of recent original articles in microbiological literature. May be repeated with change of content.

MCY 751—Research Conference (1) Same as MED 751. Critical discussion and appraisal of research programs of faculty and students of the department. May be repeated with change of content.

MCY 799—Doctoral Research (1-15)

PROGRAM IN CELLULAR
AND DEVELOPMENTAL BIOLOGY

The Department of Microbiology offers a program in cellular and developmental biology leading to the degree of Doctor of Philosophy. Requirements for admission are the same as those for other microbiology programs.

The faculty is drawn from the Departments of Botany, Microbiology, and Zoology, and the student of biological sciences enrolled in the program may elect to work under the direction of any of these graduate faculty members; P. H. Smith, *Chairman;* J. W. Brookbank, *Coordinator;* H. C. Aldrich; F. C. Davis; J. H. Gregg; G. Karp; J. Preston; E. Previc; and I. K. Vasil.

While the program emphasizes eucaryotic and microbial systems, the research interests of the staff range from areas of cell growth and metabolism to problems of morphogenesis and cell differentiation.

For additional information students should write, indicating their areas of interest in this broad field, to the Coordinator, Program in Cellular and Developmental Biology.

MUSIC
(College of Fine Arts)

Acting Chairman: R. POOLE
Graduate Coordinator: D. Z. KUSHNER

GRADUATE FACULTY 1975-76

Professors: R. W. BOWLES; R. L. DANBURG; J. P. HALE; E. J. KEISTER; D. Z. KUSHNER; R. POOLE; E. C. TROUPIN; D. L. WILMOT
Associate Professors: W. R. BODINE, JR.; P. E. DORMAN; S. P. KNISELEY

The Department of Music cooperates with the College of Education in offering courses leading to the degrees of Master of Education (emphasis in music education), Master of Arts in Education (emphasis in music history and literature, music theory and composition, applied music, and music education), Specialist in Education (emphasis in music education), Doctor of Education and Doctor of Philosophy (emphasis in college music teaching in music history and literature, music theory and composition, performance practices or music education).

During the first quarter of study, the candidate for a degree must take placement examinations in the areas of applied music, music theory, music history and literature, and music education, and must satisfy requirements for music teaching certification in Florida before the M.Ed. degree is awarded. All deficiencies must be remedied.

For additional courses in music education. see course listings ED 663, 664, 665, 666, 667.

GRADUATE COURSES

MSC 601—Graduate Music Theory Review (4)
MSC 607—Composition of Electronic Music (4) *Prereq: MSC 407.*
MSC 608—Pedagogy of Music Theory (4)
MSC 609—Topics in Music Theory (4; max: 12) Work culminating in a musical composition, arrangement, research paper, or public lecture-performance. Topics vary in different terms.
MSC 611—Methods of Musical Research and Bibliography (4) Materials and specialized techniques of research in musicology.
MSC 612—Methods of Research in Music Education (4) Materials and specialized techniques of research in music education.

MSC 613—Graduate Music History Review (4)

MSC 615—Topics in Musicology (4; max: 12) Work culminating in a research paper or article or in the public performance of a musical work of historical importance. Topics vary in different terms.

MSC 616—Topics in Music Literature (4; max: 12) Intensive study of specialized areas of music literature. Topics vary in different terms.

MSC 621—Applied Music (3; max: 18) Offered in piano, voice, organ, harpsichord, conducting, and all standard band and orchestral instruments.

MSC 622—Secondary Applied Music (3; max: 18) Offered in piano, voice, organ, harpsichord, conducting, and all standard band and orchestral instruments.

MSC 667—Topics in Music Education (4; max: 12) *Prereq: MSC 611 or 612.* Study of selected areas of music education culminating in a research paper or article. Topics vary in different terms.

MSC 669—Music in the Schools (2-9; max: 9) *Offered by extension only.* In-service training for teachers. Topics and projects vary.

MSC 670—Graduate Ensemble (1) For graduate students holding positions of leadership and participating in music ensembles.

MSC 696—Projects and Problems in Music (5; max: 15) Approved problems for study and research. May be repeated with change of content.

MSC 697—Supervised Research (1-5)

MSC 698—Supervised Teaching (1-5)

MSC 699—Master's Research or Graduate Recital (1-15) For master's degree candidates: A thesis, musical composition or group of compositions, or preparation for public performance of a graduate recital equivalent in creative work to thesis requirements. Recital must be acceptable to candidate's supervisory committee and to the Graduate School.

MSC 709—Topics in Music Theory (4; max: 12) For doctoral students. Work culminating in a musical composition, arrangement, research paper, or public lecture-performance. Topics vary in different terms.

MSC 715—Topics in Musicology (4; max: 12) For doctoral students. Work culminating in a research paper or article or in the public performance of a musical work of historical importance. Topics vary in different terms.

MSC 716—Topics in Music Literature (4; max: 12) Intensive study of specialized area of music literature for doctoral students. Topics vary in different terms.

MSC 721—Applied Music (3; max: 9) Offered in piano, voice, organ, harpsichord, and all standard band and orchestral instruments for doctoral students. Recital appearance required each term.

MSC 722—Secondary Applied Music (3; max: 9) For doctoral students. Offered in piano, voice, organ, harpsichord, conducting, and all standard band and orchestral instruments.

MSC 767—Topics in Music Education (4; max: 12) For doctoral students. Study of selected areas of music education culminating in a research paper or article.

MSC 796—Projects and Problems in Music (5; max: 15) Approved problems for study and research.

NEUROSCIENCE

(College of Medicine)

Chairman: F. A. KING; *Associate Chairman:* W. G. LUTTGE
Graduate Coordinator: W. E. BROWNELL

GRADUATE FACULTY 1975-76

Professors: R. L. ISAACSON; F. A. KING; O. M. RENNERT; B. J. WILDER
Associate Professors: J. J. BERNSTEIN; J. B. MUNSON; C. VAN HARTESVELDT; C. J. VIERCK, JR.
Assistant Professors: W. E. BROWNELL; A. J. DUNN; M. B. HEATON; W. G. LUTTGE; F. J. THOMPSON; D. W. WALKER; S. F. ZORNETZER

The Department of Neuroscience offers specialization leading to the Master of Science and Doctor of Philosophy degrees in the medical sciences. All students receive training in neuroanatomy, neurobehavioral science, neurochemistry, neuroendocrinology, neurohistology, neuropharmacology, and neurophysiology.

Prospective students should have undergraduate training in biochemistry, physiology, statistics, and behavioral sciences. Students admitted with deficiencies in these areas will be required to obtain remedial training.

GRADUATE COURSES

MED 504—Neurohumors and Behavior (4) Same as PSY 574. *Prereq: STA 320, MED 520, and PSY 371.* Synthesis, action, and metabolism of putative neural transmitters; pharmacological means of altering these; physiological or behavioral functions attributed to putative neural transmitters.

MED 505—Introduction to the Neurosciences (4) *Prereq: ZY 202 or equivalent.* Structure and basic functions of the mammalian nervous system, including neuroanatomy, neurophysiology, neurochemistry, and neuropharmacology.

MED 506—Introduction to Neurochemistry (4) *Prereq: biochemistry.* Discussion of current topics. Includes metabolism of carbohydrates, lipids, amino acids, proteins and nucleic acids, the metabolism and function of neurotransmitters, and axoplasmic flow.

MED 518—Vision (4) *Prereq: consent of instructor.* Introduction to the methodology, anatomy, and function of vision.

MED 600—History of the Neurosciences (3) Discoveries, concepts, and technical advances in the basic nervous system disciplines from ancient to modern times. Emergence of the several neurosciences as experimental disciplines providing a foundation for rational medical applications.

MED 601—Pain and Somesthesis (4) Current research on central nervous system coding and information, using somesthesis as a model, with particular emphasis on pain.

MED 603—Comparative Neuroanatomy and Neurophysiology (4) Phylogenetic development of the central nervous system of vertebrate animals considered from the anatomical, electrophysiological and behavioral points of view.

MED 622—Physiology of the Central Nervous System (4) Special and current problems in brain and spinal cord function covered in seminars.

MED 623—Neurophysiology (4) Physiology of nerve and muscle, central nervous system, and the special senses. Comparative aspects emphasized.

MED 633—Neurobiology (4) *Prereq: background in biological or behavioral sciences.* Structure and physiology of the nervous system as it pertains to control of behavior.

MED 635—Neuroendocrinology (4-6) Neural regulation of endocrine systems in vertebrate animals. Correlative study of neuroanatomical, neurophysiological, and neurochemical aspects of endocrine control.

MED 636—A Survey of Sensory Systems (4) Same as ZY 636, PSY 678. *Prereq: ZY 574 or MED 623 or MED 331 or PSY 600 or MED 767.* A group of specialists provide a survey of theories and experimental data on human and subhuman sensory reception and encoding. Auditory, visual, and cutaneous and chemical senses are included.

MED 639—Seminar in Sensory Processes (1) Same as PSY 676, ZY 638. Topics of current interest in various areas of the sensory specialties are discussed within the seminar framework. S/U.

MED 676—Neurohistology (2) Histological approaches and techniques for the study of the neuronal, neuroglial, and mesenchymal cellular components of the central and peripheral nervous system.

MED 677—Nerve as a Tissue (2) Seminar on current research problems in the area of cellular interactions in the nervous system. Readings and discussion from articles in the fields contributing to the physiology, chemistry, and anatomy of the nervous system.

MED 704—Physiology and Pharmacology of Excitable Membranes (3) Membrane ionic permeability changes underlying action and synaptic potential generation described in detail. Applications of electrophysiological and radioactive tracer techniques to analysis of drug action on excitable membranes.

MED 711—Neural-Behavioral-Endocrine Interactions (4) Interrelationships of endocrine hormones, nervous system activity, and behavior. Sample topics include the role of hormones in sexual behavior, aggression, stress, parental behavior, learning and memory, mood, and target organ physiology.

MED 712—Neurobehavioral Relations (4) Same as PSY 775. Theories and data on the central nervous system basis for higher order function. Emphasis on arousal, purposeful behavior, and learning.

MED 713—Information Storage: A Neurobiological Approach (4) Same as PSY 776. Consideration of data dealing with basic issues concerning the nature of behavioral plasticity and information storage and their central nervous system foundations. Particular emphasis on memory disruption and facilitation as an experimental tool in the study of memory processes.

MED 714—Developmental Neural-Behavioral-Endocrine Interactions (2-4) Interrelationships and roles of endocrine hormones, behavior, and nervous system activity during the perinatal period on the development of adult patterns of neuroendocrine activity and behavior.

MED 715—Neural Mechanisms of Ingestion and Energy Regulation (4) Same as PSY 770. Neuroanatomical, neurobehavioral, and neuroendocrinological mechanisms involved in the regulation of food and water consumption and regulation of body weight.

MED 716—Colloquium in Neurobiology (1-2; max: 16) Current theoretical issues that relate to the neurophysiological, physiological, chemical, and behavioral approaches to the study of the nervous system. S/U.

MED 717—Physiological Basis of Brain Rhythms (3) Analysis of the structural, physiological, and pharmacological substrates for electrical activity of the central nervous system as manifested in the normal electroencephalogram, including the development and relationship to evoked potentials.

MED 718—Neuroscience Seminar (1-2; max: 16) Readings and discussions of current topics in neuroscience. S/U.

MED 719—Special Topics in Neuroscience (1-6; max: 16) Intensive readings and lectures in specialized fields of neuroscience and allied disciplines.

MED 720—Research Methods in Neuroscience (1-10; max: 16) Research techniques in experimental neuroscience.

MED 741—Medical Neuroscience (6) Comprehensive overview of human neuroanatomy from the subcellular to the gross tissue level. Lectures cover neurochemistry, neuropharmacology, neurophysiology, neuroendocrinology and neurobehavioral biology. Clinical correlations and applications.

MED 742—Recent Advances in Neuroscience (1-2; max: 16) Seminar and group discussions of recent advances in one or more areas of neuroscience.

MED 744—Motor Systems (4) Basic mechanisms involved in motor activity; muscle spindle system and its central control by spinal cord and supraspinal mechanisms. Emphasis on normal rather than abnormal processes.

MED 745—Functional Neurochemistry (4) *Prereq: biochemistry.* Survey of molecules that play a special role in nervous system function or respond to neural stimulation. Includes studies of nucleic acids, proteins, glycoproteins, glycolipids, nucleotides and neurotransmitters and the enzymes associated with their metabolism. Results from simple systems related to those of higher brain function.

MED 746—Structure and Function of the Auditory System (4) *Prereq: MED 741 or consent of instructor.* Laboratory-seminar on the anatomy and physiology of the auditory system. Stress of brainstem nuclei and their interconnections.

MED 765—Integrative Neurobiology I: Cellular and Molecular Neurobiology (4) Cellular and subcellular structure of nervous tissue. Development of the nervous system and factors involved in its differentiation. Nervous system biochemistry including metabolism and function of neurotransmitters. Axoplasmic transport. Degeneration and regeneration and trophic functions of nervous tissue.

MED 766—Integrative Neurobiology II: Comparative Neuroanatomy (8) Lecture and laboratory course concerning general principles of vertebrate neuroanatomy and brain and spinal cord organization. Mammalian neuroanatomy stressed.

MED 767—Integrative Neurobiology III: Systems Neurobiology (8) Lecture course concerning neurobiological systems: specifically the motor systems, non-specific systems, sensory systems and neurotransmitter-neuroendocrine systems.

MED 768—Integrative Neurobiology IV: Behavioral Neurobiology (8) Lecture and laboratory course concerning the neurobiological substrates of behavior, and neurobehavioral techniques.

NUCLEAR ENGINEERING SCIENCES
(College of Engineering)

Chairman: M J. OHANIAN
Graduate Coordinator: H. D. CAMPBELL

GRADUATE FACULTY 1975-76

Graduate Research Professor: A. E. S. GREEN
Professors: E. E. CARROLL, JR.; G. R. DALTON; B. G. DUNAVANT; W. MAUDERLI; M. J. OHANIAN; R. T. SCHNEIDER; G. J. SCHOESSOW; J. A. WETHINGTON, JR.
Associate Professors: W. E. BOLCH, JR.; V. A. BROOKEMAN; H. D. CAMPBELL; N. J. DIAZ; W. H. ELLIS; C. D. KYLSTRA; C. E. ROESSLER
Assistant Professors: L. T. FITZGERALD; G. S. ROESSLER

The Department of Nuclear Engineering Sciences offers the degrees of Master of Science, Master of Engineering, Engineer, and Doctor of Philosophy with emphasis in nuclear power engineering, radiological sciences or engineering physics and thermonuclear fusion; the radiological sciences option is offered through an interdepartmental program in cooperation with the Department of Environmental Engineering Sciences and the Medical School.

Specific areas of emphasis include advanced nuclear power concepts, nuclear reactor and power plant technology and operations, reactor dynamics and control, environmental aspects of nuclear power generation, neutron and reactor physics, nuclear plasma and laser technology, thermonuclear fusion systems, and nuclear radiation chemistry, high-temperature materials, nuclear detection and instrumentation, bionucleonics, energy systems analysis, medical radiation physics, radiation biology, and health physics.

The requirement for admission to the graduate program in nuclear engineering sciences is a bachelor's degree in an approved program in engineering or in the sciences. If the student's background is considered deficient for his planned course of study, an articulation program of background courses will be required.

Depending on professional objectives, the student may omit the master's thesis and substitute 12 credits of graduate-level course work, of which at least 9 credits are in nuclear engineering sciences, including a 6-credit (minimum) special project (NES 691). In such cases the completion of 48 credits will meet the minimum requirements for the nonthesis degree.

The following *Engineering Common Courses* are also available: EGC 671—Introduction to Plasmas; EGC 672—Plasma Theory; EGC 675—Plasma Laboratory; EGC 677—Gas Lasers and Their Engineering Applications, as well as the course MSE 630—Nuclear Materials and Radiation Damage in Solids.

GRADUATE COURSES

NES 500—Fundamentals of Reactor Engineering (4) Survey of nuclear reactor concepts, instrumentation, operation, fuels, materials, and shielding.

NES 533—Isotope Separation (3) Stable isotopes important for conventional nuclear reactors, isotopes important for fusion, methods for separating them.

NES 540—Nuclear Radiation Detection and Instrumentation (4) Interaction of radiation with matter, radiation detector systems, pulse shaping, amplification, amplitude and time-analyzing circuitry; counting and measuring devices and control systems for nuclear reactors.

NES 551—Nuclear Power Reactors I (4) *Prereq: NES 403 or consent of instructor.* Study of the various types of nuclear reactors for power generation, design, construction, materials, heat transfer and cooling systems.

NES 555—Reactor Fuel Cycles (3) *Prereq: NES 402.* The fuel management problem in nuclear power reactors. Reactivity, breeding, fuel and fission product inventory as a function of life time; power distribution and fuel relocation.

NES 570—Principles of Nuclear Reactor Operations (3) *Prereq: NES 402.* Reactor start-up, reactor physics measurements and control calibrations, principles of control and operation and problems of power operation.

NES 580—Bionucleonics (3) *Prereq: one year each of college biology, chemistry, and physics or the equivalent.* Introduction to application of nuclear energy to human biomedical problems including the use of radioactive isotopes in biomedical research, medical diagnosis and therapy. Benefits to man weighed against potential hazards.

NES 584—Radiation Effects on Humans (4) *Prereq: one year each of college physics, chemistry, and biology.* Somatic and genetic radiation effects; acute and chronic radiation exposure; pathology; epidemiological aspects; fundamentals of the application of radiation for treatment of disease.

NES 585—Radioisotope Theory and Techniques (5) Same as BTY 565, MED 565, and ZY 565. *Prereq: CY 331 or consent of instructor.* The theory of radioactivity, of interaction with matter, radioactive decay given in sufficient detail to make the laboratory techniques and practices thoroughly understood.

NES 600—Nuclear Engineering Laboratory II (4) *Prereq: NES 404, 540. Coreq: NES 610.* Laboratory practice in neutron and gamma detection and analysis. Determination of basic neutron parameters in nonmultiplying and multiplying media.

NES 601—Nuclear Engineering Laboratory III (4) Laboratory practice in measurement of basic reactor parameters and the effects of reactor perturbation.

NES 610—Reactor Analysis I (3) *Prereq: NES 401, 402, 403.* Neutron diffusion theory, homogeneous and one-velocity reactors. Time-dependent behavior of the neutron flux, reactor kinetics with temperature dependence.

NES 611—Reactor Analysis II (3) *Prereq: NES 610.* Reactor analysis in terms of the slowing-down model and Fermi-age theory. Six-factor formula, reactor temperature coefficients, introduction to perturbation theory as applied to reactivity calculations.

NES 612—Advanced Reactor Analysis (3) *Prereq: NES 611.* Analytical methods of heterogeneous reactor calculations, fundamentals of control-rod theory, disadvantage factor, thermal utilization, resonance escape probability, fast fission; monoenergetic transport theory.

NES 614—Neutron Transport Theory (3) *Prereq: NES 612.* Neutron transport equation, approximations based on orthogonal functions, variational techniques, and Monte Carlo methods applied to monoenergetic and energy-dependent transport theory.

NES 616—Numerical Methods of Reactor Analysis (4) *Prereq: NES 610.* Numerical solutions to reactor analysis problems, emphasis on the solution of one-, two- and three-dimensional diffusion equations, multiregion and multigroup diffusion methods. P^n and S^n calculations.

NES 617—Computer Programs in the Nuclear Industry (4) *Prereq: NES 610, ISE 351.* Description and use of the most widely employed methods and codes used in reactor physics calculations by industry.

NES 618—Principles of Fast Reactors (3) *Prereq: NES 611.* Underlying mathematical techniques of fast reactor physics. Quantum mechanical procedures for nuclear processes involved in a fast reactor. Inelastic neutron scattering and resonance reactions.

NES 619—Fast Reactor Analysis (3) *Prereq: NES 618.* Computation of sodium void, Doppler and temperature coefficients, and fast reactor breeding ratio. Problems of fast reactor breeding.

NES 644—Nuclear Data Acquisition and Processing (4) *Prereq: NES 404, 540.* Acquisition and processing of data from nuclear detectors. Multi-input systems. Use of "on-line" digital computers for control of experiments. Special instrumentation techniques.

NES 651—Nuclear Power Reactors II (4) *Prereq: NES 551, 610.* Nuclear reactors for power generation, with emphasis on use of computer codes and an advanced set of problems.

NES 652—Reactor Technology I (4) *Prereq: NES 611.* Theories of previous courses applied to analytical design and economics of an integrated fast reactor nuclear plant.

NES 653—Reactor Technology II (4) *Prereq: NES 652.* Analysis of reactor systems by comparison of actual and predicted performance, with emphasis on use of computer codes.

NES 655—Fundamental Aspects of Reactor Shielding (3) *Prereq: NES 611.* Shielding design fundamentals. Methods of calculating gamma-ray attenuation, fast neutron penetration, effects of ducts and voids in shields, problems of heat generation and deposition in reactor components.

NES 660—Fundamentals of Reactor Kinetics (4) *Prereq: NES 611.* Dynamic behavior of nuclear reactor systems from the point of view of linear control theory. Laboratory use of analog computer to study reactor kinetics problems.

NES 661—Advanced Reactor Kinetics (3) *Prereq: NES 660.* Nuclear reactor dynamics; spatially dependent kinetics; techniques of nonlinear stability analysis; kinetics of various reactor prototypes.

NES 670—Plasma Spectroscopy (4) Spectroscopic techniques for measurement of temperature and density of plasmas, and their application to thermonuclear fusion and direct energy conversion devices.

NES 673—Advanced Plasma Theory (4) *Prereq: NES 670.* Fundamental equations of statistical plasma theory: Vlasov, Boltzmann, Fokker-Planck, and radiation transport equations, their solution, and typical applications to plasmas.

NES 674—Thermonuclear Fusion (3) Foundations of thermonuclear reactions. Methods of heating plasmas to extreme temperatures; plasma containment by magnetic fields; plasma instabilities.

NES 678—Direct Energy Conversion (4) Various direct conversion systems, with emphasis on system involving nuclear reactors or nuclear reactions.

NES 680—Radiological Physics (4) X-rays, including the production, properties, nature, circuits, and measurements; x-ray tubes, for both diagnosis and therapy; image amplifiers; the quality of x-rays, half-value layer, and x-ray filters; high energy electron accelerators and isotope therapy units.

NES 682—Medical Radiation Instrumentation and Dosimetry (4) *Prereq: NES 680 or equivalent.* Dosimetry instrumentation including ion chambers, semiconductor and luminescent devices; measurement in roentgens; measurement of absorbed radiation energy; manual and computer techniques in treatment planning for external beam therapy and implanted sources.

NES 683—Radioactive Tracer Instrumentation and Methodology (4) *Prereq: BTY 565.* Advanced techniques and theory of radioisotopes used as tracers and activation analysis in biological systems. Instrumentation, sample preparation, methods of calculation, kinetics of radiobiological investigations.

NES 685—Field Problems in Radiation Control (1-3) *Prereq: EGC 508.* On-the-job training by rotation through each phase of the radiation control program, including surveys, radioisotope receipt, storage, distribution, bioassays, personnel monitoring, record keeping.

NES 686—Nuclear Medicine Instrumentation and Procedure (5). *Prereq: NES 540 or equivalent.* Theory, evaluation, applications of detecting and imaging systems in nuclear medicine, including collimators, scintillation probes, scanners, cameras, data-processing devices; uses of radionuclides in medicine for radiopharmaceutical preparation and *in vivo* and *in vitro* diagnostic procedures; internal radiation dosimetry.

NES 690—Nuclear Seminar (1; max: 4) Discussion of research, current trends in the nuclear-related industry, government and research establishments.

NES 691—Special Projects in Nuclear Engineering Sciences (1-9; max: 18) Nonthesis research projects.

NES 692—Special Topics in Nuclear Engineering Sciences (1-9; max: 18)

NES 696—Individual Work (1-6; max: 18) Supervised study or research in areas not covered by other graduate courses.

NES 697—Supervised Research (1-5)

NES 698—Supervised Teaching (1-5)

NES 699—Master's Research (1-15)

NES 799—Doctoral Research (1-15)

NURSING

(College of Nursing)

Dean: B. I. UREY
Graduate Coordinator: D. B. PAYNE

GRADUATE FACULTY 1975-76

Professors: P. H. BARTON; M. E. HILLIARD; L. N. KNOWLES; B. I. UREY
Associate Professors: A. S. BAKER; M. E. DOUGHERTY; F. G. HARRIS; J. M. WILSON;
L. B. WILSON
Assistant Professors: P. A. CLUNN; E. E. DYKES; D. B. PAYNE; C. E. TAYLOR;
D. D. WILLIAMS

The College of Nursing offers the Master of Nursing (nonthesis) and the Master of Science in Nursing (thesis) degrees. Areas of specialization include women-infant health care, child health nursing, psychiatric mental health nursing, adult health care and the functional areas of teaching, administration, and clinical specialization.

In addition to meeting the requirements of the Graduate School, an applicant for admission must have R.N. licensure, a year's clinical experience in the area of choice, a baccalaureate degree from an accredited program with an upper-division nursing major, and a college-level course in statistics.

GRADUATE COURSES

NSG 572—Internship in Professional Nursing (4; max:12) *Prereq: admission to the internship program.*
NSG 600—Patient Evaluation for Nurses (4)
NSG 601—Developmental Theories: Implications for Nursing (4)
NSG 602—Dimensions of the Nursing Profession (4)
NSG 604—New Health-Related Roles (4)
NSG 607—A Changing Health Delivery System (4)
NSG 625—Seminar and Clinical Experiences in Psychiatric Mental-Health Nursing I (4)
NSG 626—Seminar and Clinical Experiences in Psychiatric Mental-Health Nursing II (4)
NSG 627—Seminar and Clinical Experiences in Psychiatric Mental-Health Nursing III (4)
NSG 628—Seminar and Clinical Experiences in Psychiatric Mental-Health Nursing IV (4)
NSG 631—Physical Assessment of Patient Status (4)
NSG 632—Clinical Problems in Nursing the Adult Patient I (4)
NSG 633—Clinical Problems in Nursing the Adult Patient II (4)
NSG 634—Clinical Problems in Nursing the Adult Patient III (4)
NSG 640—Pediatric Nursing: Problems of the Well Child (2)
NSG 642—Pediatric Nursing: The Ill Child (4)
NSG 643—Nursing Assessment of the Parent-Child Unit (4)
NSG 645—Seminar in Nursing Care of the Handicapped Child (4)
NSG 650—Nursing: Conception to Birth (4)
NSG 651—Nursing: Period of Early Infancy (4)
NSG 652—Nursing: Family Planning and Reproductive Health (4)
NSG 653—Seminar in Reproductive Health (4)
NSG 660—Research Methods in Nursing (4)
NSG 670—Seminar on Human Relations in Nursing (4)
NSG 671—Practicum in Nursing (4-12)
NSG 680—New Dimensions in Health in the Community (4)
NSG 690—Residency (4; max: 12) *Prereq: master's degree in nursing; admission to the residency program.*
NSG 695—Special Topics in Nursing (2-4)
NSG 696—Individual Study (1-5)
NSG 697—Supervised Research (1-5)
NSG 698—Supervised Teaching (1-5)
NSG 699—Master's Research (1-15)

OCCUPATIONAL THERAPY

(College of Health Related Professions)

Chairman: A. C. JANTZEN
Graduate Coordinator: L. A. LLORENS

GRADUATE FACULTY 1975-76

Professor: A. C. JANTZEN
Associate Professors: L. A. LLORENS; C. J. SLAYMAKER
Assistant Professor: K. W. SIEG

The Department of Occupational Therapy offers the Master of Health Science degree, with specialization in pediatric and psychiatric occupational therapy.

Preparation for positions in teaching, administration or research in occupational therapy programs is provided by means of elective options available in the curriculum.

In addition to the requirements of the Graduate School, admission to graduate study in occupational therapy requires that the candidate (1) have a bachelor's degree and (2) have completed an accredited curriculum in occupational therapy. Current registration with the American Occupational Therapy Association is acceptable as evidence of completion of an accredited curriculum.

GRADUATE COURSES

OCT 600—Research Methods in Occupational Therapy (3) Research design applicable to clinical problems and settings.
OCT 601—Proseminar (3) *Prereq: OCT 600, 613.* Preparation of proposal for investigation of clinical, academic, or administrative problems in occupational therapy. H.
OCT 603—Clinical Problems (4) Normal growth and development; diseases and disorders.
OCT 604—Clinical Problems (4) *Prereq: OCT 603.* Continuation of OCT 603.
OCT 613—Seminar: Occupational Therapy Management (4) *Prereq: OCT 603.* Evaluation techniques in occupational therapy.
OCT 614—Seminar: Occupational Therapy Management (4) *Prereq: OCT 613.* Treatment modalities in occupational therapy.
OCT 651—Advanced Specialty Practicum (3-5; max: 10) *Prereq. or coreq: OCT 613.* Field experience in clinical settings.
OCT 655—Specialty Residency (3-15) *Prereq: OCT 601.* Field experience in clinical settings approved by the department.
OCT 696—Individual Work (1-15) *Prereq: OCT 601, 651.* Project related to teaching, research, or administration.

PATHOLOGY

(College of Medicine)

Chairman: R. T. SMITH
Graduate Coordinator: B. M. GEBHARDT

GRADUATE FACULTY 1975-76

Professors: C. E. CORNELIUS; W. F. ENNEKING; R. L. HACKETT; C. MOSCOVICI; E. J. REITH; M. H. ROSS; R. T. SMITH; C. A. STETSON
Associate Professors: H. H. BAER; P. BYVOET; B. M. GEBHARDT; R. R. GRAMS; E. A. KALLENBACH; P. A. KLEIN; L. H. LARKIN; S. J. NORMANN; P. O. TEAGUE; J. C. WOODARD
Assistant Professors: C. A. CRANDALL; W. H. DONNELLY, JR.; L. L. SHAW
Instructor: J. T. FORBES

The Department of Pathology offers programs leading to the Master of Science and the Doctor of Philosophy degrees in the medical sciences, with specialization in experimental pathology. A separate program leading to advanced degrees in anatomical sciences is also offered and is described in the section entitled *Division of Anatomical Sciences.*

Specific areas of specialization in experimental pathology include immunobiology, tumor biology, molecular biology, immunopathology, infectious diseases, immunohematology, clinical chemistry, electron microscopy, virology, comparative pathology, nutritional pathology, clinical pathology, renal pathology, and neuropathology.

New graduate students in anatomical sciences and experimental pathology programs should have adequate undergraduate training in general chemistry, organic chemistry, general physics, general biology, and two or more advanced courses in the areas of physiological, developmental, or cellular biology, or, in the case of students in clinical chemistry, courses in analytical, inorganic, and physical chemistry. Students may find it necessary to remedy deficiencies in their background by taking some undergraduate courses after admission to the Graduate School. Courses in the major program will be determined by the student's advisory committee. The minor may be taken in any appropriate area.

GRADUATE COURSES

PROGRAM IN GENERAL AND EXPERIMENTAL PATHOLOGY

MED 610—Mechanisms of Disease (5) *Prereq: histology, microbiology, biochemistry, immunology, or consent of staff.* General principles of pathology and the mechanisms responsible for disease processes.

MED 611—Systemic Pathology (6) *Prereq: MED 610 and consent of staff.* Pathological processes affecting each organ or organ system.

MED 641—Special Cytology (5) Types of cells such as nerve, secretory, bone, muscle, connective tissues, blood, and lymphoid.

MED 646—Special Topics in Pathology (1-6; max: 18) *Prereq: permission of department.* Conferences and supervised laboratory work. Topics selected to meet each student's needs.

MED 647—Seminar in Pathology (1) *Required of graduate students in pathology; open to others by permission of the department.* Current research literature and research reports by graduate students, department staff, and invited speakers.

MED 648—Comparative Pathology (4) *Prereq: MED 610.* Diseases of various organ systems of domestic and laboratory animals compared and contrasted with spontaneous diseases of man.

MED 649—Nutritional and Biochemical Pathology (4) *Prereq: MED 610.* Relationships between biochemical alterations and microscopic lesions in spontaneous and experimentally induced diseases having defined nutritional or biochemical etiology.

PROGRAM IN CLINICAL CHEMISTRY

MED 640—Clinical Chemistry and Toxicology (3) Chemical techniques undertaken for diagnosis of disease. Methods of toxicology.

MED 643—Clinical Chemistry and Toxicology Rotation I (10) Participation in all phases of practical clinical chemistry and toxicology. Chemical methodology, clinical interpretation, and significance of laboratory measurements for diagnosis of the sick. Individual investigative project in clinical chemistry and toxicology. Students specializing in clinical chemistry must spend three terms on this rotation.

MED 644—Clinical Chemistry and Toxicology Rotation II (10) *Prereq: MED 643.*

MED 645—Clinical Chemistry and Toxicology Rotation III (10) *Prereq: MED 644.*

PROGRAM IN CELLULAR IMMUNOBIOLOGY

MED 642—Immunohematology (3) Immunologic, genetic, and anthropologic significance of blood group antigens and antibodies, with emphasis on their serologic and immunochemical characteristics.

MED 690—Tumor Biology (4) Pathobiology, biochemistry, and molecular biology of neoplasia; viral and chemical carcinogenesis; immunology and therapy of cancer in man and animals.

MED 691—Immunopathology (3) Abnormalities and diseases with immunological basis or component. Clinical and experimental specimens for analysis by modern immunological techniques.

MED 692—Experimental Tumor Biology (3) *Prereq: MED 690 or consent of staff.* Development of laboratory skills and fundamental techniques in the study of various phenomena in tumor biology. Students will work in direct association with members of the MED 690 staff.

MED 693—Immunobiology (5) Biological aspects of the defense·systems, specific and non-specific, cellular and humoral, amplification systems involving immune interactions; normal and abnormal conditions and sequellae; pathologic aspects of immunologic phenomena; phylogenetic and developmental aspects of immunity.

MED 694—Immunobiology Laboratory (3) *Prereq: consent of staff. Coreq: MED 693.* Project oriented. Laboratory skills and techniques in immunobiology. Each student or a small group of students works in close association with a faculty member.

DIVISION OF ANATOMICAL SCIENCES

The Division of Anatomical Sciences offers programs leading to the Doctor of Philosophy degree and, in special cases, the Master of Science degree. Areas of research and training in anatomical sciences include cell and membrane biology, cytochemistry and histochemistry, reproductive biology, dental histology, general embryology and developmental biology as well as gross, microscopic, and ultra-structural anatomy.

GRADUATE COURSES

MED 501—Gross Anatomy (6)

MED 502—Applied Gross Anatomy (7)

MED 503—Microscopic Anatomy (6)

MED 604—Advances in Submicroscopic Anatomy (4) *Prereq: histology or cytology: approval of staff.* Ultrastructure in cells and tissues of vertebrate forms. Current research trends and functional connotations where pertinent.

MED 605—Research Methods in Anatomy (1-6; max: 12) Research techniques of histo-chemistry, radiation biology, experimental embryology, teratology, endocrinology, or electron microscopy under supervision of a staff member.

MED 606—Anatomy Seminar (1-3)

MED 608—Special Topics in Anatomy (1-6; max: 15) Readings in recent research literature of anatomy and allied disciplines.

MED 609—Embryology and Organogenesis (4) *Prereq: ZY 309 or MED 501.* Human and higher mammalian development, with emphasis on maldevelopment. Physiological and clinical considerations stressed where pertinent.

MED 632—Techniques in Electron Microscopy (3-5) *Prereq: courses and/or experience in histology and cytology.* Theory and practice of electron microscopic techniques including tissue preparation, sectioning, use of the electron microscope, and photography. Offered in even-numbered years.

MED 678—Advanced Microscopic Anatomy (4-6; max: 9) *Prereq: MED 503 or ZY 521.* Histological approaches and techniques relevant to selected research areas. Lectures, micro-scopic study, and laboratory project relating structural and functional aspects of a problem.

MED 679—Advanced Gross Anatomy (3-6; max: 9) Regional and specialized anatomy of the human body taught by laboratory dissection, conferences, and demonstrations.

MED 760—Membrane Biology (3) Examination of structure, composition, and turnover of plasma and intracellular membranes; consideration of topics relating to membrane function, including pinocytosis, regulation of intracellular exchange, cell recognition, cell communica-tion, and virus formation.

MED 761—Medical Information Systems (3) Systems analysis techniques, both theoretical and practical, applied to the medical data base. Communications for health care delivery studied.

PHARMACEUTICAL CHEMISTRY
(College of Pharmacy)

Chairman: R. H. HAMMER
Graduate Coordinator: C. H. BECKER

GRADUATE FACULTY 1975-76

Professors: L. G. GRAMLING; C. H. JOHNSON; K. V. RAO
Associate Professors: R. H. HAMMER; S. G. SCHULMAN
Assistant Professor: B. D. ANDRESEN

The College of Pharmacy offers Master of Science in Pharmacy and Doctor of Philosophy degrees in pharmaceutical sciences, with specialization in pharmaceutical chemistry.

Specific areas include research in pharmaceutical analysis, analytical toxicology, drug metabolism, natural product chemistry and the synthesis of medicinal chemicals.

The applicant should have an undergraduate degree in pharmacy, chemistry, biology or premedical sciences. A background in calculus, and physical and organic chemistry is required.

GRADUATE COURSES

PCY 607—Seminar in Pharmaceutical Chemistry (1) *Required of pharmaceutical chemistry majors; open to others by permission of department.* Weekly presentation and discussion of research reports based upon programs in the college or reports in the literature.

PCY 611—Synthetic Medicinal Products I (3) Preparation of the more complex synthetic medicinals. Relationship between chemical constitution and physiological action.

PCY 612—Synthetic Medicinal Products II (3)

PCY 613—Synthetic Medicinal Products I (3) Accompanying laboratory course for PCY 611. Synthesis of organic medicinal compounds.

PCY 614—Synthetic Medicinal Products II (3) Accompanying laboratory course for PCY 612. Synthesis of organic medicinal compounds.

PCY 615—Synthetic Medicinal Products III (3)

PCY 617—Advanced Histology and Microscopy of Vegetable Drugs (5) Advanced microscopic structure and identification.

PCY 618—Microanalytical Pharmacognosy (2) Micro methods for plant constituents.

PCY 619—Cultivation and Processing of Medicinal Plants (3) Commercial sources, culture, and preparation of botanical drugs.

PCY 621—Natural Medicinal Products I (3) Chemistry of compounds derived from plants and animals.

PCY 622—Natural Medicinal Products II (3)

PCY 623—Natural Medicinal Products I (3) Accompanying laboratory course for PCY 621. Isolation and identification of plant and animal products.

PCY 624—Natural Medicinal Products II (3) Accompanying laboratory course for PCY 622. Isolation and identification of plant and animal products.

PCY 625—Natural Medicinal Products III (3)

PCY 631—Pharmaceutical Analysis I (5) Theory and applications of separation of drugs and breakdown products from dosage forms and biologic media, employing precipitation, volatilization, complexation, partition, chromatographic procedures.

PCY 632—Pharmaceutical Analysis II (5) Methods of quantitating and determing the structure of drugs and their breakdown products in any media, utilizing various spectroscopic and electronic technics.

PCY 633—Pharmaceutical Analysis III (5) Use of electrochemical and radiochemical methods of measurement in pharmaceutical systems, including potentiometry, polarography, conductimetry, neutron activation.

PCY 642—Chemobiodynamics (5) *Prereq: PCY 611.* Theoretical treatment of structure-activity relationships and approaches to drug design.

PCY 696—Research Procedures in Pharmaceutical Chemistry (2-6) *Prereq: departmental consent.* Laboratory research, advanced discussion and reading in organic pharmaceutical chemistry, analytical pharmaceutical chemistry, and natural products. Research problems of interest to the student and his program.

PCY 697—Supervised Research (1-5)
PCY 698—Supervised Teaching (1-5)
PCY 699—Master's Research (1-15)
PCY 799—Doctoral Research (1-15)

PHARMACOLOGY AND THERAPEUTICS

(College of Medicine)

Chairman: T. H. MAREN
Graduate Coordinator: C. Y. CHIOU

GRADUATE FACULTY 1975-76

Professors: H. E. KAUFMAN; K. C. LEIBMAN; T. H. MAREN; D. M. TRAVIS
Associate Professors: C. Y. CHIOU; B. P. VOGH
Assistant Professors: L. C. GARG; W. R. KEM; D. N. SILVERMAN

The Department of Pharmacology and Therapeutics offers a program leading to the degree of Doctor of Philosophy in the medical sciences, with specialization in pharmacology.

Specific areas of research specialization include autonomic and respiratory pharmacology, drug metabolism, renal and electrolyte pharmacology including transport of electrolytes into cerebrospinal fluid, carbonic anhydrase and its inhibitors, cellular neuropharmacology, and molecular pharmacology.

Applicants should present undergraduate course credits in chemistry, including quantitative analytical, organic, and physical chemistry; elementary physics and biology, and mathematics through calculus. Otherwise well-qualified students with certain deficiencies in preparation will be allowed to make these up during the first year of graduate study. In addition to elementary and advanced study in pharmacology, candidates will pursue courses in biochemistry, physiology, and other medical sciences as determined by consultation with their advisory committees.

GRADUATE COURSES

MED 566—Advanced Medical Pharmacology (6)

MED 670—Introduction to Pharmacology (5) *Prereq: elementary courses in biochemistry and physiology.* Overview of the entire field of pharmacology as the study of the interactions between living systems and foreign chemicals. Intended to prepare majors for advanced courses or to familiarize nonmajors with the area.

MED 671—Theoretical Pharmacology (5) *Prereq: MED 670, CY 342.* Physical physicochemical, and mathematical aspects of pharmacology, including the theory of drug-receptor complexes, transport and distribution kinetics and equilibria, and the kinetics of enzyme inhibition by drugs.

MED 672—Chemical Pharmacology (5) *Prereq: MED 670.* Chemical aspects of several areas of modern pharmacology, such as metabolism of foreign compounds, structure-activity relationships, the biochemistry of drug activity.

MED 673—Physiological Pharmacology (5) *Prereq: MED 670.* Influence of drugs upon physiological systems. Cholinergic and adrenergic mechanisms in autonomic pharmacology; renal and endocrine pharmacology; control of lung vasculature and smooth muscle in respiratory pharmacology.

MED 674—Seminar in Pharmacology (1) *Prereq: MED 670.* Research reports and discussions of current research literature by graduate students, faculty, and invited lecturers. S/U.

MED 701—Research Methods in Pharmacology I (1) Readings, discussions, and practical experience with modern research methods used in pharmacology. Both instrumental and biological methods.

MED 702—Research Methods in Pharmacology II (1)

MED 703—Topics in Pharmacology (1-4; max: 12) Seminars, informal conferences, or laboratory work on the use of drugs in biochemical and physiological investigations.

MED 704—Physiology and Pharmacology of Excitable Membranes (3) Membrane ionic permeability changes underlying action and synaptic potential generation described in detail. Applications of electrophysiological and radioactive tracer techniques to analysis of drug action on excitable membranes.

PHARMACY
(College of Pharmacy)

Acting Chairman: G. TOROSIAN
Graduate Coordinator: C. H. BECKER

GRADUATE FACULTY 1975-76

Graduate Research Professor: E. R. GARRETT
Professors: O. E. ARAUJO; C. H. BECKER; K. F. FINGER; F. A. VILALLONGA
Associate Professors: R. A. ANGORN; F. P. FIELD; M. A. LEMBERGER; R. B. STEWART; G. TOROSIAN
Assistant Professors: E. GOLDSTEIN; W. C. MCCORMICK; M. W. MCKENZIE; M. J. MOLDOWAN; M. P. PEVONKA

The College of Pharmacy offers Master of Science in Pharmacy and Doctor of Philosophy degrees in pharmaceutical sciences, with specialization in pharmacy.

Specific areas of specialization are pharmaceutics with research in biopharmaceutics and product formulation, pharmacy administration, clinical pharmacy and hospital pharmacy administration.

New graduate students should have an adequate background in calculus and physical, organic and analytical chemistry. A Bachelor of Science in pharmacy and an interview are required for admission to the clinical pharmacy, hospital pharmacy administration and pharmacy administration areas, while an undergraduate degree in pharmacy, chemistry, biology, or premedical sciences will be accepted in the other areas.

GRADUATE COURSES

PHY 552—Principles of Endocrinology (5) *Prereq: course in physiology.*

PHY 566—Dermatological Protectives (5) *Prereq: PHY 307.*

PHY 601—Hospital Pharmacy Administration (3) Development, functions, responsibilities, organization, and administration of the hospital and the hospital pharmacy department. Viewpoint of administrative responsibilities of the hospital pharmacist.

PHY 602—Selected Topics in Pharmacy (3)

PHY 604—Equilibria, Complexations, and Interactions of Drugs (5) *Prereq: CY 453; MS 304 or 501.* Models for drug interactions in solution. Physical chemical characteristics of drugs and their complexes in pharmaceutical systems.

PHY 605—Stability and Kinetics of Drugs (5) *Prereq: CY 644, 662, PHY 604.* Kinetics, mechanisms and prediction of stability of *in* vitro transformations of drugs, including alkaloids, vitamins, steroids, salicylates, and their pharmaceutical formulations; application of analog computer.

PHY 606—Pharmacokinetics and Biopharmaceutics (5) *Prereq: PHY 605 and a course in pharmacology, or by special arrangement. In vivo* transformations of drugs and compartmental analysis with analog computer; absorption, transfer, protein binding, metabolism, excretion, receptor site interaction, and biological availability from the dosage form.

PHY 607—Advanced Topics in Pharmaceutical Sciences (1-2; max: 6) Oral reports on·the pharmaceutical sciences; discussion and critical review of such topics; written and oral presentations of research designs, protocols, papers, and critical appraisals.

PHY 611—Hospital Pharmacy Seminar (1) *Required of hospital pharmacy residents, but not more than 3 credits are allowed.* Oral reports related to hospital pharmacy. Discussion of problems.

PHY 621—Drug Information (4) Survey of drug information sources; analysis; evaluation and communication of drug data; and survey of manual and automated drug information resources. The course will provide practical experience in the College of Pharmacy's statewide Drug Information Service, and will include discussions concerning its operation and administration.

PHY 627—Advanced Topics in Clinical Pharmacy (2; max: 6) *Prereq: 7PH classification.* Recent literature and new drug entities relevant to the practice of clinical pharmacy.

PHY 631—Advanced Pharmaceutical Law (5) History, philosophy, requirements, administration, and enforcement of the Federal Food, Drug and Cosmetic Act and various state and local laws applicable to manufacturers, wholesalers, and other distributors of drugs and drug-related products, with analyses of recent court decisions.

PHY 633—Health Sciences Liability Law (3) Liability of health sciences practitioners, including hospitals, physicians, pharmacists, nurses, medical technologists, and dentists.

PHY 635—Pharmaceutical Law Seminar (1; max: 3) Selected recent cases and materials having impact on the drug industry, health professions, health-care services, and consumers with respect to the effects of these new decisions on socioeconomics and public health.

PHY 637—Topics in Pharmaceutical Administration (3) Analysis of special topics and recent developments in pharmaceutical administration, including innovations in the distribution of drugs and health-care services such as third-party prescription payment plans and extended health-care facilities.

PHY 643—Pharmaceutical Equipment and Machinery (4) Industrial pharmaceutical machinery and equipment such as colloid mills and homogenizers, sifters, pulverizers, centrifuges, tablet machines and ampul washers, fillers and sealers. Manufacture of pharmaceutical products on a pilot-plant scale in the laboratory.

PHY 645—Pharmaceutical Machinery and Product Formulation (4) Continuation of PHY 643 with rationale and design of some pharmaceutical dosage forms, particularly on inherent physical and chemical problems, stability and biopharmacy. Selected formulas prepared for evaluation on a laboratory and pilot-plant scale.

PHY 647—Pharmaceutical Product Formulation (4) Continuation of PHY 645. Rationale and design of some pharmaceutical dosage forms, such as inherent physical and chemical problems, stability and biopharmacy. Selected formulas prepared for evaluation on a laboratory and pilot-plant scale.

PHY 653—Parenterals (5) Techniques of preparation, administration, and testing of materials designed for parenteral injection.

PHY 655—Clinical Pharmacy (4) Professional attitudes, skills, knowledge and understanding necessary to provide patient-oriented pharmaceutical services in community and institutional health care facilities. Conferences and discussion periods.

PHY 656—Therapeutics in Clinical Pharmacy I (3) Disease-oriented aspects of rational drug therapy. Case materials and clinical problems related to drug therapy. Oral reports, informal conferences, and critical review of papers.

PHY 657—Therapeutics in Clinical Pharmacy II (4) Disease-oriented aspects of rational drug therapy. Case materials and clinical problems related to drug therapy. Oral reports, informal conferences, and critical review of papers.

PHY 696—Research Methods in Pharmaceutical Sciences (2-6) *Prereq: MS 302, CY 451.* Students acquire proficiency in research techniques and instrumentation used in physical pharmacy, drug stability, kinetics and pharmacokinetics, under supervision of a staff member.

PHY 697—Supervised Research (1-5)

PHY 698—Supervised Teaching (1-5)

PHY 699—Master's Research (1-15)

PHY 799—Doctoral Research (1-15)

PHILOSOPHY
(College of Arts and Sciences)

Chairman: E. S. HARING
Graduate Coordinator: M. B. ZWEIG

GRADUATE FACULTY 1975-76

Professors: E. S. HARING; H. MEHLBERG *(emeritus);* C. W. MORRIS *(emeritus);* J. J. ZEMAN
Associate Professors: R. P. HAYNES; A. L. LEWIS, JR.
Assistant Professors: J. M. ALLEN; R. D'AMICO; A. N. GALLOIS; S. A. MCKNIGHT; T. W. SIMON; M. B. ZWEIG

The department offers programs leading to the M.A., M.A.T., and Ph.D. degrees.

GRADUATE COURSES

PPY 509—Graduate Special Topics (1-4; max: 12) An occasional course offered according to current interests of the faculty.
PPY 515—Studies in Early Greek Philosophy (4; max: 12) Examination of the first, i.e., pre-Socratic, stages of Western philosophy—with some reference to both cultural context and later influence.
PPY 516—Studies in Plato (4; max: 12) Intensive study of at least one major dialogue together with related writings.
PPY 517—Studies in Aristotle (4; max: 12) Advanced introduction to central theories and themes.
PPY 519—Studies in Medieval Philosophy (4; max: 12) Representative works from the period c. 400-1400.
PPY 524—Studies in Modern Philosophy (4; max: 12) Dominant themes and representative figures from the modern period.
PPY 525—Studies in Kant (4; max: 12) One or more of Kant's major philosophical works.
PPY 526—Studies in 19th-Century Philosophy (4; max: 12) One or more figures or schools of thought from the post-Kantian period.
PPY 527—Studies in Pragmatism (5; max: 15) Consideration of the extent to which the work of Peirce, James, Dewey, Mead, and Lewis forms an organized philosophical position.
PPY 528—Studies in Phenomenology I (4; max: 12) Theory and practice of phenomenology as a philosophical method.
PPY 529—Studies in Phenomenology II (4; max: 12) Major writings of one or more phenomenologists.
PPY 530—Graduate Symbolic Logic (5; max: 15) *Prereq: PPY 330.* Advanced deductive techniques. Detailed consideration of formal systems and related topics.
PPY 541—Studies in Theory of Knowledge (4; max: 12) Examination of positions and issues, usually with a contemporary emphasis.
PPY 542—Studies in Metaphysics (4; max: 12) Examination of positions and issues, usually with a contemporary emphasis.
PPY 546—Studies in Analytic Philosophy (4; max: 12) One or more major works or themes in recent British-American philosophy.
PPY 550—Studies in Theory of Value (4; max: 12) Examination of positions and issues, usually with a contemporary emphasis.
PPY 557—Studies in Philosophy of Science (5; max: 15) Examination of contrasting positions relating to physical and/or biological and/or social science.
PPY 560—Advanced Philosophy of History (4; max: 12) Investigation of controversial topics related to history; e.g., explanation, general laws, objectivity, and relativism. One or more classical theories of history examined.
PPY 565—Studies in Philosophy of Culture (4; max: 12) Contemporary philosophic perspectives on the nature and formation of culture.

PPY 570—Studies in the Philosophy of Art (4; max: 12) Exploration of one or more issues concerning the function of art, the role of artists, and the relation of different arts to one another.

PPY 580—Studies in the Philosophy of Religion (4; max: 12) Examination of positions and issues, usually with a contemporary emphasis.

PPY 596—Individual Work (1-5; max: 15) *Prereq: 12 hours' work in philosophy and consent of department.*

PPY 609—Special Topics (1-5)

PPY 616—Seminar in Ancient Philosophy (5; max: 15)

PPY 617—Seminar on Themes in Classical/Medieval Philosophy (5; max: 15)

PPY 624—Seminar in Modern Philosophy (5; max: 15)

PPY 625—Seminar on Kant (5; max: 15)

PPY 626—Seminar in 19th-Century Philosophy (5; max: 15)

PPY 628—Seminar in Phenomenology (5; max: 15)

PPY 629—Seminar in 20th-Century European Philosophy (5; max: 15)

PPY 630—Seminar in Logic (5; max: 15)

PPY 643—Seminar in the Philosophy of Mind (5; max: 15)

PPY 646—Seminar in Analytic Philosophy (5; max: 15)

PPY 650—Seminar in Problems of Value (5; max: 15)

PPY 659—Psychology and Philosophy of Science (5; max: 15)

PPY 665—Seminar in Epistemology and Social Theory (5; max: 15)

PPY 670—Seminar in the Philosophy of Art (5; max: 15)

PPY 696—Individual Work (1-5; max: 15)

PPY 697—Supervised Research (1-5)

PPY 698—Supervised Teaching (1-5)

PPY 699—Master's Research (1-15)

PPY 799—Doctoral Research (1-15)

PHYSICAL EDUCATION, HEALTH, AND RECREATION

(College of Physical Education, Health, and Recreation)

Chairman: W. F. UPDYKE
Graduate Coordinator: O. J. HOLYOAK

GRADUATE FACULTY 1975-76

Professors: R. H. ALEXANDER; C. A. BOYD; D. A. HICKS; N. M. LEAVITT; C. A. MOORE; W. T. SANDEFUR; D. K. STANLEY; B. K. STEVENS; W. F. UPDYKE; I. F. WAGLOW; C. W. ZAUNER
Associate Professors: R. E. ALLEN; O. J. HOLYOAK; D. A. KAUFMANN; H. A. LERCH; B. C. SMITH; P. R. VARNES
Assistant Professors: S. W. FAGERBERG

Graduate degrees are offered in Health Education and in Physical Education.

HEALTH EDUCATION

Master of Health Education (nonthesis) and Master of Arts in Health Education (thesis) degrees are offered by the college. Since the health education program is individualized, applicants with bachelor's degrees from a wide variety of related fields are accepted into the program. Previous work will be evaluated in light of the student's goals, with any deficiencies to be made up soon after entering Graduate School.

GRADUATE COURSES

PHR 545—Current Topics in Physical Education, Health Education or Recreation (1-5) *Prereq: permission of department chairman.* Offered, upon request, to meet special interests not adequately covered in other courses.

PHR 605—Research Methods in Physical Education, Health Education, Recreation (5)

PHR 610—Evaluation Procedures in Physical Education and Health Education (3) Measurement and evaluation as applied to physical education and health education.

PHR 645—Workshop Series (1-10) Special problems in physical education or health education.

PHR 660—Organizations and Practices in Programs of School and Public Health (5) Community development of the broad spectrum of health programs and services for the total community, including organization and operation, cooperative planning, and interagency coordination.

PHR 661—Scientific Foundation of Health (5) *Prereq: PHR 261, 262.* Independent study and investigation of current problems and advances in health sciences applied to personal and community health.

PHR 662—Health Education Programs and Processes in School and Public Health (5) Nature and role of health education in changing health behavior, with emphasis on development of educational programs compatible with stated purposes, target groups, and appropriate settings.

PHR 663—Trends and Issues in Health Education (5) Educational approaches to health, with emphasis on controversial topics. Physical, social, economic, and legal aspects of problem causes, prevalence, and control.

PHR 697—Supervised Research (1-5)

PHR 698—Supervised Teaching (1-5)

PHR 699—Master's Research (1-15)

PHYSICAL EDUCATION

The Master of Arts in Physical Education (M.A.P.E.) degree provides a program of study with emphasis in one of several areas of physical education, including anatomy, biomechanics, curriculum and instruction, exercise physiology, motor learning and motor behavior, and statistics and evaluation. If the emphasis is related to curriculum and instruction, credentials appropriate for teaching certification are normally expected. A thesis is required. The Master of Physical Education (M.P.E.) degree provides a program of study established for teachers of physical education primárily interested in curriculum and instruction. Credentials appropriate for teacher certification are normally expected. A thesis is not required.

GRADUATE COURSES

PHR 545—Current Topics in Physical Education, Health Education or Recreation (1-5) *Prereq: permission of department chairman.* Offered, upon request of students, to meet special interests inadequately covered in other courses.

PHR 601—Interpretations of Physical Education (3) Biological, psychological, sociological, and educational implications needed to interpret the function of physical education in contemporary democratic society.

PHR 603—Nature and Bases of Motor Performance (5) Principles relating to development of motor skill, with emphasis on conditions affecting its development and retention in physical education activities.

PHR 605—Research Methods in Physical Education, Health Education, Recreation (5)

PHR 606—Individual Work (1; max: 10) *Prereq: PHR 605.* Individual research projects under faculty guidance.

PHR 607—Seminar in Physical Education (2-4) Research implications for the field of physical education.

PHR 610—Evaluation Procedures in Physical Education and Health Education (3) Measurement and evaluation as applied to physical education and health education.

PHR 612—Physiological Bases of Physical Education (5) Application of fundamental concepts of human physiology to programs of physical education and sports. Recent research developments in sports physiology.

PHR 613—Practicum in Exercise Physiology (3) *Prereq: PHR 612.* Applied and experimental work emphasizing practical problems.

PHR 616—The Physical Education Curriculum (5) Principles and practices of developing an integrated physical education curriculum in grades K to 12.

PHR 618—The College Physical Education Program (5) Philosophy, program content, administration, and methods of conducting the required, intramural, and professional preparation programs of physical education in colleges and universities.

PHR 620—Problems in the Administration of Athletics (5) Intercollegiate and interscholastic athletic programs; relationships between athletics, education, and physical education; the administrator, control organizations; budget; equipment and facilities; intramurals; public relations; legal liability.

PHR 633—Problems in Physical Education (5) *Prereq: PHR 605.* Emphasis on research developments.

PHR 645—Workshop Series (1-10) Special problems in physical education or health education.

PHR 665—Biomechanics of Human Motion (5) *Prereq: PHR 365; CMS 171 or MS 102.* Application of principles of statics, kinematics, and kinetics to kinesiological systems of the human body in movement and sports skills.

PHR 696—Individual Work (1; max: 10) *Prereq: PHR 605.* Individual research projects under faculty guidance.

PHR 697—Supervised Research (1; max: 5)

PHR 698—Supervised Teaching (1; max: 5)

PHR 699—Master's Research (1-15)

PHYSICS

(College of Arts and Sciences)

Chairman: F. E. DUNNAM
Graduate Coordinator: B. S. THOMAS

GRADUATE FACULTY 1975-76

Graduate Research Professors: A. E. S. GREEN; P.-O. LÖWDIN; J. C. SLATER
Professors: E. D. ADAMS; T. L. BAILEY; S. S. BALLARD; J. S. BLAKEMORE;* A. A. BROYLES; C. R. BURNETT;* T. D. CARR; F. E. DUNNAM; J. W. FLOWERS; H. P. HANSON; J. B. MCGUIRE;* D. A. MICHA; A. H. NEVIS; N. Y. ÖHRN; G. C. OMER, JR.; R. PEPINSKY; T. A. SCOTT; A. G. SMITH; R. F. STETSON*
Associate Professors: R. A. BLUE; J. R. BUCHLER; J. B. CONKLIN, JR.; J. W. D. CONNOLLY; J. R. COX;* J. W. DUFTY; C. F. HOOPER, JR.; R. C. ISLER; B. LAMBORN;* M. T. PARKINSON; L. R. PETERSON; J. R. SABIN; S. B. TRICKEY; H. A. VANRINSVELT; G. D. WARD; H. R. WELLER
Assistant Professors: S. W. BRUENN;* W. P. KIRK, JR.; G. R. LEBO; M. A. LYNCH; B. S. THOMAS

These members of the faculty of Florida Atlantic University are also members of the graduate faculty of the University of Florida and participate in the doctoral degree program in the University of Florida Department of Physics.

The Department of Physics offers the Master of Science and the Doctor of Philosophy degrees. The nonthesis degree Master of Science in Teaching is also available with a major in physics. A wide choice of specializations is available.

The courses including PS 601, 611, 612, 621, 622, 643, 644, and 645 are designed ‐o provide graduate students with a solid background in basic physics. Doctoral candidates must take all these core courses, and upon their completion (which usually requires four quarters) are expected to take the qualifying exams. Students who are unprepared for these courses may take the appropriate 500-level courses in the department. Master's degree candidates must take at least six courses numbered 600 or above.

A reading or functional knowledge of French, German, or Russian is required of candidates for the Ph.D. degree in physics.

GRADUATE COURSES

PS 500—Intermediate Dynamics (3) *Prereq: PS 400.* Kinematics of two-particle collisions, motion in noninertial reference frames, dynamics of rigid bodies, small oscillations, vibrating strings, and the wave equation.

PS 510—Electric and Magnetic Fields (3) *Prereq: PS 410.* Solutions to Maxwell's equations, including selected topics relating to static and dynamic electric and magnetic fields, and an introduction to the emission and propagation of electromagnetic waves.

PS 515—Electronics I (3) *Prereq: PS 310 or equivalent.* Class and laboratory. Experiments include vacuum thermionic emission, gas and solid-state conduction, properties of amplifiers and related circuits.

PS 516—Electronics II (3) *Prereq: PS 515.*

PS 520—Fundamentals of Statistical Physics II (3) *Prereq: PS 420.*

PS 530—Classical and Modern Optics (4) *Prereq: PS 410 and 430 or equivalents.* Advanced course in physical optics; includes such modern topics as coherence, lasers, holography, and nonlinear optics.

PS 541—Modern Physics III (3) *Prereq: PS 440 or equivalent.* Introduction to quantum mechanics, with emphasis on atomic structure.

PS 542—Optical Spectra (3) *Prereq: PS 340 or equivalent.* Vector models and spectra of atoms and diatomic molecules, continuous spectra. Applications of spectral intensities and line widths to the analysis of plasmas and stellar atmospheres.

PS 550—Introductory Solid-State Physics (3) *Prereq: PS 541.* General introduction to solid-state physics for nonspecialists. Crystal structure; thermal, electrical, and magnetic properties of solids.

PS 560—Nuclear Physics (3) *Prereq: PS 440.* Static properties of nuclei, descriptive aspects of radioactivity and nuclear reactions, nuclear systematics, nuclear models, and nuclear forces.

PS 566—Laboratory Techniques in Nuclear Physics (2) *Prereq: PS 465.* Special and advanced topics in nuclear instrumentation and methods.

PS 570—Introduction to Particle Physics (3) Particle states, conserved quantum numbers, invariance principles.

PS 596—Individual Work (3-5; max: 15) Assigned reading program; special topics, or development of a special experimental problem. Work selected to meet needs and interests of the student.

PS 601—Classical Mechanics (3) Review of Lagrangian mechanics; special relativity, Hamiltonian mechanics, canonical transformations, Hamilton-Jacobi theory, action angle variables, mechanics of continuous media.

PS 603—Special Relativity (3) Same as ATY 603. Introduction to Einstein's special theory of relativity employing tensor analysis, general invariance and the background of the general theory of relativity.

PS 604—General Relativity (3) Same as ATY 604. Einstein's general theory of relativity and relativistic cosmology.

PS 611—Electromagnetic Theory I (3) Electrostatics, magnetostatics, and Maxwell's equations.

PS 612—Electromagnetic Theory II (3) *Prereq: PS 611.* Diffraction, radiation theory, covariant formulation of electromagnetic theory.

PS 615—Electrical Activity of the Nervous System (3) Same as EE 615. *Prereq: MS 305, PS 415 or EE 333. Coreq: PS 420.* Analysis of the electrical signals of peripheral nerve and brain, with application of systems engineering techniques.

PS 616—Biophysical Models of Nerve Impulse Propagation (3) Same as EE 616. *Prereq: PS 615 or EE 615.* Analysis of chemical, electrical, hydrodynamic, and solid-state models of axonic and synaptic nerve transmission.

PS 621—Statistical Physics I (3) *Prereq: PS 601.* Gamma and mu spaces, ergodic theory, Liouville equation, B-B-G-K-Y hierarchy, Boltzmann equation, Euler's equations, ensemble theory, application of ensemble theory to ideal and imperfect gases.

PS 622—Statistical Physics II (3) *Prereq: PS 621, 643.* Foundations of quantum statistical physics, Liouville-VonNeumann equation, quantum nonequilibrium problem, quantum ensembles, Slater sum, density matrices, applications of ensemble theory to quantum systems.

PS 629—Chemical Physics (3) Same as CY 629. Interatomic and intermolecular forces. Energy transfer and reaction in molecular collision processes. Computational aspects of scattering theory.

PS 633—Radiopropagation and Ionospheric Physics I (3) Same as ATY 633. *Prereq: PS 410.* Propagation of electromagnetic waves in magnetoionic media, with emphasis on the terrestrial ionosphere, and cosmic conditions such as solar corona, interstellar media, etc. Propagation of pulse conditions. Nonlinear effects in the radio-wave propagation in the ionosphere. Plasma resonances as observed from topside sounders, whistler propagation.

PS 634—Radiopropagation and Ionospheric Physics II (3) Same as ATY 634. *Prereq: PS 633.* Ionospheric electron density and ion composition profiles; diurnal, seasonal, and global variations; pre-sunrise effects; electron and ion temperatures; traveling disturbances; solar flare and magnetic storm effects.

PS 636—Atomic Physics of Planetary Atmospheres (3) Same as ATY 636. *Prereq: basic physics course and mathematics courses through integral calculus.* Atomic and quantum theory, quantum mechanics and the central field problem, atomic and molecular spectroscopy, collisional cross sections for aeronomy.

PS 637—Physics of the Earth's Upper Atmosphere (3) Same as ATY 637. *Prereq: PS 636.* Solar-terrestrial relations, aurora, airglow, and ionospheric phenomena. Remote sensing of atmospheric emissions and scattered solar radiation.

PS 638—Physics of Planetary Atmospheres (3) Same as ATY 638. *Prereq: 637.* Radiative transfer in planetary atmospheres, from the x-ray to radio regions. Discussion of recent studies of the atmospheres of Venus, Mars, Jupiter, and other planets.

PS 642—Theory of Optical Spectra (3) *Prereq: PS 645.* Theory of angular momentum applied to the structure and spectra of atoms.

PS 643—Quantum Mechanics I (3) *Prereq: MS 501, 502, PS 541.* The Schrödinger equation. WKB approximation, properties of operators and eigenfunctions, matrices, angular momentum, hydrogen atom.

PS 644—Quantum Mechanics II (3) *Prereq: PS 643.* Variational principle, elementary perturbation theory, degenerate perturbation theory. Dirac notation and spin. Quantum theory of measurement.

PS 645—Quantum Mechanics III (3) *Prereq: PS 644.* Scattering theory, identical particles, quantized amplitudes, positron hole theory, addition of angular momentum, symmetry principles. Topics may be shifted among PS 643, 644 and 645.

PS 647—Quantum Theory of Matter I (3) Same as CY 647. *Prereq: PS 541 or CY 601.* Quantum mechanics of atoms. Hartree-Fock theory. Interaction of radiation and matter. Relativistic theory.

PS 648—Quantum Theory of Matter II (3) Same as CY 648. *Prereq: PS 647.* Diatomic and polyatomic molecules. Symmetry properties and group theory.

PS 649—Quantum Theory of Matter III (3) Same as CY 649. *Prereq: PS 648.* Special topics in the quantum theory of atoms, molecules, and solids.

PS 660—Seminar in Experimental Nuclear Physics (1; max: 20) Current literature of nuclear-structure physics from an experimental viewpoint.

PS 661—Theoretical Foundations of Nuclear Physics (3) Schrodinger's equation and the independent particle model of the nucleus, velocity-dependent potentials, relations of IPM to resonances, doorway states, direct reactions, the N-N interaction, and nuclear structure.

PS 662—Experimental Foundation of Nuclear Physics I (3) *Prereq: PS 645.* Radioactivity, radiation detection, nuclear decay, accelerators, basic nuclear reaction studies. Nuclear spectroscopy.

PS 663—Experimental Foundations of Nuclear Physics II (3) *Prereq: PS 662.* Nuclear structure, with emphasis on information obtained through nuclear reactions. Application of experimental results to various nuclear models. Scattering.

PS 671—Relativistic Quantum Mechanics (3) *Prereq: PS 645.* The inhomogeneous Lorentz group. One-particle relativistic wave equations for spins O, ½, and 1 and their Greens's functions (Feynman propagators). Photon-electron interaction and Feynman diagrams.

PS 672—Quantum Electrodynamics (3) *Prereq: PS 671.* Renormalization, the Bethe-Salpeter equation, the hydrogen atom, natural line breadth, and the Compton effect.

PS 680—Seminar in Modern Physics (1; max: 20) Recent developments in theoretical and experimental physics. S/U.

PS 681—Computer Methods in Physics (3) *Prereq: PS 541; an elementary knowledge of Fortran programming.* Numerical techniques useful in solving physical problems. Aspects of advanced Fortran programming. Use of the computer.

PS 682—Low-Temperature Physics (3) *Prereq: PS 644.* Methods of producing and measuring low temperatures. Experimental and theoretical aspects of quantum liquids and solids (He-3 and He - 4) and superconductivity.

PS 685—Seminar in Experimental Low-Temperature Solid-State Physics (1; max: 20) Recent developments in low-temperature solid-state physics.

PS 695—Departmental Seminar (1) Physics, astrophysics, and astronomy topics presented by local staff members and visiting scientists. S/U.

PS 696—Individual Work (3-5; max: 18) Assigned reading program or development of an assigned experimental problem. Work selected to meet needs and interests of the student.

PS 697—Supervised Research (1-5)

PS 698—Supervised Teaching (1-5)

PS 699—Master's Research (1-15)

PS 703—Advanced Classical Mechanics (3) *Prereq: PS 601.* Rigid rotators; elasticity; vibrations, normal modes, waves.

PS 713—Advanced Electromagnetic Theory (3) *Prereq: PS 612.* Special topics. Content varies, but may include radiation reaction, Lineard-Wiechert potentials, Cerenkov effect, nonlinear optics.

PS 722—Advanced Statistical Mechanics I (3) *Prereq: PS 622.* Irreversible processes, many-body problem, Ising model, cluster expansions, phase transitions.

PS 723—Advanced Statistical Mechanics II (3) *Prereq: PS 722.*

PS 741—Atomic and Molecular Collisions I (3) *Prereq: PS 645.* Classical and quantum theories of collisions of atoms and molecules, with emphasis on low-energy collisions. Approximate theoretical methods and recent experimental developments.

PS 742—Atomic and Molecular Collisions II (3) *Prereq: PS 741.*

PS 753—Physics of the Solid State I (3) *Prereq: PS 621, 622, 644.* Band theory and symmetry properties.

PS 754—Physics of the Solid State II (3) *Prereq: PS 753.* Photons, transport properties, and electron dynamics.

PS 755—Physics of the Solid State III (3) *Prereq: PS 754.* Magnetism.

PS 756—Theory of Atomic and Molecular Structure I (3) Same as CY 756. *Prereq: PS 649.* Mathematical techniques used in atomic, molecular, and solid-state theory. The one-electron approximation and the general quantum-mechanical many-body problem. Selected advanced topics.

PS 757—Theory of Atomic and Molecular Structure II (3) Same as CY 757. *Prereq: PS 756.*

PS 764—Theory of Nuclear Spectroscopy (3) *Prereq: PS 661.* Racah algebra; single-particle shell model; two, three, or more particle systems; electromagnetic properties of nuclei.

PS 765—Theoretical Meson Physics (3) *Prereq: PS 661.* Experimental and phenomenological aspects of n-p and p-p scattering, the meson theory of nuclear forces, the N-N interaction in the inelastic region.

PS 766—Theoretical Meson and Nuclear Physics (3) *Prereq: PS 765.* Advanced topics related to the nucleon-nucleon interaction, the nuclear many-body problem, Hartree-Fock approach, meson-theoretic approach; current topics involving nuclear and meson fields.

PS 767—Advanced Topics in Meson and Nuclear Physics (3) *Prereq: PS 766.* Strong-interacting particles, relativistic wave equations, the nucleon anti-nucleon problem, two-boson systems, advanced topics.

PS 768—Theory of Nuclear Spectroscopy and Nuclear Reactions (3) *Prereq: PS 764.* Deformed nuclei, particle-hole couplings, angular correlations, nuclear reactions, R matrix and dispersion theory, the optical model.

PS 769—Direct Reactions and Nuclear Theory (3) *Prereq: PS 768.* Direct reactions and nuclear reaction mechanisms, numerical programs for nuclear reactions and nuclear spectroscopy, advanced topics in nuclear reactions, nuclear spectroscopy, nuclear structure.

PS 771—High Energy Theory I (3) *Prereq: PS 672.* Field theory, particles, scattering theory, LSZ theory.

PS 772—High Energy Theory II (3) *Prereq: PS 771.* Dispersion theory, form factors, current topics.

PS 781—Advanced Topics in Theoretical Physics (4; max: 16) Special studies in the application of various theoretical/mathematical methods to physical problems, with emphasis on problems of current interest.

PS 782—Advanced Topics in Experimental Physics (4; max: 16) Application of advanced techniques to the solution of various experimental problems, including instrument design and data analysis.

PS 790—Special Topics (3; max: 18) Assigned reading program, seminar, or lecture series in a new field of advanced physics.

PS 799—Doctoral Research (1-15)

PHYSIOLOGY
(College of Medicine)

Chairman: A. B. OTIS
Graduate Coordinator: M. J. FREGLY

GRADUATE FACULTY 1975-76

Professors: S. CASSIN; W. W. DAWSON; M. J. FREGLY; M. J. JAEGER; A. B. OTIS; W. N. STAINSBY
Associate Professor: J. B. MUNSON
Assistant Professors: M. J. FISHER, JR.; W. W. NICHOLS; P. POSNER

The Department of Physiology offers a program leading to the degrees of Master of Science and Doctor of Philosophy in the medical sciences, with specialization in physiology.

Areas of specialization within the Department of Physiology include neurophysiology, sensory physiology, endocrinology, respiration, circulation, physiology of muscle, environmental physiology, comparative physiology, and neonatal physiology.

Undergraduate majors appropriate as foundations for the study of physiology are biology, chemistry, engineering, mathematics or physics. The following courses are especially useful as a background for the study of physiology: general biology, vertebrate biology, general chemistry, analytical chemistry, organic chemistry, physical chemistry, general physics, calculus, and statistics. Students usually find it necessary to remedy deficiencies in their background by taking undergraduate courses after admission to Graduate School.

GRADUATE COURSES

MED 518—Vision (4) *Prereq: consent of instructor.* Introduction to methodology, anatomy, and function of vision.

MED 520—Principles of Physiology (5) *Prereq: MED 331 or equivalent.* Physiology of mammalian organ systems, with special reference to the human.

MED 521—Laboratory in Physiology (2) *Coreq: MED 520.* Laboratory course designed to illustrate the principles of physiology. Students perform exercises coordinated with course topics under discussion in MED 520.

MED 619—Physiology of Respiration (3) Gas exchange in lungs and tissues. Ventilatory mechanics. Respiratory functions of body fluid. Physiological regulations. Comparative physiology of respiratory mechanisms.

MED 620—Physiology of the Circulation of Blood (3) Physiology of the component parts of the circulation, relation of structure and function, emphasis on control mechanisms.

MED 621—Renal Physiology (3) Seminars on comparative physiology, aspects of renal structure and function.

MED 625—Body Temperature Regulation (3) Neural and endocrine aspects of temperature regulation, hypo-and hyperthermia, adaptation to cold and heat, hibernation. Comparative physiology of temperature regulation stressed.

MED 626—Recent Advances in Physiology (3; max: 15) Content varies from year to year but covers recent advances in physiology.

MED 627—Research Methods in Physiology (2-6; max: 9) Special needs of each student are met by conferences and laboratory work.

MED 628—Seminar in Physiology (1) S/U.

MED 629—Neonatal Physiology (3) Physiological regulation in newborn mammals.

MED 636—Survey of Sensory Systems (4) Same as PSY 623. *Prereq: MED 623 or PSY 600.* Theories and data on human sensory reception and encoding. Audition, vision, and the chemical and cutaneous senses.

MED 637—Seminar on Vision (4) Same as PSY 679. Current research and theory in visual function. Literature survey and design of an experiment relevant to recent theory.

MED 638—Physiology of the Mammalian Thyroid Gland (3) Production, secretion, control, and function of thyroid hormones; interaction with other hormones.

MED 704—Physiology and Pharmacology of Excitable Membranes (3) Membrane ionic permeability changes underlying action and synaptic potential generation described in detail. Applications of electrophysiological and radioactive tracer techniques to analysis of drug action on excitable membranes.

MED 731—Cardiac Electrophysiology (3) Study of the normal electrophysiology and ionic mechanisms involved in various regions of the heart.

MED 732—Basic Cardiac Electrophysiology (3) Basic introduction to cardiac electrophysiology and current research and techniques on genesis and control of cardiac cell potentials.

MED 733—Electrophysiological Basis of Cardiac Dysrhythmias (3) Study of normal cardiac cellular electrophysiology and changes which result in cardiac dysrhythmias. New techniques in diagnosis and management of dysrhythmias.

PLANT PATHOLOGY
(College of Agriculture)

Chairman: L. H. PURDY
Graduate Coordinator: R. E. STALL

GRADUATE FACULTY, 1975-76

Professors: A. A. COOK; P. DECKER; T. E. FREEMAN; H. H. LUKE; H. N. MILLER; R. S. MULLIN; D. E. PURCIFULL; L. H. PURDY; D. A. ROBERTS; N. C. SCHENCK; R. E. STALL

Associate Professors: J. A. BARTZ; S. M. GARNSEY; E. HIEBERT; T. A. KUCHAREK; R. A. SCHMIDT; F. W. ZETTLER

Assistant Professors: R. CHARUDATTAN; D. J. MITCHELL; D. R. PRING

The Department of Plant Pathology offers graduate studies leading to the Master of Agriculture, Master of Science, and Doctor of Philosophy degrees. A superior student with a baccalaureate degree may begin graduate study toward a higher degree in the basic areas of plant pathology with emphasis on plant diseases, plant pathogens, or plant physiology. Specializations within these areas include biochemical aspects of host-pathogen systems, epidemiology, etiology, genetics of host-pathogen systems, physiology, and taxonomy. The diversity of cropping sequences coupled with an environment ideal for plant disease development in Florida is unexcelled and offers the student opportunities of study with diseases of unique crops as well as diseases of crops of national and international importance. Intimate knowledge can be gained of diseases of field, forage, forest, fruit, ornamental, pasture, range, turf, and vegetable crops in temperate, sub-tropical, and tropical environments. Students who anticipate study in plant pathology at the University of Florida should include in their undergraduate pro-gram training in botany (anatomy, cytology, physiology, systematics), chemistry (through organic), introductory bacteriology, physics, zoology, one foreign language, and mathematics.

After completing PT 501 in the first or second quarter of residence, all students will be given an oral examination covering the general and specialized areas of plant pathology. Course requirements will be determined for each individual based on his performance on the examination as well as his background and objectives.

The Departments of Botany and Entomology-Nematology offer courses in, respectively, mycology and nematology.

GRADUATE COURSES

PT 501—Intermediate Plant Pathology (3) *Enrollment limited to students whose major or minor field is plant pathology. Prereq: PT 301 or equivalent.* Lives and times of ten destructive plant parasites.

PT 541—Tropical Plant Pathology (4) *Prereq: PT 301 or equivalent and consent of instructor.* Application of plant pathological techniques to disease control.

PT 600—Colloquium in Principles of Plant Pathology (1; max: 6)

PT 611—Plant Virology Lecture (3) Principles of plant virology; symptomatology, transmis-sion, insect vector relationships, properties of viruses, purification, electron microscopy, morphology, serology, and control of viral diseases.

PT 612—Plant Virology Laboratory (2) *Prereq. or coreq: PT 611.* Methods of research in plant virology.

PT 621—Bacterial Plant Pathogens (5) *Prereq: MCY 302.* Plant pathogenic bacteria, with emphasis on bacteriological problems unique in plant pathology.

PT 623—Fungal Plant Pathogens (5) *Prereq: PT 402, BTY 521.* Diseases caused by fungi, emphasizing taxonomy and variability of the pathogen, symptomology, host responses to infection, and factors influencing disease development.

PT 625—Physiology of Parasitism (5) *Prereq: PT 301.* Physiological aspects of the host-pathogen interaction in plant diseases.

PT 627—Epidemiology of Plant Disease (5) *Prereq: PT 301.* Principles of ecology of plant diseases with emphasis on the effects of the climatic environment on the development of disease in populations of plants and the implications with regard to the strategy of disease control.

PT 629—Pathogen Variability and Host Resistance (5) *Prereq: PT 301, BTY 521, MCY 302, AY 465, STA 320.* Concepts, methods and problems associated with development and utilization of disease-resistant germ plasm.

PT 650—Seminar in Plant Pathology (1) Discussion of the literature, techniques, and research pertaining to plant pathology. S/U.

PT 691—Field Plant Pathology (2) Examination of Florida plant diseases, with field trips to observe the predominant diseases of economic crops in most agricultural production areas.

PT 692—Plant Disease Diagnosis (2) Methods used in diagnosing plant diseases caused by fungi, bacteria, viruses, and inanimate conditions.

PT 696—Problems in Plant Pathology (1-5; max: 9) Study of any field of plant pathology, including diseases of all major crop groups.

PT 697—Supervised Research (1-5)

PT 698—Supervised Teaching (1-5)

PT 699—Master's Research (1-15)

PT 799—Doctoral Research (1-15)

POLITICAL SCIENCE
(College of Arts and Sciences)

Chairman: V. A. THOMPSON
Graduate Coordinator: A. B. CLUBOK

GRADUATE FACULTY 1975-76

Professors: E. R. BARTLEY; A. B. CLUBOK; M. J. DAUER; J. M. DeGROVE;* D. S. GATLIN;* R. J. HUCKSHORN;* K. R. LEGG; R. LEMARCHAND; O. R. McQUOWN; W. A. ROSENBAUM; J. W. SPANIER; A. SUAREZ; O. SVARLIEN; B. E. SWANSON; V. A. THOMPSON; J. E. VINCENT*
Associate Professors: R. B. BAILEY; D. P. CONRADT; A. J. DAMICO; M. W. GILES;* J. F. MORRISON; R. D. THOMAS;* E. R. WITTKOPF
Assistant Professors: L. C, BERKSON; J. S. FITCH III; W. A. KELSO; W. G. MUNSELLE; R. K. SCHER; D. M. STETSON;* G. C. WRIGHT, JR.*

*These members of the faculty of Florida Atlantic University are also members of the graduate faculty of the University of Florida and participate in the doctoral degree program in the University of Florida Department of Political Science.

The Department of Political Science offers the Master of Arts degree with both a thesis and a nonthesis option and the Doctor of Philosophy degree in political science or international relations. The Master of Arts in Teaching degree is also offered with a major in political science or international relations. In addition, Master of Arts and Doctor of Philosophy degrees in political science are offered in urban problems with the cooperation of urban-related departments and in African studies with the Center for African Studies. The Doctor of Philosophy degree in political science can also be taken in cooperation with the Center for Latin American Studies.

The formal areas of specialization for the Ph.D., M.A. and M.A.T. within the department include American government and politics, comparative politics, international relations, public administration, public law, political theory, and methodology. Individual programs composed from these areas can be used to prepare students for careers in teaching, research, and government service. The department offers a specialized M.A. program in political science with an emphasis in public administration. For further information on special degree programs offered through the department, see the section entitled *Special Programs.*

Admission to graduate study in the Department of Political Science normally requires the completion of an undergraduate major in political science or its equivalent. Students without this preparation will be required to make up deficiencies early in their graduate work. All degree programs, except for the special program emphasizing public administration, require evidence of a year of satisfactory work in an approved foreign language. For further information and detailed requirements, prospective students are invited to write for the departmental brochure on graduate programs in political science.

Study for the Ph.D. degree in political science at the University of Florida by qualified master's degree recipients at Florida Atlantic University is facilitated by a cooperative arrangement in which appropriate members of the faculty of FAU are members of the graduate faculty of the University of Florida.

GRADUATE COURSES

PCL 505—Government of the Soviet Union and Eastern Europe (5)
PCL 506—Eastern European Communist States (5)
PCL 508—Modes of Politics in Western Europe (5)

PCL 511—Smaller European States (5)

PCL 514—Problems of Administration and Policy (5) *Prereq: PCL 411.*

PCL 516—Administration of Justice (5)

PCL 517—Legislative Politics (5) *Prereq: PCL 201.* Advanced study in the legislative process. Recruitment of legislators. Formal and informal rules of behavior. Legislative-executive relations. The committee system. Impact of political parties, interest groups, and constituents on the legislative process.

PCL 524—Comparative Foreign Policy (5) *Prereq: PCL 209.* Intensive study of special topics in international relations and foreign policy such as broad-based comparative analysis of foreign policy behavior, comparative international subsystems, reinterpretation of concepts such as nationalism and imperialism.

PCL 527—International Institutions (5) *Prereq: PCL 209, 404, 405, and 406.* In-depth analysis of the political and functional aspects of international organization and administration, alternating emphasis on either global organizations such as the United Nations, or regional organizations such as the European Economic Community.

PCL 530—Special Topics (5)

PCL 540—International Politics of Latin America (5) *Prereq: PCL 209 or advanced standing in Latin American Studies.* Intensive analysis of the international politics of Latin America. Relations with U.S. and nonhemispheric powers. Foreign policies of Latin American states.

PCL 541—Political Systems of Latin America: Modernization, Authoritarianism, Revolution (5) *Prereq: PCL 340 or equivalent.* A comparative analysis of political responses to modernization in Latin America. Emphasis on authoritarian regimes in Argentina and Brazil and the role of revolution in Mexican and Cuban development.

PCL 542—Contemporary Problems in Latin American Politics (5) *Prereq: PCL 340 or 541 or equivalent.* Intensive analysis of major themes and issues in the study of Latin American politics; the breakdown of democratic systems, dependency and imperialism, revolutionary movement and regimes. Offered with changing content.

PCL 547—American Military Policy and Strategy (5)

PCL 550—Political Socialization (5)

PCL 551—Politics of Education (5)

PCL 555—Politics of Planning (5)

PCL 560—Urban Administration (5)

PCL 596—Individual Work (5)

PCL 601—Political Science Scope and Method (5) *Prereq: permission of department.*

PCL 604—Public Administration Problems (5) *Open only to students working for terminal master's degree in public administration to qualify for federal, state, or local government management.* Organizational structure; recruitment; development of leadership; development of organizational effectiveness.

PCL 605—Public Administration Procedures (5) *Open only to students working for terminal master's degree in public administration to qualify for federal, state, or local government management. Prereq: PCL 604.* Decision making; budget planning and formulation; ethics in administration.

PCL 606—Internship in Government (5) *Prereq: consent of department.*

PCL 607—Practicum in Applied Political Science (5)

PCL 609—Problems in Political Theory (5)

PCL 613—The Conduct of Inquiry (5) Empirical research methodology in political science.

PCL 615—Survey Research (5) Same as SY 648. *Prereq: STA 320.* Methods of survey research in context of field investigation. Formulation of research hypotheses; construction of measuring instruments; collection, analysis of data.

PCL 616—Seminar in Political Theory I (5) Problems in political theory. Idealism vs. pragmatism. Theories on the scope of government. Authority vs. individualism.

PCL 617—Seminar in Political Theory II (5) Theories of political causation and absolute government.

PCL 618—Seminar in Political Behavior: Polimetrics (5)

PCL 619—History of American Political Theory (5) Background of American theory. Historical treatment from the Mayflower Compact to the contemporary period.

PCL 620—Latin American Political Theory (5) *Prereq: reading knowledge of Spanish, and undergraduate work in Latin American government.* Writings and theories of the leading

Latin American political thinkers from Alberdi, Sarmiento, and Marti to contemporary figures.

PCL 621—Political Model Building (5) *Prereq: STA 602.* Mathematical and statistical applications of political model building, including computer simulation.

PCL 622—Seminar in Public Administrative Behavior (5) Public administration, with emphasis on the units of analysis and contributions of each approach to general understanding of the field.

PCL 623—Seminar in Public Administrative Behavior (5) Major methodologies used in the approaches covered in PCL 622.

PCL 624—Seminar in Comparative Public Administration (5) *Prereq: PCL 622; advanced courses in comparative government.* Organization and approaches, especially as determined by varying political, social, and economic environmental factors, among bureaucracies in various parts of the world.

PCL 627—Seminar in International Relations and Organization I (5) Basic forces, problems, and developments in international politics and organization.

PCL 628—Seminar in International Relations and Organization II (5)

PCL 629—Empirical Political Theory (5) Competing contemporary empirical theories, their relationship to values and to systematic analysis.

PCL 630—Special Topics (5)

PCL 639—Seminar in Public Law (5; max: 10) Judicial interpretation and enforcement of written constitutions. Separation of powers. The American federal system. Powers of the federal government. Due process and equal protection.

PCL 643—Seminar in International Law (5; max: 10) International law, including the law of international organization.

PCL 650—Seminar in Government and the Planning Process (5; max: 10) Case studies of federal, regional, state, and local planning agencies. Planning as governmental process.

PCL 652—Community Analysis (5; max: 10) Development of social, economic, and political profiles in understanding the trends, projections, and public policy alternatives.

PCL 653—Seminar in American Federal Government (5; max: 10) The major institutions, functions, and problems of the American political system. Methodology and bibliography of American government and politics.

PCL 654—Seminar in State Government and Politics (5; max: 10) The bibliography, methodology, and research topics of American state and local governments.

PCL 655—Seminar in Political Parties (5)

PCL 660—Seminar in Comparative Government (5) The major institutions, functions, and problems of representative major foreign political systems. Methodology and bibliography of comparative government and politics.

PCL 662—Comparative Studies in Western European Political Systems (5; max: 10) *Prereq: PCL 660.*

PCL 664—Seminar in Far Eastern Governments and Politics (5) Chinese and Japanese governments and politics.

PCL 666—Seminar in Russian and Eastern European Governments and Politics (5) Political heritage of the Revolution. Structural features of the Soviet system. Lawmaking and public administration. The Soviet state and the individual.

PCL 668—Seminar in African Governments and Politics (5) *Prereq: PCL 326 or 343.*

PCL 670—Seminar in Latin American Government and Politics I (5) *Knowledge of Spanish or Portuguese is required; French may be substituted with consent of instructor.*

PCL 672—Seminar in Latin American Government and Politics II (5)

PCL 674—Seminar in Brazilian Government and Politics (5) *Prereq: reading knowledge of Portuguese, graduate standing in Latin American Area Studies, and PCL 541.*

PCL 681—Special Topics in American Government (1-5; max: 15)

PCL 682—Special Topics in Public Law (1-5; max: 15)

PCL 683—Special Topics in International Relations (1-5; max: 15)

PCL 684—Special Topics in Comparative Politics (1-5; max: 15)

PCL 685—Special Topics in Public Administration (1-5; max: 15)

PCL 686—Special Topics in Urban Affairs (1-5; max: 15)

PCL 687—Special Topics in Political Theory (1-5; max: 15)

PCL 688—Special Topics in Methodology (1-5; max: 15)
PCL 696—Individual Work (1-5)
PCL 697—Supervised Research (1-5)
PCL 698—Supervised Teaching (1-5)
PCL 699—Master's Research (1-15)
PCL 799—Doctoral Research (1-15)

POULTRY SCIENCE
(College of Agriculture)

Chairman: R. H. HARMS
Graduate Coordinator: H. R. WILSON

GRADUATE FACULTY 1975-76

Professors: J. L. FRY; R. H. HARMS; H. R. WILSON
Associate Professors: B. L. DAMRON; C. R. DOUGLAS; R. A. VOITLE
Assistant Professor: D. M. JANKY

The Department of Poultry Science offers major work for the degrees of Master of Agriculture and Master of Science. Programs leading to the Doctor of Philosophy degree, with emphasis on problems related to poultry science, may be obtained through the Department of Animal Science, with staff members from the Department of Poultry Science directing the program.

Areas of specialization for both master's and Ph.D. degrees are management, nutrition, physiology and poultry products technology.

A departmental prerequisite for admission to graduate study is a sound background in the biological sciences.

The following courses in related areas are acceptable for graduate credit as part of the candidate's major: AL 607—Physiology of Reproduction; AL 650—Advanced Methods in Nutrition Technology; AL 653—Vitamins; AL 655—Mineral Nutrition and Metabolism; AL 657—Non-Ruminant Metabolism; DY 604—Endocrinology; FS 607—Food Chemistry; FS 641—Advanced Human Nutrition; VY 622—Veterinary Physiology I; VY 623—Veterinary Physiology II.

GRADUATE COURSES

PY 607—Topics in Poultry Production (2-4; max: 9) *Prereq: ADP 311, 312.* Offered primarily to agricultural extension workers and vocational agriculture teachers, with one of the following topics specified: production principles, principles of handling and marketing, or nutrition.

PY 612—Avian Physiology (3-5) *Prereq: VY 321.* Environmental physiology, ovulation cycle and egg formation, reproductive efficiency, experimental physiological techniques.

PY 614—Advanced Poultry Nutrition (4) *Prereq: ADP 312, PY 414.* Current topics in poultry nutrition; research techniques; formulation of experimental diets; linear programming procedures and practice.

PY 631—Advanced Poultry Management (4) Poultry management presented on a seminar/short course basis utilizing lecturers currently working in areas under discussion. Field trips made to a variety of commercial operations.

PY 660—Graduate Seminar in Poultry Science (1; max: 3) Discussion of current literature and developments in poultry science.

PY 664—Topics in Genetics (2-4; max: 12) Same as AL 664, AY 664, BTY 664, ZY 664. See AY 664.

PY 696—Problems in Poultry Science (1-4; max: 12) Individual problems in fields of nutrition, genetics, physiology, poultry and egg marketing and/or technology, and management.

PY 697—Supervised Research (1-5)
PY 698—Supervised Teaching (1-5)
PY 699—Master's Research (1-15)

PSYCHOLOGY
(College of Arts and Sciences)

Chairman: M. E. MEYER
Graduate Coordinator: M. E. SHAW

GRADUATE FACULTY 1975-76

Graduate Research Professors: Y. BRACKBILL; J. M. ENOCH; W. B. WEBB
Professors: R. J. ANDERSON; B. BARGER; L. D. COHEN; H. C. DAVIS, JR.; W. W. DAWSON; D. A. DEWSBURY; J. C. DIXON; H. A. GRATER, JR.; W. H. GUERTIN; E. P. HORNE; R. L. ISAACSON; F. A. KING; J. M. KOLARIK; T. LANDSMAN; C. M. LEVY, JR.; N. N. MARKEL; R. K. McGEE; M. E. MEYER; H. S. PENNYPACKER, JR.; N. W. PERRY, JR.; P. SATZ; P. G. SCHAUBLE; A. S. SCHUMACHER; M. E. SHAW; D. C. TEAS; W. D. WOLKING; R. C. ZILLER
Associate Professors: F. R. EPTING; J. R. GOLDMAN; E. E. HALL, JR.; E. F. MALAGODI, JR.; L. J. SEVERY; D. I. SUCHMAN; R. M. SWANSON; V. D. VAN DE RIET; C. VAN HARTESVELDT; C. J. VIERCK, JR.; W. A. YOST
Assistant Professors: C. K. ADAMS; B. L. BALDRIDGE; A. M. BELL; W. K. BERG; M. N. BRANCH; W. R. CUNNINGHAM; I. S. FISCHLER; M. K. GOLDSTEIN; R. A. GRIGGS; S. L. HOFFMAN; R. H. HORNBERGER; R. L. KING; B. M. LESTER; M. H. McCAULLEY; J. I. MORGAN; D. D. NEVILL; W. C. RASBURY; B. R. SCHLENKER; T. M. SKOVHOLT; D. W. WALKER

The Department of Psychology offers the Master of Arts and Master of Science and the Doctor of Philosophy degree. Students are not accepted for a terminal master's degree.

Doctoral areas of specialization include the teaching and research areas of cognition and perception, comparative, developmental, experimental analysis of behavior, personality, psychobiology, and social psychology, and the professional areas of clinical and counseling. The training programs in clinical and counseling are APA approved. A predoctoral internship of one year is required for the clinical and counseling psychology specializations.

Undergraduate preparation should include at least one course in experimental psychology and one course in statistics. Other courses in psychology should include at least three or four of the following: developmental, learning, perception, personality, physiological, and social. Applicants with GRE scores lower than 1200 are usually not admitted to graduate study in psychology.

GRADUATE COURSES

Note: *When followed by the same course numbers, the prefixes PSY and CLP refer to the same courses.*
PSY 500—Seminar: Contemporary Issues in Developmental Psychology (4) *Prereq: STA 320 and consent of instructor.* Examination of recent developments and current issues in developmental psychology, such as the role of early experience, psychological development of infants, behavior genetics, and sex role development.
PSY 520—Advanced Experimental Analysis of Behavior I (4) *Prereq: PSY 320, STA 320, and consent of instructor.* Advanced study of principles of behavior analysis, contemporary theory, experimental findings, and research methods in operant behavior.
PSY 522—Laboratory Methods in Psychology (4) *Prereq: PSY 320, 334, 371, or 377.* Basic instruction in the construction and programming of psychological laboratory apparatus. Includes coverage of mechanical, electromechanical, digital, and computer-assisted apparatus.
PSY 525—Motivation (4) *Prereq: PSY 320, STA 320 or consent of instructor.* Development of varying problems in the field of motivation as approached in the different areas of behavior analysis.

PSY 544—Personality and Somatic Psychology (4) *Prereq: PSY 345, STA 320, 321.* Study of various psychophysiological relationships. Emphasis on psychological modulation of physiological responses. Relevant topics are psychological set, hypnosis, biofeedback, and some of the techniques of somatic psychology.

PSY 545—Studies of the Person (5; max: 15) *Prereq: STA 320, consent of instructor.* Seminar designed to examine various topics of current interest in the field of personality development and dynamics.

PSY 546—Individual Difference (5) *Prereq: PSY 345, STA 320.* Intensive study of individual and group differences essential to evaluation of test results and vocational/educational adjustments. Influence of differences in intelligence, age, sex, and ethnic and cultural background on behavior.

PSY 547—Measurement of Ability (4) *Prereq: PSY 345, STA 320.* The psychological test as a means of assessing behavior. Principles and procedures in interpretation and evaluation of tests.

PSY 548—Measurement of Personal Attributes (4) *Prereq: STA 320, PSY 345.* Tests of general and special abilities; personality and interest inventories; selection and classification tests.

PSY 549—Current Theories and Research in Personality (4) *Prereq: STA 320, consent of instructor.* Issues and problems in description, development and organization of personality.

PSY 570—Drug Use and Abuse (4) *Prereq: 10 hours of psychology and STA 320.* Objective, informational approach to the commonly used and abused drugs. Psychological, physiological, social, medical, legal, and historical aspects.

PSY 572—Advanced Laboratory Topics in Physiological Psychology (4; max: 16) *Prereq: PSY 371 or 682 and consent of instructor.* Laboratory training in basic experimental techniques and procedures.

PSY 573—Seminar in Physiological Psychology (3-5; max: 15) *Prereq: PSY 371 or MED 505, STA 320.* Selected topics on current research, methods, and theory.

PSY 574—Neurohumors and Behavior (4) Same as MED 504. *Prereq: STA 320, PSY 371.* Synthesis, action, and metabolism of putative neural transmitters; pharmacological means of altering these; physiological or behavioral functions attributed to putative neural transmitters.

PSY 575—Biology of Human Behavior (3) *Prereq: STA 320, PSY 371.* Biological theories and models of mental retardation, schizophrenia, and affective disorders; treatments of these conditions.

PSY 576—Behavioral Pharmacology (4) *Prereq: PSY 320, STA 320.* Experimental analysis of the mechanisms based on interactions of drugs with environmental variables controlling behavior.

PSY 577—Seminar in Comparative Psychology (4) *Prereq: PSY 377, STA 320.* Intensive study of selected topics. Seminar format with emphasis on individual participation.

PSY 578—Vision (4) Same as MED 518. *Prereq: PSY 371 or ZY 574 or equivalent, with consent of instructor and STA 320.* Visual process and supporting systems approached from the orientation of human vision.

PSY 579—Introduction to Psychophysiology (4) *Prereq: consent of instructor.* Survey of research literature and procedures in psychophysiology and elementary anatomy and physiology of the autonomic nervous system. Topical areas include orienting response, conditioning of autonomic responses, biofeedback, lie detection, and arousal.

PSY 580—Developmental Psychobiology (4) *Prereq: PSY 371, STA 320.* Basic principles of neural and behavioral development stressing the correlations among structural, chemical, endocrine, and behavioral events during maturation.

PSY 594—History of Psychology (5) *Prereq: 20 quarter hours of psychology and STA 320.* Survey of psychology from the time of the Greeks to the present, covering its background in philosophy, emergence as a modern, experimental science, and the contributions of movements such as structuralism, functionalism, behaviorism, and Gestalt psychology.

PSY 604—Special Topics in Developmental Psychology (2) In-depth exploration at graduate level of important issues and topics in the field. (Repeatable with change in content).

PSY 605—Seminar: Adult Development and Aging (4; max: 12) Topics in the psychology of aging, with emphasis on theory, research, and methodology.

PSY 606—Children's Behavior Disturbances (4) *Prereq: PSY 449; PSY 549 or 684.* Behavior disturbances. Theory, research, and implication for practice.

PSY 607—Seminar: Special Topics in Developmental Psychology (4; max: 16) Examination of theory and research in selected topics.

PSY 609—Seminar: Current Research Methods in Developmental Psychology (3; max: 15) *Prereq: PSY 685.* Current research, theory, methodology, instrumentation, and instructional techniques.

PSY 611—Advanced Social Psychology I (4) *Prereq: PSY 313; PSY 413 or equivalent.* Literature of social psychology, with emphasis on individual behavior.

PSY 612—Advanced Social Psychology II (4) *Prereq: PSY 611.* Literature of social psychology, with emphasis on interpersonal relations.

PSY 613—Theories in Social Psychology (4) *Prereq: PSY 413, STA 320.* Consideration of modern theories in social psychology in relation to experimental evidence.

PSY 616—Seminar: Social Psychology (4; max: 16) *Prereq: PSY 612.* Topics in social behavior, with emphasis on current theory and research.

PSY 617—Laboratory in Social Psychology I (4) *Prereq: PSY 616.* Design and analysis of experiments pertaining to social phenomena, with emphasis on recent developments in the field.

PSY 618—Laboratory in Social Psychology II (4) *Prereq: PSY 617.*

PSY 620—Research Tactics in Experimental Analysis of Behavior (4) *Prereq: PSY 520 or 683.* Strategies, tactics, and methods of laboratory research in the experimental analysis of behavior.

PSY 621—Applied Behavior Analysis (4) Continuous, direct recording of human behavior. Tactics of behavior management. Research methods in applied behavior analysis.

PSY 622—Seminar: Special Topics in Experimental Analysis of Behavior (1-5; max: 15) *Prereq: PSY 683.* Current research, theory, and instructional techniques.

PSY 623—Seminar: Strategies & Tactics of Human Behavioral Research (4) *Prereq: PSY 621.* Advanced study of a scientific approach to investigating human behavior in applied settings.

PSY 624—Literature in Applied Behavioral Analysis (4) *Prereq: PSY 620 or 633.* Introduction to literature in the analysis of behavior in applied settings with attention to political, personal, and historical dimensions of the area.

PSY 625—Theoretical Foundations of Behavior Analysis (4) *Prereq: PSY 520 or 683 and consent of instructor.* Examination of current theoretical issues in behavior analysis, with emphasis upon systematic integration of behavior principles into general behavior theory.

PSY 626—Measurement and Assessment of Behavior (4) Theory and practice of direct measurement of human behavior with application to clinical, social, and educational evaluation.

PSY 632—Psychophysics (4) *Prereq: PSY 334, STA 320 or consent of instructor.* Methods used to measure organisms' abilities and capabilities, including classical psychophysics, theory of signal detection, scaling, information theory, and modeling.

PSY 633—Mathematical Modeling in Psychology (4) *Prereq: consent of instructor.* Examination of the use of mathematical methods to investigate psychological problems.

PSY 634—Retention and Forgetting (4) *Prereq: PSY 434 and STA 320.* Consideration of models of memory, paradigms utilized in the study of stimulus antecedents, organismic and response variables which influence retention and forgetting.

PSY 635—Seminar: Perception (4) Conditions, mechanisms, forms, and functions of perceptual processes.

PSY 636—Seminar: Verbal Learning and Verbal Behavior (2-5; max: 15) *Prereq: PSY 434, 634: SCH 596 or consent of instructor.* Consideration of various aspects of the process of acquiring and elaborating language and other verbal skills.

PSY 637—Seminar: Current Issues in Cognition and Perception (2-15) *Prereq: consent of instructor.* Examination of selected major contemporary issues and data of current interest in the areas of cognition and perception.

PSY 638—Seminar: Cognition (2-5; max: 15) *Prereq: PSY 438 or consent of instructor.* Selected topics in the areas of thinking, problem solving, and reasoning.

PSY 639—Seminar: The Teaching of Psychology (1-5; max: 15) *Prereq: consent of instructor.* Examination and evaluation of contemporary approaches to teaching psychology. Laboratory and field experiences.

PSY 640—Seminar in Personality (4; max: 12) *Prereq: PSY 549 or 684 or equivalent.* Personality development and dynamics.

PSY 644—Research Methods in Personality I (4) *Prereq: PSY 684 or consent of instructor.* Theoretical, methodological, and procedural aspects of research in personality. Emphasis on issues related to measurement of personality variables.

PSY 645—Research Methods in Personality II (4) *Prereq: PSY 684 or consent of instructor.* Theoretical, methodological, and procedural aspects of research in personality. Emphasis on issues frequently encountered in the design and analysis of experiments.

PSY 646—Advanced Topics in Factor Analysis (4) *Prereq: EDF 664, STA 623 or consent of instructor.* Advanced topics in factor analysis, including direct factoring techniques, procrustes rotation to hypothesized target matrices, factor scores, and methods of establishing factorial invariance.

PSY 647—Psychology of Women (4) Theoretical and clinical aspects of female personality and psychobiology, including normal development and problems related to hormonal changes, menstruation, sexuality, pregnancy, motherhood, menopause, and gynecologic surgery. Focus on counseling women.

PSY 648—Test Construction (4) *Prereq: PSY 548 or equivalent.* Theory and practice in construction of tests of general aptitude, special aptitude, and personality traits. Psychophysical theory and techniques.

PSY 649—Seminar on the Self (4) Developmental organization and change in selected dimensions of self are considered through the life span; methods of study, theory, and research.

CLP 651—Practicum in Professional Psychology I (5; max: 15) *Prereq: CLP 658, 665, admission to program in clinical, counseling, or school psychology.* Supervised training in appropriate work settings relating theoretical understanding of personality to case handling and consultation through a variety of psychological assessment and treatment procedures. Designed as a sequence of 3 quarters paralleling academic course work. Each succeeding registration requires increasing levels of competence and responsibility. Fifteen credits or equivalent demonstrated competence are recommended for admission to internship, CLP 769.

CLP 652—Practicum in Professional Psychology II (5; max: 15) *Prereq: CLP 651.*

CLP 653—Introduction to Clinical Psychology (3-5; max: 10) Seminar on issues and concepts in clinical psychology. Concurrent with field observation and participation.

PSY 654—Seminar in Psychopathology (4) *Prereq: PSY 334, 549.* Review of recent research on developmental, somatic, and cultural factors associated with selected mental disorders. Emphasizes experimental psychopathology.

PSY 655—Seminar: Psychology of Deviant Behavior (4; max: 8) Analysis of specific deviant life styles, with emphasis on theory and research related to diagnosis and clinical management.

CLP 656—Personality Assessment I (4) Basic procedures in assessing personality structure and dynamics, including diagnostic interview, case history, objective and projective tests.

CLP 657—Personality Assessment II (4) *Prereq: PSY 681, 682, 683, 684, 685, 686.* Advanced procedures in assessing personality structure and dynamics, including diagnostic interview, case history, objective tests.

CLP 658—Personality Assessment III (4) *Prereq: CLP 657.*

CLP 659—Personality Assessment IV (4) *Prereq: CLP 658.* Advanced techniques in assessment and prediction.

PSY 661—Seminar: Current Topics in Counseling Psychology (1-5) *Prereq: PSY 684, EDC 614 or consent of instructor.* Selected topics in various aspects of counseling psychology. Emphasis on theoretical background and implications for applied work.

CLP 664—Development and Appraisal of Vocational Choice (4) *Prereq: PSY 547.* Theories of vocational development and methods of appraisal in assessing vocational choice.

CLP 665—Personal Counseling (4) Current theories and practices in personal counseling; role of the counselor and nature of the counseling relationship.

PSY 667—Sexual Identity in the Counseling Process (4) *Prereq: PSY 684 or consent of instructor.* Study of the components in the development of sexual identity: biological, psychosexual, social-learning, cognitive-developmental, and cultural. Covers sex roles, sex differences, and current implications for counseling psychology.

PSY 670—Research Methods in the Sensory Systems (4; max: 8) Same as MED 627, ZY 637. *Prereq: MED 636, PSY 678, or ZY 636.* Participation in laboratory experiments typical of several major areas of sensory systems. Laboratory experiences are provided in the facilities of several of the faculty participating in the program. These include visual, auditory, chemical and somesthetic and pain sensory specialties. May be repeated for participation in extended experimental studies and/or learning of technical skills of specific sensory specialty.

PSY 671—Seminar: Current Topics in Sensory Processes (1-5; max: 16) *Prereq: consent of instructor.* Readings in contemporary topics of interest.

PSY 672—Advanced Psychophysiology (4) *Prereq: PSY 579 or consent of instructor.* Advanced literature and procedures in psychophysiology. Heavily oriented toward developing skills and knowledge of the laboratory tools. Students do an independent laboratory project.

PSY 673—Advanced Physiological Psychology (4; max: 8) Current research and theory in physiological psychology, with emphasis on physiological bases of learning, memory, motivation, emotion, and reinforcement.

PSY 674—Human Brain Function (4) *Prereq: PSY 682.* Recent advances in theory and experimental methods.

PSY 675—Psychophysiology of Hearing (5) Same as SCH 692. Physiological representation of acoustic events within the auditory system. Anatomical information and analysis of electrophysiological literature.

PSY 676—Seminar in Sensory Processes (1) Same as MED 639, ZY 638. Topics of current interest in various areas of sensory specialties. S/U.

PSY 677—Comparative Psychology (4; max: 12) *Prereq: PSY 682.* Survey of literature in comparative psychology.

PSY 678—A Survey of Sensory Systems (4) Same as MED 636, ZY 636. *Prereq: ZY 574; MED 623, 331, PSY 681, 682; MED 767.* A group of specialists provide a survey of theories and experimental data on human and subhuman sensory reception and encoding. Auditory, visual and cutaneous and chemical senses included.

PSY 679—Seminar on Vision (4) Current research and theory in visual function. Literature survey and design of an experiment relevant to recent theory.

PSY 681—Literature in Social Psychology (4) Empirical and theoretical foundations of social psychology.

PSY 682—Literature in Physiological and Comparative Psychology (4) Empirical and theoretical foundations of physiological and comparative psychology.

PSY 683—Literature in Experimental and Applied Behavioral Analysis (4) Empirical and theoretical foundations of various areas in experimental analysis of behavior.

PSY 684—Literature in Personality (4) Empirical and theoretical foundations of various areas of the psychology of personality.

PSY 685—Literature in Developmental Psychology (4) Empirical and theoretical foundations of developmental psychology.

PSY 686—Literature in Cognition and Perception (4) Empirical and theoretical foundations of cognition and perception.

PSY 694—Contemporary Systems in Psychology (4) *Prereq: PSY 594.* Differences in theoretical viewpoint which give rise to the emphasis responsible for the delineation of distinct systems in modern psychology. Original work of leading theorists and its impact on the science of psychology.

PSY 696—Individual Work (1-5; max: 15) Reading or research in areas of psychology.

PSY 697—Supervised Research (1-5)

PSY 698—Supervised Teaching (1-5)

PSY 699—Master's Research (1-15)

PSY 700—Seminar in Developmental Psychology: Cognitive Processes (4) *Prereq: PSY 681, 682, 683, 684, 685, 686, STA 602.* Development of cognitive processes in relation to other psychological processes.

PSY 704—Infancy and Early Childhood (4) Research findings in the development of psychological processes during the first five years of life, including prenatal, perinatal and postnatal influences on development.

PSY 706—Theories of Child Development (4) Theoretical perspectives and major theorists in child and developmental psychology.

PSY 710—Research Methods in Social Psychology (4; max: 16) *Prereq: PSY 618.* Experimental studies in social perception, social influence, attitudes, leadership, interpersonal perception, and related social processes.

PSY 711—Seminar: Research in Social Psychology (1-5; max: 20) *Prereq: consent of instructor.* Consideration of theory, research design, analytical procedures and substantive findings in selected areas of social psychology, such as prosocial behavior, attitudes, personal space, impression management, attitude formation and change, leadership, small group behavior.

PSY 718—Multidimensional Scaling for Market and Societal Analysis (5) Same as MKG 774. *Prereq: STA 603 or equivalent and fundamentals of matrix algebra.* Derivation of utilities from preferential choices; measurement of spatial attributes underlying utility; principal components and distance decompositions; scaling categorical judgments in survey research.

PSY 719—Social Psychological Research in the Community (4) *Prereq: PSY 616.* Consideration of problems and techniques of experimentation in natural settings.

PSY 720—Advanced Seminar: Experimental Analysis of Behavior (4) *Prereq: PSY 520, 683, and consent of instructor.* Restricted areas of experimental analysis of behavior such as schedules of reinforcement, stimulus control, current issues in research methods, and complex repertoires. May be repeated with change of content.

PSY 721—Advanced Seminar: Precise Behavioral Management (4) Clinical application of behavior analysis and innovative behavior change techniques; treatment in the natural environment and family setting is stressed.

PSY 722—Seminar in Behavioral Medicine (4) *Prereq: 6 hours of human biology and consent of instructor.* Analysis of daily activities contributing to chronic disease states such as smoking, alcohol consumption, overeating, etc., is undertaken with review of relevant literature.

PSY 723—Advanced Seminar in Behavioral Medicine (4) *Prereq: PSY 722, 6 hours of human biology and consent of instructor.*

PSY 728—Experimental Psychopathology (4) *Prereq: PSY 520 or 683, and consent of instructor.* Normal and pathological effects of aversive control (punishment, avoidance, escape, complex contingencies, etc.).

PSY 729—Advanced Seminar: Applied Analysis of Behavior (4) Literature and methods in special applied settings and populations.

PSY 737—Research Methods in Cognition and Perception (2; max: 16) *Prereq: consent of instructor.* Current research techniques and methods in the area of cognition and perception.

PSY 740—Advanced Theories in Personality (4; max: 12) Theoretical orientations in personality and research developments; particular groups of theorists examined.

PSY 745—Advanced Research Seminar in Personality (1-5; max: 20) Investigation of research areas involving literature and laboratory experimentation.

PSY 749—Field Work in Personality Research (4) Field experience which allows students to involve themselves as personality psychologists in settings where human beings are undergoing change or crisis, or whose background differs from theirs.

CLP 751—Seminar: Current Clinical Literature (4; max: 12) Reading based on selected topics.

CLP 752—Issues in Psychological Treatment (4; max: 8) *Prereq: CLP 651, 665.* Seminar and case discussion based on critical issues.

CLP 756—Seminar: Theory and Research Methods in Community Psychology (4) Principles of community psychology, including those related to community and program evaluation, consultation, mental health education, early identification, and intervention. Research methods and current research literature.

CLP 757—Theory and Practice of Psychological Consultation (4) Concepts and practices, including multiple roles and intervention strategies utilized by consultants as agents of organizational and social system change. Field experience in actual consultation settings in the community.

CLP 758—Seminar: Advanced Research Methods in Community Psychology (4) *Prereq: CLP 756.* Analysis of a community through methods of epidemiological and demographic data collection. Design of research for program evaluation and planning in the community.

CLP 760—Current Methods of Psychological Treatment (5) Seminar on integration of theory and methods in the treatment of individuals and groups. Emphasis on contemporary psychotherapies.

CLP 761—Advanced Current Methods of Psychological Treatment (5; max: 10) Emphasis on practical experience and techniques.

CLP 762—Psychological Treatment Through Community Intervention (4; max: 8) Theory and strategy of methods developed specifically for utilization in the practice of community psychology. Required client contact in appropriate community agency.

CLP 763—Psychological Treatment of Children's Behavior Disturbances (4) *Prereq: PSY 681, 682, 683, 684, 685, 686.* Theories and practices.

CLP 764—Psychological Treatment of Adolescent Behavior Problems (4) Behavior problems in adolescents and young adults examined with regard to developmental theories and in terms of psychopathology. Emphasis on theory, research, and clinical treatment.

CLP 765—Psychological Treatment with Groups (4) Current theories and practices in group therapy as a form of treatment. Exploration of intervention techniques.

CLP 766—Psychodiagnostic Appraisal and Assessment (4) *Prereq: CLP 658.* Synthesis of theory and practice of psychodiagnosis. Utilization of personality test batteries and other data oriented toward individual case study and group assignment.

CLP 769—Internship (5) *Required of all doctoral students in clinical, counseling, and school psychology. Prereq: CLP 651.* Student in applied specializations placed in approved intern settings. Designed as a sequence of 3 quarters which must include a minimum of 1500 work hours. Reading assignments and conferences.

PSY 770—Seminar: Neural Mechanisms of Ingestion and Energy Regulation (2-4) Same as MED 715. Neuroanatomical, neurobehavioral, and neuroendocrinological mechanisms involved in the regulation of food and water consumption and regulation of body weight.

PSY 772—Current Research Methods in Physiological Psychology (4; max: 16) Advanced training in new electrophysiological and neurochemical techniques used in studying the biological basis of behavior.

PSY 773—Seminar in Neural Mechanisms and Behavior (4) *Prereq: PSY 673.* Recent and specialized topics in brain-behavior relations.

PSY 774—Advanced Seminar in Higher Brain Function (4) Advanced seminar in research and theory with special emphasis on inter- and intrahemispheric processing.

PSY 775—Neurobehavioral Relations (4) Same as MED 712. *Prereq: MED 741.* Theories and data on the central nervous system basis for higher order function. Emphasis on arousal, purposeful behavior, and learning.

PSY 776—Information Storage: A Neurobiological Approach (4) Same as MED 713. Consideration of data dealing with basic issues concerning the nature of behavior plasticity and information storage and their central nervous system foundations. Particular emphasis on memory disruption and facilitation as an experimental tool in the study of memory processes.

PSY 777—Advanced Seminar in Comparative Psychology (3; max: 15) *Prereq: PSY 677.* Restricted area of current importance.

PSY 779—Seminar in Psychophysiology (1-4; max: 15) *Prereq: PSY 579 or consent of instructor.* In-depth study of specialized topics.

PSY 799—Doctoral Research (1-15)

REAL ESTATE AND URBAN LAND STUDIES
(College of Business Administration)

Chairman: C. A. MATTHEWS
Graduate Coordinator: H. C. SMITH, JR.

GRADUATE FACULTY 1975-76

Professors: C. A. MATTHEWS; H. C. SMITH, JR.
Associate Professors: C. C. CURTIS; L. A. GAITANIS

The Department of Finance, Insurance, Real Estate and Urban Land Studies offers the nonthesis degree Master of Business Administration and the thesis degree Master of Arts in real estate and urban land studies, with the option of a certificate in urban studies. It also offers a major and minor in the Doctor of Philosophy degree in business administration.

For admission to courses listed below, the student must have had undergraduate courses in fields pertinent to the graduate courses selected; or, where necessary, special arrangements may be made with the approval of the department chairman.

GRADUATE COURSES

RE 650—Seminar in Real Estate Valuation (4) Advanced theories and methods of appraisal. Statistical inference, market simulation, and application of specialized appraisal theory to appraisal problems.

RE 660—Seminar in Real Estate Investment and Development (4) Case course illustrating advanced applications of real estate investment analysis to both existing properties and new development. Emphasis on problem identification, analysis, and prospective solutions.

RE 670—Seminar in Land Use Analysis (4) Economic factors which provide the basis of urban economy and urban growth. Urbanization; regional planning; locations of cities and industries; private and public controls over urban land utilization and their impact upon the future of cities.

RE 680—Seminar in Real Estate Financial Analysis (4) Mortgage risk analysis, mortgage risk rating; trading on equity; long- and short-term financing; problems encountered in slum clearance, subdivision, and urban redevelopment.

RE 691—Real Estate Research and Reports (2) *Prereq: BA 690.* Supervised preparation of a report on a topic of current interest in real estate. Required of all candidates for the M.B.A. with a real estate concentration.

RE 696—Individual Work in Real Estate (1-5; max: 10) *Prereq: permission of department and Director of Graduate Studies.* Reading and/or research in real estate.

RE 697—Supervised Research (1-5)

RE 698—Supervised Teaching (1-5)

RE 699—Master's Research (1-15)

RE 790—Real Estate Research Workshop (4; max: 8) Analysis of current research topics. Paper presentation and critiques by doctoral students, faculty, and visiting scholars.

RE 799—Doctoral Research (1-15)

REHABILITATION COUNSELING
(College of Health Related Professions)

Chairman & Graduate Coordinator: J. D. BOZARTH

GRADUATE FACULTY 1975-76

Professors: J. D. BOZARTH; J. E. MUTHARD
Assistant Professors: J. G. JOINER; J. P. SAXON

The Department of Rehabilitation Counseling offers the Master of Health Science degree, with special emphases in (a) generally disabled, (b) mentally ill, (c) mentally retarded, (d) criminally incarcerated, (e) severely disabled. The areas of special emphasis are primarily related to practicum work and internship. Special courses are taken for electives. Graduates are prepared for work in vocation rehabilitation agencies, mental health centers, prison systems, rehabilitation facilities, and other community, state, and federal settings. The program consists of five quarters, including a one-quarter internship in an agency setting. Practicum is required each of the four academic quarters. Practicum and internship sites vary depending upon the individual's interests and objectives.

In addition to the requirements of the Graduate School, acceptance in the program is dependent upon demonstrated interest and background in the helping professions, and demonstrated motivation.

GRADUATE COURSES

RC 500—Introduction to Rehabilitation Counseling (5) Orientation to the rehabilitation process, including a survey of history, principles, philosophy, and legal aspects of rehabilitation and related fields.

RC 501—Psychological and Sociological Aspects of Rehabilitation (5) Social and personal problems of the handicapped; psychological aspects of physical and mental disabilities.

RC 602—Occupational Analysis and Placement Aspects of Rehabilitation Counseling (5) Vocational structure of society, occupational skills, occupational entry requirements, and physical and emotional demands. Adaption and application of occupational information to rehabilitation counseling, including job analysis, placement, and follow-up techniques.

RC 603—Medical and Related Aspects of Rehabilitation Counseling (5) Medical implications for rehabilitation counselors, including anatomy, physiology, pathology of human systems; physical restoration and etiology, prognosis and therapy of the various disabling conditions.

RC 604—Rehabilitation Evaluation and Counseling with the Disabled (5) *Prereq: PSY 637 or EDC 614, 620.* Application of evaluation, counseling theory and techniques to rehabilitation of disabled. Approaches in counseling the disabled; emphasis on techniques in practical situations, interviewing and specific testing procedures as vehicles of counseling. Limited classroom experience in counseling.

RC 605—Seminar in Rehabilitation Counseling with the Disabled Disadvantaged (5) *Prereq: RC 500 or consent of department.* Emphasis on development of skills and techniques in the provision of rehabilitation counseling services to individuals and families who are welfare recipients or from deprived backgrounds.

RC 607—Supervisory Techniques in Rehabilitation Counseling (4) Variables in organizational and community relationships, program planning, and supervisory functions related to the rehabilitation process.

RC 644—Research in Vocational Rehabilitation (4) Departmental research study in the vocational rehabilitation of the disabled.

RC 660—Rehabilitation Client Services Practicum (1-4; max: 12) Study of agency process and client services. Involvement in vocational evaluation, personal and social adjustment skills, and vocational and personal planning with clients.

RC 661—Rehabilitation Counseling Practicum (1-6; max: 12) Supervised individual counseling in a rehabilitation facility or agency. Intensive counseling regarding client's personal and adjustment problems. Emphasizes counselor-client relationship and the process and outcome of counseling procedure.

RC 680—Internship in Rehabilitation Counseling (10) *No student will be allowed to begin internship until 60 credits of degree requirement are completed and/or consent of the graduate faculty of the department is obtained.* Supervised field work in a recognized rehabilitation facility, including counseling case studies, contacts with community social agencies, and the vocational placement of disabled individuals.

RC 696—Individual Work (3-6; max: 6) Allows graduate students in rehabilitation counseling to pursue work not available in other courses.

RC 697—Supervised Research (1-5)

RC 698—Supervised Teaching (1-5)

RELIGION
(College of Arts and Sciences)

Chairman & Graduate Coordinator: S. S. HILL, JR.

GRADUATE FACULTY 1975-76
Professors: M. V. GANNON; R. H. HIERS; S. S. HILL, JR.; D. L. SCUDDER
Associate Professor: A. B. CREEL
Assistant Professor: S. R. ISENBERG

Graduate students may minor in the field of religion. For many years religion has been chosen as a minor by both master's and doctoral students working in such diverse departments as English, education, sociology, philosophy, and history.

Concentrations of strength exist in several areas, including the religions of India, religion in American culture, religion and society, and Jewish studies, with additional strength in biblical studies, philosophy of religion, and religious ethics.

While prerequisites are indicated for only a few of these courses, students with insufficient previous training in a given area in religion are urged to consult either the instructor or the graduate coordinator.

The *Undergraduate Catalog* should be consulted for a listing of courses in religion for which credit toward a minor may be given.

ROMANCE LANGUAGES AND LITERATURES
(College of Arts and Sciences)

Chairman: J. W. CONNER
Graduate Coordinators: J. J. ALLEN *(Spanish);* R. GAY-CROSIER *(French)*

GRADUATE FACULTY 1975-76

Graduate Research Professor: I. A. SCHULMAN
Professors: J. J. ALLEN; J. W. CONNER; R. GAY-CROSIER; A. HOWER; I. R. WERSHOW
Associate Professors: D. A. BONNEVILLE; J. CASAGRANDE; H. DER-HOUSSIKIAN; G. T. DILLER; F. IBARRA; M. M. LASLEY; B. SACIUK; A. B. SMITH
Assistant Professors: G. B. COULSON; W. M. DAVIS; M. RICE

The department offers programs leading to the Ph.D. in Romance Languages and Literatures, with specialization in French or Spanish; the M.A. in French or Spanish (either with or without thesis); the M.A.T. in French or Spanish.

Candidates for the master's degree in French or Spanish have a choice of two options, one oriented toward literature, the other toward language. In conjunction with their master's or doctoral work, students specializing in Spanish may also earn a certificate in Latin American Studies. Though a degree is not given in Portuguese, extensive course offerings permit students to develop a strong minor in Portuguese language and literature (particularly Brazilian).

Prerequisite for admission to graduate work is an undergraduate major in the language, including advanced courses in both literature and language. Candidates for the Ph.D. are required to take FLE 619 and FH or SH 610.

The foreign language requirement varies with degree and specialization; for details, consult the graduate coordinator. Every degree candidate is given the opportunity to gain teaching experience, either through a teaching assistantship or through participation in a departmental internship program.

GRADUATE COURSES

FLE 619—Introduction to Romance Linguistics (5) Comparative study of the major Romance languages and their development from Latin.
FLE 625—Medieval Romance Lyric Poetry (5) Reading of representative lyrics, with attention to their cultural setting and to problems of origin and influence.

FRENCH
GRADUATE COURSES

FH 505—Advanced French Composition (5)
FH 506—The Structure of French (4)
FH 512—History of the French Language (4)
FH 545—French Realism and Naturalism (4)
FH 560—20th-Century French Literature (4)
FH 600—Special Study in French Literature (4) Selected topic or problem (varied each quarter).
FH 602—Beginning French for Graduate Students I (4) For students with no formal preparation who need a reading knowledge. S/U.
FH 603—Beginning French for Graduate Students II (4) *Prereq: FH 602 or the equivalent.* For students who need proficiency in reading. S/U option.

FH 604—Advanced French Phonetics (4)
FH 606—Special Study in French Linguistics (4)
FH 610—Introduction to Graduate Study and Research (4) Tools, problems, and methods of literary and linguistic research.
FH 615—Literary Criticism in France (4)
FH 618—Old French Literature I (4)
FH 619—Old French Literature II (4)
FH 620—French Poetry of the Renaissance (4)
FH 621—French Prose of the Renaissance (4)
FH 622—17th-Century French Prose (4)
FH 623—17th-Century French Drama (4)
FH 630—The Philosophic Movement (4)
FH 631—The Novel of the 18th Century (4)
FH 641—Baroque and Preclassicism (4)
FH 642—The Romantic Period (4)
FH 645—French Classical Comedy (4)
FH 650—Modern French Poetry (4)
FH 660—The French Symbolist Movement (4)
FH 670—Contemporary French Novel (4)
FH 671—Contemporary French Theater (4)
FH 680—20th-Century Caribbean and West African Literature of French Expression (4; max: 12)
FH 696—Individual Work (2-5; max: 15) *Available only by special arrangement with graduate adviser.*
FH 697—Supervised Research (1-5)
FH 698—Supervised Teaching (1-5)
FH 699—Master's Research (1-15)
FH 799—Doctoral Research (1-15)

PORTUGUESE
GRADUATE COURSES

PE 600—Special Study in Brazilian or Portuguese Literature (3-5; max: 15) Selected topic or problem (varied each quarter).
PE 651—The 19th-Century Brazilian Novel (4)
PE 652—The 20th-Century Brazilian Novel (4)
PE 653—Brazilian Poet$_{ry}$ (4)
PE 654—Brazilian Drama (4)
PE 660—Medieval and Renaissance Portuguese Literature (4)

SPANISH
GRADUATE COURSES

SH 505—Advanced Composition and Syntax (5)
SH 506—The Structure of Spanish (4)
SH 575—Introduction to Spanish-American Literature I (4)
SH 576—Introduction to Spanish-American Literature II (4)
SH 577—Introduction to Spanish-American Literature III (4)
SH 600—Special Study in Spanish or Spanish-American Literature (4) Selected topic or problem (varied each quarter).
SH 602—Beginning Spanish for Graduate Students I (4) For students with no formal preparation who need a reading knowledge. S/U.
SH 603—Beginning Spanish for Graduate Students II (4) *Prereq: SH 602 or the equivalent.* For students who need proficiency in reading. S/U option.
SH 604—Advanced Spanish Phonetics (4)
SH 606—Special Study in Spanish Linguistics (4)
SH 610—Introduction to Graduate Study and Research (4) Tools, problems, and methods of literary and linguistic research.

SH 612—History of the Spanish Language (4)
SH 618—Old Spanish Literature I (4)
SH 619—Old Spanish Literature II (4)
SH 621—Spanish Drama of the Golden Age (4)
SH 623—Spanish Prose Fiction of the Golden Age (4)
SH 625—Spanish Poetry of the Golden Age (4)
SH 631—Spanish Drama of the 19th Century (4)
SH 632—Spanish Novel of the 19th Century (4)
SH 635—Lope de Vega and His Contemporaries (4)
SH 637—Cervantes (4)
SH 640—The Picaresque Novel (4)
SH 641—The Generation of '98 (4)
SH 650—Contemporary Spanish Literature (4)
SH 655—Argentine Literature (4)
SH 660—The Modernist Movement (4)
SH 665—The Spanish-American Essay (4)
SH 667—Contemporary Spanish-American Novel I (4)
SH 668—Contemporary Spanish-American Novel II (4)
SH 679—The Spanish-American Novel from Origins to Criollismo (4)
SH 685—Contemporary Spanish Novel (4)
SH 686—Contemporary Spanish Theater (4)
SH 696—Individual Work (2-5; max: 15) *Available only by special arrangement with graduate adviser.*
SH 697—Supervised Research (1-5)
SH 698—Supervised Teaching (1-5)
SH 699—Master's Research (1-15)
SH 799—Doctoral Research (1-15)

SOCIOLOGY

(College of Arts and Sciences)

Chairman: G. R. LESLIE
Graduate Coordinator: J. S. VANDIVER

GRADUATE FACULTY 1975-76

Graduate Research Professor: G. F. STREIB
Professors: F. M. BERARDO; B. L. GORMAN; G. R. LESLIE; M. SCHWARTZ;* G. A. SOARES; C. R. TITTLE;* J. S. VANDIVER; G. J. WARHEIT
Associate Professors: E. W. BOCK; D. W. BRITT;* J. D. KASARDA;* A. R. ROWE*
Assistant Professors: M. A. BADEN; L. BEEGHLEY III; C. E. FRAZIER; G. G. HENDERSON; R. D. HENDERSON; A. J. LA GRECA; W. B. SANDERS; C. O. THOMAS; I. C. TOUHEY;* F. J. TRAINA; H. O. VERA

These members of the faculty of Florida Atlantic University are also members of the graduate faculty of the University of Florida and participate in the doctoral degree program in the University of Florida Department of Sociology.

The Department of Sociology offers the Master of Arts and the Doctor of Philosophy degrees with specialization in demography, Latin American area studies, social organization, social psychology, sociological theory and methods, and urban studies. The Master of Arts in Teaching degree is offered also.

Specific areas of specialization include the sociology of the family, deviance, social gerontology, medical sociology, and minorities.

Admission to the master's degree program requires at least 36 quarter credits of undergraduate study in the social sciences, including 18 quarter credits in sociology. Students planning to apply for admission should take the Graduate Record Examination at the earliest possible date.

Study for the Ph.D. degree in sociology at the University of Florida by qualified master's degree recipients at Florida Atlantic University is facilitated by a cooperative arrangement in which appropriate members of the faculty of FAU are members of the graduate faculty of the University of Florida.

GRADUATE COURSES

SY 596—Individual Work (1-5)
SY 598—Special Study in Sociology (4)
SY 603—Development of Sociological Thought (4)
SY 604—Advanced General Sociology (4)
SY 605—The Development of Sociological Theories (4)
SY 606—Basic Sociological Theories (4)
SY 607—Theory Construction (4)
SY 608—Ethnomethodology (4)
SY 609—The Sociology of Human Sexuality (4) *Prereq: SY 201.*
SY 613—Social Gerontology (4)
SY 614—Social Factors in Health and Illness (4)
SY 615—Comparative Studies in Health Systems (4)
SY 616—Health Facilities in The Modern Community (4)
SY 617—Health Professions in The Modern Community (4)
SY 618—The Sociology of the Aged (4)
SY 619—Sociology of Death and Survivorship (4)
SY 622—Social Inequality (4)
SY 629—Complex Organizations (4)
SY 632—The American Family (4)
SY 633—Comparative Family Systems (4)
SY 634—Seminar in Family Theories (4)
SY 635—Seminar in Family Research (4)
SY 642—Methods of Social Research (5)
SY 643—Social Research Methods (4)
SY 648—Survey Research (5) Same as PCL 615. *Prereq: STA 320.*
SY 651—Seminar in Metropolitan Growth and Development (4) *Prereq: 12 hours in social sciences.*
SY 652—Seminar in Urban Ecology (4)
SY 653—Seminar in Comparative Urbanization (4) *Prereq: SY 350.*
SY 658—Seminar: Sociology of Rural Development (4)
SY 660—Comparative Sociology: Theory and Methods (4)
SY 663—Modernization in Latin America (4)
SY 664—Seminar in Spanish-American Societies (4)
SY 665—Seminar in Brazilian Society (4)
SY 670—Population Policy (4)
SY 672—Seminar in Population (4) Same as GPY 651.
SY 673—Seminar in Latin American Population (4) *Prereq: SY 471.*
SY 674—Seminar in Demographic Processes and Methods (4)
SY 680—Seminar in Symbolic Interaction (4)
SY 681—Collective Behavior (4)
SY 682—Social Movements (4)
SY 683—Personality and Social Structure (4)
SY 684—Research Problems in Deviance (4)
SY 685—Deviance (4)
SY 686—Criminology (5)
SY 687—Juvenile Delinquency (4)
SY 691—Seminar in American Minority Groups (4)
SY 695—Seminar in Contemporary African Societies (4)
SY 696—Individual Work (1-5) *Designed to permit work on subjects not available in currently offered courses.*
SY 697—Supervised Research (1-5)

SY 698—Supervised Teaching (1-5)
SY 699—Master's Research (1-15)
SY 701—Seminar in the Sociology of Knowledge (4)
SY 725—Research in Educational Sociology (5) Same as EDF 725. Prereq: EDF 625, or any one of the following: EDF 660, 661, 663, 664, or STA 310 and SY 442 or 642, and specialization in sociology of education.
SY 749—Seminar in Methods of Social Research (4; max: 12)
SY 797—Advanced Study in Sociology (5; max: 10) Prereq: M.A. or equivalent degree in sociology.
SY 798—Special Study in Sociology (4; max: 12)
SY 799—Doctoral Research (1-15)

SOIL SCIENCE
(College of Agriculture)

Chairman: C. F. ENO
Graduate Coordinator: D. F. ROTHWELL

GRADUATE FACULTY 1975-76

Professors: W. G. BLUE; R. E. CALDWELL; V. W. CARLISLE; J. M. DAVIDSON; C. F. ENO; J. G. A. FISKELL; N. GAMMON, JR.; L. C. HAMMOND; C. C. HORTENSTINE; H. L. POPENOE; W. L. PRITCHETT; W. K. ROBERTSON; D. F. ROTHWELL; D. O. SPINKS; T. L. YUAN
Associate Professors: H. L. BRELAND; D. H. HUBBELL; R. S. MANSELL; W. H. SMITH
Assistant Professors: F. G. CALHOUN, JR.; D. A. GRAETZ; P. G. ORTH; B. G. VOLK

The Department of Soil Science offers the Master of Science and the Doctor of Philosophy degrees with emphasis in soil chemistry, soil genesis and classification, soil microbiology, soil physics, or soil fertility. The nonthesis degree Master of Agriculture is also offered.

The interests of the student and the facilities available will determine the area of specialization for the research problem. Students will present a thesis or dissertation in their major field; however, Ph.D. candidates will be expected to qualify in all areas of soil science.

Prerequisites: Students who expect to do graduate work in the Department of Soil Science should present the bachelor's degree from a recognized college of agriculture with a major in soils or the equivalent in other sciences. Their background should include at least one course in each of the following: general soils, soil fertility, soil genesis and classification, general bacteriology, general botany, plant physiology, general field crops, general inorganic chemistry, qualitative analysis, and organic or biochemistry. Those not meeting the above requirements will be required to make up any deficiency early in their graduate work. Students will be held responsible for such basic undergraduate courses as are deemed necessary for the pursuit of their special program.

GRADUATE COURSES

SLS 525—Tropical Soils (3) Prereq: SLS 330 and SLS 421. Characteristics of tropical soils, emphasizing properties and processes in contrast to those of other areas.
SLS 600—Topics in Soils (4; max: 8) Prereq: SLS 330. Variable content; offered by arrangement to qualified students at continuing education centers.
SLS 621—Soil Chemistry (5) Prereq: SLS 421, CY 331, 341. Clay minerals and their ionic environment. Factors affecting availability and losses of plant nutrient elements.
SLS 622—Soil Microbiology (3) Prereq: SLS 422. Microorganisms of mineral and organic soils; their ecological relationships and metabolic processes.

SLS 623—Soil Genesis and Classification (4) *Prereq: SLS 423.* Origin and application of the most recent USDA soil taxonomy. Includes diagnostic soil properties and soil characterization data.

SLS 624—Soil Physics (4) *Prereq: SLS 424, PS 215, 216, 217, MS 304.* Basic physical concepts of the movement and retention of water, chemical solutes, heat, and air, with major emphasis upon water.

SLS 626—Soil Fertility (4) *Prereq: SLS 421.* Plant response to variations in soil environment.

SLS 627—Laboratory Methods of Soil Chemical Analyses (4) *Prereq: SLS 421, CY 331.* Instrumental and analytical procedures.

SLS 628—Soil Organic Matter and Organic Soils (5) *Prereq: CY 362, 363, SLS 621, 622, 626.* Chemistry of soil organic matter; techniques of identification; formation and management of organic soils.

SLS 630—Forest Soils (4) Same as FRC 630. *Prereq: SLS 330, FRC 381 or equivalent.* Soil as a component of forest ecosystems. Soil chemical, physical, and biological properties influencing forest growth, biochemical and hydrological cycles as they relate to forest land use.

SLS 631—Colloidal and Physical Chemistry of Soils (5) *Prereq: CY 342, SLS 621.* Theoretical treatment of ion exchange and activities of ions in solution and in suspension; energy relationships in soil colloids; aluminum chemistry; water properties; application of thermodynamics to the physico-chemical aspects of soil colloids.

SLS 632—Soil Microbiology Laboratory (3) *Prereq: MCY 302 and/or consent of instructor. Coreq: SLS 622.* Laboratory experiments on soil-plant-microorganism relationships.

SLS 634—Advanced Soil Physics (5) *Prereq: MS 305, CY 342, SLS 624.* Analysis of mathematical solutions to selected boundary value problems encountered during transport and storage of water, solutes, heat, and air in soils.

SLS 636—Micronutrients in Soils (3) *Prereq: SLS 421, BTY 310.* Chemistry of micronutrients and micronutrient fertilizers in soils, with special reference to factors involved in their utilization by plants and animals.

SLS 637—Morphology of Florida Soils (1) *Prereq. or coreq: SLS 437.* Field studies relating the influence of morphological characteristics on the suitability of Florida soils for agricultural and urban uses. Extensive trips required.

SLS 641—Soil Mineralogy (5) *Prereq: SLS 621 and GY 611.* Composition and properties of soil minerals; techniques of identification and analysis of mixed mineralogical systems; relations of composite mineralogical characters to soil properties.

SLS 651—Seminar (1; max: 4) Presentation of literature, methods of proposed thesis research, and selected topics.

SLS 696—Nonthesis Research (1-6; max: 9) *Prereq: 15 credits of soil science.* Study and research in a particular aspect of soils.

SLS 697—Supervised Research (1-5)

SLS 698—Supervised Teaching (1-5)

SLS 699—Master's Research (1-15)

SLS 799—Doctoral Research (1-15)

SPECIAL EDUCATION
(College of Education)

Chairman and Graduate Coordinator: W. R. REID

GRADUATE FACULTY 1975-76

Professors: M. CUNNINGHAM (*emeritus*); W. R. REID; W. D. WOLKING
Associate Professors: C. J. FORGNONE; C. L. REICHARD; J. E. WHORTON
Assistant Professors: M. K. DYKES; C. D. MERCER; S. E. SCHWARTZ

The department offers programs leading to the Master of Education or Master of Arts in Education degrees, the sixth year Specialist in Education degree, and the Doctor of Education or Doctor of Philosophy degrees.

Program specializations include the emotionally disturbed, the mentally retarded, specific learning disabilities, physically impaired/multiply handicapped, speech pathology and therapy, and administration of special education. For the latter, students should see courses listed in this *Catalog* under the Department of Educational Administration: EDA 620—Administration of Special Education; EDA 720—Seminar in Administration and Supervision of Special Education; EDA 721—Practicum: Special Education Administration.

GRADUATE COURSES

EDH 600—Teaching Exceptional Children (4) Care, treatment, and education of childre with problems and handicaps.

EDH 601—Education of the Mentally Retarded (4) *Prereq: consent of instructor.* School programs for the retarded. Educational provisions for the retarded affected by environmental deprivation and sensory and other impairment.

EDH 603—Education of the Gifted Child (4) Definitions of giftedness, characteristics of gifted children, and outside-of-school influences which affect achievement of gifted children.

EDH 604—Program Development for the Gifted (4) School programs for the gifted. Educational provisions for the achieving and underachieving gifted individual.

EDH 607—Laboratory: Evaluation in Special Education (3-6; max: 6) *Open only to majors in special education. Prereq: EDH 600.* Tests and other instruments used in evaluating pupils with learning disabilities.

EDH 610—Supervised Practice in Special Education (16) *Prereq: approval of special education faculty in area of specialization and Office of Student Teaching.* Supervised teaching in selected school settings designed to serve children and youth who have been classified as having behavioral and/or learning problems. Seminars and continuous evaluation of teaching experiences.

EDH 619—Educational Aspects of Behavioral Problems in Children and Youth (3-5) *Prereq. or coreq: EDH 300; EDH 600.* An analysis of the emerging trends and procedures in providing services to children and youth who may be classified as having behavioral disorders. H.

EDH 620—Educational Theories and Practices for Children and Youth with Behavioral Problems (3-5) *Prereq: EDH 419 or 619; EDH 300 or 600. Coreq: EDH 621.* Current practices and operational rationales, administrative arrangements for present programs and evaluation of the teaching process. H.

EDH 621—Educational Programming for Children and Youth with Behavioral Problems (5) *Prereq: EDH 419 or 619; EDH 300 or 600. Coreq: EDH 620.* Structuring individualized remediation programs for children with behavioral disorders based upon psycho-educational evaluations. Curriculum materials and techniques to increase cognitive and affective dimensions of personal development. H.

EDH 622—Resource Utilization for Children and Youth with Behavioral Problems (4) *Prereq: EDH 300 or 600.* Community resources for teachers of children and youth with severe behavioral problems. Functions and operations of service agencies and the teacher's role as a facilitation of communication about children and youth. H.

EDH 631—Organization and Program Planning in Special Education (4) *Prereq: EDH 600 and consent of instructor.* Control and management of special education programs, with emphasis on curriculum development based on needs assessment and evaluation.

EDH 651—Issues in the Education of Physically Impaired/Multihandicapped Children (2-5) *Prereq: EDH 600 or equivalent and consent of instructor.* Educational procedures and modifications required for children and youth with physical impairments including sensory, neurological, skeletal, and muscular problems. H.

EDH 652—Laboratory in Special Education Assessments of Severely Handicapped Children (3-5) *Open only to advanced students in special education. Prereq: EDH 600, 607; EDH 621, 661, or 662.* Assessment techniques, evaluation programs and prescriptive work.

EDH 653—Physiological Aspects of Physical/Multiple Handicaps (2-5) *Prereq. or coreq: EDH 600.* Educational implications and programming modifications required by physical/multiple handicaps. Relationship between educational programming and pathologies of central nervous system—motor sensory, language, and psychological disorders. H.

EDH 654—Educational Management of the Physically Impaired/Multiply Handicapped (3-5) *Prereq. or coreq: EDH 600, 653, 652, 672.* Programming and evaluation for young children with physical impairments/multiple handicaps, including curriculum, materials, habilitation, and community services H.

EDH 661—Foundations in the Field of Specific Learning Disabilities (4) Definitions, history, contributors, theories, issues, instructional strategies, delivery systems, and trends in the field.

EDH 662—Seminar: Current Literature in Specific Learning Disabilities (1-2; max: 9) Reading and discussion of current literature in the field.

EDH 663—Foundations of Clinical Teaching - Behavioral Analysis (4) Principles of behavior analysis and modification applied to the academic and classroom management problems of handicapped children. Individualized instruction based on direct and continuous analysis of the behavioral ecology.

EDH 664—Assessment of Specific Learning Disabilities (2) Task analysis, error analysis, classroom observations, and criterion-referenced tests used to provide a continuing and objective basis for individualizing the materials and conditions of instruction and classroom management.

EDH 665—Clinical Teaching: Basic Academic Skills (5) Individualized instruction of listening, speaking, writing, reading, spelling, and arithmetic skills. Materials, instructional sequences, and correction procedures for children with specific learning disabilities.

EDH 667—Program Designs for Children with Specific Learning Disabilities (4) Programs for delivering educational services: their structure, content, administrative features, and educational advantages.

EDH 668—Seminar: Early Identification and Remediation of Specific Learning Disabilities (4) Recent literature on early identification and remediation; procedures for starting early intervention programs.

EDH 670—Practicum in Special Education: Mental Retardation (4-12; max: 12) *Prereq: EDH 310 and written request six weeks prior to registration.* Tutoring mentally retarded children in educational situations appropriate to the student's professional goals.

EDH 671—Practicum in Special Education: Behavioral Disorders (4-16; max: 16) *Prereq. or coreq: EDH 419 or 619, and written request prior to registration for permission to enroll.* Working with behaviorally disordered children and youth in a variety of settings.

EDH 672—Practicum in Special Education: Physically Impaired/Multiply Handicapped (4-12; max: 12) *Prereq. or coreq: EDH 600, 651, and written request six weeks prior to registration.* Evaluation and programming for children in PI/MH programs in various settings.

EDH 674—Practicum in Special Education: Specific Learning Disabilities (4-16) *Written request is required six weeks prior to registration.* Includes supervised field experiences with children with specific learning disabilities. Supervision consists of direct observation, group sessions, individual consultation and quantified feedback on teaching effectiveness.

EDH 690—Special Topics (2-5; max: 15) *Prereq: consent of department chairman.*

EDH 696—Individual Work (2-5; max: 15) *Prereq: consent of department chairman, approval of the proposed project, and completion of at least 9 hours of graduate work.*

EDH 697—Supervised Research (1-5)

EDH 698—Supervised Teaching (1-5)

EDH 700—Seminar in Special Education (4; max: 16) *Admission limited to special education majors in the Advanced School.* Consideration of current problems.

EDH 701—Seminar: Mental Retardation (4) *Prereq: EDH 601.* Theoretical implications of mental retardation for intelligence, environment, and behavior.

EDH 702—Seminar: Current Research in Special Education (4) Problems, design, trends, issues, and implications of current research.

EDH 703—Seminar: Trends in Special Education (4) *Admission limited to special education majors in the Advanced School.* Emphasis on trends in special education and future considerations for research, and local, state, and federal priorities.

EDH 704—Internship: Special Education (3-16)

EDH 707—Seminar in Instructional Technology for Handicapped Learners (2-4) *Prereq: EDH 663.* Recent developments in programmed instruction, teaching machines, multiple channel instructional systems, and computer-assisted instruction, with particular reference to the education of multiply handicapped learners.

EDH 720—Seminar: Program Development for Children with Behavioral Disorders (4) Latest innovations in special education media, models of information dissemination and their implications.

EDH 721—Seminar: Education of the Emotionally Disturbed Child (4) *Prereq: major in special education; admission to the Advanced School.* Special issues in the education of the emotionally disturbed child.

EDH 750—Seminar: Advanced Topics in Learning Disorders (4-12; max: 12) *Prereq: EDH 661.* Review of selected literature and formulation of research problems in the area of learning disorders and instruction.

EDH 755—Seminar: Education of Physically Impaired/Multiply Handicapped Children in Public Schools (2-4) Evaluation of current research on the education of children in public school programs for the PI/MH.

EDH 756—Seminar: Education of the Severely Physically Impaired/Multiply Handicapped Child in Institutions (2-4) Evaluation of the latest innovations in programs, media, and materials for severely physically handicapped young children served in institutions other than public schools.

EDH 799—Doctoral Research (1-15)

SPEECH
(College of Arts and Sciences)

Chairman: P. J. JENSEN
Associate Chairman & Graduate Coordinator: M. BURGOON

GRADUATE FACULTY 1975-76

Professors: K. R. BZOCH; H. F. HOLLIEN; P. J. JENSEN; N. N. MARKEL; G. P. MOORE; R. E. TEW; D. E. WILLIAMS

Associate Professors: T. B. ABBOTT; D. G. BOCK; M. BURGOON; R. H. CARPENTER; A. J. CLARK; D. DEW; L. C. HAMMER; E. C. HUTCHINSON; A. PAIGE; R. J. SCHOLES

Assistant Professors: W. S. BROWN, JR.; J. K. BURGOON; W. H. CUTLER; S. H. FEINSTEIN; L. L. LaPOINTE; H. B. ROTHMAN; T. J. SAINE III: E. SCROGGIE, JR.; D. E. SELLERS; W. N. WILLIAMS

Graduate programs in the Department of Speech lead to Master of Arts, Master of Arts in Teaching, and Doctor of Philosophy degrees. Students, in conjunction with their supervisory committees, develop graduate programs to meet their specific needs and interests. Major areas of emphasis include audiology, communication sciences, communication studies, speech pathology, and language behavior.

Assistantships, fellowships, non-Florida tuition scholarships and traineeships are available.

GRADUATE COURSES

SCH 502—History of Rhetorical Theory (4) Survey of rhetorical theory from the classical period to the present, with special reference to the practical and pedagogical implications of major contributions.

SCH 503—Teaching Speech in Higher Education (4) Problems, methods, and materials in the teaching of speech in colleges or junior colleges. Courses of study, textbooks, and teaching strategies.

SCH 508—Theories of Political Communication (4) *Prereq: advanced work in contemporary history, public address, or political science.* Examination of theories of political communication. Field work investigations and assessment of individual theories.

SCH 510—Great Debates in American Life, 1650 to present (4; max: 12) Critical examination of public speaking in major controversies related to political, social, and intellectual life in America.

SCH 517—The Modern Forensics Program (4) *Prereq: experience as participant or director of forensic activities.* Methods and philosophies of administering forensics programs at the high school and college level.

SCH 540—Principles of Speech Pathology: Articulation Disorders (4) Advanced principles of diagnosis and therapy for individuals with articulatory disorders.

SCH 541—Principles of Speech Pathology: Voice Disorders (4) Advanced theory and techniques of diagnosis and therapy for voice disorders.

SCH 542—Principles of Speech Pathology: Language Disorders (4) Advanced theories and techniques of diagnosis and therapy for language disorders.

SCH 543—Principles of Speech Pathology: Stuttering (4) Advanced theories and techniques of diagnosis and therapy for stuttering.

SCH 549—Principles of Speech Pathology and Audiology: Diagnosis and Appraisal (4) Advanced analysis of interviewing principles, examination procedures, standardized testing and clinical assessment techniques.

SCH 560—Principles of Audiological Evaluation (4) Advanced procedures in speech audiometry, masking, and audiogram interpretation.

SCH 562—Theoretical Foundations in Audiology (4) *Prereq: SCH 560.* Concepts and principles relevant to audiometric evaluation and methods used in developing audiological procedures.

SCH 572—Speech and Language for the Deaf and Hard-of-Hearing (4) *Prereq: SCH 560 or consent of instructor.* Advanced principles and procedures in the development and correction of speech and language of the deaf and hard-of-hearing.

SCH 574—Auditory Training and Speechreading (4) *Prereq: SCH 572 or consent of instructor.* Advanced methods in aural rehabilitation procedures.

SCH 580—Electro-Acoustical Laboratory (3) *Prereq: EE 305.* Advanced analysis and description of electro-acoustical instruments employed in speech, hearing, and language research.

SCH 581—Applications of Digital Computers to Speech Research (3) *Prereq: ISE 350 and SCH 580.* Computational applications of digital computers to speech research: elaboration of FORTRAN, use of analog-to-digital converters, and use of small laboratory computers.

SCH 582—Man-Machine Communication (4) *Prereq: CIS 311 or 303 or ISE 350.* Interactive communication technology, natural language communication and applications in language-related research.

SCH 585—Advanced Phonetics and Phonemics (5) *Prereq: SCH 285 and 495.* Advanced study of the sounds of spoken English. Detailed examination of dialect differences, phonemic structure of English, phonemic theory, and description of non-language sounds. Includes phonetic transcription practice.

SCH 591—Auditory Perception of Speech (4) *Prereq: SCH 390 and consent of instructor.* Indepth study of the concepts and principles of speech, with emphasis on the auditory system: psychophysical methods, test materials, and basic subjective correlates of speech perception.

SCH 592—Psychoacoustics I (5) *Prereq: SCH 390.* Lectures, discussions and laboratory work on auditory stimulus, psychoacoustical methodology; general models of auditory processing. Although this course bears the same title as SCH 492, graduate students will be expected to pursue the topic in greater depth.

SCH 594—Language Acquisition (5) *Prereq: SCH 285 and 495.* Critical review of the theoretical and research literature relevant to acquisition of language. Although this course bears the same title as SCH 494, graduate students will be expected to pursue the topic in greater depth.

SCH 595—Nonverbal Communication (5) Same as APY 595. Advanced theories and methods in the experimental study of nonverbal communication.

SCH 596—Special Topics (3-5; max: 10) *Prereq: consent of major professor and department chairman.* Completion of a graduate project or research in a specific area of speech.

SCH 600—Introduction to Graduate Study (4) *Required of all graduate students majoring in speech.*

SCH 601—Seminar in Rhetorical Theory (4; max: 12) Selected topics including examination of ancient, medieval, renaissance and modern writers who have influenced rhetorical thought, criticism, speaking and writing.

SCH 605—Rhetorical Criticism (4) Principles and methods of rhetorical criticism; problems in applying critical standards in the evaluation of public address.

SCH 606—Theories of Small Group Communication (4) *Prereq: SCH 301 and 319 or consent of instructor.* Representative theories of the communication behavior of individuals in small, face-to-face, problem-solving groups, including current research on the content, frequency, duration and direction of communication in discussion groups.

SCH 608—Seminar in American Public Address (4) Selected speeches, speakers, and speaking movements which have had an impact on our history.

SCH 610—Principles and Theories of General Semantics (4) Systematic investigation of concepts and methodologies related to a broad theory of communication evaluation based on modern scientific knowledge and postulates.

SCH 611—Quantitative Research in Speech I: Applied Methodologies (4) Analysis and design of quantitative studies, with emphasis on identifying and predicting behavioral antecedents of orally transmitted messages.

SCH 612—Quantitative Research in Speech II: Laboratory Methodologies (4) Emphasis on design and analysis of speech experiments in the laboratory setting.

SCH 613—Seminar: Human Communication Theory (4; max: 12) Major ways of conceptualizing the role of communication in human affairs; process of building a human communications theory.

SCH 614—Methods of Theory Construction in Speech (4) Philosophical questions of theory construction with special emphasis associated with analysis and systematic construction of hypothetico-deductive theory.

SCH 615—Studies in the Processes of Influence (4) Examination of how communication can be used to gain influence and compliance.

SCH 616—Measurement in Speech Communication (4) *Prereq: STA 602.* Operationalizing of speech communication variables; methods of empirical evaluation for the teacher of speech communication.

SCH 618—Seminar: Organizational Speech Communication (4) *Prereq: SCH 418 or equivalent.* Analysis of speech communication variables as they operate in volunteer, commercial, governmental, and service organizations.

SCH 619—Seminar: Instructional Development in Speech (4) *Prereq: SCH 503.* History, theory, and research in the teaching of speech at all levels.

SCH 640—Seminar in Speech Pathology: Articulation Disorders (2) *Prereq: SCH 540.*

SCH 641—Seminar in Speech Pathology: Voice Disorders (2) *Prereq: SCH 541.*

SCH 642—Seminar in Speech Pathology: Language Disorders (2) *Prereq: SCH 542.*

SCH 643—Seminar in Speech Pathology: Stuttering in Adults (2) *Prereq: SCH 543.*

SCH 644—Seminar in Speech Pathology: Alaryngeal Speech (2) *Prereq: SCH 541.*

SCH 645—Seminar in Speech Pathology: Neurogenic Articulation Disorders (2) *Prereq: SCH 540.*

SCH 646—Seminar in Speech Pathology: Stuttering in Children (2)

SCH 647—Seminar in Language Pathology: Psychosocial Etiologies (2) *Prereq: SCH 542.*

SCH 648—Seminar in Speech Pathology: Special Voice Problems (2) *Prereq: SCH 541.*

SCH 649—Clinical Practice in Speech Pathology: Diagnosis (1-10; max: 10) *Prereq: SCH 549.* S/U.

SCH 650—Seminar in Speech Pathology: Myofunctional Disorders (2)

SCH 651—Seminar in Language Pathology: Aphasia in Children (2) *Prereq: SCH 542.*

SCH 653—Organization and Administration of Speech Pathology and Audiology Programs (4) Administrative problems and practices in varied speech pathology and audiology settings, community clinics, hospitals, schools, universities, training centers, and private practice.

SCH 654—Seminar in Speech, Hearing, and Language: Mental Retardation (2)

SCH 655—Seminar in Speech, Hearing, and Language: Cerebral Palsy (2)

SCH 656—Seminar in Speech, Hearing, and Language: Aphasia (2)

SCH 657—Seminar in Speech, Hearing, and Language: Cleft Palate (2)

SCH 659—Clinical Practice in Speech Pathology: Therapy (1-15; max: 15) Supervised clinical practice in speech therapy. S/U.

SCH 660—Seminar in Audiology: Diagnostic Procedures for Peripheral Disorders (2) *Prereq: SCH 560.*

SCH 661—Seminar in Audiology: Hearing Aids (2) *Prereq: SCH 660.*

SCH 662—Seminar in Audiology: Audiology for Children (2) *Prereq: SCH 660.*

SCH 663—Seminar in Audiology: Diagnostic Procedures for Central Hearing Disorders (2)
SCH 664—Seminar in Audiology: Diagnostic Procedures for Special Problems in Hearing (2) Theoretical and experimental literature and procedures for differential diagnosis of non-organic hearing disorders and other special problems.
SCH 669—Clinical Practice in Hearing Measurement (1-10; max: 10) Supervised clinical practice in hearing measurement. S/U.
SCH 670—Seminar in Audiology: Aural Rehabilitation (2)
SCH 671—Seminar in Audiology: Psychology of Deafness (2)
SCH 679—Clinical Practice in Aural Rehabilitation (1-10; max: 10) Prereq: SCH 572, 574. Supervised clinical practice in aural rehabilitation. S/U.
SCH 680—Proseminar in Communication Sciences (3) Required of all beginning students in any communication sciences area. Scientific and theoretical basis of communication sciences. Experimental phonetics, audition, psycholinguistics, experimental linguistics, and communicative factors engineering.
SCH 683—Special Topics in Communication Sciences (1; max: 10) Discussion of current topics in fields of graduate study and research. S/U.
SCH 684—Child Language (4) Advanced psycholinguistic study of early stages of syntax acquisition.
SCH 685—Experimental Phonetics I (3) Principles involved in acoustical and physiological analyses of voice production and laryngeal function. Major theories, experimental procedures. and research findings.
SCH 686—Experimental Phonetics Lab I (3) Prereq: SCH 685. Laboratory experience in experimental methods and techniques for study of voice production and analysis of voice signals. Students required to design and carry out an experiment in this area.
SCH 687—Experimental Phonetics II (3) Prereq: SCH 580. Principles of scientific analysis of speech production and recognition; major theories, experimental procedures, and research findings.
SCH 688—Experimental Phonetics Lab II (3) Prereq: SCH 687. Laboratory experience in major experimental methodologies and techniques in speech articulation, resonation, and function. Each student required to design and carry out a pilot study in this area.
SCH 689—Psycholinguistics Laboratory (3) Prereq: SCH 695. Design and analysis of experiments pertaining to the psychology of language. Areas of current research interest.
SCH 691—Psychoacoustics II (5) Prereq: SCH 592. Lectures, discussions, and laboratory work on advanced topics and current research in auditory sensation and perception.
SCH 692—Psychophysiology of Hearing (5) Physiological representation of acoustic events within the auditory system. Anatomical information and analysis of electrophysiological literature.
SCH 693—Cochlear Biophysics (5) The biophysics, anatomy and neurophysiology of the peripheral auditory system.
SCH 694—Neurobehavioral Linguistics (5) Prereq: SCH 580, 585. Nature and use of experimental method in linguistics. Evaluation of selected research topics.
SCH 695—Psycholinguistics (5) Research literature. Evaluation of theories, historical factors, geographic distinctions, and research procedures related to language development and usage.
SCH 696—Individual Study (1-10; max: 10) Prereq: consent of major professor and department chairman. Project or research course.
SCH 697—Supervised Research (1-5)
SCH 698—Supervised Teaching (1-5)
SCH 699—Master's Research (1-15)
SCH 701—Seminar in the Philosophy of Speech Communication (4; max: 12) Open to advanced graduate students in rhetoric and public address. Problems, research, and current literature in theory, criticism, pedagogy, or quantitative exploration in the area of speech communication.
SCH 706—Seminar in Group Communication (4) Prereq: SCH 606. Advanced research problems in the study of face-to-face group communication. Emphasizes content analysis, speech patterns, and temporal aspects of verbal communication.
SCH 715—Seminar: Theories of Persuasion (4) Prereq: SCH 615 or consent of instructor.
SCH 749—Practicum in Speech Pathology in a Medical-Dental Setting (3-10; max: 12) Prereq: SCH 649, 659, consent of department. Supervised training in clinical management of oral

communication problems in a medical-dental setting. Each succeeding registration requires increasing levels of competence and responsibility. S/U.

SCH 769—Practicum in Audiology in a Medical Setting (1-10; max: 12) *Prereq: SCH 669, consent of department.* Supervised training in clinical management of auditory communication problems in a medical setting. Each succeeding registration requires increasing levels of competence and responsibility. S/U.

SCH 772—Seminar in Audiology: Hearing Conservation and Noise Control (2)

SCH 780—Seminar in Communication Sciences (3) Advanced research problems.

SCH 785—Seminar in Experimental Phonetics (3) Advanced research problems in production of voice or speech.

SCH 786—Seminar in Speech Recognition (3) Advanced research problems in analysis and synthesis of speech. Emphasizes vocoders, machine translation, and computer processing of speech.

SCH 790—Seminar in Audition (3) Research problems in psychoacoustics, or acoustic physiology; recent advances in theories of hearing.

SCH 795—Seminar in Psycholinguistics (3) Theoretical and research problems in psycholinguistic processes of communication.

SCH 796—Seminar in Experimental Linguistics (3) Selected problems in linguistic theory and research, with emphasis on experimental analysis.

SCH 799—Doctoral Research (1-15)

STATISTICS
(College of Arts and Sciences)

Chairman: W. MENDENHALL III
Graduate Coordinator: J. G. SAW

GRADUATE FACULTY 1975-76

Professors: W. MENDENHALL III; Z. R. POP-STOJANOVIC; P. V. RAO; J. G. SAW
Associate Professors: J. A. CORNELL; R. C. LITTELL; F. G. MARTIN; R. L. SCHEAFFER; J. J. SHUSTER; M. C. K. YANG
Assistant Professors: A. AGRESTI; J. T. MCCLAVE; D. D. WACKERLY

Graduate programs are available leading to Master of Science, Master of Statistics, and Ph.D. degrees. Both master's programs usually require two years of course work including material covered in STA 607, 608, 609, 610, 611, 612, 619, 621.

GRADUATE COURSES

STA 505—Design and Analysis of Experiments in Biomedical Research (3) *Prereq: STA 320 or consent of instructor.* Principles of experimental design and analysis with emphasis taken from actual data and publications.

STA 509—Statistical Applications of Linear System and Time Series Models (4) *Prereq: STA 410 or 440.* Stationary and nonstationary time series models, autocorrelation and crosscorrelation analysis, spectral analysis, linear system models, applications and computing techniques.

STA 523—Computer Programs in Statistical Analysis I (2) *Prereq: concurrent registration in STA 408, 603, or 608, or consent of instructor.* Instructions for utilizing library programs with statistical interpretation of terms and parameters.

STA 524—Computer Programs in Statistical Analysis II (2) *Prereq: STA 523 and concurrent registration in STA 409, 603, or 609, or consent of instructor.* Advanced programs in statistical analysis with review of basic matrix concepts.

STA 602—Statistical Methods in Research I (4) Estimation, tests of hypotheses, basic experimental designs, least squares, regression and correlation. Some nonparametric techniques. Applications in the physical, biological, and social sciences and in business.

STA 603—Statistical Methods in Research II (4) *Prereq: STA 602.* Analysis of variance for basic experimental designs. The factorial experiment. Applications in business and in the physical, biological, and social sciences.

STA 605—Advanced Methods of Statistics (3) *Prereq: STA 603.* Complex experimental designs, including incomplete blocks, confounding, fractional replication, and response surfaces.

STA 607—Design and Analysis of Experiments I (3) *Prereq: STA 441.* Basic concepts in design of experiments. Principles of statistical inference for linear models. Method of least squares, analysis of variance, multiple comparison procedures.

STA 608—Design and Analysis of Experiments II (3) *Prereq: STA 607.* Factorial experiments, incomplete blocks, nested experiments, split plots, covariance.

STA 609—Design and Analysis of Experiments III (4) *Prereq: STA 608.* Design aspects of incomplete blocks, confounding, fractional factorials.

STA 610—Introduction to Theoretical Statistics I (3) *Prereq: MS 304.* Theory of probability. Probability spaces, continuous and discrete distributions, functions of random variables. Expectations, moment and probability generating functions. Applications.

STA 611—Introduction to Theoretical Statistics II (3) *Prereq: STA 610.* Properties of point estimators. Least squares, maximum likelihood, and Bayesian procedures. Confidence intervals, multivariate normal distributions, and introduction to the theoretical basis for analysis of variance.

STA 612—Introduction to Theoretical Statistics III (3) *Prereq: STA 611.* Tests of hypotheses, decision theory, nonparametric tests.

STA 619—Theory of Least Squares (4) *Prereq: STA 611.* Application of the Markov theory of least squares to problems of estimation and tests of hypotheses; distribution theory under normal assumptions.

STA 621—Advanced Topics in Design and Analysis (4) *Prereq: STA 609.* Random and mixed models, response surface methodology, mixture experiments, additional topics in regression.

STA 622—Sampling Theory and Application I (4) *Prereq: STA 611 or consent of instructor.* Theory of basic sampling procedures in economic and social surveys. Multistage sampling, cost functions, double sampling.

STA 623—The Analysis of Multivariate Data (4) *Prereq: STA 603 or 609.* Multivariate normal distribution; discriminant; canonical, principal component; and factor analysis.

STA 624—Sampling Theory and Application II (4) *Prereq: STA 622.* Stochastic processes as applied to sampling theory and other current research topics in sampling.

STA 626—Applied Time Series Analysis (4) *Prereq: STA 441.* Linear time series models; statistical analysis of linear stationary and nonstationary time series, with application and case studies supplemented by simulation studies.

STA 628—Problems in Statistics (1-5; max: 9) *Prereq: permission of department.* Special problems in research methods, sampling methods, and experimental design.

STA 635—Biostatistics I (4) *Prereq: STA 603 or 609.* Statistical methods in biological assay; direct assays; indirect assays; dose-response relationships; nonlinear regression; parallel line assays; potency estimation.

STA 636—Biostatistics II (4) *Prereq: STA 635.* Inferences from hospital data; nonparametric methods in medical research, including distribution free multiple comparisons, rank analysis of covariance, indices of order association; nonparametric partial correlation; multidimensional contingency tables.

STA 637—Biostatistics III (4) *Prereq: STA 636.* Multivariate problems in biostatistics; repeated measurements; discriminant analysis; diagnostic models; factor analysis; current topics in biostatistics.

STA 640—Probability Theory I (4) *Prereq: MS 543 or 649.* Measure theoretic approach to probability: random variables, probability functions, distribution functions, expectation, characteristic functions.

STA 641—Probability Theory II (4) *Prereq: STA 640.* Notions of convergence of sequences of independent random variables: continuity theorem, law of large numbers, central limit theorem.

STA 642—Probability Theory III (4) *Prereq: STA 641.* Dependence, Martingale convergence theorem, the law of large numbers and central limit theorems for dependent random variables.

STA 650—Nonparametric Statistics (4) *Prereq: STA 612 or consent of instructor.* Hypotheses testing; power and asymptotic relative efficiency of tests. Rank tests, tests of goodness of fit, robust estimators, and order statistics.

STA 652—Sequential Methods (4) *Prereq: STA 612.* Double sampling procedures, the sequential probability ratio tests, sequential tests for composite hypotheses, sequential estimation and confidence intervals.

STA 660—Stochastic Processes I (3) *Prereq: STA 610.* Discrete time and state models. Gambler's Ruin. Persistent and transient states: long-run and stationary distribution mean absorption times, mean first passage times.

STA 661—Stochastic Processes II (3) *Prereq: STA 660.* Continuous time, discrete state models. Poisson, generalized Poisson, and filtered Poisson processes. Polya process. Birth and death models. Application to the theory of queues and inventories.

STA 662—Stochastic Processes III (3) *Prereq: STA 611.* Wiener-Levy process; Ornstein-Uhlenbeck process. Integrated processes. White noise and thermal noise. Applications of stochastic processes in physical sciences.

STA 670—Multivariate Analysis I (4) *Prereq: STA 619.* Singular transformations. Multivariate normal, Wishart and multivariate beta distributions. Properties of a Wishart distributed random matrix. General linear hypothesis. Tests on a normal dispersion matrix.

STA 671—Multivariate Analysis II (4) *Prereq: STA 670.* Distribution of the latent roots of a Wishart distributed matrix. Zonal polynomials and noncentral distributions. Current topics in multivariate distribution theory.

STA 676—Stochastic Systems Analysis I (3) Same as ISE 676. *Prereq: STA 660.* Overview and classification of stochastic processes. Modeling of physical phenomena as stochastic processes. Methodology and applications from systems engineering and operations research.

STA 680—Time Series I (4) *Prereq: STA 641 or 661.* Statistical theory of stationary time series; estimation and tests of hypotheses concerning spectral density.

STA 681—Time Series II (4) *Prereq: STA 680.* Statistical analysis of parametric models; distribution of spectral estimates.

STA 682—Time Series III (4) *Prereq: STA 681.* Problems in linear estimation. Applications and recent developments discussed in journal articles.

STA 690—Special Topics in Statistics (4; max: 18) *Prereq: permission of graduate adviser.* Assigned reading of lecture series in advanced statistics.

STA 691—Seminar (1) *Prereq: permission of department.* Special topics of an advanced nature suitable for seminar treatment but not given in regular courses. S/U.

STA 696—Individual Work (1-5; max: 15) *Prereq: permission of department.* Special topics designed to meet the needs and interests of individual students.

STA 697—Supervised Research (1-5)
STA 698—Supervised Teaching (1-5)
STA 699—Master's Research (1-15)
STA 740—Statistical Inference I (4) *Prereq: STA 612.* Statistical decision theory; minimax theorem, complete class theorem, sufficiency, invariance and unbiasedness.

STA 741—Statistical Inference II (4) *Prereq: STA 740.* Hypothesis testing and multiple decision problems.

STA 742—Statistical Inference III (4) *Prereq: STA 741.* Inference with large samples, asymptotic relative efficiency, locally most powerful tests with special reference to nonparametric procedures. Sequential analysis in a general decision theoretic framework.

STA 799—Doctoral Research (1-15)

SUBJECT SPECIALIZATION
TEACHER EDUCATION

(College of Education)

Chairman & Graduate Coordinator: E. J. BOLDUC, JR.

GRADUATE FACULTY 1975-76

Professors: J. D. CASTEEL; T. W. HIPPLE; J. J. KORAN, JR.; V. MCGUIRE; W. OLSON; M. B. ROWE; E. A. TODD

Associate Professors: E. J. BOLDUC, JR.; G. D. CARR; R. C. FERGUSON; C. L. HALLMAN; A. P. NEWCOMB, JR.
Assistant Professors: D. H. BERNARD; B. R. ELLIS; M. E. FLANNERY; J. W. GREGORY; M. E. TIMMERMAN; R. G. WRIGHT

The Department of Subject Specialization Teacher Education is composed of the following specializations: art education; business education; English education; foreign language education; mathematics education; music education; science education; and social studies education.

The Department offers the Master of Education (nonthesis) and the Master of Arts in Education (thesis) degrees with an emphasis in either secondary school or community college teaching. Advanced graduate degrees, Ed.S., Ed.D., and Ph.D., are offered in all of the areas listed above.

Beyond the Graduate School requirements, beginning graduate students should have appropriate undergraduate training in professional education and in a field of subject specialization. Each graduate student is counseled during the first quarter to develop a program suited to meet specific educational objectives and designed to remove any deficiencies in previous preparation.

GENERAL COURSES

EDS 690—Special Topics (2-5; max: 15) *Prereq: permission of department chairman.*
EDS 696—Individual Work (2-5; max: 15) For advanced students who wish to study problems in secondary education under faculty guidance.
EDS 697—Supervised Research (1-5)
EDS 698—Supervised Teaching (1-5)
ED 699—Master's Research (1-15)
ED 799—Doctoral Research (1-15)

ART EDUCATION

EDE 531—Teaching Art in Elementary School I (4) *For in-service teachers. Not open to students who have taken EDE 331.* Study of art expression based on an understanding of child development. Laboratory, lecture, visual aids, class discussion, and individual projects.
EDE 532—Teaching Art in Elementary School II (4) *For in-service teachers. Prereq: EDE 531 or 331 or equivalent.* Laboratory experiences with materials. Emphasis upon ways of developing art experiences with children. Individual and group projects.
ED 671—Foundations of Art Education (4) Evolution of art education in the United States and abroad.
ED 673—Aesthetic Experience (4) Applied aesthetics. Nature of education for aesthetic experience; education of feeling. Development of a curriculum for aesthetic education.
ED 675—Curriculum in Art Education (4) Current major theories in development of the art curriculum.
ED 676—The Teaching of Art in Higher Education (4) College programs in art: objectives, problems, and approaches to teaching.
ED 678—Art Education and Related Disciplines (4) Comparative analysis of concepts derived from related disciplines and their functions in art education. Art education within the larger framework of professional education.

BUSINESS EDUCATION

EDV 640—Teaching Office Machines (4) *Prereq: EDV 346.* Functions of machines, their suitabilities for various office functions, methods of teaching operation of machines commonly used in offices.
EDV 641—Teaching Secretarial Studies (4) For teachers of business subjects. Curriculum, materials, and methods of teaching secretarial subjects.
EDV 642—Teaching Bookkeeping and Consumer Business Subjects (4) Curriculum, materials, and methods of teaching bookkeeping, economics of business, business law, salesmanship, and business arithmetic.

EDV 643—Materials and Methods of Teaching General Business (4) Objectives, content, resource materials, and methods of teaching general business in junior and senior high schools.

EDV 644—Problems in Business Education (4) Areas of interest to students enrolled are studied. Emphasis on problems in business education in Florida schools. ˙

EDV 645—Seminar and Work Experience in Business Education (8) *Prereq: permission of department.* Evaluation of effectiveness of the secondary school business education program in meeting needs of students for beginning office employment.

EDV 646—Methods and Materials for Block-Time Instruction in Office Education (4) Development of instructional plans where large blocks of time are used. Emphasis on developing concept of integrated or whole-office model and instructional materials for use in classrooms.

EDV 647—Research Seminar in Business Education (4) *Prereq: EDF 360.* Nature and purpose of research in business education. Guides for conducting research. Dissemination of research findings.

EDV 655—Cooperative Education (4) Organization and coordination of diversified cooperative training, distributive education, and cooperative business education programs.

ENGLISH EDUCATION

EDE 670—Language Arts in the Elementary School (4) Speaking, listening, writing, and language study in the elementary classroom.

EDE 671—Early Childhood Language Arts and Reading (4) *Prereq: EDE 370 or 375.* Factors influencing early language and their relationship to beginning school programs in listening, speaking, reading, and writing.

EDE 672—Children's Literature in the Childhood Curriculum (4) *Prereq: EH 491.* Evaluating, selecting, and using fiction, biography, poetry and informational books for instructional, informational, and recreational purposes.

EDS 670—Language Arts: Language and Composition (4) *Prereq: preparation in subject area equivalent for high school certification and an appropriate methods course.* Theory and practice of teaching language and composition, grades 7 to 14.

EDS 671—Language Arts: Literature (4) *Prereq: preparation in subject area equivalent for high school certification and an appropriate methods course.* Theory and practice of teaching literature, grades 7 to 14.

EDS 672—Practicum in Teaching Secondary School English (4; max: 8) *Prereq: EDS 670 or 671 or consent of instructor.* Directed field experiences based on a planned instructional unit including materials, student activities, teaching strategies, and assessment.

ED 770—Seminar in English Language Arts (4; max: 8) *Prereq: EDE 670 or EDS 670; year of graduate study.* Contemporary developments and research in language arts education.

FOREIGN LANGUAGE EDUCATION

EDS 682—Practicum in Teaching Secondary School Foreign Languages (4; max: 8) *Prereq: EDS 685.* Directed field experiences with various content emphases based on planned instructional units including materials, student activities, teaching strategies, and means of assessment.

EDS 685—Problems of Foreign Language Instruction in Secondary Schools (4) *Prereq: an appropriate methods course.* Surveys new methodology and materials through video tapes of selected teaching situations.

MATHEMATICS EDUCATION

EDE 550—Teaching Modern Math in Elementary School (4) Analysis of content, methodology, and materials for teaching modern mathematics.

EDE 650—Mathematics in the Elementary School (4) *Prereq: EDE 550.* Recent research, patterns of curriculum, techniques of teaching, and use of instructional media. Primarily for elementary teachers who desire specialization in mathematics education.

EDS 650—Mathematics in the Secondary School (4) *Prereq: preparation in subject area equivalent to requirements for high school certification and an appropriate methods course.* Patterns of mathematics curriculum; practices in teaching mathematics; preparation, selection, and use of instructional materials; laboratory experiences and classroom teaching.

EDS 654—Practicum in Teaching Secondary School Mathematics (4; max: 8) *Prereq: EDS 650 or consent of instructor.* Directed field experiences emphasizing various instructional strategies, with a focus on instructional materials, sequencing student activities, and systematizing instructional moves.

ED 655—Individualizing Instruction in Elementary Mathematics (4) Organizing a continuous progress program: objectives, diagnostic testing, placement of students, record keeping, evaluation and reporting. Includes study of the role of the teacher and team teaching as well as the development of a bank of materials, games, and activities for an individualized mathematics program.

ED 656—Laboratory Approach to Mathematics (3-6) Rationale for use of investigatory experiences with objects in the mathematics curriculum. Involvement in planning laboratory facilities and activities for classroom use. Analysis of the problems of teaching mathematics to low achievers.

ED 658—Laboratory in Diagnosing Mathematics Skills (4-8; max: 8) Diagnosis, correction, and prevention of mathematical learning difficulties: work with children in the applications of principles under study.

ED 751—Mathematics Education Seminar (4) *Prereq: EDS 650 or EDE 650.* Issues and problems in mathematics education and the investigation and planning of research relevant to selected problems.

MUSIC EDUCATION

ED 663—Music in the Elementary School (4) *Offered only by extension. In-service training course open to elementary school teachers.* Research work under supervision of the chairman of the Department of Music.

ED 664—Vocal Music in the Secondary School (4) *Offered only by extension. In-service training course open only to vocal music teachers.* Research work under supervision of the chairman of the Department of Music.

ED 665—Orchestra Music in the Public Schools (4) *Offered only by extension. In-service training course open only to instrumental music teachers.* Research work under supervision of the chairman of the Department of Music.

ED 666—Band Music in the Public Schools (4) *Offered only by extension. In-service training course open only to instrumental music teachers.* Research work under the supervision of the chairman of the Department of Music.

ED 667—Foundations of Music Education (4) Historical development and philosophy; comparison of United States with other countries and cultures; individuals, associations, and institutions that shape the music education program.

ED 767—Music Education Seminar (4) Contemporary issues and problems in music education and the investigation and planning of research relevant to selected problems.

SCIENCE EDUCATION

EDE 560—Teaching Science in Elementary School (4) Basic course for in-service teachers. Emphasis on science content, methods and materials for elementary school children.

EDE 660—Science Education in the Elementary School (4) Current problems, new materials and teaching techniques, research and recent developments in the sciences.

EDS 660—Science in the Secondary School (4) *Prereq: preparation in subject area equivalent to requirements for high school certification and an appropriate methods course.* Current problems in teaching science in secondary schools and junior college.

EDS 661—Evaluating Science Curricula in the Secondary School (4) Applications of curriculum evaluation theory and systems to contemporary science curricula.

EDS 662—Practicum in Secondary Science Curriculum (4) Directed field experience emphasizing the adoption and utilization of science curricula in the secondary schools, with a focus on instructional materials and teacher behavior.

EDS 761—Learning and Instruction in Secondary School Science (4) Selected topics in the acquisition of knowledge in science and the arrangement of conditions for science learning in the secondary schools.

EDS 762—Practicum in Learning and Instruction in Secondary School Science (4) Systematic research in learning science in the secondary school setting including the observation and modification of teacher behavior.

ED 646—The Teaching of Special Science Programs (3-6; max: 15) Preparation to teach particular science programs such as AAAS, ESS, SCIS, ESCS Patterns and Processes, CHEMS, PSSC, CAI.

ED 760—Science Education Seminar (4) *Prereq: EDS 660.* Issues and problems in science education and the investigation and planning of research relevant to selected problems.

SOCIAL STUDIES EDUCATION

EDE 620—Social Studies Education—Elementary School (4) *Prereq: graduate curriculum course.* Contributions of social education to the total elementary school program, with emphasis on social interaction and programs and procedures in social studies area.

EDS 640—Social Studies in the Secondary School (4) *Prereq: preparation in subject area equivalent to requirements for high school certification and an appropriate methods course.* Problems of teaching social studies.

EDS 642—Practicum in Secondary Social Studies Instruction (4; max: 8) *Prereq: an appropriate methods course.* Identification, definition, application, and synthesizing of component skills relevant to social studies instructions.

EDS 643—Microcriteria of Social Studies Teaching (4) *Prereq: an appropriate methods course.* Definition, identification, consequential analysis, and application of microcriteria of teacher effectiveness related to secondary social studies instruction.

ED 710—Seminar in Social Studies (4) *Open to advanced degree students in social studies education.* Application of theoretical analysis for program development and teaching strategies in social studies.

TAXATION

(College of Law)

Chairman & Graduate Coordinator: R. B. STEPHENS

GRADUATE FACULTY 1975-76

Professors: H. A. FENN; J. J. FREELAND; S. A. LIND; R. B. STEPHENS
Associate Professor: C. D. MILLER

Graduate study in the field of taxation leading to the degree Master of Laws in Taxation is available in the College of Law. Applicants for admission to the Graduate School for this degree must hold a law degree from an accredited law school but need not submit scores on the Graduate Record Examination. For further information concerning admission consult the *College of Law Catalog,* or write the College of Law, 325 Holland Law Center.

GRADUATE COURSES

LWT 601—Income Taxation I (3) Tax problems of individual taxpayers; concepts of gross income; identification of taxpayer; adjusted gross income; deductions, exemptions and taxable income.

LWT 602—Income Taxation II (3) Problems incident to the sale, exchange, and other disposition of property, including recognition and characterization concepts.

LWT 603—Income Taxation III (3) Income tax accounting principles: the taxable year, accounting methods, installment and deferred payment sales, delayed payment for services, income averaging and loss carry-overs and carry-backs.

LWT 604—State and Local Taxation (3) Nature and purpose of state taxation; comparison of property and excise taxes; uniformity of taxation; jurisdiction; assessment and collection procedures; remedies available to taxpayers.

LWⅠ 605—Corporate Taxation I (3) Tax considerations in corporate formation, distributions, redemptions, and liquidations. General consideration of tax alternatives relating to sale of corporate businesses.

LWT 606—Corporate Taxation II (3) Advanced problems including Subchapter S corporations, professional corporations, personal holding companies and punitive taxes on earnings accumulation, collapsible corporations, and taxing affiliated groups.

LWT 607—Corporate Taxation III (3) Reorganizations: mergers, consolidations and divisions, including transfer or inheritance of losses and other tax attributes.

LWT 608—Corporate Taxation IV (3) Application of the federal income tax to nonresident aliens and foreign corporations and to United States citizens, residents, and corporations investing funds abroad or conducting business with foreign persons.

LWT 609—Taxing Estates and Trusts I (3) Federal estate and gift taxes.

LWT 610—Taxing Estates and Trusts II (3) Problems of the fiduciary in allocation of receipts and disbursements between principal and income in the administration of trusts and estates; Uniform Principal and Income Act; allocation of the burden of death taxes.

LWT 611—Taxing Estates and Trusts III (3) Taxation of income of trusts and estates, with emphasis on income required to be distributed currently, equivocal distributions of income or corpus, and accumulation distributions; other fiduciary tax problems, including the treatment of income in respect of decedents.

LWT 612—Taxing Estates and Trusts IV (3) Estate planning: planning lifetime and testamentary private and charitable dispositions of property; postmortem planning; life insurance; analysis of small and large estates; eliminating and offsetting complicating and adverse factors; selection of a fiduciary and administrative provisions.

LWT 613—Partnership Taxation (3) Tax meaning of "partnership"; formation transactions between partner and partnership; determination and treatment of partnership income; sales or exchange of partnership interest; distributions; retirement; death of a partner; drafting the partnership agreement.

LWT 614—Tax Procedure I (3) Taxpayers' relationships with the Internal Revenue Service, including requests for rulings, conference and settlement procedures; deficiencies and their assessment; choice of forum; Tax Court practice; limitation periods and their mitigation; transferee liability; tax leins; and civil penalties.

LWT 615—Tax Procedure II (3) Criminal prosecution for fraud, including examination of tax offenses under provisions of the Internal Revenue Code and the Criminal Code; the interrelationship of such provisions and of civil fraud penalties; procedures in fraud cases, and constitutional and other rights of the accused.

LWT 616—Deferred Compensation (3) Tax consequences of compensation in forms other than cash paid contemporaneously with performance of services. Includes uses of employers' stock in employee compensation, nonqualified deferral compensation devices, and qualified pension and profit-sharing plans.

LWT 617—Federal Tax Research (1-2) Substantial research and writing project on a federal tax subject; instruction in tax research techniques. Students customarily register for the course and complete the project during three successive quarters. Credit is usually 1 hour each quarter but may be varied in accordance with scope and nature of project. A, H, or S/U.

LWT 618—Tax Exempt Organizations (3) Study of exemption from federal income tax accorded to a variety of public and private organizations, and tax treatment of contributions to such organizations; public policies underlying exemption from tax, and deductibility of contributions; and the broad new enforcement powers to be undertaken by the Internal Revenue Service.

LWT 619—Current Federal Tax Problems (3; max: 6) Variable content. Course involves either significant new legislation of significant developments within the existing statutory framework; emphasis on policy considerations.

LWT 696—Individual Study (1-5) May be repeated. S/U.

LWT 697—Supervised Research (1-5)

LWT 698—Supervised Teaching (1-5)

THEATRE
(College of Fine Arts)

Chairman: E. J. HOOKS
Graduate Coordinator: L. L. ZIMMERMAN

GRADUATE FACULTY 1975-76

Professor: L. L. ZIMMERMAN
Associate Professor: R. L. GREEN
Assistant Professors: E. J. HOOKS; D. L. SHELTON; A. WEHLBERG

The graduate programs offered by the Department of Theatre lead to the degrees of Master of Fine Arts and Doctor of Philosophy. The Master of Fine Arts degree permits specialization either in scene design, costume, technical theatre, or acting and directing. The Doctor of Philosophy degree with a major in theatre is awarded through the Department of Speech.

An appropriate undergraduate background in theatre, or its equivalent, is prerequisite to admission to the graduate program. In the case of deficiencies, students will be required to register for appropriate "foundations" courses. Admission to the program requires proof or demonstration of production or acting skills.

Assistantships, fellowships, and non-Florida tuition scholarships are available.

GRADUATE COURSES

THE 522—Graduate Acting I (4) Study of acting styles and their relation to theatre aesthetics.
THE 524—Summer Repertory Theatre (1-12) *Prereq: THE 322, 325, 339, 420, 423, and consent of staff.* A practical production experience in repertory theatre with direct skills application in all areas of theatre production, and special emphasis on problems of organizing a multiproduction repertory program.
THE 526—Problems in Scene Design (4) Advanced study of scene design as an art: consideration of the spatial and aesthetic factors operative in the scenic elements, with special emphasis on pragmatic consideration of the design process.
THE 527—Production Costume Design (4) *Prereq: THE 422 and 423 or consent of instructor.* Advanced application of costume design to costume requirements fostered by specific production concepts.   '
THE 528—History of the Theatre I (4) In-depth study of the development of the theatre from its beginning through the Middle Ages.
THE 529—History of the Theatre II (4) The Middle Ages to the 18th century.
THE 530—History of the Theatre III (4) The 18th century to the present.
THE 620—Advanced Problems of Stage Direction (5) Application of production theories to the problems of play direction, and a supervised problem in advanced directing techniques.
THE 621—Advanced Problems in Scene Design (5) Application of production theories to the problems of scene design, and a supervised problem in advanced scene design.
THE 622—American Plays, Players, and Playwrights I (4). Plays and their production from the Colonial period to 1860; techniques of outstanding actors and playwrights.
THE 623—American Plays, Players, and Playwrights II (4) American plays and players from 1860 to present.
THE 624—Readings in Theatrical History I (4) Selected primary source materials in the history of the theatre to 1660, and their use by theorists and historians.
THE 625—Readings in Theatrical History II (4) Selected primary source materials in the history of the theatre from 1660 to the present, and their use by theorists and historians.
THE 626—Backgrounds in Modern Theatrical Practice (4) *Prereq: THE 530.* Plays and production techniques of the modern Continental theatre.
THE 627—Art History of the Theatre (4; max: 8) Seminar in changing physical and visual conventions in the theatre, their origins in the visual traditions of the culture, and their effect on the modes of dramatic presentation.
THE 628—Seminar in Theatre Aesthetics I (4) Growth of the theatre as an art in periods through the Renaissance; the theatre's relation to the aesthetic values of the cultures involved.

THE 629—Seminar in Theatre Aesthetics II (4) Development and modification of aesthetic theory from the Renaissance to the present.

THE 631—Styles in Theatrical Art I (4) *Prereq: THE 528, 529, 530.* Styles of dramatic art through the Middle Ages.

THE 632—Styles in Theatrical Art II (4) *Prereq: THE 528, 529, 530.* Styles of dramatic art from the Middle Ages through 1850.

THE 633—Styles in Theatrical Art III (4) *Prereq: THE 528, 529, 530.* Styles of dramatic art from 1850 to the present.

THE 634—Seminar and Practicum in Modern Theatre Design and Practice (4; max: 12) Design, lighting, and costume.

THE 635—Studies in Contemporary European Theatrical Practices (4) *Prereq: THE 530, 626.* Production techniques of the Continental theatre since World War II.

THE 636—Studies in Contemporary American Theatrical Practices (4) *Prereq: THE 530, 623, 626.* Production techniques of the American theatre since World War II.

THE 637—Advanced Equipment Utilization (5) *Prereq: THE 324, 325, 326, or consent of instructor.* Designed to enable the advanced student to become conversant with the uses of special theatre construction equipment.

THE 638—Speech Research (Theatre) (4) *Prereq: permission of the department chairman.* Lecture and project course in the more complex problems in speech (theatre).

THE 639—Theories of Interpretative Reading (4) Psychological and philosophical theories of creative, artistic oral reading; the teaching of interpretative reading; practice in reading from the works of selected modern authors.

THE 640—Seminar in Production Theory Analysis and Application (4) Application of contemporary dramatic theories and production concepts.

THE 641—Graduate Acting II (4) *Prereq: Acting I, II, III or equivalent, and consent of instructor.* Designed for graduate students specializing in the areas of acting and directing. Affords advanced theoretical study of classical acting styles and studio projects involving their development and use.

THE 642—Costume Management (4) *Prereq: THE 421, 422, 423 or equivalent, and consent of instructor.* Development of professional skills essential to management of a costume shop and total costume program. Emphasis on practical skills required, workshop operation and procedures, and coordination of workshop operation with other production departments.

THE 644—Acting Ensemble (4-12) *Prereq: THE 641 or equivalent, and consent of instructor.* Students explore acting theories through intensive experiments and practicum assignments in acting.

THE 645—Directing Workshop (4-12) *Prereq: THE 328, 329, 330 or equivalent, THE 620, and consent of instructor.* Intensive exploration of specialized directing techniques, with directing projects involving varied production styles and dramatic forms.

THE 696—Individual Study (1-10; max: 10) *Prereq: consent of major professor and department chairman.* Project or research course.

THE 697—Supervised Research (1-5) *Prereq: consent of instructor and department chairman.* May be repeated.

THE 698—Supervised Teaching (1-5) *Prereq: consent of instructor and department chairman.* May be repeated.

THE 699—Master's Research (1-15)

URBAN AND REGIONAL RESEARCH
(Office of Academic Affairs)

A description of the graduate certificate program in Urban Studies may be found in the section *Special Programs.* Listings of graduate faculty with urban interests, as well as courses other than those enumerated below, may be found in departmental descriptions and in the yearly *Bulletin* of the Urban and Regional Research Center. Copies of the *Bulletin* may be obtained from the Director, Urban and Regional Research Center, 125 Building E.

Director: A. J. LaGreca

US 600—The Changing City (4) Offers an interdisciplinary examination of trends in American urbanizations and their implications for living patterns and growth policy. Special attention is focused on technological and scientific innovations, changes in population patterns and qualities of life, economic growth, social and physical flux. New forms of city government as well as the new character of urbanizing areas are studied.

US 602—Principles and Methods for Urban-Regional Studies (4) Examines the methodological foundations of inquiry into urban research in conjunction with analysis of theory construction, research design and case studies for selected urban and regional problems. Particular attention is devoted to urban models and the process of data selection.

US 610—Planning for Urban and Regional Areas (4) Emphasis on a comprehensive overview of urban and regional problems and contemporary approaches to planning. Examples of topics to be investigated include current trends in the development of urban and regional policy at all levels of government, planning for new communities and managed growth, planning and private enterprise.

US 615—Internship in Urban and Regional Development (4) Guides the student in supervised research, field work and/or work study, and offers preprofessional training in urban and regional development. Registration can be made through independent studies, supervised research, or internship course in the student's major department.

US 620—Urban and Regional Workshops (4) *Prereq: consent of instructor.* Enrollment limited to 15 in these wide-interest, interdisciplinary workshops. Potential topics for investigation include manpower planning, urban and regional information and accounting systems, land use systems, urban housing and public policy, urban and regional transportation systems, service delivery systems, urban social problems and alternatives for change. Other special areas based on the current research interests of the faculty may be approached.

VETERINARY SCIENCE
(College of Agriculture)

Chairman: C. E. CORNELIUS
Graduate Coordinator: F. H. WHITE

GRADUATE FACULTY 1975-76

Professors: E. L. BESCH; C. E. CORNELIUS; G. T. EDDS; C. F. SIMPSON; F. H. WHITE
Associate Professors: R. E. BRADLEY, SR.; P. T. CARDEILHAC; D. J. FORRESTER; J. A. HIMES; F. C. NEAL; J. T. NEILSON; W. P. PALMORE
Assistant Professors: J. M. GASKIN; K. D. LEY

Programs leading to the degree of Doctor of Philosophy with emphasis on animal disease problems, may be obtained through other departments in the University, including animal science, microbiology, zoology, and others, with faculty members from the Department of Veterinary Science directing the program.

A sound background in basic sciences is required for admission.

The Department of Veterinary Science offers programs for the degree of Master of Science. Areas of emphasis include microbiology, parasitology, pathology, pharmacology, physiology, toxicology, and laboratory animal diseases.

Students may receive financial aid through assistantships.

GRADUATE COURSES

VY 562—Veterinary Parasitology I (5) *Prereq: ZY 201, 308, 309, MCY 300, EY 420 or consent of instructor.* Selected parasitic diseases of animals, including etiology, transmission, pathogenesis, host reaction and related research techniques.

VY 563—Veterinary Parasitology II (5) *Prereq: VY 562 or consent of instructor.* Continuation study of selected parasitic diseases of animals, including diagnostic methods, therapy, prevention and control and related research techniques.

VY 602—Veterinary Pathology (5) *Prereq: degree in one of the medical sciences; suitable background in histology and approval of major professor.* Topics in pathologic conditions affecting animals, with emphasis on cellular changes.

VY 610—Animal Surgical Techniques (4) *Prereq: VY 622 or MED 741 and consent of instructor.* General surgical principles and anesthesiology including pre- and postoperative care of experimental animals. Selected surgical procedures useful in biomedical research performed to develop surgical skills.

VY 622—Veterinary Physiology I (5) *Prereq: ZY 201, 202, BCH 511 or comparable courses.* Lecture and laboratory presentation of general physiologic principles, including elements of cell physiology, and a systems approach to cardiovascular, blood, respiratory, and renal physiology.

VY 623—Veterinary Physiology II (5) *Prereq: VY 622.* Includes physiology of the gastrointestinal tract, metabolism, endocrinology, neuroendocrinology, and neurophysiology.

VY 624—Helminthology (5) Same as ZY 624. *Prereq: ZY 516 or equivalent.* Morphology, life cycles, and physiology of helminths. Emphasis on host-parasite relationship, immune responses, and related research techniques.

VY 626—Immunology of Animal Parasites (5) *Prereq: MCY 505, BCH 511, 512, ZY 516 or consent of instructor.* Biological and biochemical aspects of host resistance and immunity to endoparasites.

VY 632—Veterinary Pharmacology I (5) *Prereq: suitable background in the medical sciences; satisfactory work in physiology, biochemistry, and immunology.* Selected problems in prevention, treatment, and control of animal diseases.

VY 633—Veterinary Pharmacology II (5) *Prereq: VY 632.*

VY 634—Veterinary Toxicology I (5) *Prereq: VY 633 and suitable background in biochemistry, physiology, and pharmacology.* Effects of toxic natural products and chemicals on animals.

VY 635—Veterinary Toxicology II (5) *Prereq: VY 634.*

VY 642—Veterinary Microbiology (6) *Prereq: MCY 505, 506, 510 or equivalent and consent of instructor.* Laboratory identification of selected bacterial and viral pathogens of veterinary importance.

VY 663—Parasitic Diseases of the Tropics and Subtropics (5) Same as MCY 663, MED 663. Animal parasitology covering mechanisms of parasitic infections, physiology of parasites, and immune responses of the host.

VY 682—Veterinary Research Techniques (5) Principles of biophysical sciences, and their application to veterinary medical science.

VY 690—Seminar in Veterinary Science (1; max: 6)

VY 696—Problems in Veterinary Science (1-5; max: 10)

VY 697—Supervised Research (1-5)

VY 698—Supervised Teaching (1-5)

VY 699—Master's Research (1-15)

ZOOLOGY

(College of Arts and Sciences)

Chairman: T. C. EMMEL
Graduate Coordinator: R. M. DEWITT

GRADUATE FACULTY 1975-76

Graduate Research Professors: A. F. CARR; E. S. DEEVEY, JR.

Professors: W. AUFFENBERG; L. BERNER; P. BRODKORB; J. W. BROOKBANK; J. C. DICKINSON, JR.; J. H. GREGG; J. W. HARDY; F. C. JOHNSON II; D. W. JOHNSTON; E. R. JONES, JR.; J. H. KAUFMANN; F. J. S. MATURO, JR.; B. K. MCNAB; M. J. WESTFALL, JR.

Associate Professors: J. F. ANDERSON; W. E. S. CARR; R. M. DEWITT; T. C. EMMEL; J. T. GIESEL; C. R. GILBERT; C. A. LANCIANI; B. B. LEAVITT; F. G. NORDLIE; T. H. PATTON; J. REISKIND; H. O. SCHWASSMANN; H. M. WALLBRUNN; S. D. WEBB; S. G. ZAM

Assistant Professors: F. C. DAVIS, JR.; S. R. HUMPHREY; G. C. KARP; H. D. PRANGE

The Department of Zoology offers the degrees of Master of Science in Teaching, Master of Science, and Doctor of Philosophy with specialization in animal behavior, ecology, genetics, paleontology, physiology, and systematic biology. Specific areas of specialization include evolutionary biology, marine biology, population biology, and tropical biology.

New graduate students should have completed undergraduate courses in ecology, developmental biology, comparative anatomy, invertebrate and vertebrate zoology, genetics, physiology, one year of physics, chemistry through organic, and a sequence in mathematics or statistics. These courses constitute a core curriculum for all candidates for a graduate degree.

Each new graduate student will be given a written screening examination covering the zoological portion of the core curriculum by the departmental examining committee early in his first term of residence. The results of this examination will be used in planning the student's program.

GRADUATE COURSES

ZY 507—Vertebrate Paleontology (4) Same as GY 507. *Prereq: ZY 309.* Evolutionary history of major vertebrate groups, with special emphasis on principles of prehistoric investigations.

ZY 510—Evolution (5) *Prereq: ZY 201-202 or BTY 181 and ZY 325 or AY 362-363.* Processes and mechanisms of evolution, including population genetics, speciation, patterns of evolution and molecular evolution.

ZV 516—Animal Parasitology (5) Life cycles, morphology, and physiology of the helminth and protozoan parasites of vertebrate animals.

ZY 521—Comparative Histology (5) *Prereq: ZY 309.* Comparative aspects of both structure and function of vertebrate tissues.

ZY 529—Behavioral Ecology (5) *Prereq: ZY 307 or 405.* Behavioral adaptations of animals to their natural environment.

ZV 542—History of the Biological Sciences (3) The origins, growth and development of the major biological sciences and their influences upon society.

ZY 545—Physiological Genetics (4) *Prereq: ZY 325 or equivalent.* Nature of the gene. and its role in metabolism, specificity, differentiation, and morphological patterns.

ZY 551—Cytology (5) Same as BTY 551. *Prereq: 1 year general zoology or its equivalent. consent of instructor.*

ZV 565—Radioisotope Theory and Techniques (5) Same as BTY 565, NES 585, and MED 565. *Prereq: CY 331 or consent of instructor.* Theory of radioactivity, interaction with matter, and radioactive decay given in sufficient detail to make the laboratory techniques and practices thoroughly understood.

ZV 570—Cellular Physiology (6) *Prereq: organic chemistry, general physics and ZY 301 or equivalent. Calculus recommended.* Advanced treatment of biophysical and biochemical aspects of cell activities and specialized cell functions.

ZY 574—Animal Physiology (6) *Prereq: general physics or consent of instructor.*

ZY 579—The Biology of Marine Animals (4) *Prereq: organic chemistry, general physics. ZY 405.* Functioning and interrelationships of marine animals considered from the standpoint of comparative physiology.

ZY 601—Cellular Biology (3) Interdisciplinary course presented by the Department of Zoology to orient the student broadly in the cellular aspect of biology.

ZY 605—Tropical Biology: An Ecological Approach (12) Same as as BTY 605. Field study of ecological concepts in tropical environments. Offered in Costa Rica as part of the program of the Organization for Tropical Studies.

ZY 607—Ancient Vertebrate Faunas (4) Same as GY 607. *Prereq: ZY 507 or GY 507.* Evolution, distribution, and extinction of vertebrate faunas, with emphasis on problems in paleoecology, paleogeography, and patterns of phylogeny.

ZY 608—Seminar in Evolution (4) Same as GY 608. Processes, mechanisms, patterns, and orientation of evolution.

ZV 609—Zoogeography (3)

ZY 610—Advanced Tropical Zoology (12) Vertebrate or invertebrate group selected as basis for studies of ecological systems in the tropics. Effects of elevation and temperatures on populations, successions, microhabitat, distribution, predation, evolution, and other aspects. Offered in Costa Rica as part of the program of the Organization for Tropical Studies.

ZY 612—Marine Ecology (5) *Prereq: ZY 308; CY 213 or equivalent.* Marine communities and the physical and chemical factors that influence them.

ZY 624—Helminthology (5) Same as VY 624. *Prereq: ZY 516 or equivalent.* Morphology, life cycles, and physiology of helminths. Emphasis on host-parasite relationship, immune responses, and related research techniques.

ZV 625—Protozoology (5) *Prereq: ZY 516 or equivalent.* Ultrastructure and life cycles of protozoa. Emphasis on cellular organization, cellular functions, cellular organelles and reproduction.

ZY 626—Community Ecology (5) *Prereq: ZY 405.* Selected animal habitats, their occupants and organization. Classroom work evaluates community concept and appraises role of ecology in evolution.

ZV 627—Stream Ecology (5) *Prereq: EY 301 or 318, ZY 405 or BTY 301, CY 213, PS 213.* Physical, chemical, and biological interrelationships in flowing fresh water.

ZY 628—Limnology (5) *Prereq: ZY 405, BTY 380, CY 213.* Biological, chemical, and physical dynamics of inland waters.

ZV 629—Seminar in Ecology (2; max: 6) *Prereq: ZY 405, 626.*

ZY 632—Advanced Invertebrate Zoology (5) *Prereq: ZY 308.* Morphology, physiology, development, and life cycles of selected invertebrate groups, with emphasis on the minor phyla.

ZY 633—Principles of Systematic Zoology (4) Theory of biological classification and taxonomic practice. Laboratory experience in taxonomic procedures and techniques, including computer methods.

ZY 636—Survey of Sensory Systems (4) Same as MED 636 and PSY 678. *Prereq: ZY 574 or MED 623 or 331 or 767 or PSY 600.* A group of specialists provide a survey of theories and experimental data on human and subhuman sensory reception and encoding. Auditory, visual, and the chemical and cutaneous senses are included.

ZY 637—Research Methods in the Sensory Systems (4; max: 8) Same as MED 627 and PSY 670. *Prereq: MED 636 or PSY 678 or ZY 636.* Participation in laboratory experiments typical of several major areas of sensory systems. Includes visual, auditory, chemical and somesthetic and pain sensory specialities.

ZY 638—Seminar in Sensory Processes (1) Same as MED 639 and PSY 676. Topics of current interest in various areas of sensory specialties.

ZY 642—Physiological Ecology (5) *Prereq: ZY 570.* Physiological mechanisms that influence distribution and ecological relations, water conservation, and energy exchange in vertebrates.

ZY 644—Comparative Sensory Physiology (5) *Prereq: ZY 574 or equivalent and consent of instructor.* Classical concepts and modern research concerning the neurophysiological basis of invertebrate and vertebrate behavior.

ZY 647—Experimental Embryology (3) *Prereq: ZY 310, 570.* Problems of embryonic development and the experimental approach to their solution.

ZY 648—Experimental Embryology Laboratory (2) *Prereq. or coreq: ZY 647.* Modern techniques for the analysis of embryonic development in a wide variety of zoological material.

ZY 651—Ichthyology (5) *Prereq: ZY 306.*

ZY 652—Herpetology (5) *Prereq: ZY 306.*

ZY 653—Mammalogy (5) *Prereq: ZY 306.*

ZY 654—Ornithology (4) *Prereq: ZY 306.*

ZY 664—Topics in Genetics (2-4; max: 12) Same as AL 664, AY 664, BTY 664, PY 664.

ZY 665—Ecological Genetics (5) *Prereq: ZY 325, 405, STA 602.* Mutation, migration, selection, density, subdivision, behavior, and maintenance of variability as they affect the genetic structure of natural populations.

ZY 667—Theoretical Population Ecology (5) *Prereq: ZY 325 or AY 362 and 363; ZY 405 or BTY 501; STA 602.* Analysis of mechanisms controlling distribution and density of animal populations in terms of quantitative data and models.

ZV 668—Field Population Ecology (5) *Prereq: ZY 325; ZY 405 or BTY 501.* Interaction of population structure, genetic properties, and ecological factors in controlling the dynamics and evolutionary character of natural populations.

ZV 671—Ethology (4) *Prereq: ZY 405.* History, concepts, and methods of the comparative study of animal and human behavior. The biological substrate and classification of behavior.

ZV 673—Seminar in Animal Behavior (4; max: 12) *Prereq: ZY 529 or consent of instructor.* Special behavioral topics.

ZY 690—Special Topics in Zoology (4; max: 12)

ZV 696—Individual Studies (1-5; max: 20) S/U.

ZY 697—Supervised Research (1-5)

ZV 698—Supervised Teaching (1-5)

ZV 699—Master's Research (1-15)

ZV 799—Doctoral Research (1-15)

Index

G

H

I

J